# JOHN CALVIN

# JOHN CALVIN

## His Influence
## in the Western World

Edited by
### W. Stanford Reid

OF THE ZONDERVAN CORPORATION
GRAND RAPIDS, MICHIGAN 49506

JOHN CALVIN: HIS INFLUENCE IN THE WESTERN WORLD
Copyright © 1982 by The Zondervan Corporation
Grand Rapids, Michigan

First printing, June 1982

**Library of Congress Cataloging in Publication Data**

Main entry under title:

John Calvin, his influence in the Western world.

　　Festschrift in honor of Paul Woolley.
　　1.　Calvin, John, 1509–1564 — Influence — Addresses, essays, lectures.
2. Calvinism—Addresses, essays, lectures. 3. Woolley, Paul, 1902– . I. Reid, W.
Stanford (William Stanford), 1913– . II. Woolley, Paul, 1902– .

BX9418.J62　　　284'.2'0924　　　81-19787
ISBN 0-310-44721-6　　　　AACR2

Copy-edited and designed by Gerard Terpstra

*Printed in the United States of America*

# Contents

# Preface

The year 1979 has been a year of celebration at Westminster Theological Seminary, Philadelphia. It has been a time of commemorating both the seminary's founding in 1929 and the seventy-fifth birthday of Paul Woolley, who for most of those fifty years was registrar and Professor of Church History. The members of the Church History Department asked me, who was one of Professor Woolley's first students to specialize in his field, to undertake the preparation of this *festschrift,* a task that I have assumed with pleasure.

The rationale for this work is that it will help the Christian community understand the influence of Calvinism in the western world since the days of John Calvin. At first it was hoped that this survey would cover the whole world, but I soon realized that, because of limitations of space, we had to confine it to the Western world. In fact, even to accomplish this limited objective, I had to persuade a large number of authors to write chapters for this book.

Because some of those who agreed to contribute had other commitments, it has taken a considerable amount of time for them to complete their respective chapters. At last, however, we are presenting this book to the public in the hope that many who may not have much knowledge of Calvin or his influence will be able to understand his impact on the history of the rise of Western culture and civilization. I would like to add, however, that though I serve as editor of this work, I do not necessarily agree with everything that has been written here. But, holding to the principle of freedom of thought and expression in academic pursuits, I have been happy to have a part in this publication.

The authors wish to dedicate this work to Professor Woolley as a token of their esteem and appreciation for his faithful service to Westminster Seminary and his stimulation of their interest in the history of the Christian church, particularly of Calvinism.

W. Stanford Reid,
University of Guelph, Guelph, Ontario

# In Appreciation

Paul Wooley's reputation, like most of his convictions, runs counter to the common pattern. He is most esteemed by those who know him best! Generations of students have found their respect growing to awe at the knowledge bank of this fabulous professor who strolled back and forth, with one hand in his pocket, recreating in fascinating detail the biography of Pelagius or summarizing the *Summa Theologica* of Thomas Aquinas or following Finney's campaigns in Western New York. Those who took his courses in the days before computers were invented were not surprised to find that his data storage included the timetables of the major railroads in the United States, as well as such convenient information as local train and bus schedules. Only his dignity and his crisp stewardship of time prevented nearly everyone from asking him nearly everything to the neglect of the impressive reference collection that he had built up in the library.

Yet students who struggled to amass thousands of facts for his exams were jolted to find that he expected much more: not only information but interpretation. Here is a question set for an hour of writing in a final examination:

"Assuming that the work of the church is the preaching of the Gospel and the nurturing of its members in Christian living, what has been contributed to this task by each of the emphases—orthodoxy, rationalism, pietism, modernism? Discuss each contribution and illustrate with copious examples." Another question challenged students to provide a critique of the World Council of Churches by proposing changes or replacement as they thought necessary.

One can only regret that devotion to his teaching and administration tasks has made it impossible for Professor Woolley to prepare for publication the many volumes of historical digest and reflection that were delivered in class lectures over a half century. Beyond the accurate scholarship that compiled this material and the breadth of perspective that interpreted it, there came home to those who profited an attitude that was Woolley's rarest gift—his ability to combine warm understanding and appreciation for the men and movements of the history of Christ's church with undeviating commitment to biblical standards in evaluating them. His integrity as historian is only the application to his field of specialty of the principles of his Christian lifestyle. In administrative decisions or in personal relationships Paul Woolley holds scrupulously and impartially to the rules—first, of the Word of God and then of the application of that Word in the standards of Christian courtesy and justice. Yet Paul Wooley is a man who would first sit behind his desk to inform a student that the rules of scholarship assistance made it impossible for him to receive a further grant, and then pull out his wallet to offer the student a generous sum to meet his emergency.

Professor Woolley's integrity has left a lasting mark on Westminster Seminary. He respects those with whom he disagrees and assumes that where he disagrees with his colleagues, his views, too, will be respected. If Westminster Seminary has achieved some measure of success in uniting academic freedom with Reformed doctrinal commitment, it is the example of Paul Woolley that has been the most decisive influence.

Those who have enjoyed conversation in the Woolleys' home know something of the breadth of cultural interest that Paul Woolley, his wife, and their sons share. Helen Woolley's historical reminiscences, stretching back to Russian court life under the Czar, have always added a depth of personal experience and devotion to the wide-ranging discussions there. In private conversation, as in public ministry, Paul Woolley reveals that love for Christ and the gospel that moved him to volunteer for missionary service in China and, when that door closed, has sustained him in a half century of ministry to young leaders preparing to serve Christ.

> Edmund P. Clowney,
> President,
> Westminster Theological Seminary

# Calvinism
# as a
# Cultural Force

## *Robert D. Knudsen*

*Robert D. Knudsen is Associate Professor of Apologetics at Westminster Theological Seminary, Philadelphia, Pa. He holds degrees from the University of California, Berkeley (A.B.), Westminster Theological Seminary (Th.B., Th.M.), Union Theological Seminary, New York (S.T.M.), and the Free University of Amsterdam (Ph.D.). He has also studied at the University of Basle, Switzerland, and in West Germany at the Tillich Archive (Göttingen) and the Hegel Archive (Bochum). Dr. Knudsen is an ordained minister of the Orthodox Presbyterian Church. He is a member of the Association for Calvinistic Philosophy (Vereniging voor Calvinistische Wijsbegeerte), is a Fellow of the American Scientific Affiliation, and has an editorial position on the staff of their scholarly journals. He is also a member of the Evangelical Theological Society, the Hegel Society of America, and the North American Paul Tillich Society. He is the author of several books and is a frequent contributor to scholarly symposia and journals. Currently, he is the editor of* The Collected Works of Herman Dooyeweerd.

# 1

# Calvinism as a Cultural Force

Calvin was a patron of modern human rights. In his thought he anticipated the modern republican form of government. He contributed toward the modern understanding of the relationship of natural and positive law. Fully abreast of the social and political movements of his time,
he understood that the rise of the modern national state, the burgeoning
of international trade, the development of the bourgeois class, and the
vast expansion of the money market required a reassessment of the
prohibition of lending money at interest. Calvin, furthermore, stood
against the abuses of power in his time and wrestled with the problem of
the right to revolt.

The impact of Calvin and Calvinism on modern Western culture has
been well documented. This influence, it is acknowledged, has been
great. Calvin and Calvinism take their places among the major forces
that have molded our modern Western society.

Tracing these influences is important from a historical point of view.
What has the influence of Calvinism been? Precisely how far has this
influence extended? To assess Calvinism as a cultural force properly,
however, it is necessary to penetrate to a deeper level of questioning.
What is it about Calvinism that determines the peculiar fashion in which
it relates to culture? What cachet does it impress on culture? In these
respects how does it differ from other Protestant movements? Without
having asked such questions one is scarcely in a position to inquire
meaningfully into the extent of its influence.[1]

That focusing one's attention on the nature of Calvinism's impact is the more significant approach is clear when we bring to mind that any movement that has attained historical importance will have a corresponding cultural influence. That is indeed true of Calvinism. It is true as well, however, of Lutheranism, Anabaptism, Methodism, Puritanism, and the like. It is true of any movement, irrespective of the attitude it takes to culture. Even the antiworldly stance of a broad segment of the confessing Christian church has a special kind of cultural influence, though it be a negative one. The withdrawal of Christians from what is called "cultural involvement" has itself a cultural impact. More important than the question of the extent of Calvinism's influence will be that of the quality of that influence.

In treating Calvinism as a cultural force, therefore, we do not have in mind a bare description, important as that might be, of the influence that Calvinism has exerted on our Western culture. Instead, we ask what it is about Calvinism that has established the character of this influence. Why is it that Calvinism has had a positive attitude toward culture and has been able to make constructive cultural contributions? Why indeed is it that this positive attitude belongs to the very genius of Calvinism, so much so that Calvin had in view not only a reformation in doctrine, in individual life, and in the life of the church, but also a transformation of all of culture in the name of Christ?

In answering these questions we may, for the sake of convenience, organize our thoughts around four major points: (1) that in Calvinism there is no dichotomy between Christianity and culture; (2) that because of its penetrating insight into the doctrine of creation, the universality of divine revelation, and the place of law, it is impossible for Calvinism, be it ever so important to keep intact the biblical doctrine of the Creator-creature relation, to think in terms of a simple, unqualified distinction between the divine and human spheres and activities; (3) that all of life, including culture, is theonomous, i.e., it has its meaning in its being subject to God and to His law; and (4) that the power of the sovereign Creator-God also embraces the course of history, so that one can discern God's revelation also in that which pertains most immediately to culture, namely, man's forming activity.

## CALVINISM'S POSITIVE ATTITUDE TOWARD CULTURE

Calvin expressed his gratitude that at the same time that God again brought to light the gospel in its purity, He also brought into being a renaissance of the humanities.[2] It was Guillaume Budé who at the time of Calvin had sought to introduce into the French scene the humanistic learning that had arisen in the Italian Renaissance. He promoted a love for the liberal arts *(bonae litterae)* in contradistinction to the studies that prepared one to make a living (theology, law, medicine).[3] Calvin firmly agreed with Budé that the liberal arts were essential in forming man, in developing his humanity. Indeed, we find in Calvin a love for the liberal arts and a concern for training in them that in no way falls behind that of his humanistic contemporaries. One does not require many words, he said, to express how dear to us is the pursuit of the liberal arts.[4]

Calvin took a positive stance also toward rhetoric and the natural sciences. The influence of rhetorical theory on his theological method has been noted. In the introduction to his commentary on Thessalonians he acknowledges that he owes his humanistic learning and his method of teaching *(discendi rationem)* to the well-known humanist Maturin Cordier. Like rhetoric, the natural sciences are gifts of God, created by Him for the use of mankind.[5] The final source of the true science of nature is none other than the Holy Spirit.[6] Calvin was, however, a stubborn opponent of the pseudo-science of astrology, which was enjoying a vogue in his time, even as it is in ours.[7]

The spiritual climate in which Martin Luther grew up was that of the mysticism of the late Middle Ages. Unlike Calvin and Melanchthon, he remained largely untouched by the renaissance of humanistic learning of his time. In contrast, Calvin early took to humanistic studies. As a test of his competence as a humanistic scholar, he produced his famed commentary on Seneca's *On Clemency (De Clementia).*[8] Trained by the outstanding legal scholars of his time, Pierre de l'Estoile and Andrea Alciat, well conversant with the philosophy of classical culture, and himself a recognized humanistic scholar, Calvin manifested throughout his entire life a profound interest in, and mastery of, contemporary cultural developments. He continued to display an interest in man's humanity and in those good gifts of God, including art and music, that were able to contribute to its development.[9]

It is a mistake to suppose that Calvin's enduring interest in humanistic studies and in man's cultural development was a simple holdover from the time antedating his conversion to the evangelical faith. His concern for the humanities and for the human is too much bound up with his overall point of view to warrant such an interpretation. In fact, in a sense that must be well defined and carefully preserved from misunderstanding, Calvin may be called a "humanist."[10] Throughout his life he had a profound allegiance to what is human.

Indeed, Calvin turned his barbed criticisms against those whose humanism meant that they set themselves against the sovereignty of God, the authority of God's Word, the depravity of man, and the doctrines of grace. At age twenty-seven, in the famous letter that formed the introduction to his *Institutes of the Christian Religion,* he spoke out against humanism that did not share the evangelical doctrine.[11] Rather than against a Christian humanist such as Budé, he struck out at those who apotheosized the human self[12] and thought that realization of what is human can be attained only in presumed independence from God and from His revelation. Himself a humanist, Calvin rejected what was at the heart of the Renaissance idea of human personality, that man is the creative source of his own values and is therefore at bottom unable to sin.[13] If the humanities were dear to Calvin for their ability to develop human virtues, if the sciences were to be cultivated as good gifts of God, those must be opposed who thought that the arts and sciences might be employed as if they were sufficient to themselves. The thought was foreign to Calvin's mind that the arts and science could be free from religion *(non debere distrahi a religione scientiam)*.[14]

One need not suppose that Calvin's attitude to what is human and to what belongs to human cultural achievement is without any need of correction. His positive attitude to them, however, is indigenous to his thought and has profound implications for the attitudes of those who call themselves Calvinists. It helps account for the way in which Calvinism acts as a cultural force.

For Calvin, unlike other leaders of the Reformation, there is no basic dichotomy between the evangel and the world, the gospel and culture. There was in his thought, at the same time, no simple, uncritical acceptance of the products of human genius. His attitude required that they be criticized as to the conception behind them and that they be subjected to the rule of Christ.

## CALVINISM ON THE DIVINE AND THE HUMAN

Calvin confessed the absolute sovereignty of God. With the other Reformers he also confessed that by the grace of Christ the believer is related in his heart immediately to the sovereign God as He has revealed Himself in His Word. As we have already shown, this did not mean for Calvin that God's sovereign activity came to stand in a relation of indifference, or possibly even antithesis, to what is human and to what belongs to the realm of human cultural achievement. Calvin viewed God's activity in such a way as to avoid any such dualism. The God who sovereignly works in man's heart is the same God who has revealed Himself as the Creator of man and of human cultural values.

One who has a profound grasp of God's revelation of Himself as the Creator will understand that the divine and the human may not be conceived of as if they were on opposite ends of a spectrum, so that exalting the one would mean *per se* debasing the other. God is not honored by demeaning His creation, nor is His creation exalted by demeaning God. The creation is the expression of God's Creator-will. In its unspoiled state God called it good. He reveals Himself as being actively concerned with it. To glorify God one need not denigrate the creation; he need only carry out in it what answers to God's Creator-will for it.

If one has a profound understanding of the biblical revelation concerning creation, he will understand that what is at issue is not a mere emphasis on what is divine or what is human but whether or not what is human and what belongs to the sphere of human activity has been brought to conform to the will of God as expressed in His law. That is to say, he will see that what is at issue is whether they answer to what God desired for them from the beginning.

It is clear that the Reformation doctrine of the immediate working of God's grace through His Word in the human heart arose in opposition to the views that the human is a semiautonomous sphere antecedent to the divine and that performing works by one's own natural powers serves as a necessary preamble to the working of grace. By the time Luther began to set forth his doctrine of justification by faith alone the nominalist William of Ockham, in whose logic he had been instructed by Trutvetter and Usingen, and whom he called his teacher *(magister meus)*, [15] had already created a climate of thought uncongenial to the idea that nature is the preamble of grace. Ockham disallowed that anything outside the evangel might serve to judge it or act as a staging platform for God's gracious provision and for man's believing response. Luther was proud of belonging to the school of Ockham, whom he regarded as the head and the most clever of the scholastic doctors.

The nominalist position appeared to dovetail, furthermore, with his doctrines of grace. Nominalists taught that God acts directly, addressing man with an absolute, sovereign demand, without room for an exercise of natural human powers of judgment, discrimination, or choice. They taught that divine grace is not the accompaniment, even if that is understood as the divine perfection, of human works. They taught that divine grace works immediately in man's heart, in indifference to, or even in contrast to, human accomplishment.

I do not wish to suggest that Luther's understanding of the doctrines of grace arose out of, or even depended on, this nominalist teaching. This understanding, I hold, came from his reading of the Scriptures. The Ockhamist tradition, however, provided a niche for it in its criticism of the view that nature is the preamble of grace. Once these doctrines had been discovered, furthermore, the nominalist teachings were able to affect their theological outworking and to determine the conception as to how the gospel relates to culture.

It is acknowledged that Luther's view of what is called the "two kingdoms" is deeply affected by nominalism. For the sphere of nature, he taught, the widely accepted Aristotelian concept of knowledge is sufficient. For religion, however, it is only revelation that is authoritative. Here human reason has to submit itself entirely to the Word of God. The natural understanding and its logic, limited as they are to the finite, are detrimental to theology, because they do not lead to faith but rather away from it.

The manner in which this nominalist tradition distinguished between the divine and the human has indeed a point of contact with the concrete verbal usage in the Scriptures. The Scriptures often speak of the activity of God and the activity of man in such a way as to set them diametrically over against each other. It is possible, however, to adopt a usage without having penetrated to the truth behind it. This, it would appear, was the case with the nominalistic understanding of the biblical teaching concerning God and man, which was thought to parallel that of grace and nature. It was inevitable that this tradition should affect the manner in which Luther developed his theology and conceived of the relationship between Christianity and culture.

Luther correctly holds forth for the evangelical doctrine of the immediate operation through the Word of God's sovereign grace. In Luther's thought, however, there is a very marked distinction between an inner sphere of divine, spiritual activity and an outer sphere of worldly ordinances. In line with the nominalist position, this outer sphere, in contrast to the inner, is regarded as formal and conventional. At the least, it stands to the spiritual realm in a relation of indifference. Human cultural activity, which belongs to this external sphere, is acceptable, as long as its standards are not thought to apply to the spiritual realm. There is no inner connection, however, between it and this spiritual realm. Spiritual activity affects the cultural, to use a metaphor, only as it effervesces and spills over into it. In comparison with the spiritual, human cultural activity must suffer.

Within this context, it is not surprising that Melanchthon, discovering in Luther's position no inner point of contact with culture and concerned with the foundations of theology and his practical program of university reform, moved farther and farther toward an uncritical acceptance of what came to him from the secular milieu. He accommodated his position more and more to that of Aristotle, who, he said, had developed the only scientific philosophy.[16] True to the Reformation doctrines of grace in his personal confession, Melanchthon accommodated himself nevertheless to secular culture in a fashion that was impossible for Calvin.

In Calvin's thought we find no such dualism. Indeed, for him there is no relatively autonomous sphere of human activity preceding the operation of God's grace. Moreover, there is no limitation of divine sovereignty as it operates in the human heart. In Calvin's thought, however, these attitudes combine with a profound understanding of the biblical doctrine of creation. God is the absolute, sovereign Creator and Sustainer of all things. There is nothing of which He is not the Creator and that is not subject to His Creator-will. All things, including those that are apparently the most trivial, are revelatory of Him. Furthermore His sovereign Creator-will embraces what is human and what belongs to the sphere of human achievement, the course of history and of cultural development. All of them are subject to His will, as expressed in His law.

In Calvin, therefore, we do not find a simple, across-the-board—what amounts to a logicistic—distinction between God and man, between what is divine and what is human activity. Indeed, one must honor to the full the biblical distinction between the Creator and His creation. It is, however, a profound understanding of this very biblical doctrine that preserves one from using the terms "God" and "man" *en bloc,* in the simple, unqualified way against which I am warning. This pitfall is avoided if one, with Calvin, thinks within the creation, under the horizon of God's revelation, in terms of the expression of God's Creator-will in His law.

Calvin saw that everything conformable to God's will as expressed in creation has God's approval. As he answers to God's creative purpose, man answers to what is his state of nature, to that which God at the creation declared to be good. Thus Calvin could embrace with enthusiasm the program of natural science to ferret out the secrets of God's universe. Thus too, he could accept freely the products of human genius that contributed to man's being man. Granted that these things were meaningless apart from religion; they were indeed meaningful with it. They were good gifts of God, imparted by the power of the Holy Spirit.

To be sure, mankind is depraved at its heart because of sin, and culture has not developed without severe dislocations. Depravity is, however, contrary to nature. It is unnatural. What does not answer to God's Creator-will, what is not truly in conformity with His law, is an expression of that unnaturalness that has entered the world because of sin. This deformation, however, even though it is great, is not such as to have separated the world and its culture from God's purpose and plan. Nor is it such that the world no longer displays God's glory. God's good gifts are spread abroad, without any special favor to those who are of the household of faith. Truth, which is present by the influence of the Holy Spirit, must be embraced, therefore, wherever it is found. In spite of the depravity of man's heart, God has, by His common grace, kept embers burning of that which answers to His Creator-will.[17] Thus it is possible to understand that there are even brilliant accomplishments of the human spirit among those who have in their hearts little or no place for the teachings of the Word of God.

Calvin's view of the relation of God and man appears to be epitomized in his famous statement at the beginning of his *Institutes,* that there is a correlation between one's knowledge of God and his knowledge of himself *(Dei notitiam et nostri res esse coniunctas).*[18] The thought is that one knows himself truly only as he knows himself in the light of God and His revelation, with the corollary that if one knows himself truly he also knows God truly. It is not too much to draw from this correlation the thought that for man to be truly related to God religiously is to be truly related to himself and to be truly related to himself religiously is to be truly related to God.

As I understand the matter, Calvin's idea of the correlation between our knowledge of God and our knowledge of ourselves opened the way for him to meet what must have been for him a major problem, viz., that of relating the humanistic training he had received and for which he continued to have the greatest respect, to the truths of the gospel, which he embraced at his conversion. It expressed a point of view in which the danger of taking "God" and "man," the "divine" and the "human," *en bloc* had already been avoided. It allowed him, in a fashion that is truly conformable to Scripture teaching, to give full place to man's humanity and to his cultural achievements without detracting in the least from the honor and glory of God.

Calvin viewed man's humanity in its depth. Indeed, that depth-understanding was not guided by an idea of universal humanity such as that of the Renaissance, where man was thought to be autonomous personality, the creative source of his own values; instead, it was led by the revelation of God concerning His purpose in creation, the distorting effects of sin, and His provision for the redemption of man and his world. For Calvin it became possible to relate the idea of humanity to the religious antithesis portrayed in Scripture. The way was opened for the idea that man has his being in his relationship to God. Man is himself, is truly human, as he answers to what is his state of nature, to what he was created to be.[19] In this fashion it is possible to see that the *humanum* is realized not in autonomous isolation from God but in relation to him, and that sinful human autonomy, far from being the avenue to human self-realization, is itself a distortion of what is human.

Against this background it is clear that what is at issue is not a simple, relative emphasis or de-emphasis of man and the products of human activity. The issue is whether what man does and how he conceives himself conform to what God intended for him from the beginning in His sovereign Creator-will. It follows that any idea of man, of human activity, or of the products of that activity must be examined as to its religious root. Does man seek to express his humanity in conformity with the law of God, is he ready to acknowledge the unnaturalness attaching to everything human and to all human accomplishment because of sin, and is he prepared to depend in everything relating to himself and his activities on the redeeming grace of Christ and its restoring power?

From the vantage point we have now reached we are able to bring into sharper focus how Calvin's thought is "humanistic." His position does not require one, in the interests of God's glory and of the gospel of Jesus

Christ, to negate or even to depreciate what is human. In fact, man's humanity may even be exalted without detracting from the honor of God. Interest in, and concern for, the *humanum* becomes humanism in a pejorative sense only when it is thought that man's center of gravity, as it were, resides in himself, in a presumed autonomy vis-à-vis his Creator. The latter kind of humanism, as we have noted, budded during the Renaissance and flowered at the time of the Enlightenment. To this kind of humanism Calvin reacted vigorously, as its exponents were attempting with every means at their disposal to defeat the cause of the Reformation.

## CALVINISM ON THE RULE OF GOD THROUGH LAW

In the preceding we have ascertained that for Calvin God's sovereign Creator-will is without limitation. It penetrates everything, even those things that are apparently the most insignificant. Everything is revelatory of God, expressing in some way or other His majesty and glory. We have ascertained, furthermore, that this sovereign will of God is not understood apart from His revelation of Himself, apart from the expression of His will in His law, to which man and indeed the entire creation are subject. It is in line with Calvin's thought to say that man has his being in his responding to God's impartation of Himself in His revelation. Man is himself in freely responding to the call of God, in his obedience to God's sovereign will, which to be sure does not hem him in but serves as the medium within which he realizes himself.[20]

With this understanding, I turn to my third proposition: For Calvin, all of life, including what is loosely called "culture," is theonomous; that is, it has its being in its subjection to God and to His law.

What comes particularly into focus here is Calvin's view of law. If God, as the Creator, is above the law *(deus legibus solutus),* without anything outside of His own being that might limit Him, man and the entire cosmos with him are under the law, subject to it. For creaturely existence in its entirety, bounds are set up by the law of God. Apart from these bounds creaturely existence has no meaning.

Accordingly, the image that is brought to mind by Calvin's view of the divine sovereignty is not that of a despotic tyrant but that of a grand architect, a designation Calvin often applied to God.[21] When speaking of the creation, Calvin could easily refer to its architectonic, to its architecture, which is a revelation of the greatness and the goodness of God. The idea of creation brings with it for Calvin the idea of order, one in which everything is built up into a magnificent structure, a thing of beauty.[22]

This understanding makes it impossible to see in the Calvinistic idea of the sovereignty of God a sanction for any kind of unlimited human sovereignty. All creaturely existence is limited. Even though man may have authority sanctioned by God, it is bounded. Human sovereignty is always restricted to the bounds set for it.

These two facets, the all-penetrating character of God's Creator-sovereignty as He has revealed Himself in His Word and the boundedness of all creaturely existence, appear in the Reformation idea of calling.

Luther is credited with having brought about a Copernican revolution of the idea of calling as it was held in the Middle Ages. The idea of calling had been applied only to special areas, so-called "holy orders," for which a special consecration was needed. Indeed, the idea was rife that only monasticism was a true calling. Likewise, a life of spiritual contemplation was highly favored over an active life.[23] Recognizing that all of life as it reflects God's purpose is holy, Luther extended the idea of calling to embrace every legitimate activity of man.

The full impact of Luther's revolutionary conception can be felt, however, only if one escapes the kind of dualism he himself fell into with his distinction between an inner, spiritual realm and a sphere of external ordinances. Calvin, I have asserted, never shared such a dualistic view. Indeed, even as Luther did, he rejected the idea that nature is the preamble of grace and he held that God works immediately in the human heart through His Word; he was, however, untouched by the nominalist influences that affected the outworking of Luther's thought. His view, as I established in the preceding section, did not at all involve a depreciation of human cultural activity and human institutions. In Calvin the Reformation idea of calling was able to come to purer expression in its universal significance.

For Calvin, man's life in its entirety is understood as a response to the calling of God. Man is a covenant being. He has, as Luther put it, an assured rule according to which he is to live and die (*certa regula tum vivendi tum moriendi*). In every aspect of his life one is confronted with the sovereign God, before whom he must give an account of himself.

Indeed, the calling of God has this universal sense. The Reformation idea of calling does not come to full expression, however, apart from the idea that there are particular callings. The Reformation recovered the idea of the sanctity of all legitimate human activities. What is at stake, therefore, is not whether one enters a particular calling but whether in the sphere in which he is active he views his labor in the light of the divine call and serves God there with all his heart.

One of the keystones of Calvin's view of calling was his understanding that a great diversity of gifts has been given to people according to the sovereign will of the Spirit of God. Just as it is not a single ray of the sun that lightens the world, but all of the rays conjoin to perform their task, so God spreads His gifts abroad, in order to keep mankind in mutual interdependence.[24] Among men there is a diversity of gifts, leading to a diversity of functions. That one has a particular place and task presupposes that he has a calling to it. By accepting this place and its obligations one has an assured calling *(certa vocatio)*.[25] One's vocation is an obedient answer to the divine calling.[26]

In this connection, Calvin employed another figure, that of the body. This he extended beyond the church to the family and to the state.[27] The worldly callings belong to the state.[28] The members of the state as well as of the church, with their diverse gifts, are united in a body, with mutually dependent functions. Thus Calvin developed what has been called an "organismic" view of the church, the state, the family, etc.[29]

The Reformation idea of calling, especially as it was developed by Calvin, leads to the idea that sanctity attaches to what are broadly called man's "cultural activities." Man's cultural activity is thought of as being in response to a divine call and as involving a divinely given cultural task. Thus man's cultural activity is theonomous, having its meaning only in response to God and to His law, which sets its bounds and establishes its meaning. This step, in effect, was already taken by Calvin.

Calvin discerned such an organic sphere in the family. The family is a creation ordinance founded by God.[30] It is an eternal and indestructible institution of God.[31] The head of the family in the narrow sense of the word, the husband, has been given special gifts of the Spirit. Because of those gifts, he has been entrusted with an authority, which he is called to exercise in the particular sphere within which he is placed. Within the family there is a special relationship of superordination and subordination. According to the divine arrangement, the husband is the head of the wife, in such a way, however, that he should care for her as he does for his own body. Indeed, he is to love her as Christ loved the church and gave Himself for it. On her part, the wife is to be subservient to her husband in the Lord, giving him the love and obedience he should have as her head. Over both husband and wife, however, is the head of all things, Jesus Christ. Both the husband and the wife are limited in their authority and activity. Their lives as a married pair come to fruition in their obedience to the law of God as it pertains to the sphere to which they are called.

Calvin's organismic view also came to expression in his idea of the state, in which he found in this regard an analogy with the family.[32] He related to the state also his idea of the diversity of mankind as to gifts and station. The state too is analogous to a body, in which the various members have their own place and function. In the state people are gathered together in an organic unity, with different stations of life and differing functions.

Over the state is the ruler. His authority, Calvin taught, is not derived first of all from the will of the people; it is given first of all by God.[33]

The divine source of the authority of the magistrate resides in his having received the peculiar gifts of the Spirit for ruling.[34] Within the sphere of the state, therefore, there is an authority, a seat of power, that is divinely legitimated.

Calvin interacted with the ancient idea that the ruler is above the law because he is its source *(princeps legibus solutus)*. Indeed, he allowed, the ruler is the source of the positive law that is binding within his territory. Calvin spoke in this sense of the ruler as the law personified *(lex animata)*.[35] True to his conception in general, however, Calvin held that the authority of a ruler is limited. A ruler must himself submit to the positive law that holds within his territory.[36] Positive law, furthermore, is only one expression of law; besides it there is natural law, a law of nature,[37] which Calvin associated closely with fairness. Every positive law must express the principle of fairness. Apart from this it is void.[38]

What for Calvin is the meaning of natural law? The answer to this question is not a simple one. Like Luther and Melanchthon, Calvin had a warm appreciation for Roman law, which had been received widely and was interacting with current legal systems. He shared the distinction that the Roman jurist Quintilian made between the laws that have been given to everyone by nature, that is, natural right *(iustum natura),* and the laws that pertain to a folk or a people, in which context laws receive their formal juridical expression *(iustum constitutione).*[39] Calvin's openness to Roman law at this point, involving as it does a formal agreement with its idea that there is a law of nature, is in agreement with his attitude in general toward human cultural achievement and, more particularly, with his attitude toward the system of Roman law, into which he introduced very few corrections. That he accepted the idea of natural law does not mean, however, that he did not place it in a setting that would materially change its meaning. To hold a view of a law of nature, as Calvin did, was not to come into the camp of the Stoics, with their idea of universal reason, or into material agreement with Roman law, in its view of the origin and the meaning of natural law.

That Calvin could accept Roman law at all depended on his interpretation of its place in the providential plan of God, and that would of necessity involve his having reinterpreted it, placing its distinctions within the context of his understanding of Christian doctrine. Accepting it was agreeable to his idea that God had not allowed the world to go to ruin because of sin but that He had preserved it by His common grace. Calvin's acceptance of some kind of natural-law doctrine also reflects his interpretation of the Scripture teaching concerning what is understood ''by nature'' *(physei)* by those who are outside the pale of God's special revelation, those who, unlike the Jews, have not received the oracles *(ta logia)* of God. That these nevertheless do "by nature" the things that are written in the law of God is, according to Calvin, to be ascribed to the human sensibilities spread throughout mankind *(sensus communis),* which reflect the divine will and which have been preserved from annihilation by God's common grace. It follows that Calvin could not think of the law of nature as a right inhering in a universal reason, understood apart from the biblical message. The law of nature had to be related to the order of creation, through which, in spite of the ravages of sin, God continues to reveal Himself everywhere and at all times.

A ruler, then, who indeed for Calvin is the source of the positive laws inscribed on the statute books of his territory, is subject to the law of nature. According to Calvin, this law of nature is the rule and the goal of all positive laws and is that which establishes their bounds.[40] A ruler is subject, therefore, to a law whose authority far exceeds any laws that he himself might generate. In the final analysis, he is subject to God, who is the final source of all law and all authority.

Indeed, the respect Calvin had for the magistrate and for the gifts of ruling was enormous. One is obliged to approach a ruler as one who is endowed by the Spirit of God Himself with the remarkable gifts suited for ruling. This human authority, however, sanctioned as it is by divine authority, is always restricted, being bound to the limits of the calling pertaining to the office of ruler.

Calvin's view of calling, whether it be to activity in the sphere of the home, the state, teaching, or the church, always displays these two facets. There is, on the one hand, the idea that all of life is response to the universal call of God, whose sovereign will embraces all things and whose providence extends to every minutia of human existence. There is, on the other hand, the companion idea that human response is channeled by specific callings, so that each has his place and performs his function within a body.

It would remain for the great Dutch statesman and theologian Abraham Kuyper to draw together the threads of Reformed teaching and to develop the idea of "sphere-sovereignty," or, as it has been called, "sovereignty in the individual spheres of life," that God, whose absolute sovereignty extends over all of life, has ordained various spheres of society, each of which has a derived sovereignty within its own orbit.[41] Calvin already understood, however, that there was a diversity of gifts and callings and that each had to be understood in relation to God and to His sovereign will. According to Calvin, as well as Kuyper, one might serve according to his peculiar gifts, his special capacities, in his own place, and be graced with the knowledge that he was engaged in fulfilling a particular calling of God.

Calvin's view of the diversity of callings established by God makes it imperative to reconstruct a widespread notion of modern times concerning the nature of culture and society. Up to this point I have used the word *culture* in a rather general and indiscriminate sense, without throwing into question the common usage of the term. According to this usage, culture is the general term denoting the order that has been brought into being by human agency. Culture is supposed to embrace everything that does not come ready-made as part of nature. Thus it is thought to include all language, all laws, all social conventions, etc.

For the greater part, when a contemporary introduces such a topic as "Christianity and Culture," he has in mind the word *culture* interpreted in this way. Culture, embracing all human contrivance and its products, is set in contrast to what belongs to the sphere of the divine. One introduces thereby a discussion of the relationship of Christianity, as being of divine origin, to what is the product of human contrivance in the widest sense of the word.

Calvin's view of nature and of natural law suggests that this view needs reconstruction. His view does not allow all law and all structure that is not just that of nature to be understood as a product of human contrivance. Human contrivance itself, on the contrary, has its meaning within the framework established by the divine ordinances, which it is beyond human prerogative to change.

Again, Calvin's view does not allow one to consider the divine and the human *en bloc*. Human activity is meaningful only within the bounds set by God's sovereign will expressed in His law. God's law constitutes the abiding framework for human activity, apart from which it loses its meaning. Human cultural activity, indeed all of culture, is theonomous, having its meaning in relation to God and to His law.

## CALVINISM ON MAN'S CULTURAL ACTIVITY

Calvin lived in a time of ferment and change, in an age that he himself described in terms that were most unflattering. It was a time of innovations of thought, of profound social dislocations, and of religious conflict. In both the Renaissance and the Reformation there was not only a vivid awareness of returning to what had for a long time been obscured, a return to the sources *(ad fontes),* but also a consciousness that this return was to mark a new beginning, the emergence of a new age that would differ in marked degree from the one that had immediately preceded.

In the midst of such ferment it is not surprising that there also arose a sense of historical change. This awareness also gripped Calvin. His view of natural law did not prevent him from being supple with respect to the changes that were everywhere taking place around him. He knew that it was impossible to associate the will of God altogether with the existing order, for to do so would have been to sanction the forces of conservatism and of reaction. The assault characteristic of his time on well-established ideas and customs was not simply destructive and de-void of meaning. It is clear, however, that Calvin did not abandon everything to the forces of history, as our discussion of law has already shown us. That he embraced a doctrine of natural law would itself stand in the way of such an abandonment. He did not divorce his view of change from God or from His law in a fashion that would lead him down the path to revolution. Even though he was more restrained in his attitude toward them than was Luther, Calvin held in contempt those on the fringe of the Reformation who struck out with revolutionary fervor against what was established.

It is true, nevertheless, that Calvin had a sharp eye for the role of history. Furthermore, he was a modern person in the sense that he did not consider history simply the moving image of eternity. His refusal to limit the sovereign will of the Creator-God could not stop short of history. History, for Calvin, has meaning resident in itself.[42] History and historical change fall within the province of God's sovereign activity and carry out the purposes of His will.[43]

Did Calvin possess, then, a well-worked-out principle of historical change that would account for his giving prominence to history without falling, on the one hand, into a conservatism or, on the other hand, into a revolutionary stance? Did he have a clear notion of what it is that constitutes culture, so that he could see clearly how history and histori-cal culture-formation have their place within the order of the cosmos as God has created it? He was indeed fully aware of what had been done in the past toward constructing a Christian view of history, having read the church fathers, including Augustine, who is the first to have developed what might be called a Christian philosophy of history. Indeed, he himself also developed a view of history. The answer to the above questions, however, must be in the negative. Calvin did not develop a philosophy of history in the technical sense of the word.

It is better to conclude that Calvin possessed a finely tuned sense of the attitude a Christian ought to have with respect to historical change, a sense that was schooled in his study of history, in his training, and especially in his profound grasp of biblical teaching.

It is significant on this score that before his conversion to the evangelical faith Calvin was already fully involved in what was one of the most powerful modernizing forces of his time, the humanistic ren-aissance. This had already made an important impact in Roman Catholic circles—witness the fact that the leading French humanist, Budé, was a Roman Catholic—and had influenced some of Calvin's closest as-sociates. Calvin first established himself as a humanist. Only after that did he undergo the development that was to make him the grandest systematician of the Reformation. Having already planted his feet sol-idly in the modern world, Calvin's problem would not be how to enter modernity but how to relate himself and the new learning to the ancient truths of the gospel as they had again been brought to light by the Reformation and how to interpret the modern world in their light.

It must also not be forgotten that Calvin, in the interests of applying the truths of the gospel to life, was drawn into the practical arena. His principles did not have about them that air of unreality that attaches to ideal schemes that have little or no contact with actual life. There is in Calvin a healthful realism. It has been suggested that his principles had effect because he was in contact with real-life situations and was in a position to change them. [44]

We observe Calvin, for instance, attempting as much as was possible to replace canon law in Geneva with the principles of Roman law. [45] We see him, in cooperation with Marot, raising the level of appreciation for music in worship. [46] We see him entering the field of education, with the founding of the Academy in Geneva, and attempting to develop a truly Christian view of learning. [47] We find him, through his intense literary efforts, raising the level of the French language to unaccustomed heights. [48] In the introduction to his *Institutes of the Christian Religion* he addresses the king in a fashion reminiscent of that of the early apologists, pleading for the welfare of the true followers of the gospel, but stating also, in a fashion that related to the deepest concerns of the current political situation, that the true interests of the state are advanced only as there is true obedience to Christ and to the truths of His Word. [49] Truly, for Calvin, the Word of God was not to remain in the cloisters of the human heart. Its energies were to radiate out into the entire world, into all of life, including the domain of culture.

At bottom, however, it was because Calvin had penetrated so profoundly into the depths of the Christian world view that he was able to develop a proper sense of history and of its dynamics. That he had understood, as Augustine before him, the seminal meaning of the biblical doctrine of creation, that he acknowledged the sovereignty and the providence of God over all things, so that nothing escaped God's Creator-will, made it possible for him to see that this will extends also to history and to that which is central to history, man's forming activity, which is the heart of cultural development.

If one stands in the line of Calvin, it is not necessary to view human cultural activity in contrast to a presumed sphere of divine activity. Culture may be viewed as an aspect of human activity, indeed in distinction to nature, but not independent of the divine law, the divine plan, and divine calling. Human cultural activity may be viewed as a response to God's calling, even as all of life is, and may be judged as to whether it is carried out in accordance with His Creator-will. What is required is a reconstruction of the idea of culture, which views it within the context of divine revelation, the context within which it becomes meaningful. Human cultural activity, carried on in obedience to God's law is an expression of His will. It is in line with the thought of Calvin to say that what flows from it has a place in God's plan as it relates to the end of this age and the coming of a new heavens and a new earth.

# The Transmission
of Calvinism
in the Sixteenth Century

## W. Stanford Reid

*W. Stanford Reid is Emeritus Professor of History, University of Guelph, Guelph, Ontario. He holds degrees from McGill University, Montreal (B.A., M.A.), Westminster Theological Seminary, Philadelphia (Th.B., Th.M.), The University of Pennsylvania, Philadelphia (Ph.D.), Wheaton College, Wheaton, Illinois (L.H.D.Hon.), and The Presbyterian College, Montreal, Quebec (D.D.Hon.). He has served in the pastoral ministry in Montreal and as a member of the Arts Faculty at McGill University, Montreal. Dr. Reid has contributed articles to* Church History, Fides et Historia, The Scottish Historical Review, The Canadian Historical Review, Speculum, Christianity Today, The Presbyterian Record, *and many other periodicals. He has authored or edited some ten books on the Protestant Reformation and on Canadian history. He is a member of the American Society of Church History, the Canadian Society of Church History, the Scottish Historical Society, the Conference on Faith and History, the Scottish Church History Society, and the Royal Historical Society.*

# 2

# The Transmission of Calvinism in the Sixteenth Century

The problem of communication is always of importance in any civilization or culture, but it has become even more important than usual in our own society. The press, the radio, and television play a large part in our decision making and in our thinking generally. With more facilities for communication than man has ever possessed in the past, we tend to feel that our age is the only time when communication, propaganda, or whatever we may call it, is really appreciated. Yet as we turn back to the sixteenth century, we cannot but be struck by the way in which information and ideas of various kinds moved around Europe. And one of the most outstanding examples of this transmission of ideas appears in the way in which Calvinism spread from the small Swiss city of Geneva throughout a large part of Europe from the lower reaches of the Danube to the northern parts of Scotland.

Lutheranism also spread quite rapidly in the early days of the Reformation, but it soon began to recede like the ebbing of the tide, except in the more Teutonic areas such as Germany and Scandinavia. Calvin's ideas, on the other hand, moved in and often supplanted those of Luther in regions as diverse as those of France, Scotland, the Netherlands, and Hungary. Despite the difficulties of physical geography, the obstacles caused by political opposition and the persecution instigated by the Roman Catholic authorities, Calvinism succeeded in expanding its influence and in enlarging its borders to the extent that it came to be regarded as the number-one enemy of the Roman Church and of absolutist government. While there are a number of reasons for this, one very important factor was the way and means by which Calvinism was transmitted throughout the Europe of the sixteenth century.

In attempting to understand this matter of communication we must recognize that the communication of ideas is largely dependent on the society in which those ideas are expressed. We have had a rather good example of this in the jargon invented by university students and the hippie generation of the 1960s. Furthermore, the question of the technology of communication and transmission of ideas in society is of crucial importance, just as today the computer is taking on a completely revolutionary role in this very field but is understood by very few except those who have been technically trained to use it. Therefore, in order to understand the success of the transmission of Calvin's ideas and partially to explain his success in spreading them, it is necessary for us to look first at the societal background of the Reformation and the development of the means of communication.

## LATE MEDIEVAL AND EARLY MODERN DEVELOPMENTS

The two centuries from 1300 to 1500 were centuries of rapid, even revolutionary, change in the society of western Europe. If Petrarch or Dante had been able to return to visit with Erasmus, they would have found themselves in a world completely different from that which they had known. For one thing Europe had suffered the devastating attack of the Black Death, or bubonic plague, which in some countries had killed one third of the population. This tragedy had widespread implications and effects. At the same time, we must remember that in these centuries the Renaissance took place; the Great Schism and the conciliar movement in the church ran their courses; and finally geographic discoveries were made that changed much of the outlook of western Europeans—including the discovery of America and the rounding of the Cape of Good Hope, the latter opening up a direct route to the Far East. By 1500 Europe was a changed continent with a radically altered society.

One result of the Black Death was a decline in the economy of western Europe, as both the demand for goods and the hands to produce them decreased. By the mid-fifteenth century, however, as the people became more immune to the disease, population began to climb and, although the population did not reach its pre-plague numbers until well on into the sixteenth century, industry and trade began to pick up. New techniques in such industries as woolen-cloth manufacture, coal mining, and armaments production all helped to stimulate the economies, particularly of the countries in the northwest such as England and the Netherlands. Because of this, a need for a greater cash flow developed, resulting in improvements in methods of finance and the rise of important banking firms such as the Medici of Florence and the Fuggers of Augsburg. All this helped to produce a general expansion of trade after

1450, which led in turn to the formation of a communications network that was to play a considerable part during the sixteenth century in the transmission of ideas.[1]

This network arose also because of the class changes that were taking place in certain parts of Europe as a result of the economic development. While there had always been merchants and craftsmen whom we might call middle class, because they were between the nobility and the servile class, it was not until the latter part of the fifteenth century that a true middle class began to develop. Instead of a few traders and bankers, a much larger group of men interested in commerce, although perhaps on a rather small scale, began to play a part in society. In northwestern Europe in countries such as England, the Netherlands, and western Germany the new class of men were beginning to oust the nobility from their positions as those in control of society.[2] Whereas the nobility were suffering from the inflation that was taking place, the new commercial class were battening on this economic expansion and becoming the support of kings who had a growing need for a cash income.

Politically the fourteenth and fifteenth centuries saw the rapid growth of nationalist sentiment in many areas. It was the period of the attempted English expansion, both within the British Isles and across the Channel into France, that resulted in the development and consolidation, not only of English but also of French and Scottish national feeling. Toward the end of the period Spanish nationalism became strong in the struggle with the Moors. This popular nationalism in turn helped to give rise to what has come to be known as the "new monarchies." The monarchs of the developing nations, to consolidate their power both within the country and in opposition to external foes, needed an administration and armies, which could be maintained only with the financial assistance of the new middle class.[3] In this way the political balance of power in some countries was beginning to change.

A further change that took place between 1300 and 1500 was in the orientation of Western thought. The theology of Thomas Aquinas with its acceptance of the reality of universals in which the particulars participated, fell out of favor with the rise of "modern" thought as set forth by such men as Marsilio of Padua and William of Ockham. The individual or particular was regarded as the only *real* entity, while the universals were only nominal classifications. This type of thinking was further supported by the interest shown in classical thought as expressed in newly discovered or newly studied Greek and Latin writings. Renaissance humanism with its stress on the individual, particularly the man of *virtu,* gave a further stimulus to the view that the individual was the central figure in any understanding of man and his activity, a view concretely set forth by Pico de la Mirandolla in his "Oration on the Glory of Man."[4]

All these changes had their influence on the pattern of communication. To be sure, the Middle Ages had its method of transmitting ideas, but it did so to only a relatively few people, and therefore the movement of ideas was rather limited. Since the vast majority of people were illiterate, medieval society was basically an oral and visual society. The church communicated its teachings to the people by means of pictures, statues, and ceremonies. Even preaching was not common. Usually when governments found it necessary to record various acts, charters, and events, they used the services of the clergy, the one literate class. New ideas, developed in the schools of the day by such revolutionary thinkers as Peter Abelard, were usually transmitted by the students who had studied under such men. The books and writings of the time, until 1300 produced on parchment, were usually written in Latin. Therefore their readership was limited to those who had both a university education and sufficient funds to buy what were very expensive items.

The fifteenth century saw a radical change in thought. For one thing, the rediscovery of classical literature stirred up a new interest in education and learning. This interest was further assisted by the use of paper in the production of books, reducing their price considerably. Furthermore, although there was continuing international conflict, the rise of national states made it somewhat easier to move around Europe with the result that there was an increase in the numbers of students moving from university to university. The fact that Copernicus, after studying in Poland, could move to the University of Padua in Italy to study science demonstrates how the situation was changing. In addition, as the middle class was growing, it became necessary for them to have at least an elementary education if they were to carry on business. A new reading public was developing, but a public able to read in the vernacular, not in the Latin of the schools.[5]

All this provided the background for the most revolutionary development of the fifteenth century: the invention of printing. Early in the century the use of the carved wood-block had come into use for the reproduction of pictures and of relatively short written materials. While books could be produced in this way, their publication was slow and rather costly. It was around 1450, however, that a German, Johannes Gutenberg of Mainz, is said to have developed an alloy of metal that could be used to make moveable type. The result was a virtual revolution in the whole process of the transmission and communication of ideas.

Working at first in Mainz and then in Strasburg, Gutenberg achieved a reputation for his publications quite quickly. As a result, others in these two cities also took up the printing craft. From Germany the techniques of the new process soon spread to Italy, and Venice became a leading center for printed works. Soon afterward other cities, such as

Basel in Switzerland, followed suit, and by 1500 printing had become relatively common. It has been estimated that between 1450 and 1500 from 10,000 to 15,000 distinct texts were produced, amounting to between fifteen and twenty million copies. The use of paper and moveable type gave the production of books a completely different character from what it had been before 1450.

In addition to making it possible for books to be produced cheaply and in large quantities, printing helped to bring about an intellectual revolution in many other ways as well. While it is true that until 1500 most of the works printed were older Latin works, new works also began to appear with increasing frequency in the vernacular languages. This meant that the new methods of book production were directed to a new reading public. No longer were such works produced primarily for the people with a university education but also for those who could read only in their own common tongue. Perhaps of equal importance, as Marshall McLuhan has pointed out, a new frame of mind was generated by the printing revolution. While it is a little difficult to think in terms of McLuhan's linear type of thought, there is little doubt that the stress now was much more on the written word and on the intellectual understanding of that word. The visual became less important than the power to comprehend the intellectual and even the abstract type of thought.[6]

The new class of readers, receiving a different type of training from those of a century earlier, now began to think in different terms and could appreciate and grasp new ideas. Moreover, with the possibility of the rapid and cheap production of books, the new ideas could be spread more easily and could reach social classes that hitherto had paid little attention to such things. Even if many people could not read, others could read to them, thus helping to condition them to accept and appreciate not only the need for education but also the ideas that the books contained. Here was the basis for the transmission of the teachings of the Protestant Reformers and particularly those of John Calvin.

## Sixteenth-Century Developments

The sixteenth century saw the climax of the developments of the preceding two centuries in which the new cultural pattern opened up completely in preparation for the advance into the modern age. Therefore, to understand what happened in the sixteenth century, we have to keep in mind what had gone before and to recognize that new forces and elements were also having their effect on western European culture and civilization.

One characteristic of the sixteenth century was the acceleration of processes that had commenced fifty to a hundred years earlier. Inflation, for instance, seems to have accelerated partially as a result of the influx of bullion from the New World, coupled with the reopening of the

Tyrolean silver mines from which the Fuggers of Augsburg gained much of their wealth. The outcome of this inflationary spiral coupled with increasing population and other factors meant an acceleration of economic development and a rapid growth in commerce with its attendant stimulus to credit, banking, and investment. Added to this, with Europe now looking out to the West rather than to the Near East and with the rapid economic growth of such areas as the Netherlands, the Rhine River Valley, and parts of the British Isles, the balance of Europe's economy shifted more rapidly than before to the Northwest.[7]

These economic changes produced corresponding changes in the relations of the social classes as well as in their geographic distribution. During the sixteenth century the nobility found their economic position becoming increasingly more difficult, for although they were usually wealthy in land, they were short on cash. For this reason they were frequently dependent on the rising commercial elements in the population for money either directly or indirectly. Directly they might obtain loans from the merchants or the bankers, while indirectly they might find employment in the mercenary armies or in the civil service of the monarchs who were drawing an ever larger amount of their income from taxes levied on the middle class. This meant that the people who paid the piper very often called the tune. The commercial classes coupled with professional groups such as lawyers were thus gaining an increasing amount of influence in government, a phenomenon that was particularly noticeable in the areas of the Northwest.[8]

The social changes were reflected in the political arena, even in the countries where the absolutism of the New Monarchy had become most obvious. The dependence of Emperor Charles V on the Fuggers for financial assistance in his battling with the Turks or the Lutherans and the dependence of Francis I on the merchants of Paris in his attempts to maintain his power within his own country as well as in his wars with the Emperor show how important the merchant-banker class had become to the monarchs who could no longer depend on the feudal services of their vassals as soldiers or as councilors. In fact it was the refusal of the money lenders on both sides to provide more funds for the French king and the emperor that brought the Franco-Spanish War to a close in 1559 in the Treaty of Chateau-Cambresis. Other monarchs, such as Henry VIII of England and his children and the Stewarts of Scotland, all faced the same problem.[9]

One might almost say that it was the constant warfare of the sixteenth century that made it possible for the middle class to gain such power. Until 1559 France and Spain, and later the Empire, were almost constantly fighting each other, with England, Scotland, Denmark, and the Netherlands being involved on one side or the other. The involvement of the papacy in these conflicts decreased its spiritual influence. From

1560 the type of conflict began to change, for this was the age of the Wars of Religion. True, there had been fighting in Germany between the Lutheran and the Imperial forces in the 1530s and 1540s, but those conflicts were rather spasmodic, whereas the wars of religion in France and the Netherlands, with England and Scotland involved on the side, occupied most of the last forty years of the sixteenth century.[10]

Behind these conflicts throughout the latter part of the century, lay ideological differences and conflicts. New ideas were being disseminated as the Renaissance came to its full fruition in its literary, artistic, political, and social thinking. It was no accident that the great works of Michelangelo in the Sistene Chapel, the completion of St. Peter's Basilica, the writing of Machiavelli's *Prince* and Castiglione's *The Courtier* all belong to the sixteenth century. In the 1540s the work of Copernicus on the revolutions of the heavens and Vesalius's book on the fabric of the human body appeared. These were two revolutionary scientific treatises that were to cause the Roman Catholic church as well as some Protestants serious intellectual difficulties. With the increase of printing this new thought was spreading at a rapid rate, particularly among the rising middle class, which was now the reading public and which gladly accepted the humanist view that the individal was responsible for his own advancement through the use of his reason.[11]

The greatest of the intellectual changes, however, came with the Reformation. On October 31, 1517, Luther, according to tradition, nailed his Ninety-five Theses to the door of the castle church of Wittenberg. Although he did this originally as an academic exercise, challenging all comers in Latin to debate these points with him, it soon became clear that he had begun a conflict, in fact a revolution, far beyond anything he had contemplated. His declaration that the Roman Church and its doctrines were in conflict with the teachings of the Scriptures caused such a furor in Germany and beyond its borders that both he and the church were taken by surprise.

The question then arises as to how and why Luther's posting of his theses—a common academic ploy for arousing debate—should have caused such a stir. Probably the most basic reason was that Luther was first and foremost a preacher who proclaimed his views primarily in the church to the common people. He insisted that it was only by preaching that the Scriptures became the living word. Furthermore he had two groups of allies in the dissemination of his ideas: students from Wittenberg and the preachers trained and sent out from his university to tour the country preaching the doctrines they had learned in Luther's classroom.

Fully as important as the preachers and teachers of Luther's doctrines was the printed word. One of the reasons for the rapid dissemination of his Ninety-five Theses throughout Saxony was that an enterprising local printer had the document translated into German, published in considerable quantities, and sold around the country. Merchants, soldiers, and others traveling through Saxony obtained copies, which they took back to their own lands. Whether they agreed with Luther's views or bought the copies merely as curiosities, the ideas were in this way spread widely and rapidly. But Luther did not stop with his theses, for he became a prolific pamphleteer for the rest of his life, firing off pamphlets like cannon shot about every two weeks to the discomfort of the enemy and the help of friends and supporters.

Luther, however, was not a systematic thinker or writer. He dealt with problems as they arose, but never attempted a systematic statement of his theological position, which must be pieced together from his pamphlets, his commentaries, and his "table talk." The systematic work of the Lutheran Reformation was done by Philip Melanchthon, who in his *Loci Communes* (1521) sought to set forth the first Protestant systematic theology. However, although it was an important work in terms of presenting a systematic view of the evangelical faith, it never seems to have gained great popularity outside of Germany. Written originally in Latin, it was never translated into the vernacular languages as fully as many of Luther's writings were. However, Luther's and Melanchthon's works carried the new doctrines far and wide, though they were often attacked and suppressed by antagonistic ecclesiastical and political authorities.[12]

Meanwhile the Reformation had taken shape in Switzerland, where Zwingli was leading a movement for reform in Zurich. In this he was relatively successful and also persuaded some of the other cities in the German-Swiss area such as Basel and the French-speaking city of Bern to throw off the yoke of the church of Rome. He also came into conflict with Luther over the doctrine of the presence of Christ in the sacrament of the Lord's Supper. Like others involved in the Reformation movement, he wrote a number of short works, but they do not seem to have enjoyed wide popularity in his own day. Becoming involved in the political conflicts of the Swiss cantons, Zwingli died at the Battle of Kappel in 1532.[13]

Henry Bullinger, the man who took Zwingli's place in Zurich, had a much longer life and a much wider influence than his predecessor. Offering refuge to persecuted Protestants from other lands, he was able to influence many who came to find safety and to study in his city. And after they returned home, he kept up a steady correspondence with them, producing more letters than most of the other Reformers combined. To further extend the influence of Protestantism, Bullinger also wrote extensively, and, although he never produced a full systematic theology, his *Decades,* consisting of Bible studies, and his many pamphlets exercised an influence on Protestants as widely separated as the

English and the Hungarian Reformers. In these ways Bullinger, like the other Reformers, made his impact felt on the religious consciousness of western Europe.[14]

Meanwhile, in the small city of Geneva situated on Lac Leman and really part of the Duchy of Savoy, events had been moving in the direction of reform, although it seems to have been primarily a political revolt of the citizens against the authority of the bishop. How much religious interest the citizens had is hard to assess, but the important matter was that they chased out their bishop and defied the Duke of Savoy with the help of their French-speaking neighbor, Bern, to the north. In 1535 a certain Guillaume Farel, a refugee Protestant preacher from Paris, arrived in Geneva, where he immediately set about bringing in a religious reformation that would have results he probably never foresaw.[15]

## THE TRANSMISSION OF CALVIN'S IDEAS

Lest any reader of this chapter should feel that it has taken a considerable length of time to arrive at the actual topic in the title, it is necessary to point out two things. First, we cannot possibly understand the transmission of Calvin's theological and other ideas unless we have some conception of the social and intellectual climate in which he worked. It was this radically changed environment that made it possible for his ideas to spread rapidly and widely. And it is only as we see how the ideas of the other Reformers were transmitted that we can understand how within the space of less than twenty years Calvin's ideas had spread more widely than those of most, if not all, of the others.

To understand the basis of Calvin's influence, we must look back into his early training. First studying at the University of Paris, probably under such men as John Major, the Scottish scholastic, he developed an interest in the humanistic disciplines as he prepared to enter the priesthood. However, as his father had a dispute with the bishop of Noyon for whom he had been acting as a notary, Calvin suddenly received instructions to forget about becoming a cleric and move to Orleans, where he could be trained as a lawyer. In Orleans and Bourges he received legal training under the traditionalist professor Pierre de l'Estoile and under the Italian humanist Andrea Alciat. Equally important, it may have been while in Orleans or Bourges that he was converted to Protestantism, so that when he returned to Paris on his father's death to continue his humanistic studies, his outlook was rather different from what it was when he left Paris.

In the early stages of his Christian life he was asked to write the preface to a French Bible translated from the Latin by a cousin, Pierre Robert Olivétan, and it may have been about the same time that he published his first major work, a commentary on the *De Clementia* of the Roman philosopher Seneca. Shortly after this he entered the theological fray by writing an attack on the doctrine of "soul sleep" set forth by some of the Anabaptist groups. Most important at this point, however, was his writing a small work of seven chapters to assist study groups by setting forth biblical doctrine and as a defense against misrepresentation of these doctrines. This was his *Institutes of the Christian Religion,* which was published in Basel in 1536 and was the beginning of a long series of seven revised and enlarged editions until 1559.

Calvin's original intention was to spend his time studying and writing in the fields of theology and philosophy, but this was not to be. While passing through Geneva in 1536 he was effectively stopped by Guillaume Farel who insisted that he help him in effecting the Reformation in that city. Although unwilling to do so, Calvin eventually consented. However, he and Farel sought such a thorough reformation not only of beliefs but also of morals, manners, and practices that in 1538 they were told to leave. Calvin no doubt took his departure with considerable pleasure, as he hoped that in Strasbourg he would have peace and quiet for study. This, however, was not to be, for Martin Bucer pressured him into becoming the pastor of the French refugee congregation in Strasbourg and also had him take part in some of the Protestant-Roman Catholic meetings held at that time. Then to cap it all, when Cardinal Sadoleto wrote the people of Geneva urging them to return to the Roman fold, they sent his letter to Calvin with a request that he answer it. He did so with great effectiveness.

Partially as a result of Calvin's reply to Sadoleto, when Geneva was in a state of virtual anarchy in 1540, the city council decided to call Calvin back to give guidance and leadership. When Calvin replied that he did not wish to return, the Genevan authorities wrote Farel, who had gone to Lausanne, and he finally persuaded Calvin to return in 1541. Calvin remained in Geneva until his death in 1564. It was from this rather small city at the headwaters of the River Rhone—a city with little economic, political, or intellectual prestige—that Calvin exercised a wide influence over western Europe's religious Reformation, the effects of that movement still being felt to the present day. In the fifty-five years of his life he made an impact on his own age and succeeding ages, an impact equalled by very few in history. The question is, how and why was he able to do this? Calvinists would of course reply, as did John Knox, that he was "a notable servant of the Lord." But there were also certain worldly aspects to his work and situation that in the providence of God enabled him to wield his influence widely and effectively.[16]

Probably the most important factor in the spread of Calvin's ideas was the character of the man himself. He was a systematic thinker and writer. As one reads even his first edition of the *Institutes,* written at the age of twenty-five, one cannot but be impressed with his carefully worked-out position and statement. Although some might accuse Calvin of being a rationalist, the fact of the matter is that he was logical in his thinking, seeking to avoid false deductions and analogies. Yet at the same time, he was quite prepared to acknowledge that he did not have all the answers, since he was dealing with the mystery of God Himself. He was, therefore, always willing to draw a line and say, ''Thus far and no farther.'' In this he showed a mixture of systematic logic and a sense of mystery into which he would not delve. His *Institutes,* his biblical commentaries, his letters, and his pamphlets all show these characteristics, which did not appeal to some but which spoke to the hearts of many.

We may perhaps understand Calvin's structure of thought if we look at his principles of thought as a theologian. The formal principle was the authority of the Scriptures of the Old and New Testaments. He believed that the Bible was the Word of God written. While some have endeavored in recent years to enlist his support for various formulations of doctrines of verbal inspiration, inerrancy, and the like, Calvin does not set forth anything clearly on this subject. His view was that the Bible is recognized as the Word of God, not by logical deductions or by empirical observations and proofs, but because the Holy Spirit testifies to the believer that it is the Word of God. And because it is the Word of God, it must have final authority over all other forms of knowledge as to man's nature and his relation to God, his Creator and Sovereign.[17] With regard to man's knowledge and understanding of nature, man finds out by means of empirical investigation, always of course remembering that the Bible gives the ultimate interpretation of all things (cf. his comments on astronomy in Genesis 1:16).[18]

The material principle of Calvin's thought was the sovereignty of God. As the Creator, Sustainer, Ruler, and Redeemer, God is sovereign over all His creatures and all their actions. This doctrine formed the basis of, and foundation for, all other doctrines. If any formulation of a doctrine tended to infringe on the Sovereignty of God, it was to be either reworded or rejected completely. Thus his systematic statement of the Christian faith grew naturally out of his doctrine of God's sovereignty. However, all statements of belief must necessarily be governed and limited by the teaching of the Scriptures. In formulating a doctrine such as election, for example, though it is based on the sovereignty of God, and one may be tempted to include many logical implications of the doctrine, he held that it is improper, in fact sinful, to go beyond what the Bible has to say on the matter. Even though this limitation leaves certain paradoxes in the Christian faith, they are to be accepted, he said, and ideas that seem irreconcilable should be held in tension, since the sovereign God had spoken through His prophets and apostles. While this position does not satisfy the rationalist, Calvin, following his two basic principles, could do no other.[19]

Calvin, however, was not just a theoretician without any practical interests. As a lawyer who at one point was the prime mover in the reform of Geneva's laws and as a controversialist constantly battling to maintain and strengthen the Reformation movement, he had to be practical in his application of his theological principles. As one reads his letters, his *Institutes,* his commentaries, and his pamphlets, one gains a strong impression of a man who was very much alive to the events taking place in his world. His pamphlet on astrology and his letter on the taking of usury reflect practical thinking, as do the applications he made of his texts in his sermons. It is not surprising, therefore, that not only scholars but also the hard-headed businessmen of his day responded to his views with considerable enthusiasm.

In order to understand Calvin's widespread influence, we must look not only at his style of expression and method of thought but also at the means he used for communicating his ideas. Preaching and teaching were basic means of propagating his views, but equally important were his personal contacts and, most important of all, his writings. It will be necessary to look at all these means of communication if we are to understand how he had, and for that matter still has, such a wide impact on Western thought. Furthermore, we must also obtain some knowledge of those whom he influenced, those who accepted his views and put them into action in the sixteenth century.

As mentioned, preaching was basic to Calvin's exposition and the communication of his ideas. In this Calvin was in agreement with Luther, Bullinger, Bucer, and most of the other Reformers. In fact one could almost say that the Reformation brought about the rebirth of preaching. Calvin had apparently begun preaching very soon after his conversion, for there is a tradition that he used to preach in some of the churches in or near Bourges when he was a student. On his return to Geneva in 1541, preaching became one of his chief occupations, as he occupied the pulpit of St. Pierre not only on Sundays, but also as often as three times during the week. This gave him a great opportunity to present his interpretation of the Scriptures both to the burghers of Geneva and to strangers either living in the city or passing through.

Probably because he had to preach so frequently, Calvin apparently was not in the habit of writing out his sermons, although we know that on one occasion he wrote out some sermons after preaching them and sent them to Elizabeth, queen of England. His usual practice seems to have been to spend considerable time thinking about the meaning of his text. Then he would go into the pulpit prepared to give a homily on a passage of from five to fifteen or twenty verses. This consisted of a running commentary on the passage with an application of the material to the Christian's everyday life, but particularly to his spiritual growth and appreciation of his relationship to God.

In accord with his systematic approach to his work, Calvin usually followed the plan of preaching right through a biblical book, section by section and Sunday by Sunday. This meant that there was continuity of instruction both in expounding and in applying the Scriptures. Calvin was careful to keep his explanations and application within the context of the book as a whole and also within the context of its historical situation. He did not interpret Scripture allegorically. He always brought the hearers back to the fact that the center of the Christian life is Christ Himself.

Calvin's hearers often wished to have copies of his sermons in print for their own reading or to give to others, but Calvin did not comply, partly because he wrote out very few of his sermons. Consequently, despite his opposition, some of his congregation employed a certain Raguenier of Bar-sur-Seine, a French refugee, who took down Calvin's sermons in a sort of shorthand. Some of the Genevan printers then wished to print these sermons, but Calvin was strongly opposed to this at first. Finally in 1557 he gave Conrad Badius, brother-in-law of publisher Robert Estienne, permission to print his series of sermons on the Ten Commandments. The following year, again after considerable pressure and argument, he allowed his sermons on the life and work of Christ to be published. But many of them were never published and have only recently been discovered. Those that were published, however, were soon translated into various vernacular languages and became an important means of spreading abroad the teachings of the Genevan Reformer.

In this way Calvin's sermons began to serve a double purpose. Naturally they influenced those who heard them, for we are told that after he had preached, people thronged about him to speak to him about what he had said and would often form a procession to accompany him to his home. But the sermons also influenced those who read them in other countries, either in the original French or in their own language. In this connection it is interesting to note that Richard Bannatyne, John Knox's secretary, reports that as Knox lay on his deathbed, some of the sermons of "Messire Jean Calvin" were read to him in French, which he understood very well. They were probably the sermons on "La Passion de Notre Seigneur." Sermons, then, were a primary means by which Calvin's ideas were spread.[20]

Closely related to his work as a preacher was his work as a teacher. While in Strasbourg, he had been in close contact with Jean Sturm and Martin Bucer, both of whom were very much interested in developing an educational system that would provide instruction for all the children of the city. When he returned to Geneva, he worked on their ideas for some time, until at last in 1559 he had established a full system of education. Out of his efforts grew the Academy of Geneva, which later became that city's university. Calvin not only took a prominent part in its completion, but he was also one of the professors who taught theology to those who planned to enter the ministry. For many years he gave lectures, expounding the various books of the Bible. The person in charge of the Academy was Theodore Beza, who had come over from Lausanne.[21]

Calvin's work both as preacher and as teacher was extremely effective in Geneva, for one may see by a study of the city's history during this period that much of the change that he brought about was through these activities. It is true that until 1555 he faced strong opposition to his views, particularly on church discipline, from those who agreed neither with his doctrines nor with his views on morality. But since he occupied the principal pulpit in the city from which he preached up to five times a week besides giving biblical lectures, he had the most effective means of putting over his ideas. As a result, by 1555 he had won the battle and from that year to the day of his death in 1564 his theological and moral influence dominated Geneva.[22]

There was more, however, than a general influence that he wielded in and over Geneva. The city's population of around nine thousand was almost doubled by the number of refugees who had flocked there to obtain respite from persecution in their own countries. The French congregation was the largest, and in some senses the most unpopular, but there were also Spanish and Italian congregations, and to these was added the English congregation under John Knox during the reign of Mary Tudor. Then there were the students who came to study under Calvin and his fellow-teachers. They came from many different countries but particularly from France, the Netherlands, Germany, England, and Italy. Many of them returned to their own lands later and carried on the work of Reformation there. After the establishment of the Academy, the influx of students became even greater, as they came to study not only theology but also law and to obtain a general education. When these students returned home, they brought with them Calvin's ideas, which they sought to proclaim, not infrequently ending their careers at the stake.[23]

While most historians of Calvin's influence stress the importance of his preaching and teaching, a few seem to feel that his personal relationships with people were of importance. Calvin is usually pictured as very austere, humorless, and even bad tempered. Yet the accounts of those who visited Geneva and came in contact with Calvin give a much different picture. He apparently possessed a sense of humor with a somewhat satirical cast, as we can see from some of his writings, such as his pamphlet on the necessity of taking an inventory of all the religious relics in Europe. While he suffered from a number of chronic diseases, including ulcers, he nevertheless seems to have been hospitable. A report says that he was even well enough to enjoy bowling.[24] But above and beyond all this, the fact that he could gain the almost fierce loyalty of widely differing personalities indicates that in his personal relationships he was able to communicate his ideas effectively and dynamically.

Calvin received many visitors from many lands who visited Geneva for a short time, very often just to meet him. John Foxe, the English martyrologist, and Bishop Coverdale are good examples. But Calvin was also in constant communication with the other Reformers—particularly Bucer, Bullinger, Melanchthon—with whom he constantly exchanged ideas. It was as a result of his relationship with Bullinger that these two men signed the *Consensus Tigurinus* of 1549 in which they set forth a statement concerning the "real" presence of Christ in the Lord's Supper as being effected by the Holy Spirit, through the reception of the elements by the believer. In this way a position was taken midway between Luther's *consubstantiation* and Zwingli's purely symbolic interpretation.[25]

Besides his contacts with his students and some of the other Reformers, Calvin kept up a large correspondence with men and women all over Europe, from kings and their councilors to people of the lower classes who wrote to him for help or advice. Perhaps there is no better place to see the *real* Calvin than in these letters. The letters are always practical and very much to the point. He wrote a letter of comfort to John Knox on the death of Marjorie, his wife. And he wrote a strong letter of rebuke to an erstwhile friend, Louis du Tillet, who had deserted the cause and returned to the church of Rome. He also wrote letters of encouragement to those facing persecution and conflict for the faith, such as the five students of Lausanne who were going to their deaths at the stake in Lyon. He wrote letters giving advice to Protestants planning to establish a congregation. He sent a letter also to a minister who had written him for counsel concerning some of his problems. In all of these letters one sees his many-sidedness: his warmth, his compassion, his anger at times with those who proved untrustworthy, and his intellectual integrity and strength. There is little doubt that these letters did much not only to manifest his personality but also to spread his ideas throughout the length and breadth of Europe.[26]

But though we speak of Calvin's preaching and teaching, his personal contacts, and his letter-writing, undoubtedly the most effective means of the transmission of his ideas was his formal writings. One may say that the other means of communication formed the spring from which his formal writings came, for on more than one occasion it was as a result of the reaction to his own experiences as a preacher or teacher, or as a consequence of his personal contacts, that he felt it necessary to write. And it was his writings that had the widest circulation and the most lasting effect, as we can see from the fact that many of them are still being republished in the twentieth century in different countries and in many different languages.

Undoubtedly of all his writings the *Institutes of the Christian Religion* was, and still is, the most important. Originally published in 1536, it was later revised and republished seven times in both Latin and French, growing from a small monograph of seven chapters to a work of seventy-nine chapters in the edition of 1559. At first he sought to follow the order of the Apostles' Creed but later, finding this unsatisfactory, he changed the whole structure of the work, expanding and applying his thoughts more fully in each new edition. As one reads the work in the latest English edition edited by J. T. McNeill and Ford Lewis Battles in the Library of Christian Classics, keeping one's eyes open for the indications of the different editions, one can easily see that Calvin, the constant student, added to it in each edition the exegetical and theological material that he had accumulated since the previous edition. Constantly studying both the Scriptures and other writers such as Bernard of Clairvaux and many of the church fathers, Calvin added an increasing number of references to them in edition after edition.[27]

Of the greatest importance in this process was the fact that from 1541 on he was, for the purpose of his preaching and teaching, preparing commentaries on the various books of the Bible. Refusing the fourfold allegorical method of the medieval commentators and eschewing the sermonizing of Luther's commentary on Galatians, he followed the typical humanist technique of the historico-grammatical exegesis, sticking closely to the historical context of the books and seeking to understand exactly what they were saying. His was, in a true sense, an empirical method. And as he accumulated more knowledge from these studies, he was able to use it in the revision of his *Institutes*. In his lifetime he wrote commentaries on most of the books of the Bible, although he avoided some of the more difficult writings such as the Song of Solomon and the Book of Revelation. He appears to have been unwilling to make clear assertions about what these books actually meant. The complete set of his commentaries was finally issued in Geneva in the latter part of the 1570s and the early 1580s and had a wide dispersion.[28]

Calvin was also a pamphleteer. One of the first editions of his collected pamphlets, owned by the present writer, forms a folio volume of over one thousand pages. His pamphlets were not only numerous but also varied in subject and purpose. Exposition was one of Calvin's first objectives, as he sought to set forth in a small format the meaning of some of the Christian doctrines and practices. One of his pamphlets was his *Forme des Prières,* which was really a directory of worship for the church services in Geneva but which had considerable influence on the liturgical practices of Reformed churches in Geneva and France and also in Scotland, the Netherlands, and other countries where his ideas had been received. Perhaps more of a true pamphlet was his exposition of the meaning of the Lord's Supper. This pamphlet was partially responsible for the signing of the *Consensus Tigurinus,* and Luther said it would have prevented the conflict between himself and Zwingli.

Calvin's primary reason for writing pamphlets, however, seems to have been polemical. Naturally one of his principal targets was the Roman Catholic church. It was in 1541 that he wrote his letter in reply to Cardinal Sadoleto, who had urged the Genevans to return to Rome. In this letter he pointed out that Rome had forsaken biblical Christianity. Two years later he published his satirical article on relics and another urging the Emperor Charles V to stop the persecution of the Protestants. After the first session of the Council of Trent he wrote a pamphlet attacking its actions. And of course we must remember that the *Institutes* with the dedicatory letter to Francis I of France pleading for toleration of the Protestants was itself a pamphlet, albeit a rather bulky one.

Calvin did not limit himself to controversy with the Roman Catholics. One of his first pamphlets, *Psychopannichia,* attacked the doctrine of soul sleep as set forth by some of the Anabaptists. In a later pamphlet he took some shots at the group of spiritual anarchists known as the Libertines. In another he wrote a devastating criticism of astrology, which was as popular in his day as it is in ours, and largely for the same reason: a decline in Christian faith. Thus while immersed in the problems of preaching, teaching, writing commentaries, and revising his *Institutes,* Calvin found time to deal with the current problems facing the Protestant movement. One wonders how he did it and can hardly be surprised that he died at the age of fifty-five!

Most of his pamphlets first appeared in Latin, as they were frequently addressed to the more educated, academic class. It was never very long, however, before the pamphlets appeared also in French, sometimes translated by Calvin himself and sometimes by one of the publishers in Geneva. Usually shortly after a pamphlet's appearance in French it was also published in some one of the other vernacular languages. One of the earliest translations was that of his pamphlet against Pope Paul III, which appeared in German in 1541. In 1545 his catechism appeared in Latin, French, and Italian almost simultaneously. In 1546 there was a Czech version of another pamphlet, and from 1548 on his pamphlets began to appear in English, Spanish, Dutch, and even Greek. In this way they had a widespread effect on the Reformation movement.[29]

Calvin's writings had a wide readership because they were published both in Latin and in the various vernacular languages. Quite naturally, since Latin was the language of scholarship, academics and theologians could read his works when they originally appeared in Latin. This, however, would have had relatively little effect on the common people. The important thing was that there was now a literate middle class who were able to read works in their own languages, even if they were unable to read Latin. It was to this class that Calvin made his greatest appeal. Coming from a middle-class, professional background, he knew how to speak to that element as well as to the academics, and so he gained their attention right from the beginning.

One of the important factors in Calvin's successful propagation of his ideas was his style and method of presentation. He was not interested in making a name for himself as a great literary figure but was primarily concerned that he would be able to put his ideas across to his readers. He wanted to be crystal clear in what he had to say. He held that the most important basic characteristic of a good style was clarity, and he practiced what he preached. The result was that he was understood very well both by those who heard him and by those who read his works. And even today his style, when compared with that of many of our contemporaries, is clearer and more to the point than theirs. His clarity and directness undoubtedly played an important part in the spread of his thought.[30]

However, Calvin did not owe his influence only to his style. As Pierre Chaunu has pointed out, reform movements in the church have two stages. The first is the evangelistic, and the second, the systematic. Luther was the evangelist of the Reformation. Moreover he was clearly teutonic in his approach and conservative almost to the point of being archaic, following the principle that nothing in the church should be changed but that which conflicted with the Word of God. Calvin, on the other hand, trained as a humanist and a lawyer, was the systemizer *par excellence*. Furthermore, his insistence that in the field of theology and church practice nothing should be retained that was not required in the Scriptures, was much more radical than anything Luther favored. In addition, Luther allowed the civil authorities to have much more to say in the church than Calvin was ever prepared to allow them.[31] Thus Calvin's whole approach and position fitted much more readily into the frame of thought of the more radical elements in the western European scene.

Like Luther, Calvin was primarily interested in the religious and theological aspect of the Reformation and on most counts he found himself in agreement with his German forerunner. There are frequent appreciative references in his works to Luther's achievements, and he constantly reiterated the German Reformer's fundamental doctrines of the sole authority of Scripture and justification by faith alone. Yet because of his systematic (one might even say scientific) approach to theology, he not only made Luther's views clearer but he also developed other aspects of the Christian faith largely ignored by Luther. In this respect he went beyond Luther, creating a wider structure of theology that appealed to many, even to some of Luther's strongest supporters such as Philip Melanchthon.[32] This is one of the reasons for Calvinism's supplanting of Lutheranism in a number of countries such as France, England, Scotland, and the Netherlands.

It was also because of this more systematic and wider theological approach that Calvin also exercised a considerable influence on the development of Western thought generally in his own and succeeding generations. He saw theology as undergirding all human thought, so that every thought might be brought into bondage to Jesus Christ. Thus one finds that he had a powerful impact on the universities, not only in a general fashion but very concretely in the work of men such as Pierre de la Ramée, Jerome Zanchius, Andrew Melville, and many others. These men sought to apply Calvin's life-and-world view to all areas of thought and endeavored to present their interpretations of the various areas of thought as seen both *sub specie aeternitatis* and *soli Deo gloria*.[33]

Calvin, as I stated earlier, did not write merely for academics, nor were his writings mere academic exercise. He was a practical man who believed that thought must produce action. In Geneva, he sought to establish a city that would manifest in its way of life a culture that recognized in all its activities the kingship of Jesus Christ. This point of view became the keynote of the thought of his followers in other lands. The result was that Calvinists in England, Scotland, France, the Netherlands, and America came to be regarded as political radicals who were constantly pushing to have a democratic form of government established. Some even went so far as to say that the subordinate magistrates making up the Estates General or Parliament could remove a king—and on some occasions they did so.[34] At the same time, it was the Calvinists in France, England, Scotland, and the Netherlands who were prepared to take the initiative in trading ventures beyond the continent of Europe, who were willing to risk even their lives in colonizing new countries, and who were always prepared to work hard in the calling to which God had called them, whatever that might be. Whatever error the sociologist Max Weber may have made in his theory of the relation of Calvinism to the rise of capitalism, he was surely right when he stressed the importance of the doctrine of calling in the thought of the Calvinist, a doctrine that we can see worked out in country after country down to the present.[35]

We must also recognize that because of this sense of calling Calvin's influence was not generated primarily by organization or by mass propaganda. His influence was spread through devoted individuals who had been gripped by Calvin's vision of the sovereignty of God and their calling to God's service and who responded in faith and obedience.

Academics such as Zanchius, Ramée, and Melville; scientists such as Ambroise Paré, Bernard Palissy, and Francis Bacon; artists such as the Dutch masters of the late sixteenth century; and many others all played their parts. Sometimes Calvinistic influence led to the organization of such groups as the Huguenot armies of Coligny and Henry of Navarre and the Scottish Lords of the Congregation of Jesus Christ, but ultimately Calvin's impact arose from the conviction of believing individuals who recognized that what he taught found its ultimate authority in the Bible, the Word of God.

Calvin's impact was not limited to his own day, but continued into the following centuries in many different parts of the world as Europe expanded through trade and conquest. In the latter part of the nineteenth century and the early years of the twentieth century, this influence tended to disappear in the face of changing patterns of thought brought on by atheistic humanism and materialism. But in recent years Calvinism has seen a revival of considerable proportions. It is beginning once again to wield an influence on the world scene. This book in some degree bears witness to its resurgence.

# Switzerland:
# Triumph and Decline

## Richard C. Gamble

*Richard C. Gamble is Assistant Professor of Church History at Westminster Theological Seminary, Philadelphia. He holds degrees from Westminster College (B.A.) and Pittsburgh Theological Seminary (M.A.) and is a Dr.Theol. candidate at the University of Basel, Switzerland. He has served as lecturer in church history at the Freie Evangelisch-Theologische Akademie in Basel. Mr. Gamble has written articles and reviews for the* Westminster Theological Journal *and the* Theologische Zeitschrift. *He is a member of the American Society for Church History, the American Society for Reformation Research, and the North American Patristic Society.*

# 3

# Switzerland: Triumph and Decline

Attempting to trace the influence of Calvin and Calvinism in any individual country is a complex task made even more difficult by the necessary brevity with which each author of such a work as this must approach his geographic area. The country of Switzerland poses some unique problems of interpretation in that Switzerland gave birth to the movement that we are tracing! We will begin with Calvin's labors in the city of Geneva, devoting the majority of the chapter, however, to a discussion of his influence on sixteenth-century Switzerland: his communications with Bullinger in Zurich (the *Consensus Tigurinus*); the Second Helvetic Confession; and the continuation of his ideas through Beza, his successor in Geneva, who died in 1605. Seventeenth-century Switzerland will receive a quick review as we examine the theologies of Wollebius and the framers of the Helvetic Consensus Formula (1675). A natural terminus to our discussion of Calvinism in Switzerland is the ascendency of J.-A. Turretin in Geneva and the victory of French rationalism over Calvinism at the university there.

The Reformation in Switzerland had its beginnings in Zurich with Ulrich Zwingli (1484–1531), whose death preceded even the first edition of Calvin's *Institutes*. More particularly, the Reformation in Geneva was begun by Guillaume Farel (1489–1565). Farel first visited Geneva in 1532, and in 1533 he held the first Protestant service there, in a garden, on Good Friday. The spread of the gospel in Geneva bore some violent fruit: in May of 1533 a riot broke out in which a canon was killed. The bishop of Geneva had the ringleaders of the riot arrested, but the city magistrates argued that in the case of murder the episcopal court had no jurisdiction. Seeing that he would not be able to try the murderers, the bishop left Geneva and never returned. The culprits were later executed.

Geneva had been in alliance with the cities of Fribourg and Bern. Fribourg, a strongly Catholic city, had protested the presence of Farel in Geneva, but Farel had the approval of the city of Bern. After various disputations and riots, it was discovered that an episcopal notary had documents signed by the bishop; these documents were to authorize the appointment of a military governor from Fribourg over the city. Infuriated by this, Geneva refused to continue the alliance with Fribourg, leaving Bern the sole protector of the city.

The bishop, however, did not give up his power in the city without a fight. He, along with Charles III of Savoy, gathered troops and attacked the city. This attack failed. A number of other attacks were attempted, all without success. The magistrates wrote to Rome, protesting the actions of their bishop, reporting his absence, and declaring the office of bishop vacant; however, Rome chose to ignore the letter. The magistrates established their own mint in 1535, thus proclaiming their independence from Roman hierarchy.

Charles III of Savoy was not ready to lose Geneva; he mustered a troop of five hundred mercenaries and besieged the city late in 1535. Geneva appealed to Bern for help but, receiving none, turned to Francis I of France. A small cavalry force was sent, but after attempting to cross the Alps during the winter and being attacked by Savoyard troops, only seven men and the commander succeeded in reaching Geneva. Their offer of protection under French rule was voted on and turned down by the city.

This futile attempt by France aroused Bern to action. Assembling a force of six thousand, she liberated Geneva from the troops of Savoy in February 1536. As a result of the preaching and disputations of Farel, the citizens of the newly liberated city voted in May to live "according to the gospel."

Although Geneva was now legally a Protestant town, it was such in name only, as Calvin bears testimony. As he was saying farewell to the Company of Pastors, he testified:

> When I first came to this church there was almost nothing. They were preaching and that is all. They were good at seeking out idols and burning them, yet there was no other Reformation. Everything was in an uproar.[1]

Certainly the city of Geneva at the time of Calvin's death could not be described in the same terms that Calvin used in describing the city on his arrival. What were some of the effects of Calvin's sojourn in this Protestant city?

In Calvin's efforts to reform the church in Geneva, he established four offices: those of pastors, teachers (doctors), elders, and deacons. The pastor was to preach the Word of God, admonish, and exhort, as well as administer the sacraments. The teacher was to "teach sound doctrine to the faithful" and "prepare youth for the ministry and for civil government." The duties of the elders were "to keep watch over every man's life, to admonish amiably those whom they see leading a disorderly life, and where necessary to report to the assembly which will be deputized to make fraternal correction." The deacons were charged with caring for the poor and sick and with putting an end to begging.[2]

The church of Geneva consisted of the "Venerable Company of Pastors" and the consistory. The Company of Pastors had strictly ecclesiastical functions, primarily the education and examination of candidates for ordination. The consistory, or presbytery, was not confined to pastors but had lay members as well, who in fact had a majority in the consistory. The duty of the consistory was to maintain ecclesiastical discipline within the city; its court was the controlling power in the church. The consistorial court, however, did not have the right of civil punishment.[3]

By reforming the church in this way, Calvin was moving to reform the society of Geneva as well. His method of reforming the city was by the use of ecclesiastical discipline. The object of Calvin's discipline was to protect the church as a body of believers, to protect the individual Christian within the church, and also to bring offenders to repentance. The manner of discipline was first through private admonition of the offender, then admonition before witnesses, and finally, when admonition failed, through excommunication. The grave sentence of excommunication was implemented for only the most serious of crimes. It is important to remember that as one of the objects of discipline was to bring the offender to repentance, care had to be taken in the community's response to those punished.

The church was further protected in that the pastors themselves were not exempt from discipline. Calvin wanted them to be liable to civil jurisdiction as well, for they should provide the very best of examples to the people.

No matter how important the citizen, the laws of Geneva were to be honored by all and were strictly enforced.[4] Calvin was no innovator when it came to these laws of morality, for nearly all of the towns of the Middle Ages had laws on their books concerning various extravagances. In many Swiss towns the laws were not formally or structurally changed, but rather certain laws came to be "ignored" and other laws were added.[5] What was new was the enforcement of these laws. Calvin's purpose in maintaining discipline within the city was as an aid to moral regeneration. In his thought, there was no separation between

Christianity and morality; a Christian city could not tolerate such sins as blatant prostitution, for example. As noted by Calvin himself when he arrived in Geneva, the pastors were preaching evangelical doctrine but no reformation of life had occurred. The two must go hand-in-hand.

Calvin's views of government and the relationship between church and state were new and radical. Philip Hughes expresses Calvin's thought succinctly:

> Indeed, the whole structure of society as conceived in Calvin's mind was based on the distinction between church and state as two separate powers whose spheres of authority were clearly defined, the former wielding the spiritual sword in the faithful proclamation of the Word of God, and the latter the secular sword in the maintaining of good and just government and the punishment of offenders against the statutory laws; and both being subject to the supreme authority of Almighty God.[6]

As we have already seen, "wielding the spiritual sword" included, among other things, the power of excommunication. This power in the hands of the pastors was a return to one of the distinctives of the church of the first three centuries, as Calvin saw it. This return was, however, not at all in line with the existing societal structures and was indeed foreign to the conception that the magistrates had of themselves and their duties. It is easy to imagine that to follow this plan boldly in church/state relations would involve a rocky road for Calvin; and it did.

Any notion that Calvin or the church of Geneva ruled the civil government is not accurate. In September 1548, the council of the city ruled that the pastors could only exhort the people, not excommunicate them.[7] In December the council went further in its attempts to usurp power by giving Guichard Roux permission to receive the Lord's Supper after being forbidden by the consistory. Calvin himself was admonished by the council on September 24, 1548, because of a letter he had written criticizing the magistrates of Geneva.[8] After various protests and efforts by the pastors, the council finally agreed on January 24, 1555, to grant the consistory the rights that were theirs as established by the Ecclesiastical Ordinances of 1541. Basically, the Ecclesiastical Ordinances established the standards by which the church would run. The times and number of church services in the city were set, as well as the frequency of the meetings of the pastors and other regulations, such as excommunication.

As mentioned above, Calvin's conception of church/state relations was new and even differed from the structures established in German-speaking Switzerland. For example, Zwingli and Bullinger denied that the church had the right of excommunication.[9] For Bullinger, excommunication was a temporal judgment and as such was an inherent right of the magistrate to prosecute.[10] In Zurich, the church was governed in this manner: within the canton, there were at first eight and then nine chapters, each headed by a deacon (dean). Twice a year, the pastors would meet at a synod, which was first suggested by Zwingli in 1528 and finally approved in October 1532. The power of the synod was limited strictly to matters of doctrine and the morality of the clergy; eight members of the small council of the city fathers were also in attendance. A committee of examiners was also established, which included two members of the small council, two pastors, and two lectors of the Carolinum, the school of theology; the purpose of the committee was to examine pastoral candidates. If approved by the committee, the candidate would then be inspected by the council and would swear an oath of allegiance to the magistrates. The candidate would then be presented to the people of the church, having been recommended by the Christian government. The people of the church were asked if there were any objections to him and were then enjoined to help the pastor in the performance of his duties.

Zwingli and Bullinger could not agree with Calvin's idea that there should be a separation between civil government and church government.[11] Farel, who agreed with Calvin, was not successful in getting the new ideas introduced into the government of Neuchâtel. Unfortunately, even during Calvin's lifetime, the two separate powers in Geneva were not as separate in reality as they were in theory.[12]

One of the fruits of Calvin's ministry in Geneva was the missionary activity that proceeded from there and the care for the destitute who arrived in Geneva. It is clear from the records of that time that Geneva became the most famous place to which religious refugees fled.[13] We are also informed that Geneva sent out a host of well-trained missionaries, especially to France but even as far away as Brazil. The records of those missionaries who were martyred for their faith are also in our possession. Professor Hughes again summarizes well when he says:

> Here is irrefutable proof of the falsity of the too common conclusion that Calvinism is incompatible with evangelism and spells death to all missionary enterprise.[14]

## THE CONSENSUS TIGURINUS

As we consider the influence of Calvin and Calvinism on Switzerland, the *Consensus Tigurinus,* or Zurich Consensus, not only presents us with a suitable point of departure but also elucidates the theological background of Switzerland at this critical era. In German-speaking Switzerland, a mature doctrine of the sacraments had developed, especially that of the Lord's Supper, which is dealt with in the Consensus. Zwingli had thought much and debated often on the nature of the elements of the Lord's Supper; both he and Luther had rejected the Roman Catholic notion of transubstantiation, which holds that the bread and wine actually become the body and blood of Christ in such a way that a miracle takes place and Christ is then sacrificed on the altar. Calvin says, "But the question is: What is the nature of this communication?"[15]—a question that needs to be investigated if we are to understand the interpretations of Christ's words "This is my body."

Zwingli and Luther could not agree on this matter. In 1529 they had a discussion in Marburg and agreed on fourteen major points of theology, but could not see eye-to-eye on this issue. Luther's position was that the bread and wine were the body and blood of Christ; not a *transubstantiation* of the elements but rather a *consubstantiation*. *Consubstantiation* was the view that the body and blood of Christ is "in, with, and under" the bread and wine. Zwingli's view, on the other hand, was that the bread and wine are not naturally united with the body and blood of Christ; the body and blood of Christ are neither locally included in the elements nor sensibly present but are symbols through which we have communion in Christ's body and blood.[16]

Zwingli and Luther never did find a resolution to this difficulty. Later a further complication developed because of Calvin's views on the Lord's Supper, which were identical neither with Luther's understanding nor with Zwingli's. Calvin was hopeful that an agreement could be reached among the Protestants, at least among the Protestants of Switzerland. The Consensus Tigurinus succeeded in uniting Switzerland regarding the doctrine of the Lord's Supper.

Before beginning an examination of the thought of Bullinger and Calvin concerning the Lord's Supper, we will investigate the historical circumstances surrounding the *Consensus*. In 1544–45 Luther attacked the Zwinglian notion of the Lord's Supper with his "Kurzes Bekenntnis vom Abendmahl" (Short Confession on the Lord's Supper). Zwingli's successor Bullinger responded to this attack in his "Wahrhaftes Bekenntnis der Diener der Kirche zu Zurich . . . insbesondere über das Nachtmahl . . ." (The True Confession of the Pastors of Zurich . . . Concerning the Lord's Supper). As mentioned previously, Calvin's thought agreed neither with Luther nor with Bullinger, who closely followed his predecessor. Calvin was able, however, to enter into discussion with Bullinger concerning their respective views of the Supper. Bullinger gave him a copy of his "De Sacramentis," written in 1546, when Calvin was in Zurich early in 1547. As we shall see, Calvin was not in complete agreement with Bullinger's conception and submitted to Bullinger a draft of his position in twenty-four propositions, which was sent to Zurich in June 1548. Bullinger made certain annotations to this text and then sent it back to Calvin, who revised it again in January 1549. Calvin then thought the project important enough to travel with Farel to Zurich in May 1549, where consensus between Calvin and Bullinger was found within a few hours.[17] This understanding resulted in the *Consensus Tigurinus*. To help us understand the importance of this document, the convictions of Bullinger and Calvin regarding the Lord's Supper will be briefly sketched.

Bullinger, like Zwingli, rejected the Lutheran view of consubstantiation. Besides rejecting the idea that the sacrament can be a direct means of grace, Bullinger saw the fundamental principle of the Lord's Supper as being a religious illustration and a stimulant to faith; the entire content of the sacrament consists in the remembrance of Christ.[18] For the believer, the real presence of Christ is in the Supper, but the unbeliever receives only bread and wine.[19] It is through the Holy Spirit that it is possible for believers to be partakers of Christ.[20]

Looking at Calvin's formulations concerning the Lord's Supper, we remember that Calvin's position lies somewhere between those of Luther and Zwingli. His view did not satisfy the extremists of either party. Calvin was first influenced by Luther, perhaps more strongly than by Zwingli; the prospects of agreement with the Zurich Reformers were therefore not very great.[21]

Yet it is clear from Calvin's writings that he rejected the Lutheran notion of consubstantiation.[22] While rejecting that notion, however, he affirmed with the Lutherans that the flesh of Christ is given in the Lord's Supper.[23] Christ is present in the sacrament.[24]

How can this be? Calvin also very clearly affirmed that the body of Christ remains in heaven and retains its human properties.[25] The answer to this question is found in the Holy Spirit's action in regard to the Supper; Christ does not come down to us from heaven but by the power of the Spirit lifts us to Himself in heaven.[26] We then partake of Christ in the Supper in a spiritual, heavenly manner.[27] There is a real presence of Christ in the Lord's Supper, yet it is a heavenly mode of presence.

Calvin is quick to point out that this presence of Christ is not received by a nonbeliever.[28] It is not that the nonbeliever is not offered the body and blood of Christ, as both evil and good are offered it,[29] but true reception is by faith alone, the receiver himself being the obstacle that keeps him from enjoying the gift.[30] The partaking by the nonbeliever does not mean that he receives it to his own detriment, however, as some Lutherans maintained.

What can be concluded from an analysis of the contents of the *Consensus Tigurinus?* Are we capable of determining whether Calvin's understanding of the sacrament of the Lord's Supper became normative throughout Switzerland? Two differing conclusions have been drawn concerning the *Consensus*: either it was a triumph for Calvin's doctrine or there was honest give and take between Bullinger and Calvin in their agreement. To say that there is no Bullingerian influence in the *Consensus* is not accurate, although it is also clear that Calvin's understanding of the Lord's Supper is what is presented in the *Consensus Tigurinus*.

The *Consensus* asserts that in the sacrament there is a real life union with Christ and that the signs are not "empty"; they are means of grace and convey the benefits of redemption.

After the writing of the *Consensus Tigurinus,* Calvinism began growing in strength in Switzerland; in the city of Zurich, where Bullinger was still the *antistes* or head pastor, Calvinism had in some ways replaced Zwinglianism as the leading theological school. The earliest Reformer of the town of St. Gallen, Vadian (Joachim von Watt, 1484–1551), was personally influenced by Zwingli and had heard of Calvin as early as 1536. Vadian had thought it important for Calvin to be united with the Zurich theologians concerning the nature of the Lord's Supper, and Calvin found him possessing keen judgment in desiring that union. Calvin had high regard for him and dedicated his work *"De scandalis"* to Vadian. As Calvin's letters of the time indicate, he was deeply touched by Vadian's death. Another Reformer of St. Gallen, Johan Kessler (1502–74), was of a humble spirit and earnestly desired a visit from Calvin. Although that meeting never occurred as far as we know, Kessler was a faithful defender of Calvin throughout his life. Basel, however, was under the ecclesiastical headship of Simon Sulzer, who had Lutheran tendencies; therefore, the city of Basel was not very receptive to Calvin or his theology until the next *antistes.* [31]

Within Switzerland after a few years the attention given to the nature of the Lord's Supper, although not entirely submerged, had dwindled into secondary importance with the emergence of a new controversial issue, the doctrine of predestination. Beza brought this doctrine to the fore as an important point of discussion when he maintained that God first decreed that some people should be saved by His mercy and the others consigned to misery, and after that decree and in subordination to it He created man. This doctrine became known as supralapsarianism. In Zurich especially, the topic of predestination and its implications became a matter of acute conflict. Theodore Bibliander (1504–62), professor of Old Testament at the university there, taught a difference between predestination and the foreknowledge of God and attempted to stress above all the universality of love. Peter Martyr Vermigli (1500–62), newly called to Zurich from Strasbourg, took offense at this teaching. He propounded double predestination, an election to damnation as well as to eternal bliss, and therefore sharply criticized Bibliander. Even though Bullinger usually wanted only to stress election to salvation, the theology faculty of Zurich found itself in agreement with Vermigli and had Bibliander dismissed on February 8, 1560. [32]

While conflict was brewing within Zurich over predestination, Bern and Geneva were at odds on another issue. The disagreement was not concerning either the sacrament of the Lord's Supper or predestination;

there was relative peace on those fronts. The area of conflict centered in the dispute over the nature of church/state relations, which were interpreted differently by the major theologians of the two cities. Wolfgang Musculus (1497–1563), professor of theology and Greek in Bern since 1549, led the Bernese camp, which was convinced that it was correct to unite the state and the church, with the church in subordination to the government and the servants of the church employees of the government. In his strivings for a Christian government, he thought it his duty to fight against any separation of church and state, whether he had to fight against Rome or Geneva.[33] The concept of *ius reformandi* was one of the most important parts of Musculus's thought, *ius reformandi* being the right to reform and renew the character and organization of the church. This right belonged to the magistrates and put the authority of the magistrates in the center of his system. Calvin's position was not in accord with these conclusions. Calvin saw the rights of the church belonging inherently to the church. The church, and the church alone, is responsible for the church.[34] As we continue our analysis of Switzerland, we will notice some results of the ideological conflict in church/ state relations.

As Calvinism was growing stronger in Switzerland, it was spreading to other parts of Europe as well, as other chapters of this book demonstrate. Important for Swiss history is the spread of Calvinism north into Germany, especially into the area around the city of Heidelberg. The crisis that evolved as Calvinism met Lutheranism on German soil provided the ground for the Swiss confession known as the Second Helvetic Confession.

## THE SECOND HELVETIC CONFESSION

In 1562, Bullinger had composed in Latin a personal confession of faith that was, at least at that time, intended for his private use. In 1564, he elaborated on it and added his will to it, expecting to die of the plague that had already taken his wife and was still ravaging Zurich. He survived the plague, however, and in December 1565 received a request from Friedrich III of the Palatinate for help from Zurich and Geneva in the form of a confession that would testify to his orthodoxy. Because of his Swiss Reformed theology, he was being threatened with exclusion from the Lutherans in political affairs. Bullinger was eager to reply, but solicited the aid of Beza, then head theologian in Geneva, to edit this personal testament of faith before sending it to Heidelberg as a confession of the Swiss church. Beza complied and came to Zurich; few changes were made, however, and the statement was sent to Friedrich III. This confession of faith has come to be called the Second Helvetic Confession; it apparently served the purpose for which Friedrich III intended it, for he was not impeached. His personal piety was recognized by all, and Calvinism was, at least for the time being, secure in Germany.

The importance of the Second Helvetic Confession can hardly be overestimated.[35] It was agreed on by all the Swiss churches, including Basel and Geneva. This was no mean accomplishment when one considers the diversity of Reformed theology that had been evident in Switzerland until this time. This unanimity enabled the Swiss churches to have a common formula for instruction, a formula that was used extensively for centuries and provided for unity in preaching and theological education. The Confession is the largest continental Reformed creed and, with the exception of the Heidelberg Catechism, was the most widely adopted of Reformed symbols, being approved in Hungary in 1567, France and Poland in 1571, and Scotland in 1578 and well received in Holland and England also. As to its theological merit, it is of the first rank.[36]

The Second Helvetic Confession purports to demonstrate the unity of its teaching with that of the Bible as well as that of the ancient church. Concerning its theology in general, the Confession treats the doctrines of Scripture (chs. 1–2), God and election (chs. 3–10), ecclesiology (chs. 17–23) and church life (chs. 24–28), the family and government (chs. 29, 31), as well as the sacraments (chs. 19–21). More particularly, it teaches concerning the sacraments (ch. 19) that (1) they are holy rites, with God as their author and Christ as the great object presented in them; (2) there were sacraments under the old economy as well as the new; and (3) as far as the substance is concerned, the sacraments under both dispensations are equal. Baptism, then, replaces circumcision, and the Lord's Supper the sacrifices of the Old Testament. Also of import is that this is the first Protestant confession to exclude the Apocrypha from the text of the Scriptures (ch. 1). The Confession recognizes secondary causes under the providence of God (ch. 6), eliminating the charge of fatalism that has often been placed against Calvinism.

It was as head theologian of Geneva that Beza contributed to the editing of the Second Helvetic Confession. After Calvin died on May 17, 1564, Beza was quickly called on to succeed his dear friend. As the death of Calvin ended an era in Geneva's history, we are able to observe the changes in that city after 1564.

## GENEVA AFTER CALVIN

It is apparent to us that there were many changes following Calvin's death. These changes were not only ecclesiastical but also political. For some time after Calvin's death Geneva was in search of political security. The main disruptive factor was the surrounding of the city by the Duke of Savoy in 1567; this occupation of the surrounding districts played an important role in Geneva's political activities for about twenty years.

Tensions were running high in Geneva, but fortunately for her future, a *mode de vivre* was negotiated with the Duke of Savoy, Emmanuel-Philibert. This agreement was to last twenty-three years. In 1579 a treaty with France, Bern, and the canton of Soleure also helped to assure Geneva her rights as a sovereign city in spite of her weakness. This was very fortunate for Geneva, for Emmanuel-Philibert died shortly there-after, and Charles-Emmanuel, the next duke, had little desire to permit Geneva her sovereign status.

Another treaty was struck in 1584 by Bern, Zurich, and Geneva, and this one also helped to maintain Geneva's security. Charles-Emmanuel responded some months later with an embargo on grain to Geneva that lasted nearly two years. Geneva was brought to her knees by this em-bargo; however, after receiving little help from the German-speaking cantons, the city declared war on Savoy in 1589. After four years of fighting, they made peace with Savoy; however, nothing of great import was resolved, except that Geneva retained her independence. In 1602 Savoy made a further futile attempt to scale Geneva's walls, and finally, in 1603, Geneva succeeded in obtaining a permanent truce, with her sovereignty and independence relatively secure.[37]

Within the city there were changes also. The flow of refugees con-tinued after Calvin's time, a situation difficult for any city to accom-modate; yet Geneva, like few other cities, succeeded in integrating her refugees. As in many European cities at that time, there was a strong movement toward oligarchy; the magistrates began to wear uniform dress in the 1570s and received the title of "Excellency" and other titles in the 1580s. However, this development in government owes "little or nothing to the entrenchment of Calvinism."[38] After Calvin's death, the government began to take more control of the church in Geneva. Until this time, the church had retained considerable independence from the state, unlike other churches in Switzerland.

It was actually after Calvin's death that the ministers of the city showed the most activity. They maintained their faithful watch over the people and saw themselves as "the rock of orthodoxy." The morals of the community were observed and the ministers petitioned constantly for new legislation in this area. The codification into law of Calvin's thoughts concerning morals was accomplished mainly after his death; in 1576 the famous Ecclesiastical Ordinances were revised, establishing a strict rule and order for living.

There was also revision within the Academy of Geneva, which was founded during Calvin's lifetime.[39] In 1565, a chair of law was estab-lished, though this was against the wishes of the pastors,[40] and the Academy had to be closed for a short time during the embargo against

Geneva by Savoy. However, the most important change to occur in the Academy of Geneva was its development under Beza's leadership into the most famous center of Protestant learning in Europe.[41]

As we analyze the various aspects of the situation in Geneva after Calvin, it is imperative to investigate in more detail the life and thought of Theodore Beza, the friend and successor of Calvin. Beza attempted to follow Calvin, and in many ways he did follow his guidelines and example as moderator of the Company of Pastors. Within the confines of the city itself, Beza's political activity was more modest than that of Calvin. To his credit, Beza followed Calvin's example of guarding against any one pastor's taking control of the Company of Pastors: he attempted to have a new moderator elected every year. Beza went into partial retirement in 1580, and this brought an end to a distinct epoch of Geneva's history, although he was not to retire entirely from public life until his death in 1605.

It is asserted today that there is the dawn of a new theological era with Beza. He is accused of developing Calvinism into a Reformed Scholasticism.[42] This Reformed Scholasticism is supposedly an abandonment of Calvin and his theology, not just in one or a few doctrines; it has been said that "Beza's whole theological program shows a serious departure from that of Calvin."[43] It is undoubtedly true that Beza did not follow Calvin in every point of doctrine, a good example being his propounding of supralapsarianism. Yet in no way can the thesis be proved that there was a radical difference in the basic doctrines of the two theologians. The scope and purpose of this chapter will not permit an extended defense of the unity of thought between Calvin and Beza; it must here suffice to say that the able defense of that concurrence as presented by William Cunningham in the 1800s still stands unshaken.[44] Cunningham's defense has so far been largely ignored by the proponents of the disunity theory.

## CHURCH/STATE RELATIONS IN SWITZERLAND

Having examined post-Calvinian Geneva, we look now at the effects of Calvin and Calvinism in the various cities of Switzerland, noting first the development of relations between church and state. Two similar yet distinct notions of church/state relations emerged in the early 1600s. In the French-speaking areas of Switzerland (Geneva, Neuchâtel, Lausanne) there was a clearly defined Presbyterian form of church government. The German-speaking areas (Basel, Bern, Zurich), although maintaining basically the same Calvinistic doctrine, continued in the Zwinglian tradition of church government by placing it under the state's control.

Geneva has already been examined to some extent; we have observed the gradual usurpation of the church's right by the government there. A unique situation arose concerning the relations between the church and the state in Neuchâtel, where Guillaume Farel was the Reformer. The people there were won for the Reformation, but the government was not. This situation was not normal and resulted in a church that acted independently of the state. Therefore, the church in Neuchâtel was ruled only by a Company of Pastors, first headed by Farel.

## THE INFLUENCE OF CALVIN'S THEOLOGY

The dominance of Calvin's theology in Switzerland at the end of the sixteenth century and the beginning of the seventeenth century can scarcely be denied. Calvin had representatives of his theology in the universities of all the major cities.

Johann Jakob Grynäus (1540–1607) became professor of theology at the University of Basel in 1575. Earlier he had had Lutheran tendencies because of the influence of Simon Sulzer (1508–85), head pastor in Basel, and his own study at Tübingen. Yet by the time he took his professorship, he was fully Calvinistic in his teachings and was a firm upholder of the Second Helvetic Confession. He thus changed the tide of leadership in Basel, breaking from Lutheran influence. His son-in-law Amandus Polanus a Polansdorf (1561–1610), who was also a strict Calvinist maintaining particular atonement, studied with Beza in Geneva, received his doctorate from Basel, and in 1596 became professor of Old Testament there.[45]

Perhaps one of the most important theologians of this period was Johannes Wolleb (Wollebius, 1586–1629) of Basel. He accepted the chair of Old Testament in Basel, as well as being the *antistes,* and wrote his *Compendium Theologiae Christianae* in 1626. Bromiley appreciates the importance of the *Compendium,* saying of it: "As a clear and concise statement of reformed orthodoxy in the early seventeenth century it could hardly be excelled."[46] The *Compendium* was used extensively in the seventeenth century and was translated into English and Dutch at an early date.

Theodore Zwinger (1597–1654) followed Wollebius as *antistes* of Basel. Torn between following medicine or theology, he entered the ministry after a sickness that brought him to the door of death. A strong follower of Calvin, he disputed at Heidelberg concerning unconditional election. It was during his tenure as *antistes* that Basel finally accepted the Second Helvetic Confession and implemented the use of bread instead of wafers at the Lord's Supper.

In Bern, Calvinism grew stronger and stronger. A dispute broke out between Samuel Huber (1545–1624) and Abraham Musculus (Müslin, d. 1591), the son of Wolfgang, culminating in a debate in April 1588. Huber taught a universality of grace; that is, all persons are predestined to blessedness. Those who are lost throw away their salvation through their own fault. He also held to a Lutheran conception of the Lord's Supper. Musculus asserted that each Christian is absolutely predestined to belief by the grace of God. He won a complete victory in the city, and Huber was expelled from Bern. Leaving Switzerland to live in Germany, Huber later became a Lutheran. The triumph of Musculus over Huber may be marked as the triumph of Calvinism in Bern especially in that Musculus had signed a paper asserting Beza's teaching of predestination. Later Hermann Dürrholz (Lignaridus), professor of theology in Bern from 1598, would propound a strict Calvinism for the thirty years that he taught.[47]

Geneva was saddened on October 13, 1605, when Theodore Beza rested from his labors there. The successor to Beza, Giovanni Diodati (1576–1649), had already been an instructor in Hebrew at the Academy and followed in the theological tradition of Calvin and Beza. In 1607 he produced a translation of the Bible in the Italian language. As Diodati assumed the rectorship in 1618, Theodore Tronchin (d. 1657), the son-in-law of Beza, took his place in theology. Tronchin had followed Diodati in teaching Hebrew and oriental languages when Diodati had first assumed the chair of theology. In 1644, Diodati also produced a French translation of the Bible with notes, which received a wide circulation at the time.

Zurich always remained open to the thought of Zwingli, although, as mentioned earlier, Calvinism became the dominant theology of the city. In 1575, Rudolph Gwalther (1519–85) replaced Bullinger as the *antistes*. Apparently his parents were very poor, and he was raised by Bullinger himself. In 1541 he married Regula Zwingli, the daughter of Ulrich. A number of his sermons were published, and he was responsible for seeing a number of his father-in-law's works through the press. Shortly after his death, Johann Rudolph Stumpf (1550–92) became the *antistes* of Zurich. Although Stumpf's tenure was a short one, it was especially important for the spread of Calvinism in Switzerland. Under his leadership, there was a change in the direction that Zurich took theologically; he held emphatically to limited atonement. Before this time, only Peter Martyr had held to the view of limited atonement. During the Huber controversy in Bern, Stumpf had taken a strong stand against Huber for high Calvinism. Johann Wilhelm Stucki (1542–1609) became professor of Old Testament in 1571. Stucki had learned Chaldean and Syriac with a rabbi in Padua and was an ardent supporter of Beza's teaching on predestination. Markus Bäumler (1555–1611) became professor of theology at the university in 1607 and continued the Zurich tradition of fighting with Lutherans, as exemplified by his contest with Jakob Andreae concerning the Lord's Supper. The *antistes* in Zurich after 1613 was Johann Jakob Breitinger (1575–1645), who headed the Swiss delegation at the Synod of Dort. In 1618–19 the important synod, in which theologians from Switzerland participated, took place in the town of Dordrecht.[48] Outside the Netherlands, the decrees of the synod were an obligatory expression of faith for church members in Huguenot France and Switzerland alone. This is important for Swiss history because of the position Switzerland took in relation to the theology propounded at the school of Saumer in France. In 1647 Zurich forbade its students to enter the academy in Saumer, and in 1666 Bern followed suit.

Zurich and Bern prohibited attendance there because the theologians of that school were not in agreement with the Synod of Dort though they asserted at the same time that they were Calvinists. The problem of finding a solution concerning the theology of Saumer was met in part by Johann Heinrich Heidegger (1633–98) of Zurich, Lukas Gernler (1625–75) of Basel, and Francis Turretin (1623–87) of Geneva, who composed the *Formula Consensus Helvetica,* or Helvetic Consensus Formula, in 1675 as a response to and against the theology at Saumer.

## THE HELVETIC CONSENSUS FORMULA

The Helvetic Consensus Formula[49] is the last creed of Calvinist Switzerland. It was written some 111 years after the death of Calvin. Its authority was limited to Switzerland and it ceased having authority there in 1722—less than half a century later. Its value, however, was especially seen in America in the nineteenth century; A. A. Hodge called it "the most scientific and thorough of all the Reformed confessions. Its eminent authorship and the fact that it distinctively represents the most thoroughly consistent school of old Calvinists gives it classic interest."[50]

As previously mentioned, this confession was written in response to the theology being propounded at the Saumer Academy, which was founded by Du Plessis Mornay in 1604. Important for our study are the professors Josue de La Place (Placeus, 1596–1655), Louis Cappel (Capellus, 1585–1658), and Moyse Amyraut (Moïse Amyraldus, 1596–1664). They departed from the teachings of Dort regarding verbal inspiration of the Old Testament, particular predestination, and the imputation of Adam's sin. The school ceased to exist in 1685 when Louis XIV revoked the Edict of Nantes.

Louis Cappel maintained that the vocalization of the Hebrew text came after the completion of the Babylonian Talmud and also criticized the literal integrity of the Masoretic text of the Old Testament.[51] Amyraut developed the doctrine of *universalismus hypotheticus* (hypothetical or conditional universalism). This doctrine, though contrary to Arminianism, resembled Lutheranism, which likewise taught a universal atonement and limited election.[52] Amyraut also distinguished between physical and moral necessity, an idea that was to reappear a century later in America.[53] Placeus propounded the doctrine of mediate imputation, that the ground of the condemnation of mankind is the corrupt nature inherited from Adam, not the sin of Adam.

With that brief background to the Consensus, we may investigate its contents. In twenty-six articles, the Helvetic Consensus Formula taught that the consonants and vowels of the Hebrew Old Testament and Greek New Testament are inspired by God (chs. 1–2); that Amyraldism is in conflict with the Scriptures (chs. 4–6); that there is a covenant of works between God and Adam (chs. 7–9); that the sin of Adam is passed to his posterity by immediate imputation (chs. 10–12); that the external call of God is effective in the elect (chs. 17–20); that man is unable to believe the gospel by himself (ch. 21–22); and that as well as a covenant of works between God and Adam, there is a covenant of grace between God and the elect (chs. 23–25). Article twenty-six prohibits the teaching of new doctrines. The author from Geneva, Turretin, was an important Calvinist in the era of the late seventeenth century. He deserves fuller treatment than can be offered in the space of this chapter,[54] but a recent criticism of his theology must here be addressed.

Francis Turretin was made professor at Geneva in 1648; his father, Benedict Turretin, was a pastor and professor before him. One year after the death of the younger Turretin, his three-volume *Institutio Theologiae Elencticae* was published, and in 1702 his four-volume *Opera* came into print.[55] Turretin followed the theology of Calvin and should be classified as a Calvinist of the finest sort.

As there is a charge laid against Beza as the beginner of Reformed Scholasticism, likewise Francis Turretin is accused of teaching an even more radical departure from Calvin. Some authors have asserted that in the doctrine of Scripture, for example, Calvin and Turretin held views that were antithetical to each other.[56] This is hardly the case, as these men maintained similar doctrines of Scripture and implemented basically the same arguments to demonstrate their conviction. Like Calvin, Turretin argued that the inerrant form of the Bible is a result of its divine origin and authority and that Christians are convinced that the Bible is the Word of God by the action of the Holy Spirit as well as by its internal and external marks.[57] Although more work needs to be done in this area, the theological continuity between Calvin and Turretin within a changing cultural and theological climate should be emphasized.

In many ways, the death of Francis Turretin and the ascending of his son Jean-Alfonse Turretin (1671–1737) to the first chair of church history in Geneva in 1697 and to theology in 1705 saw the end of an epoch of Swiss church history. The younger Turretin was not in agreement with his father's teaching and did not continue in the Calvinist tradition. Actually he is known as ''the liberator of Calvin's church from the tyranny of Calvinistic Scholasticism.''[58] As Geneva was the home of Calvin, because she received his guidance and care, so Geneva witnessed the demise of his theology in that city as it was replaced with the theology and spirit of the rationalist mood of the Enlightenment.

Switzerland was the birthplace of Calvinism. Calvin himself is one of her sons, and she can claim the great theologians Beza, Bullinger, Wollebius, Heidegger, and Turretin also. Calvinism made a great impact on both the social and the religious life of Switzerland during the sixteenth and seventeenth centuries, and it is from Switzerland that some of the most important Reformed creeds stem. It was on Swiss soil that many of the great debates concerning the Lord's Supper and other fundamental doctrines of Reformed Christianity took place. Certainly then, the history of Calvinism in Switzerland is an important chapter in a proper understanding of Calvin's influence on Europe and America.

# The Golden Age of Calvinism in France: 1533-1633

*Pierre Courthial*

*Translator: Jonathan Jack*

*Pierre Courthial is Professor of Ethics and Practical Theology and Dean at the Faculté de théologie réformée d'Ain-en-Provence (France). He holds degrees from the Faculté de théologie protestante de Paris and Westminster Theological Seminary (D.D.). He has served in the pastoral ministry in Paris for twenty-three years. He has written many articles and a book:* Fondements pour l'avenir, *and is co-editor of two French reviews:* Ichthus *and* La Revue Réformee. *He is a member of the WEF Theological Commission.*

# 4

# The Golden Age
# of Calvinism
# in France: 1533-1633

Why were the dates 1533 and 1633 selected to mark the beginning and the end of the golden age of Calvinism in France?

The year 1533 marks John Calvin's sudden conversion to the "evangelical" faith. This was the year in which, during a short stay with his friend Louis du Tillet, curate of Claix, Calvin put down on paper his very first notes for the future *Institutes of the Christian Religion*. On May 4, 1534, he resigned his "ecclesiastical benefices," held by the canons of the cathedral in Noyon, the town of his birth. In that same year he preached the "pure gospel" in Poitiers, thus laying the foundations of the future Reformed church of that town.

The year 1633 saw the publication of *Eirenicon seu Synopsis doctrinae de natura et gratia* by Paul Testard. This was the first work of a theologian of the Reformed churches in France to undermine, in a covert way, the faith of these churches as declared in their Confession of 1559 and the Canons of Dordrecht accepted and ratified by their National Synod at Alès in 1620. Testard's work dealt with the central issue of divine predestination. The following year, 1634, Moïse Amyraut (Amyraldus) published his *Short Treatise on Predestination and the Principal Things Which Depend Thereon*—a work that leaned even more strongly toward Arminianism. Despite the excellent warnings against the teachings of Testard and Amyraut given by Pierre du Moulin (Molinaeus) and André Rivet, the National Synod of Alençon, which met in 1637, applied no sanctions against them.[1]

The period prior to 1533 was the pre-Calvinistic period of Protestantism in France. At that time, French Protestantism was made up of two currents of thought. The first was indigenous, initiated and guarded by Roman Catholics who were more or less "evangelical" and "reformed" in spirit, such as Jacques Lefèvre d'Étaples (1450–1537) and Guillaume Briçonnet (1472–1534). The second came from Luther and especially from the French Reformer Guillaume Farel (1489–1565) and Swiss Reformers such as Zwingli. As early as 1523, Farel had established a small secret evangelical church in Paris. In this pre-Calvinistic period, the Evangelical faith already had many martyrs, such as Jean Vallières (d. 1523), Jaques Pavans or Pouent (d. 1524), Jean Leclerc (d. 1524), Louis de Berquin (d. 1529), and Jean de Caturce (d. 1532).

The period after 1633 was the period of the decline of Calvinism in France. As a Provençal proverb says, "The rotting of a fish begins with the head," and under the regrettable influence of theologians of the Academy of Saumur, such as Moïse Amyraut (1596–1664), Louis Cappel (1585–1658), and Josué de La Place (1596–1655), the faith of a growing number of pastors and churches was impregnaged with Arminian influences. People of the Reformed faith became a rarity. The golden age of Calvinism in France is, alas, over. Yet there remains the expectation and hope, which some people have always kept, of a Renaissance, the dawn of which we are beginning to see at last.

In the first heroic period (1533–62), when there was harsh persecution, in the terrible days of a thirty-year religious and civil war (from 1562 to 1593), and in a period of relative peace in the reigns of Henry IV and Louis XIII (from 1593 to 1633), the Reformed faith, sown first by the testimony and martyrdom of many, sprang forth and then overflowed from the hearts of a multitude of believers. It manifested itself in every area of human existence—in theology and philosophy, in the sciences and the arts, in town and country, in family and professional life as well as in politics. And it appeared in all social classes—among peasants and nobility, bourgeois and craftsmen. Huguenots won to Jesus Christ put into practice the exhortations of the admirable treatise on Christian living, which makes up chapters 6 to 10 of Book III of the *Institutes:*

> If we, then, are not our own, but the Lord's, it is clear what error we must flee, and whither we must direct all the acts of our life.
>
> We are not on our own: let not our reason nor our will, therefore, sway our plans and deeds. We are not our own: let us therefore not set it as our goal to seek what is expedient for us according to the flesh. We are not our own: in so far as we can, let us therefore forget ourselves and all that is ours.
>
> Conversely, we are God's: let his wisdom and will therefore rule all our actions. We are God's: let all the parts of our life accordingly strive toward him as our only lawful goal. O, how much has that man profited who, having been taught that he is not his own, has taken away dominion and rule from his own reason that he may yield it to God![2]

The first heroic period, that of heavy persecution lasting till 1562, falls into two parts: the first and longer, up to 1555, was a time of sowing. There were no established or organized Reformed churches. When the growing number of believers gathered together, it was in clandestine assemblies. The Paris congregation, for example, was not organized as a church and led on a regular basis by pastors and elders until September 1555. The very brief period of explosion in the establishment of churches lasted seven years: from 1555 to 1562. The facts speak for themselves: there were only 5 organized churches in 1555 (in Paris, Meaux, Angers, Poitiers, and Loudun); nearly 100 four years later, at the time of the first National Synod in Paris in 1559; and 2,150 in 1562, the date of the beginning of the Wars of Religion. Samuel Mours writes, "There is no doubt that if the scourge of the Wars of Religion had not stricken the country, France would have become predominantly Protestant."[3]

Up to 1555, the time that Reformed churches were "established," Calvin, who was in Geneva, did not cease praying for his country and his compatriots that they might yield themselves to the Lord and His Word, that true churches might be established in France, and that the believers in France might be strengthened to stand firm and, if necessary, become martyrs. As early as 1535, as the *Epistle to King Francis I* (destined to be inserted in the preface to the *Institutes*) testifies, the Reformer sought to help and comfort *la pauvrette Eglise* ("the poor little church") of France. It was with her in mind, and desiring "to serve our French people" by his labors, that he translated the Latin edition of 1536 (a summary of which he had published in French as early as 1537 under the title *Instruction and Confession of Faith*).[4] In the preface of the first French edition of his *Institutes* (1541) he wrote concerning his masterwork, which he continued to develop and enrich as years went by:

> First of all I put it into Latin so as to serve all men of learning, to whatever nation they belonged; then afterward, desiring to communicate what could bear fruit for our French nation, I have also translated it into our tongue.

Despite the persecutions that intensified following an edict issued by Francis I on June 24, 1539, and which became even more severe following Henry II's creation of a "burning chamber" in Paris in 1547 and similar courts in the provinces, conversions to the pure gospel and clandestine evangelical congregations continued to multiply. Here and there these congregations were already appointing leaders. This happened, for example, with the congregation in Paris, which in 1540 took as its preacher a journeyman goldsmith, Claude Le Peintre, who had just spent three years in Geneva. (After being denounced, Le Peintre was burned at the stake.) Also the congregation in Meaux in 1546 chose a simple carder, Pierre Le Clerc, as its "minister responsible for proclaiming the Word of God and administering the sacraments."[5]

How many Huguenots in those days, whenever they went visiting or on a journey, carried in a pocket of their ample coat a Bible in French or a copy of the *Institutes,* personally annotated and with key passages underlined, or some Reformed tract from Geneva or Basel! How many of them were given over to the flames of the stakes just because such works had been discovered on them or at their homes—in a table drawer, a cupboard, or some other hiding place—or at their workplace or on their farm!

A few priests or monks had become Reformed, such as Ponthus de Saint Georges, an abbot from near Couhé in Poitou; Jérôme Vindocin, in Gascony; Jean Michel in Bourges; Secenat and Ramondy, in the Cévennes. More importantly, men of virtually every trade in far greater numbers exercised "secret ministries" in those days. In clandestine congregations, the new Reformed believers met to read Holy Scripture, pray and sing psalms, making use of any preacher who should happen to come by or be found there.

Printers, such as Simon Dubois in Lyon, as early as 1528, and Robert Estienne in Paris, from 1532 to 1551, published unauthorized tracts.

Colporteurs, such as Macé Moreau and Jean Joerry, who were later burned at the stake, the former in Troyes and the latter in Toulouse, spread the French Bible, Reformed tracts (for example Calvin's *On the Lord's Supper),* and books of "spiritual songs."

The flames at the stakes burned higher, but higher still rose the flame of the Reformed faith! Jean Crespin (1500–72), in his *Martyrology* or *Book of Martyrs* of 1554, completed with additions in 1619 by Pastor Simon Goulart, tells the story of 789 martyrs and mentions the names of 2,120 other Protestants sentenced to death or murdered. Yet it is also the time in which "the streams of the Gospel, from the pure springs of the preaching in Geneva, trickle slowly out and water the land of France."

The French believers, in the midst of such severe testing, knew they had been given a mission and responsibility as evangelists and witnesses. So Calvin could rejoice that the gospel, despite all opposition, made progress in his home country. On June 10, 1549, he wrote to Madame de la Roche-Ponçay:

> How joyful we must be when the reign of the Son of God our Saviour multiplies and when the good seed of His doctrine is scattered abroad. . . . In calling us to Himself, He dedicates us so that our whole life may serve to honour Him. . . . However, may you be mindful that wherever we go, the Cross of Jesus Christ will follow us.[6]

And in a letter of September 3, 1554, he exhorted the believers in Poitou, where Reformed congregations were developing:

> May each of you try to attract and to win to Jesus Christ those he can and, afterwards, may those you have found to be capable, after proper examination, be received (into the congregation), upon the agreement of all. . . . Show that the Gospel of our Lord Jesus enlightens you to show you the right path, so that you may not err as children of darkness.[7]

The Reformer was also concerned for the final perseverance of those imprisoned for the faith. On March 12, 1553, he wrote to the five prisoners of Lyon:

> I am fully assured that nothing can shake the strength that God has placed in you. Already, for a long time, you have been meditating on the final battle which you will have to endure if it be His good pleasure to bring you to that point. Be confident that He whom you serve will rule in your hearts by His Holy Spirit in such a way that His grace will triumph over all temptations. *"He who dwells in you is stronger than the world."* Here, we will do our duty to pray to Him that He may be increasingly glorified in your constancy, and that by the consolation of His Spirit, He may sweeten and render agreeable all that is bitter to your flesh, and thus direct all your affections to Him, so that, in looking to the heavenly crown, you may be ready to leave everything that is of the world without regret.[8]

About two months later, he wrote again to the same prisoners of Lyon, who were to die as martyrs on May 16, 1553, saying one to another, "Courage, my brother, courage!":

> Since it seems that God desires to use your blood to sign His truth, there is nothing better than to prepare yourselves for this end, praying to Him to make you submissive to His good pleasure in such a way that nothing may hinder you from going where He calls you.[9]

From May 26 to 28, 1559, still in the midst of persecutions, the first National Synod of the Reformed Churches in France met secretly in Paris.

The idea of such a synod had slowly crystallized. "God inspired all the Christian [=Reformed] Churches established in France to gather together in order to agree unitedly on doctrine and discipline, in conformity with the Word of God," wrote Theodore Beza in his *Church History* (1580).[10] It was a meeting of "ministers" and faithful, held in Poitiers at Christmas 1557, at the time of the visit of the Parisian pastor Antoine de Chandieu, that defined the project of the Synod.

Another Parisian pastor, François de Morel, presided over this Synod that brought together representatives from more than sixty of the one hundred churches that could then be counted in France. This first National Synod of the Reformed Churches in France adopted a Confession of Faith and a Rule of Discipline. The Confession of Faith came from a draft of thirty-five articles prepared by Calvin. As for the Rule of Discipline, it was inspired equally by what the Reformer had written in his *Institutes* and by the example of the churches of Strasbourg and Geneva.

Four of the forty articles of the Confession of Faith asserted the following—clearly in the line of Calvin:

### Article 5 (On the Authority of the Books of Scripture):

We believe that the Word contained in these books comes from God, and takes its authority, not from men, but from God alone.

This Word is the rule of all truth and contains all that is necessary for the service of God and for our salvation; it is not therefore permitted for men, nor even for angels, to add anything to it, to excise anything from it or to alter anything of it. . . .

### Article 8 (On Divine Providence):

We believe, not only that God created all things, but that He governs and directs them, ordering everything that happens in the world and controlling everything according to His will.

Yet we certainly do not believe that God is the author of evil or that the guilt of it can be imputed to Him, since, on the contrary, His will is the sovereign and infallible rule of all righteousness and true justice. . . . [But God has marvelous ways of dealing with the demons and the wicked, turning to good the evil that they commit and of which they are guilty.] Thus, in confessing that nothing happens without the providence of God, we humbly marvel at the secrets that are hidden from us, without questioning things that are beyond us. On the contrary, to be at peace and in security, we apply to our personal lives what Holy Scripture teaches us; for God, to whom all things are subject, watches over us with such fatherly care, that not a hair from our head falls without Him having willed it. By so doing, He keeps a firm rein on the demons and all our enemies, so that they cannot cause us the slightest harm without His permission.

### Article 12 (On Election in Jesus Christ):

From the general state of corruption and condemnation in which all men are immersed, we believe that God delivers those who, in His eternal and unchangeable will, He has, through His goodness and mercy alone, elected in our Lord Jesus Christ, with no consideration as to their works.

We believe that He leaves the rest in their corruption and condemnation, to show forth His justice in them, just as He displays in the former the riches of His mercy. For they are no better than the rest, until God sets them apart, according to His unchanging purpose that He established in Jesus Christ before the foundation of the world.

Moreover, there is no one capable of obtaining such a benefit by his own means, since we are by nature incapable of any good desire, any good disposition of our wills, or any good thought, until God goes before us and gives us the right disposition for them.

### Article 36 (On the Lord's Supper):

We confess that the Lord's Supper testifies to our union with Jesus Christ. Indeed, Christ did not only die and rise once and for all for us, but He also feeds and nourishes us in a real way by His flesh and blood, so that we may be one with Him and that His life may be communicated to us.

Now, although He is in heaven until he returns from there to judge the world, yet we believe that He feeds and vivifies us—by the secret and incomprehensible activity of His Holy Spirit—with the substance of His body and blood. We firmly assert that this happens spiritually, not in order to substitute imagination or speculation for the benefit and true reality of the Lord's Supper, but because this mystery, by its greatness, is beyond our human capabilities of understanding and the whole natural order; in short, because it is heavenly, we esteem that it can only be grasped by faith.

The standard of faith, expounded and developed in the *Institutes* and summarized in condensed form in the 1559 Confession of Faith (adopted in 1571 by the seventh National Synod held at La Rochelle) never failed to encourage and strengthen all church members, pastors, elders, and teachers of the Reformed churches in France up to 1633. In the best sense of the word, all at that time were "theo-logians," men and women of the *Word* of *God,* able to give an answer to whoever asked them to give account of the hope that was in them (see 1 Peter 3:15).

Throughout the period of the persecutions, Calvin entreated the Huguenots to endure and stand firm in attacks and trials and not to rise up in revolt:

We beg you to put into practice the lesson which the Great Master has taught us, that is, to live our lives in patience. We know how hard it is for the flesh, but remember also that then is the time for fighting against ourselves and our passions, when we are assailed by our enemies. . . . Only be sure to under- take nothing that is not permitted by His Word. . . . It would be better for us all to be annihilated, rather than the Gospel of God to be exposed to the accusation that it makes men take up arms for sedition and riot, for God will always make the ashes of His servants bear fruit; but excess and violence will only bring sterility. (To the Church of Paris, September 16, 1557.)[11]

And again:

If you have to be sacrificed to sign and ratify your testimony, may you also take courage to overcome all the temptations that can divert you from it. . . . It was well said of the death of St. Peter, that he would be led to a place where he would not want to go. . . . therefore, following his example, strive valiantly against your weaknesses, in order to remain victorious over Satan and all your enemies. . . . The more the wicked try to eradicate the memory of His Name [the Name of God] from the earth, the more He will make our blood blossom by the strength He gives us. . . . Keep yourselves from with- drawing from the flock of our Lord Jesus so as to flee the cross. . . . (To the believers in France, June 1559.)[12]

And again:

> Persecutions are the real battles of Christians, to test the constancy and firmness of their faith. . . . Hold in high esteem the blood of the martyrs shed for a testimony to the truth as dedicated and consecrated to the glory of our God. . . . apply this for your edification, so that it may stir you up to follow them. (To the same, November 1559.)[13]

But the time came when a section of the Protestant nobility (some, such as the Prince de Condé, not, alas, without an element of personal ambition; the others, such as Admiral Gaspard de Coligny, after long hesitation due to their spiritual qualities) took up arms. Agrippa d'Aubigné wrote:

> As long as Protestants were put to death *under the form of justice,* however iniquitous and cruel it may have been, *they bared their throats to the dagger and did not resist.* But *when the public authorities, the magistrates, tiring of the fires (of the stakes), cast the dagger to the people,* and by the riots and great massacres in France, removed the respected face of justice and had each man put to death by his neighbour to the sound of trumpets and drums, who could forbid the unfortunate people [meaning here those under threat of massacre, outside all framework of justice] from meeting brute force with brute force, and iron with iron, and receiving the condemnation of *righteous anger* from a *fury without justice?*[14]

After many massacres, the massacre at Vassy on March 1, 1562, of an "assembly" holding its worship service caused Condé to launch an appeal to Protestants on April 12 to take up arms. We will not go into the ups and downs of a thirty-year civil and religious war, interrupted by a few moments of peace, quickly broken by new massacres and insurrections, including the famous St. Bartholomew's Massacre of August 24, 1572, which claimed between seven and nine thousand victims, among them Coligny, and which ended with the abjuration of the Protestant King Henry IV ("Paris is worth a Mass!") in 1593. During this thirty-year war between Frenchmen, some among the Protestants fought more for political or selfish motives rather than out of conviction, others apostatized out of fear, and still others indulged in executions and excesses as some of their adversaries did; but fortunately, by God's grace, the Reformed faith remained and became more and more deeply rooted in the hearts of many. Whenever, because they were crushed by the Roman Catholic troops, a large number of churches disappeared from certain regions (Normandy, for example), they developed elsewhere, and their synods continued to be held, watching over the doctrine and lives of all believers in accord with Holy Scripture. Reformed academies (i.e., universities) were founded, as well as hundreds of schools ("The churches will make it their bounden duty to establish schools and will insist that young people receive instruction," said the Articles of Discipline).

Among the theologians of the Golden Age of French Calvinism, whose names it is essential to know, and with whose works one ought to be acquainted, there are:

1. *Those of the First Generation.* Guillaume Farel (1489–1565) from Gap was a forerunner of Calvinism and afterwards a Calvinist. Being hounded from place to place after he had evangelized the Dauphiné, his home province, and Guyenne, he fled into exile as early as 1524. It was he who detained Calvin in Geneva in 1536. After his expulsion from Geneva with Calvin in 1538 he became a pastor in Neuchâtel in Switzerland for nearly thirty years and died there. The following among his works deserve mention: *Summary and Brief Declaration of Some Points of Doctrine of Great Importance for a Christian* (1530); *The Practice of Administering Holy Baptism* (1533); *The Sword of the Word* (1550); *Concerning the True Use of Crosses* (1552).

John Calvin (1509–64) from Noyon—of course!

Theodore Beza (1519–1605) from Vézelay fled into exile at the time of his conversion in November 1548. However, he returned to France several times: to head the Protestant delegation to the Colloquium of Poissy (which brought together Protestants and Roman Catholics in 1561), to be chaplain to Condé's army during the first of the wars of religion, and to be president of the National Synod at La Rochelle in 1571. As a theologian, he is the author of a number of works, including *The Christian Confession of Faith* (French version: 1558; Latin version: 1560),[15] which he composed in the hope that it would help toward the conversion of his father "in his advanced old age." This little theological and literary masterpiece was adopted as the "confession of faith" of the Reformed churches of Hungary in 1562 and of those of Transylvania in 1563. Article 24 of Part III says the following about Christ:

> He came down to earth to draw us up to heaven. From the moment of His conception to His resurrection, He bore our sins in order to relieve us of them. He perfectly fulfilled all righteousness to cover our unrighteousness. He fully revealed to us the will of God His Father, by His words and the example of His life in order to show us the true way of salvation.
>
> Finally, to crown His atoning work for our sins which He took upon Himself, He was bound in order to release us, condemned so that we might be absolved. He suffered infinite shame in order to deliver us from all anguish of guilt. He was nailed to the Cross, there to nail our sins. He died bearing the curse which was our due, in order to satisfy for ever the wrath of God by His unique sacrifice. He was buried to make His death real for us and to vanquish death on its home ground. . . . He rose victorious so that, with all our corruption dead and buried, we might be renewed to a newness of spiritual and eternal life. . . .

As a jurist, Beza, after the St. Bartholomew's Massacre (1572), launched an appeal for a just resistance against tyranny: *De Jure Magistratum*. As a historian, he is the author of a *Life of Calvin* (1575), and probably of the *Ecclesiastical History of the Reformed Churches of the Kingdom of France* (1580). As a dramatist, he composed a remarkable "mystery play": *Abraham's Sacrifice* (1550). As a poet, he put into French verse many psalms, several of which have remained unsurpassed (Ps. 42, 47, 68, 72, 116, 121, 144, 149).

2. *Those of the Second Generation.* Lambert Daneau (1530–95) from Beaugency was a pastor and a professor of theology abroad (Geneva, Leyden, Ghent) as well as in France (Gien, Orthez, Castres). He wrote more than seventy books and concerned himself particularly with Christian ethics. He is the author of *A Brief Remonstrance on Gambling* (1574), of a study on ethics in three books (1574), and of *A Treatise on Dancing* (1579). Thoroughly grounded in the Word of God, he refused excessive strictness. Thus he writes in his *Brief Remonstrance:*

> When we entertain ourselves lawfully in order to take care of and conserve our health and strength, to recover our physical powers and refresh our spirits, so that we might the better carry out more cheerfully and efficiently the work to which it has pleased God to call us, this activity also redounds to the glory of God. In this way, we can serve Him more faithfully and serve the good of our neighbor, whom we can more easily help according to our means, being ourselves fresh and well-disposed in mind.

Michel Berault, or Beraud, (1537–1611) was a professor at the Reformed Academy of Montauban. He exalted the righteous and merciful greatness of divine predestination and, in reply to the attacks of the Roman Catholic theologians, published a book on the vocation of ministers of the gospel.

Simon Goulart (1543–1628) from Senlis was at one and the same time pastor in Geneva, theologian, eminent scholar, and poet. He wrote many historical and theological books, among which are his *Theses on the State of France* (1576). He was one of the greatest "poet-theologians" of Calvinism. Speaking of his conversion, he writes:

> An heureux, heureux mois, jour heureux, heureuse heure,
> Que mon Père céleste ayant de moi souci,
> A haute voix cria à mon coeur: "Me voici,
> Je veux, pour l'avenir, faire en toi ma demeure!"
> (Oh happy year, happy month, happy day, happy hour,
> When my heavenly Father, being mindful of me,
> Cried aloud to my heart: "Here am I,
> From now on will I make my dwelling-place in thee!")

3. *Those of the Third Generation*. Philippe du Plessis-Mornay (1549-1623) was a politician and leading Protestant of remarkable wisdom. One of Henry IV's friends and collaborators, he was also an excellent theologian (being an untiring reader of the Bible and the church fathers and a disciple of Calvin). At the age of twenty-eight he published *A Treatise on the Church,* but his masterpiece is a book of apologetics: *A Treatise on the Truth of the Christian Religion* (1581), which in some respects anticipates Pascal. He also wrote a work on *The Eucharist and the Early Church* (1598), which did not have the good fortune to please the renegade Henry IV.

Daniel Chamier (d. 1621) was a professor at the Reformed Academy of Montauban, where for a while he proved capable of masterfully teaching, at the same time, dogmatics, philosophy, Hebrew, and Greek! He also wrote a four-volume *Pantrastae Catholicae,* a universally applicable order of battle. His death on the ramparts of Montauban during a siege prevented him from composing a fifth volume—on the church. In his *Pantrastae Catholicae,* he remarks as a pioneer exegete that "the evangelists did not use the Attic language, but the common language of the people." In passing, it is worth noting that on this point he was supported by the Protestant philological scholar Saumaise (1588-1658), who asserted at the same time that the New Testament authors had used the colloquial Greek idiom of their time.[16]

Pierre du Moulin (1568-1658), one of the best-ever French theologians and controversialists, expressed himself in language of classical purity. He was pastor, churchman, and chaplain to Madame—Catherine de Bourbon, sister of King Henry IV. (The title Madame was given to the sister of a king or queen in France at that time.) He visited England several times. His works are many: books on theology and philosophy, letters, sermons, and poems.[17]

Du Moulin saw the great dangers for the church of any drift toward Arminianism. In 1620 he presided over the National Synod of Alès, which, in adopting the Canons of Dort, rejected and condemned "the doctrine of the Arminians, seeing that it makes divine election depend on the will of man; weakens and destroys the grace of God; elevates man and the powers of his free will, in order to cast him down; brings back Pelagianism; disguises Popery; and overthrows all certainty of salvation."

In his *Newness of Popery* (1627), a magnificent reply to the attacks of Cardinal du Perron, du Moulin writes:

> They want the people to follow their leaders without questioning whether or not they are following the right path and teaching true doctrine. How can one be expected to join the congregation of believers without knowing what it means to be a believer? And how will one know what it means to be a believer, without knowing the doctrine of faith? How shall I know what is

true and pure, if people hide from me the rule of truth and purity by preventing me from reading Holy Scripture, which alone is the source of these rules?

The Church is not the judge of Holy Scripture, but only a witness to it and a guardian of it.

Why should we be afraid of giving too much praise to God or attributing too much to His grace, or humbling ourselves too much before Him? Why should we make man enter into a partnership with God, to attribute some of this praise to man? True religion is that which gives all praise to God and all the benefits to man. It humbles man so as to glorify God.

Let us return to Jesus Christ, and we shall find complete rest in His expiation, if, in giving God the glory, we want to find rest for our consciences.

André Rivet (1572–1651), an ardent Calvinist, was a pastor in France and then a teacher in the Netherlands. His *Introduction* to the study of Scripture lays the foundations of an exegesis that avidly seeks the exact meaning of the text.

Antoine Garrissoles (1587–1650), a professor at Montauban, was, along with some others, the author of a well-structured book entitled *The Imputation of Original Sin,* in which he replies to the far-out ideas of Josué de La Place, who turned original sin into a simple matter of heredity by which each person was no longer implicated as a responsible individual.

Philosophical and scientific research was stimulated and developed among Reformed people who saw the glory of God displayed in the wonders and secrets of His creation. In his writings Calvin defended this legitimate curiosity, commanded by God already in the first two chapters of Genesis, against the obscurantism

of a mass of enthusiastic minds that cry out against all the liberal arts and honest sciences as if they were good for nothing except making men proud and were not highly useful means as much towards the knowledge of God as for the conduct of human life.

In his *Catechism* Calvin adds:

Because God has manifested Himself to us in His works, we must search for Him in them. For we are incapable of understanding His essence. But the world is like a mirror for us in which we can contemplate Him insofar as it is expedient for us to know Him.

Pierre de la Ramée, or Ramus (1515–72),[18] played a major role as a scholar and especially as a philosopher in the scientific advances of the sixteenth and seventeenth centuries that took place notably in the Protestant countries. His great struggle, which earned him many enemies, was waged against the "maladie de l'Ecole" (the *morbus scholasticus* of Scholasticism), the almost superstitious, slavish following of Aristotle at that time. In his "antischolastic" works (*Dialecticae partitiones; Aristotelicae animadversiones; Oratio pro philosophica disciplina;* et al.) Ramus was astonished and dismayed that the Christian religion was being founded on a pagan philosophy; that Aristotle, rather than Holy Scripture, was the source of instruction in ethics; and that the coherence of an argument was more highly esteemed than its faithfulness to the two books of God—the Bible and the created universe. Converted to the Reformed faith after the Colloquium of Poissy (1560), Ramus was unpopular with the Geneva school, especially with Theodore Beza, as long as the latter, though an excellent theologian for the most part, maintained his defense of Aristotle as the point of departure for knowledge and scholarship.

Ramus was interested in questions of semantics and linguistics. He demanded the definitions be as clear and as simple as possible. He renewed the system of logic by distinguishing between "invention" and "judgment." He defined an empirical method for approaching, examining, and understanding created realities, so that they might no longer be tied to the "hypotheses" of Scholasticism. In all this, despite a certain unfortunate leaning toward rationalism, Ramus did effective work in epistemology in the Reformed tradition.

He drew up systems of *arithmetic, geometry,* and *algebra* that were used into the seventeenth century. He unhesitatingly adopted the system of Copernicus.

Toward the end of his life, after becoming a theologian, he wrote *Commentaries on the Christian Religion.* Thus the man who had defined physics as the science that studies "first the sky, then the meteorites, minerals, plants and trees, fish, birds, beasts, and men" discovered also the science that studies, in prayerful and obedient submission, the Word of God. Ramus was killed in the St. Bartholomew's Day massacre.

Bernard Palissy (1510–90),[19] a contemporary of Ramus, was a great man. He died in the Bastille in Paris where he had the honor of being imprisoned for his Reformed faith. He too replaced the reasonings of Scholasticism with a practical and living Christian faith. For him the Creation is a "book of marvels" in which divine words can be read and from which may be derived "a wisdom necessary for all the inhabitants of the earth." In his books Palissy expresses his praise for the works of God and tells of the scientific discoveries that God has permitted him to make.[20]

His wide scientific interests led to a number of noteworthy achievements. In ceramics he improved the transparent lead glazes used in pottery and increased the quality and range of color. He produced mottled polychrome works of pottery, covering them with designs of stones, shells, fish, and reptiles. His rustic figurines were imitated virtually everywhere in the centuries that followed. He launched the first course in geology at the Sorbonne with lessons on water, stone, and metals. In his study of hydrology, he gave a correct interpretation of the water cycle, especially in regard to the feeding of springs by rain. In palaeontology he defied the whole Scholastic school by asserting that fossil shells were real shells and that real animals, including fish, had given their forms to fossil stones. In plant physiology he noted that plants do not absorb only water and humus from the soil but also "salts" and that some of these salts are beneficial to them. That was the first time that the mineral nutrition of plants was set forth.

Filled with wonder at the beauties, secrets, and manifold laws of Creation, Palissy defined two unified goals of scientific research: the glory of God and the well-being of men.

Ambroise Paré (1509–90), a self-taught man, was nicknamed "the father of modern surgery." From the age of twenty, he began to practice this demanding and difficult profession for the love of God and his fellow man. In about thirty works, he wrote all that he had learned through careful investigation.[21]

At the time of the St. Bartholomew's Massacre (1572), Paré was under the protection of King Charles IX. Brantôme (1537–1614) relates how "the king was shouting incessantly: 'Kill, kill!' never intending to spare one of them, except Master Ambroise Paré, his foremost surgeon and the foremost of Christendom. He sent for him to come to his bedroom and wardrobe that evening, commanding him not to move from there. . . ."

Paré touched on most areas of medicine and surgery. In his foreword "to the reader" prefacing his *Introduction or Entrance Into How to Reach a True Knowledge of Surgery,* he wrote:

> I have occasion to praise God for the fact that it pleased Him to call me to the medical practice that is commonly called surgery, which cannot be bought by silver and gold but by perseverance and long experience. . . . The laws of venerable medicine are not subject to those of kings or other overlords, nor to custom, as medicine has its origin in God, who I pray may be pleased to bless this enterprise of mine, to His eternal glory.

Besides such scholars as Palissy and Paré, I should also mention Olivier de Serres (1539–1619), a deacon in the Reformed Church of Berg. He turned his estate of Pradel into a model agricultural enterprise and, even during the "Wars of Religion," he improved the science of agronomy. He proceeded with the same brilliant Christian empiricism as Palissy and Paré had done in their fields. Serres produced three major works. The first one was *The Collecting of Silk by the Feeding of the Worms That Make It* (1599). It was a Protestant from Nîmes, François Traucat, who had encouraged the growing of mulberry trees throughout the south of France. Serres also wrote *Agricultural Enterprise and Field Management* (1600), which, it is said, King Henry IV liked so much that he had a few pages of it read to him every evening. This work defines a thorough reform of agriculture, not actually put into practice until the nineteenth century. A third work was *An Additional Value of the White Mulberry* (1603).

There were also noteworthy sculptors and architects in the golden age of French Calvinism.[22] Ligier Richier (1500–67) has been called the most accomplished and skilled workman in the art of sculpting ever seen. Among his works are the excellent *Entombment* in the Church of Saint-Etienne at Saint-Mihiel (his birthplace in Lorraine); the funerary statue called *Death* or *The Chill of Death* or *The Skeleton,* for the Mausoleum of René de Chalon, Prince of Orange; and the *Recumbent Figure of Philippe de Gueldre* at the Franciscan monastery in Nancy.

Pierre Bontemps (1507–63) carved the praying figures of the Dauphin François and Charles d'Orléans and remarkably precise bas-reliefs representing the battles of the reign of François I.

Jean Goujon (c. 1510–c. 1565) created the bas-reliefs of the *Four Evangelists* and the *Entombment of Christ* in the Museum of the Louvre. He also contributed the following to the embellishment of the palace of the Louvre: bas-reliefs of *War* and *Peace* in the Cour Carrée; bas-reliefs of *History, Victory, Renown,* and *The Glory of the King* on the side-projections of the façade; the four statues in the gallery of the *Caryatids;* and the *Henry II Stairway.* He was responsible for the elegant *Fountain of the Innocents* in the Square of the Innocents in Paris and for *The Good Shepherd,* a sculptured wood panel embellishing a door at the Church of Saint-Maclou, in Rouen. Goujon, also an engraver, illustrated the first French edition of the *Ten Books of Architecture* by Vitruve. "My work," he said, "is according to the knowledge that God gave me."

Jacques Androuet Du Cerceau (1510–85) was an architectural engraver and the author of *The Finest Buildings in France* (1576–79), a weighty work, the third volume of which remained unfinished. He wrote several other books that exercised a major influence.[23] He built two houses in Orléans as well as two châteaux, which have since been destroyed.

Salomon de Brosse (1571–1626), a maternal grandson of Jacques Du Cerceau, worked on the château of Montceaux (for Gabrielle d'Estrées and afterwards for Marie de Médicis), Verneuil, Blérancourt, and Coulomniers-en-Brie. From 1615 he was the architect of the new Palais du Luxembourg and, in 1618, of the Great Hall of the Palais de Justice in Paris. In the same year he assisted in the completion of Brittany's parliament Building in Rennes. In 1623 he built the second Protestant

Church of Charenton, which, unfortunately, was destroyed in 1685 at the time of the revocation of the Edict of Nantes.

Other people deserving mention are Charles du Ry, who built the Saint-Honoré Gate in Paris; sculptors Abraham Hideaux, Barthélémy Prieur, and Slaximilien Poultrain; and architects Jacques Aleaume and Salomon de Caus.

Still in the highly diverse field of the arts I should mention three others. Jacob Bunel (1558–1614) was a remarkable portrait artist and distinguished painter whose work has unfortunately been lost. He painted the décor of a cloister at Escurial and the great gallery of the Louvre. He was also responsible for frescoes at Fontainebleau.

Another artist was Claude Vignon (1593–1673), whose painting *Esther before Ahasuerus* can still be seen at the Louvre. He was an acquaintance of Rembrandt.

Abraham Bosse (1602–76) produced extraordinary and renowned engravings, portraying in painstaking and minute detail the everyday life of the period: *Marriage Contract, French Nobleman's Garden, Town Wedding, Blessing of the Meal, Bloodletting, Schoolmaster, Four Ages of Life, Prison Visit,* and others. He also wrote *A Treatise on Methods of Copper-plate Engraving.*

Furthermore, three French Protestant composers should be mentioned. Loys Bourgeois (c. 1510–c. 1560) was the cantor at St. Peter's in Geneva and collaborated for a while with Calvin. He composed polyphonic psalms and wrote *The Straight Path of Music* (1550), which makes it possible for sixteenth-century music to be properly understood and interpreted.

Claude Goudimel, who was killed in Lyon in the St. Bartholomew's Day Massacre in 1572, set to music all the psalms that Clément Marot and Theodore Beza had translated into French. He also composed several *Magnificats.* The tenor nearly always carries the melody (the soprano carries the melody only seventeen times). Goudimel particularly had family singing at home in mind in his compositions.

Claude Le Jeune (c. 1530–1600) was a composer who could handle a great variety of musical genres. His style, full of vivacity and precision, did full justice to the psalms in the French texts of Marot, Beza, Baïf, and Agrippa d'Aubigné.

An explosion of literary activity has testified in particular to the faith of the French Calvinists during their golden age.

Of great value, among other works, are the *Mémoires,* diverse and yet of the same basic character, of Pierre de La Place, Louis Regnier de La Planche, Antoine La Roche de Chandieu, and Simon Goulart. Captain Francois de la Noue (1531–91) included them all in his *Political and Military Discourses* (1587), enabling us to relive this age of faith, bloodshed, and fire.

The greatest writer of the period—one of the foremost French writers —is without doubt Théodore d'Agrippa d'Aubigné (1552–1630), the author of two masterpieces: *Universal History* (1616–20) and *Les Tragiques,* a poem begun in 1577, when he was twenty-five, and published in 1616, when he was sixty-four.

Agrippa d'Aubigné was a child prodigy. At the age of six he could read French, Latin, Greek, and Hebrew and at eight he could read texts of Plato. As a friend and advisor to King Henry IV, whose abjuration of Protestantism he forever deplored and never forgave, he undertook to write, after the King's death, his *Universal History,* which, despite its title, is in fact the history of Protestant France from 1550 to 1601. An ardent Calvinist, d'Aubigné nevertheless tried to be as objective as possible, always giving priority to the precise and detailed reporting of facts before the demands of style. He wrote, "When truth puts its dagger to our throat, we must kiss its white hand though it be stained with our blood."

*Les Tragiques* is an epic poem that recalls Dante and anticipates Victor Hugo, who often read and studied it. In serried ranks of nearly ten thousand lines of poetry, its impetus still carries today's reader along. A twentieth-century critic, Thierry Maulnier, was able to write about d'Aubigné: "No other French poet has such momentous breadth, this inspired giant's voice, this breath made for the trumpets of cosmic disasters, for the gathering of the clouds of the Flood, the fall of besieged walls, the call of the dawn of Jehoshaphat."[24]

I will restrict myself here to quoting the last four lines of *Les Tragiques:*

Mes sens n'ont plus de sens, l'esprit de moi s'envole,
Le coeur ravi se trait, ma bouche est sans parole.
Tout meurt; l'âme s'enfuit et reprenant son lieu,
Extatique se pâme au giron de son Dieu.
(My senses have no more sense, my spirit from me flies,
My raptured heart falls silent, my mouth without speech lies.
Death engulfs all; my soul takes its flight and finds its own abode,
And falls in raptured ecstasy in the bosom of its God.)

Nourished and molded by the Bible, filled with compassion for the downtrodden, and terrible in his attacks against the powerful, d'Aubigné is the very essence of the French Calvinist, the Huguenot.

Besides d'Aubigné, and of almost the same stature, is the French Milton, Guillaume de Saluste du Bartas (1544–90), who expressed himself in a very different style. *The Week or the Creation of the World,* which he published in 1579, is a long poem of seven songs praising the Author and the wonders of the universe.

Another name to be mentioned is that of Antoine de Montchrestien (1576–1621), who, strangely, was at the same time tragic playwright and economist. He wrote *Sophonisbe, The Lacenae or Constancy, David, Aman, Hector,* and in 1605 a real masterpiece, the *Scottish Lady or Mary Stuart.* He was one of the first people to grasp the necessity for industrialization. He himself set up a metallurgical factory specializing in cutlery at Chatillon-sur-Loire. He is the author of *A Treatise of Political Economy* (1615).

Among the poets, one should not forget Simon Goulart, Jean Tagaut, Christophe de Gamon, and Bernard de Montmeja, all of whom eulogized the wonders of God's Creation, described the great misery of the fallen human race, and extolled the saving work of the one and perfect Mediator. Albert-Marie Schmidt, a leading critic, wrote of these disciples of Calvin that they "integrated into their very personalities the doctrine of their master, to the degree that their poems harmonize an unaffected simplicity of testimony with the precision required of all theological reflection. This blend of aesthetic perfection, dogmatic rigor and confiding humility is absolutely unique in the history of French poetry."[25]

Thus, for the duration of a century, from 1533 to 1633, France could count hundreds of thousands of spiritual sons and daughters of John Calvin. They sought to celebrate the glory of the Creator and Savior God in every area of life, for the joy of the church that had been reformed according to His Word.[26]

# Calvin and Calvinism in the Netherlands

*W. Robert Godfrey*

*W. Robert Godfrey is Professor of Church History at Westminster Theological Seminary, Escondido, California. He holds degrees from Stanford University (A.B., M.A., Ph.D.) and Gordon-Conwell Theological Seminary (M.Div.) and is a minister in the Christian Reformed Church. Dr. Godfrey has written articles for the* Archive for Reformation History *and the* Westminster Theological Journal *and a volume of essays entitled* Discord, Dialogue, and Concord. *He is a member of the American Historical Association and the American Society for Reformation Research.*

# 5

# Calvin and Calvinism
# in the Netherlands

Calvinism has penetrated and influenced the Netherlands fully as much as any other country in the world, if not more. The Netherlands has been a center of Calvinist living, thinking, and renewal, and Dutch Calvinists have made many contributions to the Reformed community throughout the centuries. Dutch Calvinists provided a model of courage and faithfulness in Holland's struggle for independence from Spain in the sixteenth century. They confronted and answered the threat of Arminian theology in the early seventeenth century at the great Synod of Dort. They spoke a timely, prophetic word to post-revolutionary society in modern Europe from the nineteenth to the twentieth century through the work of Guillaume Groen van Prinsterer and Abraham Kuyper. Recently Dutch Calvinism has inspired the encyclopedic philosophical efforts of Herman Dooyeweerd.

Each of these contributions and many more make up the fabric of Dutch Calvinism. This study will seek to examine some of the ways in which that fabric has been woven through the centuries. From the early impact of Calvin himself this study will investigate the developing pattern of Calvinism's reform of the church and society of the Netherlands.

## Reform Before Calvinism

The pattern for reform in the Netherlands was set in many ways by its distinctive political and religious history. Politically the Netherlands in the sixteenth century was composed of seventeen provinces in the area of modern Belgium, the Netherlands, and northern France. These provinces, known as the Low Countries, or *Belgica,* were bound together by common participation in a States General and by economic, cultural, and ethnic ties. By the middle of the sixteenth century each province acknowledged Charles V, the Holy Roman Emperor and king of Spain, as its sovereign.

Concern for the religious reform of the Roman Catholic church had deep roots in the Netherlands before the Reformation began. Early expressions of the need for reform date from the fourteenth century when Jan van Ruysbroeck expressed his concern for renewal among Christians in terms of a mystical relationship with God. His greatest pupil, Geert Groote (1340–84), formed the fellowship known as the Brethren of the Common Life, which stressed practical Christian living in devotion to Christ. The Brethren based their ethos on monastic principles but did not bind anyone by oath to the fellowship. Their commitment to the value of education for the Christian life was evident in their work of copying manuscripts and establishing schools.

The spiritual environment fostered by the Brethren gave birth to the great devotional work of Thomas à Kempis, *The Imitation of Christ* (1418). The *Imitation*'s stress on the spiritual, internal relationship between the soul and Christ and on the importance of the moral life remained typical of most reforming movements in the Netherlands. Yet in the work of Wessel Gansfort (1419–89), also influenced by the Brethren of the Common Life, there was an additional element of concern for doctrinal reform. He seemed to have a more spiritual view of the Lord's Supper, and Luther looked back to Gansfort as a forerunner of his teaching on justification. On the eve of the Reformation the Brethren helped educate the great humanist scholar, Desiderius Erasmus (c. 1469–1536). Erasmus too had a vision of a reformed church in which a more spiritual, moral, and biblical piety would flourish.

The long history of calls for positive reform and for the correction of abuses in the church laid a foundation of concern on which the Protestant Reformation would build so successfully. Thus the prompt response, both negative and positive, to Martin Luther in the Netherlands was not surprising. In November 1519, for example, the theological faculty of the University of Louvain became the first group in Europe to condemn Luther's teaching. On the other hand, two Augustinian monks heartily advocated Luther's reform and became early martyrs to the cause when they were burned in Brussels in 1523. The divisions between proponents and opponents of the Reformation in the Low Countries intensified in the course of the sixteenth century, and the Roman Catholic government of Charles V and his son and successor, Philip II of Spain, ordered what became some of the most severe persecutions of Protestants in Europe.

If the response to Luther was rapid in the Netherlands, it was not widespread. Lutheranism never became a large, popular movement in the Low Countries. Neither did the second manifestation of Protestantism in the Netherlands, Sacramentarianism. Sacramentarianism attracted a small humanist elite and continued a rather Erasmian approach to reform. The most important influence of this movement was through the statesman Cornelius Hoen, who wrote "A Most Christian Letter." In this letter he proposed a spiritual and memorial view of the Lord's Supper that was rejected by Luther, but greatly influenced Ulrich Zwingli's eucharistic theology.

The first expression of Protestantism that gained a large Dutch following was Anabaptism. A number of prominent Anabaptist leaders came from the Netherlands, from revolutionary followers of Melchior Hoffman such as Jan Matthys of Haarlem and Jan Beuckelszon of Leiden, who led the uprising at Münster, to the pacifists David Joris and Menno Simons. These early Anabaptists laid down deep roots among the people of the Netherlands and bore the brunt of the persecution by the Roman Catholic authorities. Anabaptism was the dominant form of Protestantism in the Netherlands in the 1530s and 1540s, but ultimately Calvinism supplanted Anabaptism as the most popular expression of reform in the Netherlands.

## CALVIN'S CONTACT WITH THE NETHERLANDS

John Calvin (1509–64) was a Frenchman who spent his most creative years in Geneva. But his concern for the church of Jesus Christ was not limited to France and Switzerland. His voluminous correspondence testifies to his concern for the advancement of the Reformed cause throughout Europe, including the Netherlands. Indeed through personal associations he had close contacts with the Low Countries. During his exile in Strasbourg Calvin grew to know the Netherlander Johannes Sturm quite well. In Geneva at different times he met several leaders of the Dutch reform: Peter Dathenus, Guido De Brès, Philipp Marnix van St. Aldegonde, Franciscus Junius, Jean Taffin, and Pierre Loiseleur de Villiers. In addition to these contacts, Calvin himself had ethnic affinities with the Netherlands. His mother and wife were born in the Low Countries, his mother in Cambrai, and his wife in Liège. Calvin was born in Picardy, a French province that borders on the Netherlands. His home city of Noyon was only about thirty miles from the border of *Belgica*. In one letter to Heinrich Bullinger Calvin even remarked, "I am a Belgian too."[1]

Calvin was also involved in sending the first known preacher of Calvinism into the Netherlands. Late in 1544 Calvin urged Pierre Brully to go to preach in Tournai and Valenciennes. Calvin had known Brully in Strasbourg, and Brully had succeeded Calvin as the pastor of the

French refugee church there. Brully had preached in the Netherlands only three months when he was captured and burned to death for his faith. But his courageous work in building a visible church initiated a slow but steady penetration of the Reformed movement into the southern part of the Low Countries.

Calvin's influence on the Netherlands was not limited to personal contacts, however. His writings, which were well known and widely distributed, were also very important in spreading the Reformed faith. The definitive edition of the *Institutes* was translated into Dutch in 1560 and was probably, after Bullinger's *Decades,* the most influential book published there by a Reformer. Calvin also addressed several treatises specifically to the Low Countries. Three of them—written in 1543, 1544, and 1562—discussed how a faithful person should live among Papists. Two other treatises analyzed Anabaptism and spiritualism, as they were a threat to the Reformed movement in the Netherlands.

His first work directed to the Netherlands was his 1543 treatise, "A Short Treatise showing what a faithful man knowing the truth of the Gospel ought to do when he is among the Papists." This work cautioned against outward conformity to Roman Catholicism while inwardly embracing the Reform. Calvin's vision of the Christian life as expressed in this treatise left a profound impact on the Dutch Reformed churches.

Calvin's argument in the work is clear. The ceremonies of the Roman church, including the Mass, baptism, pilgrimages, prayers for the dead, and images, were idolatrous. Calvin urged the true Christian to flee idolatry not only in his heart but also in his external actions. This mandate became characteristic of Dutch Calvinism: "My doctrine is that the faithful man must sanctify and consecrate himself to God, as much with his body as with his spirit. . . ."[2] To support this teaching Calvin referred twice to Romans 10:9–10. To serve Christ with the heart but not the body is "carnal prudence."[3] This was not right for the true Christian: "For if the heart is good, it will produce its fruit outwardly."[4] Calvin insisted that real trust in God would make such difficult obedience possible: "God loves above all things this confidence: that in observing his commandments we should entrust the end to his providence and that in this our spirit rests."[5] He insisted that only martyrdom or exile were the options of the faithful Christian when compelled to conform to idolatry. He declared with passion: "You say you are forced. Do you think then that he [God] does not much more esteem his glory than your life?"[6]

In this treatise Calvin laid down what became guideposts for the program of the Dutch Reformed churches. Life must be lived to the glory of God whatever the cost. The true Christian must face every danger with absolute confidence in God's providence. He must be committed to the truth of Reformed doctrine and must give visible expression to his faith whatever the consequences. This vision of the disciplined, militant Reformed church remained at the heart of the ideal embraced by many Calvinists in the Netherlands, an ideal that guided their actions for centuries to come.

## CHURCHES UNDER THE CROSS

The character and growth of the Reformed congregations in the Netherlands from the 1540s through the 1560s is difficult to determine. These congregations were "under the cross," that is, suffering persecution. Many of their activities were secret, and few records survive from which the historian may reconstruct the situation.

Two points are clear from this period, however. First, there were significant differences within the Reformed community on practice and doctrine. Calvin's treatise on the Christian obligation to practice the faith openly was rejected as too rigorous and harsh by some, while others championed Calvin's vision for the church. On doctrinal matters there were some who espoused a more Erasmian theology, while others followed the high Augustinianism of Calvin. The tensions between those sometimes called "the national Reformed" and the strict Calvinists continued throughout the sixteenth century, manifesting themselves again in the Arminian controversy. The strict Calvinists seem to have been a sizeable majority, but in days of persecution they were unable to achieve uniformity in doctrine or practice in the Reformed community.

Secondly, it is clear that the growth of the Reformed movement in numbers and organization was significant in these decades in spite of persecution. The greatest numerical growth was in the south, particularly the provinces of Flanders and Brabant. Penetration into the north (the Netherlands of today) came more slowly and cannot be clearly discerned until the 1560s.

As the movement spread, there were efforts to organize the congregations both internally and in relation to one another. There were communication and mutual support through a limited synodical system. But a recent study has shown that this organization was much more limited than scholars had previously thought.[7] Calvinism had not become a highly disciplined revolutionary party. The widespread public preaching, the hedge preaching, and the wave of iconoclasm that swept the Netherlands in August 1566 were not the result of well-orchestrated Reformed planning. The hedge preachers were as often itinerant laymen as ministers, and the Reformed ministers were divided among themselves about the propriety of the iconoclastic violence.

The late 1560s and early 1570s, however, saw significant movement toward greater organization and doctrinal discipline among the Dutch Reformed. Determined efforts were made to realize Calvin's vision of the church. A group of Dutch Calvinists gathered at Wesel in 1568 for a conference on the church. Although it was not actually a synod, the conference adopted influential articles to guide the church. These articles were entitled, "Certain chapters or articles which ministers of the Dutch Church have judged to be in part necessary and in part useful in the ministry of the church."

Concern for the unity and well-being of the Reformed church culminated in the calling of the church's first national synod, which met in Emden in East Friesland in 1571. This synod officially laid the foundation for the church order of the Dutch Reformed churches. Building on the conference of Wesel and on the structure of the French Reformed Church, the acts of the Synod of Emden show the Reformed zeal for order and discipline in the life of the church. The second article declares that the participants have signed both the Belgic Confession and the French Confession to testify to their unity with one another and with the French in their commitment to the Reformed faith. Article 4 calls on all ministers present and future to sign the confessions also. Article 5 requires the use of the Genevan Catechism in French-speaking churches and the Heidelberg Catechism in the Dutch-speaking churches, although the Synod allowed other catechisms that conformed to God's Word to be used in churches where they were already used.

The next articles deal with the organizational structure of the church. Article 6 requires that every church have a consistory composed of a minister, elders, and deacons and that the consistory meet at least once a week. Article 7 calls for meetings of classis every three or six months. According to article 8, regional synods should be held every year. Article 9 states, "Finally an assembly of all the Dutch churches together will be held every second year."[8] The intention of the Synod of Emden clearly was to erect a full synodical structure for the church.

The Emden Synod called for a disciplined church not only in terms of organization but also in terms of the supervision of the lives of the members of the churches. Articles 25–34 of the church order stressed the obligation of moral discipline as part of the calling of the minister and outlined the ways of dealing with private and public sins; the stages of discipline leading, if necessary, to excommunication; and the discipline of office-bearers who failed to discharge their duties properly.

The adoption of the Belgic Confession and the catechisms as doctrinal standards for the church by the Synod of Emden was of special importance for regulating the teaching of the church. The synod endorsed the Belgic Confession, which had been written in 1559 and revised for distribution in 1561 by Guido De Brès. The Confession was significantly modeled on the French Confession of 1559, which had been written under the supervision of John Calvin. The Belgic Confession was to be a summary of the Reformed faith to instruct those within the church and to inform those outside the church. By it De Brès sought to differentiate the Reformed clearly from the Anabaptists in particular, who were the object of much official and popular mistrust. He sought to demonstrate the biblical and catholic character of Reformed Christianity.

The theology of the Belgic Confession is distinguished from the French Confession in very little except on the marks of the church. The Belgic Confession, following the theme of Calvin's early treatise to the Netherlands, stressed the importance of the church and its discipline in the face of opposition. Article 28 insisted: "It is the duty of all believers . . . to join themselves to this congregation, wheresoever God hath established it, even though the magistrates and edicts of princes be against it; yea, though they should suffer death or bodily punishment." In addition De Brès maintained that there are three marks of the true church: the faithful preaching of the Word, the faithful administration of the sacraments, and the faithful exercise of discipline.[9] Although Calvin had often referred to the importance of discipline in the church, the French Confession does not make discipline a mark of the church. The Belgic Confession, then, has gone farther in stressing the importance of the church, its discipline, and the visible expression of faithfulness.

The Heidelberg Catechism, which was also mentioned by the Synod of Emden, came to occupy an important place in the Dutch Reformed Church. This catechism prepared in the Palatinate by Zacharius Ursinus and Caspar Olevianus in 1563 gave a warm and pastoral introduction to Calvinism. Some of the particular emphases of Calvinism, especially that of predestination, are not prominent in the catechism. But a strongly Calvinist perspective suffuses the work. By regularly teaching it to the young and preaching it to the congregations, the Reformed ministers made it an important tool for impressing the Reformed faith on the Dutch.

There are no reliable figures for the size of the Reformed movement in the Netherlands when the Revolt against Spain broke out in earnest in 1572. But it was clearly still a small minority even in its areas of greatest strength. Yet the zeal and devotion of its adherents gave it a significance far beyond its numbers. Well on its way to unity in organization and confession, it had already demonstrated its strength of character in the nobility of its martyrs (including Guido De Brès), and in the activism of its adherents (in public preaching and nocturnal psalm singing).

## The Church in a New State

In order to follow the development of Dutch Calvinism, it is essential to understand the political situation in which it grew. In 1566, the year of the iconoclasm, there was significant political reaction to King Philip's economic, administrative, and religious policies in the Netherlands. Some of the lesser nobility entered into a league and called on Philip to restore the ancient privileges of the Low Countries and to end religious oppression. In response Philip sent the Duke of Alva and Spanish troops to quell opposition, and in the skirmishes of 1568 Alva was successful. But in 1572 when the revolt led by William of Orange broke out in earnest, the situation became more difficult for Philip. He found it difficult to get fresh troops into the Netherlands because the rebels held all the ports. To add to his woes, Philip was always short of money to pay the troops already on the scene and to keep them fighting.

Though aided by Philip's troubles, William and the rebels were hampered by their own problems. They were short of money to fund the revolt and short of allies. All Europe feared Spain and assumed that it was only a matter of time until the revolt would be quelled. Other powers were reluctant to support the rebels. German Lutheran princes refused to support the revolt unless the leaders agreed to sign the Augsburg Confession. The militant Calvinist contingent in the revolt would not agree to that. Hopes for French support died with Gaspard de Coligny who perished in the St. Bartholomew's Day massacre. Elizabeth of England offered limited support with some troops and funds but was more eager to give moral support, which was less expensive and less entangling.

Despite the difficulties he faced, William was clear in his own mind on the goals for the revolt. He desired to regain the ancient rights of the Netherlands promised in the coronation oaths of its sovereign and he sought an end to religious persecution. He wanted to pursue those goals and to prevent the revolt from becoming a Protestant crusade that would only alienate the Dutch nobility, which was still largely Roman Catholic. Yet, on the other hand, William recognized that realistically his most dependable core of support came from the Reformed community in the Netherlands. To achieve his ends William needed to hold together the tenuous alliance of Roman Catholic nobles and Reformed zealots.

The revolt was initially conducted in the name of the king, but in 1581 that legal fiction was abandoned when the States General, made up of the representatives of the provinces, abjured Philip's sovereignty. For a time the States General cast about unsuccessfully for a sovereign. But by 1584 the United Provinces (basically composed of the seven northern provinces of Holland, Zeeland, Utrecht, Friesland, Gelderland, Overijssel, and Groningen) became a *de facto* republic. They were bound together by the Union of Utrecht of 1579, which had been written not as a constitution, but as a defensive alliance that William had hoped would unite all seventeen provinces.

The United Provinces evolved as a republic in response to the exigencies of the war with Spain, which dragged on until 1608, when the United Provinces gained *de facto* independence. Thus the new Dutch state, born of the needs of the moment, grew with a number of internal and unresolved contradictions. For example, in due course William's son, Maurice, received the official title of *Stadhouder* (something like a viceroy) of various provinces. But the constitutional role of the *Stadhouder* in the absence of a monarch was never clearly defined. Another example is the position of John Oldenbarnevelt. Shortly after William's death in 1584 most of the real political power passed into the hands of Oldenbarnevelt, who was Advocate of Holland. The office of Advocate carried little constitutional power or official standing, but by exercising his abilities and political skills Oldenbarnevelt became the functional head of the government. A situation rife with such constitutional ambiguity was bound to produce tensions, and the clash between Maurice and Oldenbarnevelt in the seventeenth century over the Arminian question was inevitable.

If the political institutions of the Netherlands had ambiguities, the status of the Reformed church in the United Provinces was also uncertain. Article 13 of the Union of Utrecht declared that religion was a matter for each province to decide and recognized the legal rights of the Reformed church explicitly only in Holland and Zeeland. The Union had also declared that important questions affecting all of the provinces could be settled in the States General only by unanimous vote. The States General applied these provisions of the Union to the calling of national synods, a decision that seriously limited the independence of the church in exercising discipline.

Despite the potential conflict between the new state and the church on the calling of national synods, the Reformed church came quickly to dominate the religious affairs of the provinces, with power quite disproportionate to its size. By the end of the sixteenth century the public exercise of the Roman Catholic religion had been outlawed in all of the United Provinces. Yet the Reformed church remained a minority. Until 1610 even in the centers of Reformed strength, Holland and Zeeland, the majority of the populace remained outside the Reformed church. Not until as late as 1650 did at least 50 percent of the population of the United Provinces belong to the Reformed church, and only in 1800 did the figure reach as high as 60 percent.

The power of the Reformed church and the close cooperation on some matters between church and state did not mean that the church had become officially a state church. While the cooperation between the church and state was close in certain matters, tensions continued on the matter of doctrinal discipline. The state often sought control of the life of the church in accordance with the views of Thomas Erastus, while most leaders of the church sought greater independence for the church, particularly in matters of discipline. Here the Reformed church in the Netherlands showed herself a true daughter of Calvin. The church wanted regular meetings of synods with rights to judge the orthodoxy of office-bearers. But the government at times blocked such discipline. Such interference most often occurred on the provincial or local level. For example, in 1591 Herman Herbertsz, a minister in Gouda, was suspended by the church, but the local authorities kept him in his post until he was reconciled with the church authorities in 1593. Beyond this local interference lay the continuing government insistence that major problems in the church could be resolved only at national synods and that national synods could be called only by unanimous vote of the States General.

## ARMINIUS AND CONFRONTATION

The tensions between the church and the state in the United Provinces remained relatively minor in the sixteenth century. But the differences over questions of discipline left a potential for deep division and sharp confrontation in Dutch society. That potential was realized in the Arminian controversy—a conflict so bitter that it brought the United Provinces to the very edge of civil war.

In 1603 Jacob Arminius (1560–1609) was appointed to a chair in theology at the University of Leiden. This appointment evoked some scattered protest in the church. Leiden had become an important and internationally recognized Reformed university. The church was concerned to preserve unquestioned orthodoxy in the theological faculty there. On the surface, Arminius seemed reliable. He had studied in Geneva, returned with a fine letter of recommendation in hand from Theodore Beza, and had served well as a pastor in Amsterdam. But some ministers raised questions about his theology. In sermons on Romans 7 and 9 he had presented views on the unregenerate will and on predestination that were disturbing to some. In 1603 Franciscus Gomarus, a strict Calvinist and, after the death of F. Junius and L. Trelcatius from the plague, the sole surviving member of the Leiden theological faculty, offered to interview Arminius. After the interview Gomarus declared that he was fully satisfied with the views of Arminius, and Arminius was installed at the university.

Within a short period of time, however, rumors began to circulate in the university about Arminius's teaching. In 1605 the local synod sought to investigate but was prevented from doing so by university authorities. In the same year all the provincial synods called for a national synod to investigate the matter, but the government refused to call a synod for this purpose. Instead, Oldenbarnevelt organized nonecclesiastical conferences in 1608 and 1609 in which he hoped discussions could resolve the problems. The strict Calvinists insisted that Arminius had deviated seriously from orthodox Calvinism in the matters of justification and election. Charges of Socinianism, Pelagianism, and Papist sympathies were hurled at Arminius. The controversy was halted only temporarily by Arminius's death in 1609.

The theology of Arminius defied thorough analysis in the early seventeenth century, for much of his important writings had not been published. In retrospect his views were neither Socinian nor Pelagian but did differ from confessional Reformed orthodoxy. He was concerned to uphold the goodness and mercy of God. He feared that supralapsarianism tended to make God the author of sin. He wanted to stress the importance of faith and holiness in the Christian life and feared that some elements of Calvinist theology undermined morality. In his work "An Examination of the Treatise of William Perkins Concerning the Order and Mode of Predestination" (written in 1602) he showed his non-Calvinist approach to election. He wrote, "In the second place, you assert, that 'divine Election is the rule of giving or withholding faith. Therefore Election does not pertain to believers, but faith rather pertains to the elect, or is from the gift of Election.' You will allow me to deny this, and to ask for the proof, while I plead the cause of those whose sentiment you here oppose. Election is made in Christ. But no one is in Christ, except he is a believer. Therefore no one is elected in Christ, unless he is a believer."[10] He also questioned whether special and efficacious grace was necessary for one to come to faith, and he challenged the doctrine of perseverance.[11]

The death of Arminius only delayed the eruption of controversy in the church. Indeed his followers continued resolutely to labor for toleration of their views within the church. A group of forty-three Arminian ministers, led by John Uytenbogaert, met in 1610 to draw up a petition, a remonstrance, to the States of Holland asking for protection for their position. They stated their views in five points, declaring, first, that God did not elect individuals but rather the group of those who believe and obey; second, that Christ died for all men and every man; third, that faith is a gift of God, but, fourth, that the gift of faith is resistible; and fifth, that they were uncertain about the doctrine of perseverance. This document evoked a vehement reaction from the strict Calvinists who produced a seven-point statement that they called the Counter-Remonstrance. From that point on the two groups were largely known by contemporaries in the Netherlands as Remonstrants and Counter-Remonstrants.

The government continued to try to deal with the situation through conferences, but both the church and the society only grew more polarized on the issue. The Counter-Remonstrants included the large majority of the ministers and members of the church. The Remonstrants represented a small minority who were protected by the government, particularly by Oldenbarnevelt and others who promoted the Erastian perspectives of Holland's merchant patricians.

The strict Calvinists experienced growing frustration over the Arminian controversy. They believed that the Arminians denied basic truths of the gospel, compromising the orthodoxy of their churches, and that the government was preventing church leaders from fulfilling their right and responsibility to discipline the doctrinal offenders. In some cities the Calvinists took the extraordinary action of withdrawing from churches with Remonstrant preachers and either visiting neighboring towns or holding their own preaching services outside the city walls. The tensions in some towns were so great that riots broke out. In 1615 some ministers began to talk of organizing secret synods and withdrawing from the state-dominated church.

The polarization of Dutch society seemed complete when in July 1617 Prince Maurice openly identified with the Counter-Remonstrant cause by refusing to worship any longer in the Court church at The Hague where Uytenbogaert was the preacher. Maurice to that point had not been actively involved in the theological controversy raging in the churches. His cousin, William Louis of Friesland, had been pressing the merits of the Calvinist cause, but political considerations were probably more influential with Maurice. Maurice saw in the controversy an opportunity to gain political advantage over his rival Oldenbarnevelt, with whom he was already feuding over the question of peace with Spain. Maurice wanted the war to continue until the country was unified again, whereas Oldenbarnevelt wanted permanent peace with Spain for the sake of the commercial well-being of the United Provinces.

Maurice supported the call for a national synod to settle the Arminian problem and in November 1617 the States General voted four to three to call such a synod. Holland insisted that a unanimous vote was required and that the action of the States General was invalid. When Maurice began to put military pressure on the government, Oldenbarnevelt threatened to raise a civilian army to fight the prince. The threat of civil war passed when Maurice arrested Oldenbarnevelt on August 29, 1618. Several leaders of the Remonstrant cause fled the country. With Maurice firmly in control, the States General's decree of the previous year was immediately implemented and the national synod was called to meet at Dordrecht (Dort) in November 1618.

## THE SYNOD OF DORT

The Dutch Calvinists were sensitive to the Remonstrants' claim that they would not receive a fair trial at the national synod and that only local personality problems had caused the conflict. To insure and to demonstrate the fairness of the proceedings, therefore, the Dutch decided to invite delegations from sister Reformed churches throughout Europe to participate as full members of the synod. The synod was organized in terms of delegations or colleges. The Dutch colleges were from the synods of Gelderland, South Holland, North Holland, Zeeland, Utrecht, Friesland, Overijssel, Groningen, Drenthe, and the Walloon churches. There was also a delegation of Dutch professors of theology—Johannes Polyander, Franciscus Gomarus, Anthonius Thysius, Antonius Walaeus, and Sibrandus Lubbertus. The international colleges were from England, the Palatinate, Hesse, Nassau, Bremen, Emden, the German-speaking Swiss (Zurich, Bern, Basel, and Schaffhausen), and Geneva. Invitations were also sent to France and Brandenburg, but political problems prevented delegations from coming.

The foreign delegations exercised considerable influence on the work of the Synod, particularly the college from Great Britain. King James of England had been a faithful military ally of the Dutch, and the Dutch were eager to show every respect for his representatives to the Synod. The Church of Scotland was unhappy that it was not invited separately from the English. James did add one Scot to the delegation belatedly, but this delegate, Walter Balcanqual, was himself a member of the Church of England. The Dutch had determined, however, wherever possible to send invitations to the Synod to the heads of state and allow them to determine the delegation from their own dominions.

The Synod of Dort, which convened on November 13, 1618, was certainly unique from several perspectives. For example, the gathering at Dordrecht was undoubtedly the only Dutch synod to which a bishop (George Carlton from England) was a delegate. More significantly, however, it was the only truly ecumenical synod that the Reformed churches have ever had. Most of the Reformed churches of the world were represented and their delegations were full members of the synod, able to discuss and vote on the doctrinal issue. The Synod's decisions on Arminian theology were unanimous and were widely hailed throughout Reformed Europe as a clear articulation of biblical truth and a victory for Reformed orthodoxy.

The basic work of the Synod was to judge the views of the Remonstrants. The Remonstrant leaders who had not fled the Netherlands were summoned to present their views to the Synod. Through their spokesman, Simon Episcopius, the Arminians tried several tactics to delay the work of the Synod and to divide the delegates. After listening to their protests and presentations for over a month, the President of the Synod, Johannes Bogerman, dismissed the Remonstrants and declared that the Synod would reach its decisions on the basis of their written works. Each of the various colleges drew up its own response to the Arminian doctrines and a committee that included the more prominent delegates prepared the final form of the Canons that was adopted.

Some problems and differences among the orthodox delegates to the Synod emerged as they worked on their responses. Both infralapsarians and supralapsarians were present; they compromised by writing canons that were acceptable to both sides. More difficult were the differences on the extent of the atonement. The theological differences that surfaced on this question came as a surprise to many and angered some. But in the end the synod worked out a compromise that united the delegates against the Arminians without fully resolving their own differences.

In their final form the Canons were divided into Five Heads of Doctrine answering the five points of the Remonstrance. Because the third point of the Remonstrance was erroneous only in relation to the fourth point, the Canons have a Third and Fourth Head of Doctrine as one unit. The Canons declared that God's electing purpose was not conditioned by anything inherent in or done by sinful men; that Christ's death was sufficient to save the world, but was efficient only for the elect; that fallen man is totally unable to help himself and that the Spirit therefore sovereignly and irresistibly gives the gift of faith to the elect; and that those justified and regenerated will be preserved to the end and glorified. These five Heads of Doctrine have often been called the five points of Calvinism. Yet they are not a summary of the fullness of Reformed Christianity. They are better seen as Calvinism's five answers to the five errors of Arminianism.

The Canons have been caricatured as an expression of a rigid, arid Reformed scholastic theology. Anyone who reads the Canons will find quite a different reality. The Canons are profoundly pastoral in character and were deliberately written in popular language for the edification of the church. They are not speculative, but begin with the misery of the human condition and focus on God's gracious and effective provision of salvation in Christ. The theme of the consolation of the believer is a recurring one. This quality of the Canons of Dort can be seen, for example in Canons I,13: ''The sense and certainty of this election afford to the children of God additional matter for daily humiliation before Him, for adoring the depth of His mercies, for cleansing themselves, and rendering grateful returns of ardent love to Him who first manifested so great love towards them. The consideration of this doctrine of election is so far from encouraging remissness in the observance of the divine commands or from sinking men in carnal security, that these, in the just judgment of God, are the usual effects of rash presumption or of idle and wanton trifling with the grace of election, in those who refuse to walk in the ways of the elect.''

The work of the Synod was not limited to the issues raised by the Arminians. Since no national synod had met since 1586, many other issues for the life and work of the church needed resolution. An overview of the additional work of the Synod provides useful insights into the concerns and character of the Dutch Reformed Church in the early seventeenth century. This additional work of the Synod was divided into the *Pro-Acta* and the *Post-Acta,* i.e., the work done before the Armi-nians arrived and the work completed after the Canons had been adopted. The *Pro-Acta* included five basic dispositions. First, the Synod decided on a new official translation of the Bible into Dutch. The result ultimately was the *Statenvertaling,* a version nearly as influential in the Netherlands as the King James Version was in the English-speaking world. Second, the Synod provided for regular catechetical instruction for the young and regular preaching of the catechism in the churches. Third, the Synod decided that pagan children of the servants in the households of Christian merchants in the Far East should not be baptized as infants, but should first be instructed in the faith. The fourth issue related to the preparation necessary for candidates for the ministry, and the fifth decision regulated the censuring of dangerous books.

In the *Post-Acta* the Synod dealt with three major issues. First, the Synod established a definite text of the Belgic Confession for the church. Second, it responded to growing tensions in the Dutch churches between a strict Puritan Sabbath observance and the less strict conti-nental observance. The Synod, issuing a six-point declaration that took a mediating position, ruled that there was a continuing moral dimension to the fourth commandment that prohibited ordinary work and prohib-ited recreation that interfered with public worship.[12] Third, the Synod adopted a new church order that incorporated Calvin's concern for the right of the church to discipline itself. This church order, based on that of the early Synod of Emden, did not end the functional Erastianism practiced by the state in the Netherlands, however. Indeed, no national synod met in the Netherlands for nearly two hundred years after Dort.

The Synod of Dort marked the triumph of Calvinist orthodoxy in the theology of the Dutch Reformed Church and manifested Calvinist zeal for a disciplined church in its decisions on polity and ethics. Its counsel, however, was not always determinative of the actual course of events in the Dutch church and society in future centuries. Yet its actions and conclusions expressed anew the vision of John Calvin, demonstrated the vitality of Reformed Christianity, and provided a rich source of wisdom from which the church's Calvinism drew strength and was renewed.

## Pietism and Scholasticism

The Synod of Dort resolved the most serious theological problem confronting the Reformed church in the Netherlands in the early sev-enteenth century and spoke to a number of pressing practical issues in the life of the church. Yet many other tasks and opportunities awaited action by the church. The church continued to examine the life and piety of her members, to clarify her theology, and to develop a mandate for missionary concern to spread the gospel beyond the boundaries of the Netherlands.

Concern for the piety of the church is inherent in Reformed Christianity. As F. E. Stoeffler has remarked, "Calvinism was intrinsically oriented toward piety."[13] In the early days of the Reformation there had been no particular tension between doctrine and life. The risk involved in adopting the Reformation principles usually welded belief in doctrine and comitment of life together. Yet even early in the Reformation era, Protestants recognized the difference between "historic faith"—a purely formal intellectual assent to doctrine—and "living faith"—a wholehearted commitment to Christ. As Protestant churches became established and socially required in certain areas, churches had to face the growing problem of members whose relation to the church was purely formal. This was true in the Netherlands as well, and for many of the Dutch, English Puritanism offered the model for linking piety to doctrine.

One Dutch Calvinist who addressed the concern for piety in the church was William Teellinck (1579–1629), who became known as the father of Reformed Pietism. During his travels in England he had embraced Puritan theology. When he returned to the Netherlands, he labored effectively as a preacher and pastor calling individuals to a life of greater commitment. The call to new life in Christ, self-denial, and the felicity of knowing God were the key themes of his work.[14] Although he was sometimes criticized before the Synod of Dort for not being sufficiently militant in his opposition to Arminianism, his theology was orthodox Calvinism. Teellinck, like later Pietists in the Netherlands, believed that the Canons of Dort in stressing the necessity and radical character of regeneration supported efforts to continue the moral reform of the church.[15]

The Dutch Pietists looked especially to William Ames as the theologian of their movement. Ames (1576–1633), a student of William Perkins, was himself an Englishman, but after 1610 he spent his life in exile in the Netherlands for his nonconformity. He taught theology at the University of Franeker from 1622 until shortly before his death. His two most famous and influential works, *The Marrow of Theology* (1623 and 1627) and *Conscience with the Power and Cases Thereof* (1622 and 1630) showed the character of his thought and his concern for piety in the Reformed churches. Following the logical manner of the French Calvinist Peter Ramus, he divided his thought into two parts: faith and observance. He insisted on the importance of openly living and manifesting the regenerate life. His casuistry, i.e., his work of determining the application of biblical law to the Christian life, was the ethical foundation for Dutch precisionism. This precisionist concern for exact, legal obedience in the Christian life always carried with it the danger of legalism in later Dutch Pietism.

Other important figures demonstrate continued concern for greater piety in the Dutch Reformed church. Jadocus van Lodensteyn (1620–77) took the principles of precision and self-denial to even greater lengths than his predecessors had done and was even attracted by some forms of medieval piety. He labored both as a pastor and as a writer of devotional literature for Christians. T. G. Brakel (1608–69) and his son William (1635–1711) began to place greater stress on feelings in the Christian experience. Later Pietists of strong precisionist convictions tended even more to lose the balance between doctrine and life, putting excessive emphasis on rigorous living, while others overemphasized the role of feelings and religious experiences.

While Pietists worked to improve the moral and spiritual life of the church, others met the church's needs for continued work in systematic theology. The articulation and refinement of Reformed theology were fundamental in days of vigorous polemics against Roman Catholics, Socinians, and others. But as the seventeenth century wore on, Reformed theologians also had to face new philosophical challenges to their work. The emergence of Descartes's thought marked a special challenge to Reformed dogmaticians as Cartesian philosophy confronted the Aristotelianism often used to express Reformed systematic theology in the universities. Thus theology moved in a more technical and scholastic direction in response to the polemical and philosophical climate of the day, but also in response to the basic Reformed conviction that theology was a science.

One of the most important early products of this continuing theological reflection was a handbook of Reformed theology published shortly after the Synod of Dort. The *Synopsis Purioris Theologiae* (1625) was written by J. Polyander, A. Rivetus, A. Walaeus, and A. Thysius. This *Synopsis,* organized in fifty-two loci remained an influential summary of Reformed systematic theology for years.

## VOETIUS

The developing scholastic theology cannot be caricatured as an arid and irrelevant academic exercise at odds with the life and piety of the church. The life and work of Gisbertus Voetius (1589–1676), the dominant theologian in the Netherlands in the middle of the seventeenth century, demonstrates the harmonious union of Scholasticism and Pietism and provides a mirror that reflects many aspects of the Dutch Reformed church in his day.

Voetius grew up in an atmosphere fraught with the tensions and problems of Dutch society in the late sixteenth century. He was born in Heusden near the border with the Spanish Netherlands, and his father was killed in 1597 while fighting for Prince Maurice. Voetius studied at Leiden from 1604 to 1611 where he showed keen interests in philosophy, theology, and Semitic languages. He became a determined

Aristotelian in philosophy and, after the model of his teacher Gomarus, he became a strict Calvinist as well.

In his first two pastorates Voetius worked hard to combat the errors of Romanism and Arminianism. His effectiveness as a pastor earned him an appointment to the Synod of Dort despite his youth. His work as a pastor was phenomenal. In addition to visiting members of his congregation and catechizing the youth, he preached eight times in a week and took on private students as a teacher of theology, logic, physics, metaphysics, Hebrew, Syriac, and Arabic. He also took two days a week for personal study. During his second pastorate, at Heusden, he published his first work, *Proof of the Power of Godliness* (1634). He also served for a time as a chaplain with the forces of Prince Frederick Henry in the war against Spain. When the city of Den Bosch was captured by the prince, Voetius went with other chaplains to reform the population. This drew Voetius into a polemical exchange with the bishop of Ypres, Cornelius Jansenius, but this exchange produced no understanding between those two Augustinians.

In 1636 Voetius was called to teach theology and oriental languages at the Academy of Utrecht. When the Academy was elevated to the status of a university a few years later, Voetius was made a professor. He summed up his concerns in his inaugural lecture: "On Piety Joined With Science." Both his teaching and preaching in Utrecht drew wide attention, and he attracted many students. His fame and influence were so widespread that the university was often called the *Academia Voetiana,* and his writings disseminated his thought throughout the land. He wrote against compromise with Arminians or Romanists and even opposed the peace with Spain (1648) because it left the southern Low Countries in bondage to Rome.

In the 1640s Voetius turned his energies to lead the attack on the growing influence of Cartesianism in the Dutch universities. Descartes personally answered Voetius's attacks in his *Letter to the Very Famous Man Gisbertus Voetius.* Voetius's dedication to Aristotle in both philosophy and science today seems simply reactionary and obscurantist. But in his own day Voetius slowed the spread of new ideas that he regarded to be inimical to the faith. He failed to help the church develop tools for effectively understanding and coping with modern systems of thought, but as John Beardslee has commented, "It is true that the theologians did poorly in dealing with the new questions that were to dominate the next development of European culture. . . . But if this 'secular' world was not their interest, neither was it that of the common man."[16]

Later in his life Voetius faced a new dispute within the church. This revolved around Johannes Cocceius (1603–69), a Bremen-born theologian, who first taught at Franeker and later at Leiden. Cocceius began to take a new approach to the Old Testament. He endeavored to deal with the Old Testament in a more historical and contextual and a less dogmatic way. Voetius believed that Cocceius's claim of having a more covenantal and Christocentric approach to the Old Testament in reality undermined both strict Calvinist dogmatics and precisionism for Christian living. The Cocceian method of interpretation meant that the Old Testament could no longer be easily used as proof of dogmatic conclusions or as a source of Christian moral law. The church rapidly divided into two camps. The division really reflected a difference of spirit as much as anything—the inflexible versus the flexible. For example, differences on how strictly and precisely the Sabbath was to be observed were typical of the division.

Voetius's vigorous efforts to promote the doctrinal purity and moral improvement of the church never undermined his devotion to the visible, institutional church. His relationship with Jean de Labadie (1610–74) illustrates his concern for the unity as well as the purity of the church. De Labadie's preaching had been the source of spiritual revival in Reformed churches in Switzerland. Voetius, excited by this news and hoping for a similar revival in the Netherlands, engineered de Labadie's call to Middelburg in Zeeland in 1665. But de Labadie soon came into conflict with church authorities and began to move in an increasingly schismatic direction. Voetius, while sympathetic to the vision of a pure church, was horrified by separatism and took up the pen against de Labadie. Beyond such occasional writing against separatism, Voetius's fullest statement on the church and its unity was his notable three-volume work *Politica Ecclesiastica* (1663–76). The striking feature of this work was Voetius's clear rejection of Erastianism and his demand that the church be completely independent of the state and of all patronage.

Voetius articulated a clear vision of a pious and orthodox Reformed church dominating Dutch society. But the changes of the seventeenth century brought many other influences to bear on life in the Netherlands. The United Provinces were clearly one of the leading countries of Europe in the middle of the seventeenth century and had achieved considerable political stability and security. Economically the Netherlands flourished, dominating world trade. Culturally her art and literature blossomed, producing such greats as Rembrandt and Vondel. Many varied intellectual currents flowed through the Netherlands. Voetius stoutly set himself against novelty and diversity and continued to pursue in quite medieval terms his ideal of a fully Reformed society.

## Missions

In addition to the internal problems of theology and piety with which the church wrestled, a whole new opportunity in foreign missions was opened to the church by Dutch economic enterprises in the Orient. Throughout the sixteenth century the Dutch had been involved in the spice trade in Europe, buying spices in Lisbon and distributing them in northern Europe. Late in the sixteenth century they sent their first expeditions to the Far East and found the trade so profitable that they began an active rivalry with the Portuguese. In 1602 the United East India Company received its charter and a monopoly of the trade for the Dutch. The first charter contained no mention of an obligation to spread the faith and not surprisingly the company always placed its commercial interests first. However, the renewed charter of 1622 obligated it "rightly to further the common faith."[17] The company undertook responsibility for the training and supervision of all missionaries in the East.

The opening of the East to the Dutch helped stimulate thought in the church on the task of missions. Adrian Saravia (1531–1613), once a Reformed minister and friend of Guido De Brès, expressed the importance of taking the Gospel to pagans in his famous work *De Diversis Gradibus Ministrorum* (1590). This treatise, written after he had joined the Church of England, also defended episcopacy, insisting that missions were linked to the episcopal office. More characteristic of Dutch perspectives on missions were Jean Taffin the Younger, William Teellinck, Justus Heurnius, and Voetius—seventeenth-century Pietists who stressed the importance of missions in the work of the church. From these Dutch thinkers came the first significant Protestant theory of missions.

Many practical problems faced the church when the United East India Company began to request clergy for its ships and trading communities in the East around 1609. In response to the growing need for missionaries, an institute for training men for ministry in the East opened in Leiden in 1622 under Antonius Walaeus. This institute was probably the first Protestant school for missionaries, but survived only until 1633 and graduated only twelve students. The interference of the company in the work of the missions no doubt contributed to the failure of the school.

The history of Dutch missions in Indonesia was hardly glorious. The number of converts was very small and serious errors in theology and practice developed in the Indonesian church. The responsibility lay in large part with the church at home whose zeal and vision were so often limited. But the negative interference of the company in the mission efforts limited and undermined the work even more. Ministers who went east found that the company kept the church in the East from any creative or independent action and even prevented effective communication with the church at home. The result was that during the first 120 years of company monopoly in Indonesia the church grew from 40,000 (whom the Portuguese had brought into the Roman Catholic church) to only 55,000.

## ENLIGHTENMENT, REVOLUTION, AND REVIVAL

In the eighteenth century the intellectual and religious climate in the Netherlands began to change even more rapidly and significantly than in the seventeenth. The individualism and rationalism of the French Enlightenment infiltrated Dutch society and the Dutch church. The Enlightenment triumphed in the Netherlands when revolutionary France went to war with the United Provinces in 1793. The victorious French reorganized the Netherlands as the Batavian Republic from 1795 to 1806. The new republic instituted a radical separation of church and state that created ethical and financial difficulties for the church and the clergy. The state was regarded as secular and the church was treated as just another private organization. This was hardly the end of Erastianism that Voetius had envisioned. When Napoleon created the Kingdom of Holland in 1806 and then annexed the Netherlands to France in 1810, the conditions for the church were not significantly changed.

After the defeat of Napoleon, the triumphant European powers established the House of Orange as the monarchy of the Netherlands in 1813. In 1816 King William I issued a new constitution for the kingdom that granted all religious groups equality before the law. The constitution declared that the state had a special concern for the Reformed church. The king gave the Reformed church a new church order that was hierarchical rather than presbyterian in nature and that gave the state authority to supervise various aspects of the work of the synods. Traditional Calvinists viewed these developments with dismay, feeling that Erastianism had been imposed on them in a worse form than ever before.

While the external structure of the church was being changed, strict Calvinists were experiencing spiritual renewal through the religious revival, the Awakening, that was affecting many parts of Europe in the 1820s. Many Dutch Calvinists were strengthened in their convictions that the church had been weakened by its new church order and that its foundations of discipline and doctrine had suffered erosion from Enlightenment principles. Among those who spoke out against the new spirit of the age was the poet Willem Bilderdyk. Like others who called for a national revival, Bilderdyk (1756–1831), himself a product of the Awakening, wrote of the glories of Holland's Calvinistic heritage. Isaac Da Costa echoed this theme as he lamented the present decline in the discipline of the church.

Strict Calvinists came to see a focal danger to the church in the new form of subscription to the church's doctrinal standards. The new form of subscription of 1816 was ambiguous and vague. Some office-bearers in the church insisted that they subscribed to the doctrinal standards because *(quia)* they conformed to God's Word. This interpretation imposed strict Calvinism on all subscribers. Others claimed that they subscribed in so far as *(quatenus)* the standards conformed to God's Word. This interpretation allowed a much more liberal approach to doctrinal issues. This conflict on the nature of subscription caused some of the strict Calvinists, influenced by the Awakening and Dutch Pietism, to despair of the future of the church. After some years of heated conflict over such laxity, a secession (the *Afscheiding*) occurred in 1834. It was led by Hendrik de Cock, H. P. Scholte, and others. Within a few years some twenty thousand orthodox Calvinists had joined the secessionist movement, but many more remained in the Dutch Reformed church and continued to press the claims of Reformed orthodoxy in that body.

Conflicts within the Dutch church in the early nineteenth century reflected the unstable social and cultural condition of Dutch society in general. The growing pluralism, secularism, and fragmentation of society were all products of the spirit of modern, postrevolutionary Holland. In this new cultural environment a Calvinist thinker emerged who faced the problems of the modern world squarely and opened a new era in the development of Reformed thought and life. This man, Guillaume Groen Van Prinsterer (1801–76), was an aristocrat raised in a liberal environment. Influenced by the Awakening, Groen came to embrace the orthodox Reformed faith. He devoted himself to work as a historian (in 1832 he was appointed archivist for the House of Orange-Nassau) and a statesman (serving in the Parliament and founding the Anti-Revolutionary Party). In all these activities he sought to relate his Christian commitments to his work. Although he did not join the *Afscheiding*, he did share many of its concerns over the growing lack of discipline in the Reformed church. He called for legal toleration for the *Afscheiding* and labored for independence and proper doctrine for the Reformed church.

Groen was influenced in the development of his thought by the conviction that the spirit of the French Revolution was the greatest threat in his day to Christianity and to Dutch society in general. This spirit, whether manifested in absolutist or individualistic notions of sovereignty, opposed the sovereignty and law of God to which all Christians must adhere. For this reason he was convinced that Christians must be "anti-revolutionary." He expressed his belief about the destructive force of the revolutionary principle quite strongly: "The history of the irreligious philosophy of the past century is in its source and its results, the teaching which, freely developed, destroys Church and State, society and family, produces disorder without ever founding liberty or reestablishing moral order, and, in matters of religion, infallibly leads its conscientious followers to atheism and despair."[18]

Yet Groen also insisted that the Christian could not return to a seventeenth-century theocratic ideal or maintain a static conservatism.

He rejected both revolutionary and counter revolutionary absolutism. He argued that sovereignty in society is derived from and resides ultimately in God alone, and not in the state, the people, or a monarch. In service to the sovereign God the Christian must seek actively to promote justice and goodness according to the unique circumstances and opportunities of his own time. The Word of God must be applied to historical reality. In this sense he championed the slogan: "It is written and it has happened." Groen believed that conservatives made a tragic mistake when they continued to "cling to the old and obsolete forgetting that life is only preserved by growth, that all that lives is subject to change, that existence is revealed by movement and progress, and would be willing to undo the conquests of the modern mind and improvements which in spite of the revolutionary spirit, have been good and laudable results of the social commotion—freedom of religion, abolition of excessive privilege, equality before the law, civil rights, political centralization. . . ."[19]

Groen was convinced that Reformed Christians needed to articulate their own principles and programs according to their own unique religious insights and then needed to pursue them without compromise. His conviction on Reformed distinctiveness in politics became something of a motto for the Anti-Revolutionary Party: "In our isolation is our strength."

## KUYPER

Groen's influence reached into many areas of Dutch life, but undoubtedly his most faithful and powerful colaborer and successor was Abraham Kuyper (1837–1921). Kuyper, like Groen, had undergone a spiritual pilgrimage before becoming a staunch Calvinist. As a university student he had accepted the religious liberalism of his day and only in his first pastorate in the Dutch Reformed church did he turn to the orthodox Reformed faith. He soon turned his great talents to restoring the Reformed character of the church and to increasing the impact of Christianity on Dutch life generally. He embraced the old Calvinist ideal of a disciplined church and a Christian society, but adopted the modern, progressive form of that ideal found in Groen's work.

Kuyper was a profound thinker, a great organizer, and an effective communicator with the common people. He effectively used his talents as a powerful and prolific writer in periodicals and theological works. In 1870 he became the editor of the religious weekly *De Heraut,* which was a vehicle for expressing his views throughout his life and through which he sought to restore the health of the church. In 1872 he founded and began to edit the daily paper *De Standaard* to present a regular Reformed perspective on all problems facing Dutch society. For the English reader the full range of his vision of modern Calvinism is summarized in the lectures that he delivered at Princeton in 1898, printed as *Calvinism: Six Stone Foundation Lectures.*[20]

His growing concern about social and political questions in the Netherlands drew him into Dutch political life. In 1874 he was elected to Parliament, and this necessitated his retirement from the ministry. He reorganized the Anti-Revolutionary Party, making it the first party in the Netherlands to move away from being a rather elitist club toward becoming a truly popular party with involvement of the rank and file. His political successes led him to the post of prime minister from 1901 to 1905. His greatest personal political concerns included an extension of suffrage, state support for Christian schools, and social legislation to help protect working people.

He also saw the need for a Reformed university to promote Christian intellectual development. In 1880 he helped found the Free University of Amsterdam (free from both state and church control). There Kuyper himself taught theology, homiletics, Hebrew, and literature.

Although he could no longer serve as a minister, his concern for the church never faded. Kuyper served as an elder in the church in Amsterdam where he endeavored to improve the discipline and faithfulness of the church. The majority of the Amsterdam consistory, of which Kuyper was a part, came into conflict with higher church authorities when the consistory refused to admit liberal catechumens to church membership. In 1886 the higher authorities removed Kuyper and the majority of the consistory from office for their stand. This disciplinary action against the orthodox precipitated a new secession. Some two hundred congregations left the Reformed church and formed the churches of the *Doleantie,* the churches grieving or mourning. These churches initially hoped that changes in the Reformed church would enable them to return someday. When hopes for reform faded, the churches of the *Doleantie* united in 1892 with most of the churches of the *Afscheiding* to form a denomination called The Reformed Churches in the Netherlands. The new church was committed to traditional Calvinism as expressed in the theology of the Three Forms of Unity—the Belgic Confession, the Heidelberg Catechism, and the Canons of Dort—and the traditional church order of the Synod of Dort.

In all of Kuyper's work certain basic convictions remained consistent. He insisted on a radical antithesis between Christian thought and non-Christian thought. Christians must seek their own distinctive understanding of God and His world based on His revelation in Scripture and in nature. Yet he recognized that by God's common grace the effects of sin had been restrained in the world so that there was truth to be found and used in the work of non-Christians, an idea that permitted some political coalition with non-Calvinists.

His work as church reformer, educator, and politician was based on his idea of "sphere sovereignty." Each sphere of life (church, state, family, etc.) has its own area of responsibility, which is derived directly from God, and those within each sphere are accountable only to God. He saw this principle as the essential bulwark against all forms of modern totalitarianism and the foundation of a proper modern pluralism. Yet the Christian must labor to see Christ honored in every one of these spheres. As he wrote in *Pro Rege:* "In the total expanse of human life there is not a single square inch of which Christ, who alone is sovereign, does not declare, 'That is mine.'"[21]

## ANTITHESIS OR ACCOMMODATION

The spirit and work of Kuyper renewed and revitalized Calvinism as a vital force in the church and society of the Netherlands. Kuyper had many co-workers and followers, of whom only a few can be mentioned here. Herman Bavinck (1854–1921), the son of an *Afscheiding* minister, was, with Kuyper, one of the great theologians of the revived Calvinism. He taught at the *Afscheiding* theological school at Kampen from 1883 until he went to the Free University in 1902. His greatest work was his brilliant systematic theology, *Gereformeerde Dogmatiek* (four volumes, first edition, 1895–99, second edition, 1911).

Perhaps the most profound thinker of later generations among the Dutch Calvinists was Herman Dooyeweerd (1894–1977). From 1926 he worked as Professor of Law at the Free University. He sought to develop a fully Reformed philosophy in the tradition of Kuyper's stress on the antithesis and sphere sovereignty. He stressed especially the function of law both as the boundary between God and His creation and as the structure of the created world. He gave the fullest expression of his complex philosophical thought in *A New Critique of Theoretical Thought* (four volumes, 1953–58).

While Dooyeweerd sought to extend the thought of Kuyper in the area of philosophy, the most notable successor of Kuyper and Bavinck in theology has been G. C. Berkouwer (born 1903). In 1945 he succeeded Valentinus Hepp in the chair of Dogmatics at the Free University. The work of Berkouwer began strongly in the orthodox tradition of his predecessors. His works in the 1930s and 1940s were directed against the theologies of liberalism, Romanism, and neoorthodoxy. He has furthered his reputation as a thoughtful and influential theologian in his multi-volume, *Studies in Dogmatics*. But in the 1950s and 1960s the work of Berkouwer, like many of the institutions of Dutch Calvinism, began to show a milder attitude toward non-Reformed religious expressions. Berkouwer wrote of the triumph of grace in Barth's theology. He attended the Second Vatican Council and wrote sympathetically of developments in the Roman Catholic church. He raised questions of the deforming effect of Aristotelianism in the confessional standards of the

Reformed churches. His most recent works on Scripture, the church, and theology—especially *A Half Century of Theology* (1974)—show significant deviation from the Reformed orthodoxy that marked his earlier work.

Berkouwer is somewhat symbolic of the meandering of the Dutch Calvinist tradition of the past few decades. The vision of Calvin and his early Dutch followers of a strong, orthodox, disciplined church and of a just society seems to be declining. The Reformed churches in the Netherlands seem unwilling to maintain their doctrinal standards. The Free University in many areas has abandoned its commitment to and search for distinctively Christian learning. As at other points in the history of the Netherlands, the creative powers of true Calvinism for the whole society seem on the decline. Accommodation to modern liberalism seems to be replacing the principle of antithesis.

The historian is no prophet. He can only wait to see if the present decline represents a temporary setback or a permanent departure from Calvinist roots. Followers of the development of Calvinism in the Netherlands may still see new forms of Calvinism in the Netherlands in the future. Yet whatever the future brings, Calvinism certainly has not ceased to be an important key to understanding modern Dutch life and thought.

# The Reformed Church of Germany: Calvinists as an Influential Minority

## D. Clair Davis

*D. Clair Davis is Professor of Church History at Westminster Theological Seminary, Philadelphia, Pennsylvania. He holds degrees from Wheaton College (B.A., M.A.), Westminster Theological Seminary (B.D.), and Georg-August Universität, Göttingen, Germany (Th.D.). He has served on the faculties of Olivet College, Michigan, and the Wheaton Graduate School of Theology. He has been editor of the* Westminster Theological Journal, *and has written articles for it and for* Christianity Today, Eternity, *and the* Journal of Pastoral Practice. *He is a member of the American Society of Church History and the Evangelical Theological Society.*

# 6

# The Reformed Church of Germany: Calvinists as an Influential Minority

The German Reformed church has not attracted much attention in the English-speaking world. Perhaps that is because Calvinist nostalgia tends to focus on the countries where Reformed churches were dominant or were even the state churches, as in Scotland and the Netherlands or, on a smaller scale, the city-state of Geneva and that of the Massachusetts Bay colony. When such a focus is made, there is manifest discontinuity between the halcyon years of Calvinist control and the present situation of small, near-irrelevant churches submerged in a pluralistic society. So the other face of the history of the Reformed churches is well worth our attention today, not only for the professional historian but also for all those who are concerned and committed to a working Calvinism today.

The Reformed churches are best understood as second-generation phenomena. Not for them is the excitement of a single-issue campaign, whether that of the Lutheran recapture of the heart of the gospel in justification by faith alone or that of the Anabaptist zeal for the life of radical discipleship. For Calvinists the goal must always be grasping *all* of the Lord and His salvation, of going on from the good beginning, of not being weary in well doing, of "finishing the Reformation." This means that it is not just Rome who must be answered, but also Renaissance humanism; Calvin's *Institutes* clearly wages the war on both fronts.[1] Because of its multifaceted character, it is not surprising that the usual role for a Reformed church is that of a minority. However, this hardly means an unnoticed minority; rather, it constitutes a visible reminder to all Christians that there are other biblical options that demand exploration and that it is wrong to be content with even a Protestant traditionalism.

This is in a particular way true of the Reformed church in Germany. Because of the continued existence there of smaller feudal governing units, many of these could serve as areas where Reformed theology and practice could be encouraged, but they were so close to Roman Catholic and Lutheran territories that interaction with them was almost certainly insured. This phenomenon served as a continuation and expansion of the already-useful ''pilot-project'' churches of Calvinist refugees, which had already come into being in Geneva and Strasbourg. In these cities it became possible for congregations of Calvinist refugees from France, England, and Scotland to put into immediate practice the radical reforms in worship and church government and discipline that would have been impossible at home but which they could attempt to implement on a nation-wide scale after their return to their homelands. But these smaller arenas were always somewhat artificial.

Ordinarily these congregations worshiped exclusively in their mother tongues—that is, in languages largely unknown in the communities in which they were. Further, the city-state size often led not only to immigrations of foreigners with no lasting commitment to their new temporary homes but also to wholesale departures of the old inhabitants who left in disgust because of their unwillingness to adapt to the comprehensive changes the newcomers had instituted and perhaps also because they saw themselves losing control of their place in the socio-economic power structure of their communities. So while such micro-expressions of Reformed churches ultimately proved invaluable in learning how to apply the new Calvinist insights to the creation of a biblical church in a practical way, they could ultimately be misleading as to how that church was to be established in a larger, more pluralistic society. It is there that the ''medium-size'' churches of the German principalities, with their indigenous character, were to be more useful. It is there that Calvinism's identity over against Lutheranism was to be more clearly seen, not only in theology but also fully as much in the practical expression of that theology in the life of the church.

This is true even more than in the British context, where the conflicts over the proper worship and government of a biblically reformed church became too often a matter of political and even social struggle. In Germany theology was much more vitally related to the real issues surrounding the Lord's Supper, and this led to the proper appreciation both of the true humanity of Jesus Christ in His ascended, exalted state, and of the truly historical character of His ascension and return. That is, as one considers the Reformed church in its German context, one learns to define its essence in terms of the *continuing* relationship of Jesus

Christ to His people and not just in terms of His eternal election or sovereign work in bringing the individual to faith at the time of his conversion, as is so easily understood in the British-Dutch Calvinist focus against Arminianism.[2] Perhaps only when the British-Dutch and the German emphases are combined can later Calvinism, that of our own day included, be as truly biblically comprehensive in its response to all that our Lord has done for us as it was in the original vision of John Calvin himself.

The Reformed church of Germany is not an abstraction but involved many committed people in many different places. As suggested above, the beginning of the Reformed church in Germany was at Strasbourg, a free city in the southwest. First Matthew Zell in 1521 and then Capito began the great work of biblical preaching, but Martin Bucer arrived to take over the real leadership and became pastor in 1524. Soon he was in close contact with the three ministers of the refugee French Reformed church there, including Farel. Later contacts with Zwingli led Bucer to take his side against Luther at the Marburg conference, where attempts at Swiss and German agreement broke down over the differing understanding of the nature of the Lord's Supper and hence of the human nature of Christ. When in 1530 the Diet of Augsburg was held and Melanchthon was asked to prepare what became known as the Augsburg Confession to represent the Protestant position, Strasbourg had hoped that the confession would be broadly enough formulated so that Strasbourg could sign it and therefore be protected by it. But since that could not be, it needed its own confession, the Tetrapolitan, drawn up by Bucer and Capito. This became the first German Reformed confession. It emphasizes that "Christ offers to his followers his very body and blood as spiritual food and drink," but says little on the question so important to the Lutherans: the relation of the bread and wine to the body and blood of Christ. Yet it goes beyond the Augsburg Confession in stressing the need for biblical support for all aspects of worship and it denounces the worship of images, while Lutherans continued to retain religious statues in their churches.[3] In practice Strasbourg substituted the simple table for the altar.

Calvin himself was involved in developments there, arriving in 1538 after his expulsion from Geneva. The more consistent presbyterianism in the French refugee church of which he became pastor did much to influence the pattern of government and worship in the other churches in the city; the Genevan prototype thus formed the Strasbourg prototype! Calvin's stay in Strasbourg was also of great importance for his own development, for it was there that he came to understand first-hand the German Lutheran point of view, particularly as it concerned the theology of the Lord's Supper.

In 1549 when the Interim was forced on Strasbourg, with its reintroduction of Roman Catholic practices into worship, Bucer left for England, where he became a professor at Cambridge and exerted considerable influence in the formulation of the Second Book of Common Prayer and in what was to become the Thirty-nine Articles, the creed of the Anglican church. Again the lessons learned in Germany were to be of great use elsewhere in the Reformed world. Unfortunately, when the high Lutheran, or anti-Reformed, Formula of Concord was forced on Strasbourg in 1581, this good beginning came to an end, and the Reformed church found it necessary to find other homes in Germany. But at least some understanding of the plainer, simpler style of worship came to be known throughout the Protestant movement. The recognition of Calvinistic as well as Lutheran churches as legitimate (in contrast to the less-orderly Anabaptist groups), worthy of toleration and perhaps interest, was of enormous value in protecting the Reformed from the worst persecution. It also helped to establish among Lutherans some appreciation of the Reformed.

In particular, this tendency toward tolerance was to have a special effect on the attitude of the church in Hesse. There is no question that the preliminary encounters at Strasbourg between Reformed and Lutheran leaders had much to do with the comparative unity at the Marburg Conference. While the question of the Lord's Supper remained unresolved, it is often forgotten that the Lutherans originally were suspicious of the Reformed views of original sin and justification, and it was soon apparent to all that on these questions there was a fundamental agreement that united all of Protestantism. Indeed, Landgrave Phillip of Hesse insisted that the conference go on record to this effect in the fifteen Marburg articles. His suggestions for a mediating statement on the Supper to which all could agree were later adopted by the Lutheran theologian Melanchthon in his "variation" of the Augsburg Confession. It was primarily because of his influence that the Augsburg Confession did not explicitly brand Zwinglianism as a heresy. Even though the Hessian church itself was Lutheran, Zwinglians and Calvinists were allowed in it, and its government approached a presbyterian one, with synods but no elders.

Further, it is only on the basis of this background that the later Lutheran Pietist dependence on English and Dutch Pietism is at all explainable.[4] Indeed, the whole Pietist concept of "finishing the Reformation," that is, going on to complete biblical doctrinal orthodoxy and perfecting biblical worship and living, has to be understood from the perspective of Lutheran interest in the Reformed example, as that came to be first evident in Strasbourg.

We have already alluded to the German contribution to the development of presbyterianism as the Reformed church government. One must not think that that necessarily meant the same thing as it does today, with the emphasis on the local church and its "lay" elders. Rather it referred primarily to the "upper" structure of church government, the synod. There the issue was the whole church-and-state question: Who was ultimately responsible for the doctrinal alignment of the territory, for the discipline of ministers, and the like? Should it be the secular ruler and his representatives, or the church itself, or should there be some compromise solution? This question is of life-and-death importance in a time of persecution or war, as it involves political issues that from one point of view are better negotiated by the civil authorities. To a large extent this problem and its various solutions are the same everywhere in the Reformed world.

On the more basic, fundamental level, however, a very good case can be made for the unique contribution made by the German Reformed church to the meaning and importance of the local elder, especially as John Laski (à Lasco) in the Frisian church in northwestern Germany clarified it.[5] While most Reformed communities (e.g., in Geneva, London, and Amsterdam) discovered in the Bible the basis for a city-wide governing unit composed of ministers and elders who would administer the affairs of all the neighborhood churches (a presbytery without sessions!), and while the authority of an assembly or synod over presbyteries was generally accepted as at least a reasonable goal (with Scotland achieving it), it was left to Laski to coordinate the responsibility of presbytery and congregation and of congregation and elders. He also defined the elder's district within a congregation. Laski was a Polish nobleman whose uncle had been archbishop of Gnesen and primate of all Poland, and who himself had been offered a Polish bishopric. Through the influence of Zwingli and other Swiss leaders, he became Reformed and settled in East Friesland in 1540. In 1543 he was offered the position of superintendent of Friesland. Not only did he then introduce Reformed simplicity into worship, but in particular he began a weekly meeting of all the clergy in the area from Easter to Michaelmas (September 29). There the faith and life of all ministers were inquired into, sermons were heard and discussed, and a discussion of a doctrinal issue was carried on, with different ministers leading each week. It had a tremendous effect on the congregations to learn that church discipline was exercised among the ministers themselves and that ministers were training each other in pastoral care. A ministers' meeting was more than a business meeting; it was a truly spiritual exercise! When the emperor attempted to reimpose the superstitions of Catholicism on the Frisian churches, these ministers stood firm against them, refusing to accept even the compromises that Lutherans could accept. But when Laski's international ties led to a charge of treason against him, he left for London to take charge of the refugee church there.

There his development of presbyterianism went even further. Since he had many different ethnic groups together in one congregation, he found it convenient to make practical use of these natural subdivisions. This was accomplished by appointing elders from each group, giving them responsibility for particular oversight over their group, with the obligation to report to the whole body of elders. Out of such reports developed quite naturally elders' discussions of the doctrinal and practical questions confronting the whole church. Just as in Friesland ministers' meetings had been directed at resolving the problems of ministers, so in London elders' meetings wrestled with elders' issues.

Again, here is a development of long-range significance for the Reformed churches, particularly in the present day. It is not difficult to show that churches have shown great growth of all sorts whenever their people have been organized in small groups for mutual edification and training in service. Whether one thinks of the Puritan "prophecying," the Scottish "exercise,"[6] the Pietist "conventicle," or the Wesleyan or Calvinistic Methodist "class," the principle and the value seems the same. But it is also true that such groups have a reputation, sometimes well-deserved, for being subversive of the worship and life of the "real" church. Such subversion occurs when these groups consider themselves not as supplementing or supporting the work of the whole church, but rather as doing something that the church should be doing but is not. There is almost inevitably a judgmental tone about such groups. Conversely, not every church looks with favor on the existence of such groups in its midst, as they seem to be replacing the official preaching of the Word with teaching by untrained, schismatic people. These questions are still with us. One of the great strengths of the "charismatic" movement is its stress on developing and making use of the spiritual gifts of every believer, and this naturally leads to the desire for small, more informal worship situations in which the gifts of many people can be given expression. Within the presbyterian churches today the great unresolved question is the precise line between the office of minister and that of elder—or is there no line at all?

To a very great extent, Laski's solution is still very helpful. If presbytery and session business is not dominated by concerns other than the pastoral or "spiritual," then there are natural opportunities for the concerns of the churches or of the elder groups to come to expression. Thus the work of the groups under their elders cannot be in any way detrimental to the work of the church, but rather is a vital aspect of that church. No longer can the elders appear to have only an advisory role to the one pastoral officer of the church, the minister, for they all share truly pastoral oversight. And since the only "rule" in a Protestant church is a spiritual one—that is, based on communicating the teaching of the Bible—an elder's ability to rule therefore is really his ability to teach. Therefore the line between minister and elder is not nearly so sharp. This is what presbyterians have always sensed and even articulated, but have had so much difficulty in putting into practice. It is this that Laski and the Frisian Reformed church were able to begin to put into effect.

Again, the later influence of Reformed practice on Lutheran Pietism is unmistakable. While lay spiritual leadership hardly fits into Lutheran practice (except in the far-off day yearned for by Luther himself when Christians would possess sufficient spiritual maturity to make such a thing possible), Reformed practice can only encourage it, for elders are not "laymen" anyway but are officers of the church. As such they can hardly subvert the church but rather support it. While Pietists may never have formally endorsed Reformed church government, they certainly learned from it and used it, as they had seen it expressed in Britain and the Netherlands, probably without ever realizing its German source. The Puritan/Pietist relationship goes far beyond such questions of structure, however. Lutherans seem to have a built-in fear of too great a stress on sanctification, obedience to the law of God, and the like.[7] This is understandable against the legalistic background of Luther himself and others from the first generation of the Protestant movement, for they could hardly think of obedience to God in any other terms than as a basis for forgiveness. But the living example of the Reformed in Germany and elsewhere made clear that vital concern with the details of the Christian life need not undermine the foundation of the Reformation, justification by faith alone. After all, both Lutherans and Reformed were agreed in principle to something like Reformed structure and discipline, and the Lutherans' belief that its implementation should be delayed obviously lost much of its force as time went by.

Even more important than presbyterian structure is Reformed doctrine. Certainly the most influential and continuing contribution of the German Reformed church is her great creed, the Heidelberg Catechism. Technically speaking, there is no such thing as an international Reformed statement of faith, the equivalent of the Lutheran Formula of Concord. Instead, there are three families of creeds: the Swiss First and Second Helvetic Confessions, the British Westminster symbols, and the German/Dutch Heidelberg Catechism and the Dutch Belgic Confession and Canons of Dort. All attempts to draw up a truly international creed have failed, almost always because of the recognition that such a creed would be totally unnecessary, for "everyone knows what Calvinism is."[8] But the creedal representation that most clearly gives expression to what international Calvinism in all its simplicity confesses is certainly the Heidelberg Catechism. More than any other Reformed creed, it transcends the passing controversies of the day and concentrates on the positive biblical faith known as the Reformed faith. It is simultaneously a catechism for children and the only creed for ministers and theologians that the German church knows. It facilitates catechetical preaching in the Reformed churches, for it is admirably suited and organized for practical doctrinal instruction.

So Heidelberg and the surrounding territory of the Palatinate are especially significant in the history of Calvinism in Germany. While the achievements in Strasbourg, Hesse, and Friesland were important, the most lasting effects, for the German church at least, were at Heidelberg. While in other places Calvinism owed its strength to the ministers and the people, being essentially a minority faith as far as the higher levels of government were concerned, it can be said that it was founded at Heidelberg and owes its strength to the Elector Frederick III, the most powerful statesman in Germany next to the emperor. Apparently his own Protestant faith was largely due to the influence of his Lutheran wife. When he succeeded to power, he was confronted by a religiously divided state; Protestants were divided among themselves, with the high Lutherans the least tolerant. A brief discussion of the central point at issue, the physical presence of Christ in the Lord's Supper, should be useful at this point. How is it possible that a question that seems peripheral today (to Calvinists at least) could then have seemed so central?

To high Lutherans nothing less than the gospel itself seemed to be at stake. First of all the authority of Scripture seemed to be in question. If the Bible clearly reads, "This *is* my body," then any attempt to explain that away by alluding to metaphorical language opens the door to allegorizing away the gospel itself, which is precisely what medieval interpretation had done! Reformed repudiation of the clear words of Scripture was nothing more than rationalism, making of man's understanding an idol before which God's Word was being asked to bow. Lutherans not only were concerned with such a potential attack on the gospel but they also believed that the denial of the incarnate Christ's physical presence in the Supper was in itself a rejection of the gospel. For if all that is offered is a spiritual Christ, of what value is that to us, who are threatened by the death of our *bodies?* No, said the Lutherans, with such a Christ we will have nothing to do, but only with the concrete, historical Christ, our Savior. To the Reformed ear this sounded like nothing but a caricature. For it was precisely because the Reformed were concerned with the incarnate, historical Christ that they placed so much stress on His now being ascended and hence *not* present in the Supper in the same way that He was when He was on earth in the days before His ascension, and as He will be again after His return. Only as they maintained this could they maintain also the reality of Christ and his work. "Spiritual" for the Reformed did not mean "less than complete" but rather referred to the ongoing work of Christ by His Spirit. Far from being a denial of the completeness of Christ's work, it expressed His continuing work for His people. The Reformed felt that they were affirming all that the Lutherans affirmed, but in a clearer, more biblical way. The Lutherans, on the other hand, believed that any compromise on this question was impossible. It was this ecclesiastical situation that confronted the Elector.[9]

Initially Frederick attempted to go the way of Melanchthon's mediating party, which would neither affirm nor repudiate the Reformed view, but would remain carefully ambiguous. When other German princes who had favored that approach abandoned it, this left Frederick with no alternative but to support the Reformed position. This was underlined when the new Heidelberg University granted a degree to a student who defended Calvinistic theses, which thereby committed the university itself. In addition, Reformed practices were introduced to foster a biblical, nonsuperstitious worship, and civil legislation was enacted along the lines of Genevan discipline. There remained only the composition of the new creed to complete the foundation for a Reformed church.

This was to be the task of two great theologians, Zachary Ursinus and Kaspar Olevianus. Ursinus had been greatly influenced by Melanchthon and had used his textbook in teaching in his home city of Breslau. When high Lutheran opposition to his teaching arose, he determined to study in Switzerland, where he came to respect Peter Martyr, who had clarified the Reformed understanding of predestination and election. When Martyr declined a call to Heidelberg, he nominated Ursinus in his place. Olevianus, a native of Trier, began to associate with the persecuted Calvinist groups in France, the churches "under the cross." After studying with Calvin, he returned to Trier to preach the new message. But after the Reformation was crushed there by its Catholic elector, he accepted a call as court-preacher in Heidelberg. These were the men Elector Frederick selected to formulate his new creed, with the intent that unity and purity of doctrine might exist in his realm.

After its completion and approval by the elector (he himself was actively involved in its final formulation), he called a synod of theologians and pastors in December 1562 for their examination and approval of the catechism. When this was completed, the Heidelberg Catechism appeared in early 1563 and was circulated throughout Germany. It met with immediate opposition from Lutherans as well as Catholics, partly because of an accompanying document that advocated the use of bread instead of wafers in the Supper. When the Lutherans asserted that the Augsburg Confession had been rejected by Heidelberg, Frederick replied that much of its material had been taught earlier in Heidelberg by the Lutheran theologian Brenz and that it was high Lutheranism with its new doctrine of ubiquity (that the body of Christ partakes of the divine attribute of omnipresence) that was the departure, not his catechism.

When a conference was held in Maulbron between Lutheran theologians and representatives from Heidelberg, it soon became apparent that the Reformed would not accept ubiquity, and the conference collapsed. However, the minutes of the conference made clear to the mediating Lutheran party, the Melanchthonians, how greatly they themselves were threatened by the proponents of ubiquity, and encouraged some to look to Calvinism as their natural home.

More significant, though, are those developments that resulted in the recognition of the Reformed church. Since the only recognition of Protestantism up to this point was that granted by the 1555 Peace of Augsburg to those giving allegiance to the Augsburg Confession, with its Lutheran view of the Lord's Supper, how could the Reformed be recognized, with all that that implied for legal protection? When Frederick was accused in 1566 of having violated that agreement, he replied that he did give allegiance to Augsburg, that he interpreted it in the Melanchthonian way, that Strasbourg had interpreted it that way without being rejected, and that therefore the Palatinate should be under its protection. But Emperor Maximilian decreed that Frederick should give up his Calvinism and the Heidelberg Catechism along with it and revert to Lutheranism. This Frederick refused to do, asserting that the Catechism was based on Scripture and could be overthrown only by being refuted from Scripture. Further, it was improper for Catholic princes to determine what was orthodox Lutheranism, and his statement of support for Augsburg should be taken seriously. At this the sentiment in the Diet moved to support Frederick, and Calvinism was recognized under the protection of the Augsburg Confession. From then on the Reformed church, though small, has been understood to be a legitimate (state) church in Germany.[10]

What is this Catechism that had now become the backbone of German Calvinism? Its dual role of practical catechism and theological confession of faith has already been noted. The practical life-centered orientation of Calvinism is a well-thought-out theological foundation. As one works through the Catechism, one cannot help be moved by its unique themes. There is above all its central concern with man's need and the way that need is met by the gracious provisions of the gospel. The facts and doctrines central to the work of Christ are continually defined in terms of the "benefits" we receive from them (Questions and Answers 36, 43, 45, 49, 51) and "comforts" (57, 58, 59), culminating in the magnificent fifty-ninth:

> Q. But how does it help you now that you believe all this?
> A. That I am righteous in Christ before God, and an heir of eternal life.

Almost every question speaks of the effects of Christ's work "for me." Indeed, the very outline of the Heidelberg Catechism, as expressed in Answer 2, demonstrates even more clearly its personal orientation:

> Q. How many things must you know that you may live and die in the blessedness of this comfort?
> A. Three. First, the greatness of my sin and wretchedness. Second, how I am freed from all my sins and their wretched consequences. Third, what gratitude I owe to God for such redemption.

What significance has this approach to theology had for the German Reformed church? Is it possible to speak of an analytical orientation, a teleological-eschatological one, and a German Reformed *methodology* that corresponds to its theology? This can be a complex discussion; not only is the methodology and structure of the Catechism not uniquely Reformed in its origins, but its more lasting impact was on Lutheran theology with its soteriological emphasis! There is, moreover, the concern of English Puritans, William Ames in particular, in a similar theological direction; the Puritan attempt to regard theology as an art, not as a combination of art and science, seems to run parallel with the Heidelberg Catechism. When all the dust has settled, the ultimate issue seems to be: Just what role can the doctrine of election play in theology? Does its essential *unknowability* forbid its inclusion in a theological approach that focuses precisely on the possibility and necessity of the Christian's *experiencing* the grace of God? If so, does the necessity for the inclusion of election mean then that the analytical approach is ultimately unsatisfactory for Calvinism for the same reason that it is so satisfactory for Lutheranism, which deliberately omits discussion of consistent predestination from its theological concerns? Perhaps Calvinism's inability to employ the analytical method with election led to its subsequent preoccupation with the question of the subjective beginning of faith; it would seem that failure to apply to the individual's personal life the biblical doctrine of election led to a substituted application of a nonbiblical interest in the genesis and morphology of faith.[11]

That is to say that while the Heidelberg Catechism has so much to say about the believer's belonging to Christ and partaking of all His benefits, it has nothing to say about the dark side of predestination, the rejection of the nonelect. Indeed, it was precisely because of this potential ambiguity that the church of the Netherlands found it necessary to supplement Heidelberg with the clarifications of the Canons of Dort. Is there indeed something sub-Reformed about a solely positive presentation of God's decrees? At least it must be observed that Calvin himself proceeded in much the same way. The great bulk of his discussion of election in the *Institutes* is located not in Book I, concerning the doctrine of God, but in Book III, concerning the Christian life. There it is taken up in connection with the most practical issues of all—the believer's perseverance and assurance throughout his struggle with suffering and temptation. Too often modern scholarship attempts to drive too large a wedge between early and later Calvinism; it is more reasonable to see continuity between the pastoral theology of Calvin and that of Heidelberg and to recognize the value of this "analytic" approach.

It is also wise to look to the parallel with the Puritans, with their own variety of practical Calvinism. There is certainly a link between the two developments, particularly in the influence that the philosophy of the French Huguenot martyr, Petrus Ramus, had on both.[12] His practical, anti-Aristotelian empiricism not only flourished among the Puritans in Old and New England but it was also for some time the dominant position in Heidelberg and its successor institution, the Reformed academy at Herborn. This approach was characterized by the reduction of complicated logical arguments to the simple disjunctive syllogism. This prevented any argument from divorcing itself totally from reality, as it was subject to the constant monitoring of an either/or dialectic (either this is true or not; either it advances the glory of God or not). While this methodology can lend itself to trivialization, it was an international Reformed attempt to avoid the blurring of the line between God and man so common to the older Aristotelian approach, and did prove to be of use. Both German and English Calvinism, then, stood together against rationalism and for a practical empiricism. While the influence of the Heidelberg Catechism itself in Britain was minimal, certainly its kind of thinking was not. It is likely that German Christians whose thinking had been shaped by the Heidelberg approach would find themselves open to the Puritan approach to theology and life as introduced by the Pietists. And it is not surprising that the Pietists with their practical, or even pragmatic, approach to theology were led to see in the Reformed understanding of the Lord's Supper something more congenial to their faith. So the Heidelberg approach at its beginning provided a way to see the continuity between the heart of Lutheranism and the heart of Calvinism. It also provided the foundation for the later cooperation of Lutherans and Reformed in Pietism. Pietism goes far to explain the later unity among those of diverse ecclesiastical backgrounds in the various "awakenings" and revivals of the modern age of the church and hence to explain also the basic biblical ecumenicity of the contemporary evangelical movement.

The subsequent history of the Reformed church of the Palatinate is not as encouraging. Continuing rejection of the Reformed churches by their fellow German Lutherans led to such a weakness of the Protestant cause that the Roman Catholic church was bound to attempt to regain territory by military means and to succeed in large measure. Continued Lutheran animosity to the Reformed in a time when both were literally fighting for their lives is even harder to understand. Lutherans were willing to make use of Reformed military support but, rather than helping the Reformed in turn, they took advantage of Reformed exhaustion, exploiting the situation and taking over for themselves Reformed territory. To summarize much too briefly, in light of the horrible suffering it endured, the Reformed church was virtually obliterated in the Palatinate. This led to emigrations of survivors, to the profit of many other churches, not the least the Reformed community in America.

While the greatest theological contribution to the church must remain with the Palatinate, in almost every other way the greatest Reformed success was in Brandenburg, one of the predecessor states to Prussia, which eventually became the dominant state in Germany. Because of the comparatively unsettled character and tolerant spirit of Brandenburg, many Calvinist refugees and merchant families had settled there from almost the beginning of the Reformation, including people and ministers from the Netherlands, Strasbourg, and Poland. The real breakthrough, though, was when its ruler, Elector John Sigismund, joined the Reformed Church in 1613. While he may have had some political motives, including securing disputed territory in Western Germany for his state, his conversion must be seen as coming out of conviction, based on his personal acquaintance with neighboring Reformed people and particularly his impression of the Reformed faith in Heidelberg. Almost immediately, in 1614, he proclaimed liberty of conscience in his realm and made no attempt to compel his Lutheran subjects to become Reformed. This antedates other better-known victories for freedom of conscience, as in England or Rhode Island.[13] Indeed, after the Thirty Years' War, it was again the Elector of Brandenburg who secured rights for the Reformed under the Treaty of Westphalia, and at a later point he was the only great protector of the Protestant faith in Germany.

Brandenburg was the great place of refuge not only for German Calvinists, but also for Calvinists from all of Europe. Under the "Great Elector," Frederick William, Brandenburg interceded for persecuted Waldensians in Savoy, for Calvinists in Anhalt, and also for Hungarian galley slaves in Naples. When William of Orange went to England to take the throne, 9,000 troops from Brandenburg were sent to accompany him. Perhaps most important, the Elector welcomed the Huguenot refugees, who were to become so influential in the expansion of Berlin and of Prussia itself. But apparently religious pluralism does not function as well in Europe as in America, for in the interest of unity in the nineteenth century the Prussian Union church was established, combining the larger Lutheran and the smaller Reformed. Apparently in the centuries of living side by side the Reformed leaven had not leavened the whole lump, for in the Union, Lutheran liturgical practices were imposed and fewer opportunities for churches and theological schools of a Reformed character remained available. Perhaps this was because in a union of a narrower and a broader body, the narrow ways prevail. The romanticism of the age gave encouragement to stressing traditional Lutheran practices, as well. Probably the basic reason for the Reformed collapse, however, was just the draining effect that years of nationalism had had on theology; if Calvinism lives or dies by her theology, and if it has become weak, then almost inevitably the only real issues in a union are those of practice. It is also true that the Reformed refugee communities tended to remain closed societies, definitely of upper-middle class character, and the great mass of the working class people were hardly aware at all of the Reformed presence in their midst.

There remains one final Reformed community whose impact is worthy of consideration, that of the small city-state of Bremen in the northwest.[14] The Reformed faith came there in 1547 through the preaching of Hardenberg, a friend of Laski. Perhaps his views on the Lord's Supper were originally unknown, but soon the Lutherans applied the usual pressure to conform to the doctrine of ubiquity. Melanchthon advised that such irrelevancies be avoided, but this did not prevent serious upheavals that resulted in first one party and then the other being in control. When there was an attempt to force Bremen into the high-Lutheran camp, the city under the leadership of the dynamic pastor Pezel resisted Catholic-Lutheran pressure and adopted his strongly Reformed Bremen Confession in 1595.

The theological significance of Bremen is seen in its introduction of covenant theology, or biblical theology.[15] The development of this theology in the Netherlands is better known, yet the fact that its founder was John Koch from Bremen and that it has a German Reformed background makes an understanding of the movement much clearer. First of all, covenant/biblical theology wishes to avoid the Lutheran/Reformed dilemma over the Lord's Supper. Endless arguments over metaphysical questions such as in what sense Christ was in heaven and in what sense in the Supper at the same time, and how the two senses qualify each other, appeared to be leading nowhere. The Reformed had always affirmed that such metaphysical questions must be subordinate to the historical reality of the ascension and the return of Christ; that is, no "presence" of Christ now must be permitted to relativize away His very real "absence" and His coming again. Historical concerns must be foremost. It is the very gracious nature of God's work for us that it changes, develops, and becomes in history *more* than it has been before. Perhaps this is just a particularly dramatic way of affirming what Calvinist debaters in the Supper controversy have always affirmed, that the fact of the ascension is more basic than the nature of Christ's presence in the Supper. Certainly there is here also the customary Reformed stress on the work of the Spirit of Christ in this age, over against the Lutheran stress on the continuing work of the incarnate Christ.

But covenant theology does suggest a new beginning in evangelical theology in general around the structure of God's self-revelation and action throughout the unfolding plan of salvation presented in the Bible. For example, in the continual question of the relation between Old and New Testament ethics, covenant theology helped by determining the line between the "ceremonial" and the "moral" law (typically, it was used to support the Swiss and German contention that the Lord's Day is *not* the Sabbath).[16] Questions of great practicality concerning the psychological character of saving faith could be explored by comparing the concept of salvation in the Old and the New Testaments. In general, one could attempt a more scientific theology in which to a greater extent than before all theological conclusions would have to be rooted in Scripture itself and Scripture understood as an organic whole, not as a collection of isolated proof texts. This could lead to the fulfillment of the great Reformed ecumenical dream: a truly united Protestant church. However, in the Netherlands the more traditionalist Puritan/Precisianist party strongly opposed this approach (for example, concerning the Sabbath question), and it required some time before the two parties realized that biblical theology and Reformed piety could work very well together. This was not the case in Germany, where the Reformed wing of the Puritan/Pietist movement immediately made much use of the method. It is no accident that this went far to remove Lutheran hostility and greatly fostered the growth of Lutheran Pietism. As the covenant approach seems to be easily understood, inasmuch as it does not require mastering a philosophical foundation first, it lent itself immediately to the purposes of small-group Bible study with "lay" elder leadership. Hence the theology of northwest Germany was grafted on to its Laskian polity.

Germany, however, like the other Protestant countries, did not remain true to its Reformation heritage. Is it useful to discuss the sense in which the liberal Schleiermacher or Karl Barth may be considered Reformed?[17] If there is value in taking up that question at all, the task transcends the scope of this chapter. Yet we should keep in mind that the stance of the theologians or most famous preachers of a church does not always represent the view of the grass roots. True, the Pietist *Stillen im Lande* (the quiet ones in the country, the "silent majority") did not remain unscathed by modern liberalism, but they did have their own Bibles, their biblical theology, their small groups, and definitely their Heidelberg Catechism, and when the Lord raised up an evangelical Reformed standard, they were there to rally to it. This was certainly true in the nineteenth century, when officially Germany was captive to Schleiermacher and Ritschl, but when Reformed piety and theology nevertheless lived on. While they are less visible today, *die Stille* are still there.

So although the prospect of building great German Reformed universities is hardly before us today, and we do not expect an evangelical Reformed theological breakthrough or even large churches with famous preachers vigorously faithful to the Heidelberg Catechism, yet there is great value and encouragement to be gained from a final look at German Reformed Pietism. Pivotal Calvinist influence apparently comes to bear through other churches and parachurches. The example of earlier Pietism provides continuing encouragement. As has already been seen in connection with Friesland, the presbyterian concept of the elder and elders' meetings is admirably suited for grass-roots religion. It is not surprising that the concept would be very useful later on, when Lutherans would call into question the very possibility of biblical instruction being carried on outside of official preaching. In such circumstances the Reformed could provide the successful, nonsubversive examples. In particular, the Reformed inculcation of practical catechetical instruction was of great service in the formation of an evangelical Confirmation for young people in Lutheranism; it provided a "respectable" means of addressing the fundamental question of the presence or absence of a knowledgeable saving faith among the youth of the church. Perhaps this was itself the most effective antidote to dead orthodoxy in the whole Pietist movement. Reformed Pietism took its devotional poetry and set it to music, creating the hymns that have done so much to keep the evangelical spirit alive. Best of all, the biblically based spirit of practical Christianity was fostered and communicated by the Reformed and the Lutheran groups, even while they were surrounded by "official" rationalism and unbelief. Perhaps such an expression of faith could be termed other-worldly or unscholarly, but more likely it was and is the expression of German Reformed, Heidelberg, and covenant theology and faith, which refuse to take seriously any movement that does not itself take biblical orientation in faith and life seriously.

This is the great legacy of the German Reformed. It is at bottom little different from any other Calvinistic or soundly evangelical movement. But in God's providence that church was called on to define very significant issues in a vital, practical way, and to a large extent it succeeded. That heritage still blesses God's church everywhere as it confesses its "only comfort in life and in death."

# The Helvetic Reformation in Hungary

## Kálmán D. Tóth

*Kálmán D. Tóth is a retired Presbyterian minister in Ottawa, Ontario. He served as missionary and minister in various places in Canada from 1947 to 1978. He has received the following degrees: B.D., at the Theological Seminary of the Reformed Church, Budapest; Th.M., at Princeton; and Th.D., at Union Seminary, New York. He has written several theses, including* The Dialectic in the Political Ethics of Calvinism *published in Budapest in 1941. He has written articles on church history and church life. For ten years he was editor of the monthly* New Life.

# 7

# The Helvetic Reformation in Hungary

The sixteenth century, with all its tragedies, its struggle for survival, and the light of the gospel shining in the darkness, a generation ago was considered a clearly documented and well-known epoch in Hungarian church history. We would have said that Calvinism was fairly well established by 1545 and the giants of the Hungarian Reformation were peacefully settled in their respective Lutheran and Calvinist camps.

Recent translations of Reformation literature from Latin to Hungarian and the consequent research of historians, however, have shattered some of the traditional views, classifications, and statements regarding the theology of individual Reformers and also the theological trends they represented.

Hungarians (*Magyars* in the vernacular) are of Finn-Ugor and Ogur Türk ethnic origin. After three thousand years of moving westward, the two people united into one nation at the time of Christ in the Tobol area. Driven further west by the Great Migration, the new nation, under Árpád, entered the Carpathian Basin in 896.[1] By this time, their religion centered around the worship of *Is-ten,* the "Great Mighty Lord."

After preliminary contact with the Eastern Church, the Árpáds decided for Western Christianity. Géza's son, Vojk, who was baptized "Stephen," established a strong Christian kingdom in the Danubian Basin in A.D. 1000. In spite of fierce rebellions, which were crushed by the merciless hand of the saintly king, royal rule and Christianity were generally accepted. The Árpáds gave several "saints" to the Christian church: Stephen, Emery, Ladislaus, Elizabeth, and Margaret.

Reaction against the church, which was corrupt in ignorance and luxurious and immoral in living, soon appeared in the movements of the Albigenses, Bogomili, and Cathari along the southern border and in the Waldensian movement throughout the land. Peter Waldo, for some years a refugee in Bohemia, sent suitable preachers *("idoneos verbi divini ministros")*[2] to Hungary, so that by the mid-thirteenth century, Bible-studying Waldensian communities of modest and industrious lifestyle were found in the northern, western, and southwestern regions and, in 1303, even in Buda itself. These communities survived severe persecutions until, in the fifteenth century, they were absorbed into the Hussite communities.

John Hus's teachings spread rapidly through returning Hungarian veterans of the Hussite war and students attending Prague University.[3] From among the three Hussite factions, the *unitas fratrum* found refuge in the northern Carpathians. In 1410 Jerome of Prague preached in Buda. After 1420 there were Hussite communities not only in the north but also in the central, eastern, and southern counties and even in Buda. The first translation of the Bible into Hungarian, the ''Hussite Bible,'' was the work of two priests in Moldavia in the 1430s—Thomas Pécsi and Bálint Ujlaki, who were Hussite refugees.[4]

The Renaissance king, Matthias Hunyadi (1458–90), organized Giskra's Hussite guerillas into his famed ''Black Legion.'' He also resettled Hussite refugees from Moldavia in the Danube-Tisza region.

At the turn of the century lower and higher nobility joined the movement. The Hussite General Synod in 1508 presented a statement of its faith to King Wladyslas II (1490–1516).[5]

### IN THE DECADE OF THE MOHÁCS DISASTER

Luther's Ninety-five Theses were distributed in Hungary as early as 1518[6] and they were well received, first in German cities, then in Hungarian cities. In 1521 the archbishop of Esztergom ordered that the papal bull against Luther be read in every pulpit. Also in 1521, Stephen Werböczy, head of the National Party, gave a banquet in Luther's honor at the Imperial Diet of Worms and tried to persuade him to withdraw his teachings.[7] In the same year, Simon Grynaeus, later professor in Heidelberg and Basel, at the invitation of Margrave George of Brandenburg began to teach at the University of Buda. The next year Paul Speratus of Würtzburg followed suit to escape persecution. Evangelical preaching and the denunciation of the pope became more outspoken in Sopron, Nagyszeben, Körmöc, and Löcse, while Eperjes expelled an indulgence salesman. At the same time two students, Baumheckel of Beszterce and Martin Czirják of Löcse, registered at the University of Wittenberg. They were followed by five others before 1526 and by six hundred more during the rest of the century. Both the Margrave of

Brandenburg, the Hungarian king's guardian and one of the signers of the Protestation in Speyer in 1529, and Queen Maria were sympathetic to the Reformation. In 1523 the queen appointed the evangelical Conrad Cordatus and John Henckel as court preachers. Papal envoys arrived in 1524 and in 1526, however, to silence evangelicals, and Vid Vinshemius, a professor of evangelical conviction in Buda, was expelled in 1524. Others, including Grynaeus and Henckel, escaped, while John Kresling and Conrad Cordatus were imprisoned.[8]

Since the Reformation was at that time considered a German cause dividing the Hungarian nation, the national Diet of 1523, at the insistence of the National Party, took harsh measures against the followers of the movement. It decreed that "all Lutherans be punished by death and confiscation of property," while the 1524 and 1525 Diets resolved that "all Lutherans be burned."[9] A few executions followed, but the law did not really take effect. The Diet of 1526, disillusioned by the nonsupport of the pope against the Turks, annulled the resolution and allowed some freedom for evangelical preaching.

In 1525 Kresling was preaching in the mining cities of the north. Preaching among the Germans and Hungarians began in the ancient capital city of Székesfehérvár and Trencsén county in the north. Popular preference following the "Holy Year 1525" was indicated by the offerings, which amounted to one-thirtieth of the previous "Holy Year," and by notes found in the collection boxes criticizing and ridiculing the pope and clergy.

In the year of Mohács, 1526, the queen and the royal court came to the center of attention again. While George of Brandenburg corresponded with Luther, the Reformer dedicated four psalms of his own translation to the queen, under the title: *Vier tröstliche Psalmen an die Königin von Ungern* (1526). Pope Clement VII complained to Charles V concerning his sister's empathy toward the "heresy," while Queen Maria allowed the emperor's envoy, Schneidpeck, to openly propagate his evangelical convictions at court. At the 1530 Augsburg Diet she tried to persuade Charles to be lenient to the followers of the Augsburg Confession.[10]

There are also indications of Zwinglian influence in the country during the 1520s. When John Bugenhagen's open letter to John Hess of Breslau was published in 1525, before Zwingli himself could reply, a strong and well-argued anonymous reply left the press in Augsburg, presumably written by Conrad Reyss von Ofen of Buda. It was reprinted soon in Zurich and in Strasbourg.[11] The other Zwinglian, whose name appears about this time in the records as "John," was reported by the people of Kisszeben in the year 1530 for his teaching on the Lord's Supper in the spirit of Zwingli.[12] The increasing number of the followers of Zwingli and Oecolampadius after the defeat of the Hungarians at

Mohács is indicated by the severe punishment imposed on them in King Ferdinand's decree of 1527.

## THE EFFECTS OF MOHÁCS

Sultan Suleiman II in his drive to the West did not want to conquer Hungary, only the Balkans. He sought only to use Hungary as a friendly vassal state, as a buffer between the Ottoman and Habsburg empires. However, he demanded tribute of King Louis II. But after his delegation to Buda returned empty-handed in 1521, he pursued his goal by force. At Mohács (1526), his army of 200,000 annihilated the Hungarian force of 26,000. The king and the leading nobility fell, and the nation collapsed. Looting, plundering, and killing followed. The Turks marched north, entered Buda, and withdrew, leaving devastation in their wake and 200,000 dead.

Based on a 1505 law,[13] John Szapolyai, the voivoda of Transylvania was elected king by the National Party, while, on the basis of dynastic agreement with the Jagellos, Archduke Ferdinand of Habsburg was elected by the pro-western faction: both in 1526. Between the western (Habsburg) kingdom and the eastern (national) kingdom the Sultan ruled the major, central segment. After the death of King John in 1540, Ferdinand sought to control Buda. So did the sultan in support of the dowager Queen Isabella and her infant son, John II. In order to avoid a bloody confrontation, Suleiman, under a sly pretense, peacefully entered Buda, and the Turks held it for a century and a half. By this the tripartition of the country was sealed.

Conditions in the three segments of the country were by no means the same, both with regard to the physical welfare and security of the people and the advancement of the cause of the gospel. Under Turkish occupation the people suffered unbelievable hardship.[14] Unwarranted heavy fines were added to the already exacting burden of taxation, according to the whim of the Turkish officer. Leaders of communities, among them most of the Reformers, suffered imprisonment and beating, from which ransom was practically the only way of escape. Masses of people, including women and children, were driven into slavery. Villages were raided and burned. For compromisers coexistence meant deplorable morals.[15] Physical conditions of life, on the other hand, were fair under the Habsburgs and good in the national kingdom.

As far as religious freedom was concerned, there was considerable freedom under the Turks, who sometimes attended the Protestant service or even arbitrated religious debates. There was much less freedom of worship under the Habsburgs, and Protestant preachers often suffered imprisonment. Religious freedom was greater in the national kingdom, especially after 1556. Between 1544 and 1574 in Transylvania, the lighthouse of this freedom, the National Diet guaranteed the freedom of religion twenty-two times, most comprehensively in 1557 and 1568.[16]

Generally speaking, preachers were always on the move, not only seeking where they could preach, but also in their missionary zeal looking for opportunities to win converts. Religious disputes were also frequent, first, between papists and Protestants; later, between Lutherans and Sacramentarians, as followers of the Helvetic Reformation were called; and, lastly, between the latter and the Antitrinitarians. In these public debates, the popular polemical dramas, the widely spread church schools, and the numerous products of printing presses the people as a whole were much involved.

Psychologically, the tragic political conditions and the inhuman suffering of the bulk of the nation had beneficial effects throughout the land. Aristocracy, nobility, and the common people were brought close together. They also learned to identify the cause of the Christian faith with that of the nation. Therefore, when preachers declared the devastation of the land and the suffering of the people to be the judgment of God for former idolatry, the people accepted the chastisement with sincere repentance and the consolation of the gospel with a joyful, positive response.[17]

## MARTIN KÁLMÁNCSEHI SÁNTA (c. 1500–57)

The influence of the Zwinglian Reformation in Hungary is indicated by Conrad Reyss's defense of Zwingli (1526) and King Ferdinand's decree of 1527 prohibiting Zwinglian teaching. The most prominent representative of this school was Martin Kálmáncsehi Sánta in Debrecen.

Kálmáncsehi was probably born in Kálmáncsa, Baranya, in lower Transdanubia, about the turn of the century. In 1523 he registered at the University of Crakow, where in 1525 he was honored with the office of "senior" by the "Hungarian Bursa,"[18] After returning home with a Master's Degree in 1538, he became a canon and headmaster of the Cathedral School of Gyulafehérvár (Alba Julia). This Cathedral chapter played an important role in the history of the Reformation in Transylvania, since it had strong leanings toward reforms and, in due time, toward the Reformation movement. The clue to this may have been the broadmindedness of the provost, the humanist Anthony Verancsics, and the hostility toward the Roman Catholic bishop, John Statileo. More probable, however, was the impact of the puritanical atmosphere of the chapter, which was endeavoring to return to the apostolic simplicity of the New Testament church.[19]

Canon Peter Kolozsvári and three other outstanding members of the chapter became prominent leaders in the Reformation movement. From this shelter of erudite and enlightened clergy, Canon Martin rose to prominence as the Helvetic Reformer of Debrecen.

Kálmáncsehi came to the foreground when he was appointed by King John as an arbiter of a Protestant–Roman Catholic debate in 1538 at Segesvár. An outspoken man, he spoke his mind even to the king: "I can only say that he [the debater Stephen Szántai, reformer of Kassa] disputes and teaches nothing but the truth. He speaks and treats the pure Scripture, while the matter of the monks and priests is nothing but fable, human opinion, and vain blabbery."[20] It is assumed that this debate was the turning point in Kálmáncsehi's life. He made the decision to join the Reformation. In the early 1540s he was minister in Mezőtúr. In the later 1540s he worked in Sátoraljaújhely and in 1551 he moved to Debrecen.

In that part of the world these were difficult years for the Reformation, especially for those holding the Helvetic position. Although "Frater George" Martinuzzi Utyeszenovics, the Roman Catholic bishop of Nagyvárad with pro-Habsburg leanings but at the same time the most powerful councilor of the queen and one of the guardians of the young King John II, was assassinated in 1551, his like-minded successor, Matthias Zabárdy, succeeded in gaining a victory over the Protestants. He defeated in battle Peter Petrovics,[21] one of the wealthiest landowners in the country and the only surviving councilor and guardian of John II, who was also a Protestant strongly in favor of maintaining the independence of the Hungarian kingdom. Under Zabárdy, the Lutherans gained another chance, and the ban of the Diet of 1548 against "sacramentarians," as followers of the Swiss Reformation were called, was revived. The tables were turned, however, when in 1556 Zabárdy died, and Nagyvárad, after a long siege, was taken by Petrovics's forces in 1557. This year marks the turning point in favor of the Helvetic element and for the whole of Transtibiscia, the area east of the Tisza River. Peter Petrovics emerged as the most powerful man in the kingdom. He leaned heavily on the sturdiest element of the Hungarians, the followers of the Helvetic Reformation.

Against this political backdrop, Martin Kálmáncsehi Sánta ran his own course and fought his own battles. As "plebanus" (senior minister) in Debrecen from 1551, in his puritan Zwinglian zeal he purged the city of Roman Catholicism and Lutheranism, perhaps prematurely. Within a year he found himself excommunicated by his Protestant brethren at the Lutheran Synod of Köröslány. He in turn excommunicated them.[22] In 1552 he left Debrecen for Munkács in the northeast, where, under the protection of Peter Petrovics, he left traces of his influence in a moderate representation of the Helvetic views at the two Synods of Beregszász (1552). Ultimately, the Lutheran majority, protected by the law of 1548, confirmed the position set forth in the Acts of the Synod of Erdőd (1545) and the *Confessio Pentapolitana* (1549), both Lutheran statements. They did show a spirit of moderation and compromise, however, and various synods during the next few years followed their example, though they by no means accepted fully the Swiss position on the Lord's Supper. Their compromises must have been hard on the radical Kálmáncsehi and his numerous followers, even though by 1552 his Zwinglianism had probably mellowed in the spirit of the 1549 *Consensus Tigurinus*.[23]

In the early 1550s Kálmáncsehi came under attack by the Roman Catholics. George Draskovich—later archbishop, cardinal, and chancellor—while studying in Padua wrote his *Confutatio eorum quae dicta sunt a Joanne Calvino sacramentario,* published in 1551. The next year Draskovich, as canon of Nagyvárad, reported to the Royal Chancellery that in his diocese there were many sacramentarians as well as Lutherans. The chief exponent of their teaching was Martin, a priest of Debrecen. Resurrecting the views of Berengar, he taught that Christ's body was in heaven since His ascension and therefore it could not be present in the sacrament. From Draskovich's account, it is evident that Kálmáncsehi taught in the spirit of the Helvetic Reformation, but it is difficult to ascertain if his was a Zwinglian view or if he followed Oecolampadius's, Bucer's, and Calvin's doctrine.[24]

Early in 1556, Kálmáncsehi returned to Debrecen and was elected bishop of Transtibiscia.[25] In the same year, after Queen Isabella's return, Petrovics, a faithful patron and follower of Kálmáncsehi, purged the Kolozsvár church of Roman Catholic paraphernalia and invited the Reformer to Transylvania to teach the Helvetic doctrine, especially on the Lord's Supper. His Saxon Lutheran opponents challenged him to an open debate, but, realizing his minority position, he declined. Then the Lutheran leaders Francis Dávid and Caspar Heltai attacked him in their *Responsum . . . ad scripta varia Martini a Calmancsa* (1556),[26] Matthias Hebler followed suit in his *Elleboron ad repurganda Phanaticorum . . . Capita qui primum in Transylvania Calvinismi semina spergere coeperunt authore M. Kálmáncsehi,* published in the same year.[27] Bálint Wagner the following year criticized him in his *Odia calviniana* (MS).[28] Challenged again by the Lutherans in 1557, Kálmáncsehi set out for Transylvania. His grave illness, however, turned him back to Debrecen, where he died at the end of the year.

In spite of the odds against the Helvetic trend, 1557 was the turning point in the history of Transylvania and of religious freedom. The Diet of Transylvania that year repeated its proclamations, once in Kolozsvár and again in Torda, that "everyone may follow the faith of his choice." The Diet of Torda, however, the next year ruled against the sacramentarians. But the overwhelming preponderance of the followers of the "Hungarian religion," as Calvinism was named by Kálmáncsehi, made the implementation of this law impossible. The final declaration of freedom was the glory of the Diet of Torda in 1568.[29]

## STEPHEN SZEGEDI KIS (1505-72)

Szegedi was born in Szeged on the Lower Tisza. After a rectorate in the area, he studied in Vienna and in Crakow, where he held an assistant professorship. In 1543 he entered the University of Wittenberg, where he enjoyed the friendship of Luther and Melanchthon and, in the same year, earned his doctorate in theology with supreme distinction. From 1545 he held rectorates in Cegléd and Lower Transtibiscia. In Transtibiscia he began to teach in the spirit of the Swiss Reformation, probably under the influence of Martin Kálmáncsehi, whom he succeeded in Mezötúr. He suffered severe persecution and was driven from place to place. In 1552, with his Helvetic orientation already formulated, he found refuge as rector of Tolna College. For his scholarship, "Master Szegedi" earned the title *"Magister Hungariae."* In Tolna and in transit to the pastorate of Laskó on the lower Danube (1554-58), he fought his most difficult battle and won his most rewarding victory: he won over from the Luther-Brenz camp to the Helvetic Reformation one of his students, Peter Mélius Juhász.[30] In Laskó, he was elected bishop of Baranya District, whose 120 churches his predecessor, Michael Sztáray, had won over to the Reformation. After four years he moved farther west in lower Transdanubia and, with his parish in Kálmáncsa, he served the frontier area on both sides of the Turkish-Hungarian line. At this time he drew up the *Canons of Baranya,* which, in his Helvetic revision, were to become the *Canons of Hercegszőlős*[31] (1576). He was arrested by Turkish officials, but after two years of suffering in cruel Turkish prisons, he was released by a ransom collected nationwide. Following this, he faithfully served the Ráckeve church and, as bishop, the larger Danubian district, devoting much of his time to theological scholarship.

This "most scholarly Hungarian Reformer"[32] is the author of a number of works, all published posthumously and abroad: *Assertio vera de trinitate* (Geneva 1573, 1576), *Speculum Romanorum pontificum* (Basel 1584, 4th ed. 1602), *Tractatus brevis de traditionibus quibusdam pontificum Romanorum* jointly with the previous one; *Questiones de verbis coenae Domini* (Zurich, 1584), *Theologiae sincerae loci communes de Deo et homine* (Basel, 1585, 5th ed. 1608), *Doctrinae papisticae* appended to the previous one, *Confessio verae fidei de uno vero Deo* attached to the 4th and 5th ed. of *Loci Communes,* and *Tabulae analyticae* (Shaffhausen 1592, 2nd ed. London 1593, 5th ed. Basel 1610).[33]

The analysis of his magnum opus, *Loci Communes,* by G. Kathona,[34] will serve the purpose of demonstrating his theological genealogy in relation to the western Reformers, especially the representatives of the Helvetic trend, and the channels through which, by the mediation of

Szegedi's scholarship, Reformation theology flowed into the life of the Reformed church in Hungary.

After Melanchthon's *Loci Communes* (1521) several *Locis* followed, especially in the Helvetic camp. The most important one is that of Wolfgang Musculus (1597–63)[35] in 1560. In fact, Szegedi used it as a model for his work. Musculus, a former deacon in Strasbourg, minister in Augsburg, and, after 1549, professor in Bern, formulated his theology under the influence of Bucer and Capito in his earlier years. During his professorship in Bern he was also influenced by Bullinger and Calvin, especially in his teaching on predestination. Through correspondence and personal contact he exerted a strong influence on various Hungarians, among them Szegedi Kis and his *Loci Communes*. Szegedi, however, goes beyond Musculus in his theological conclusions and extends his scope to related fields, including ethics, politics, sociology, and economics.

His sources are the key theologians of the Helvetic Reformation.[36] The only outsider is Melanchthon, whom Szegedi considers the Musculus of the Lutheran camp. Szegedi plays Musculus's mediating role supremely well by his eclectic approach to theology. He only rarely identifies his sources, but he draws from them liberally. Musculus's name is mentioned only three times, although his *Loci Communes* of 1560 can be traced all through Szegedi's work. It is evident that Musculus is his favorite theologian. Peter Vermigli Martyr's name is mentioned thirteen times, mostly in connection with secondary issues, while his views were adopted by Szegedi on key subjects like predestination, election, sin, reprobation, and others. John Calvin's name occurs only once, in condemning immoral dancing, but he is not mentioned in the exposition of the Lord's Prayer, which was borrowed by Szegedi in all its essential elements. Theodore Beza's name never occurs, although his Confession of 1560 is essentially incorporated into Szegedi's work. Heinrich Bullinger's name is mentioned three times, on law and marriage, but his views on the sacraments, the Lord's Supper, covenant, angels, civil authority, and heretics are incorporated into Szegedi's *Loci*. Melanchthon's name occurs four times, with reference to marriage, although his teaching is reflected also under penitence, good works, and free will.

Further analysis reveals that in Szegedi's presentation of twenty-six key doctrines, Musculus dominates in twenty-one—in seven exclusively, in fourteen prominently. Apparently Szegedi had an empathy with his favorite theologian, due to their common theological conviction and endeavor to build an ecclesiastical bridge between Wittenberg and Geneva.

We gain further insight into Szegedi's theological thinking by considering his way of selecting, emending, and emphasizing his material. Musculus's views on sin and salvation agree with those of Calvin; they are considered part of the same decree. Musculus says very little about God being the author of sin. Szegedi, however, goes farther in his search for the solution. He turns to Vermigli who considers sin God's means of pointing to salvation. In deviating from Musculus's gloomier view, Szegedi presents, parallel to him, Melanchthon's teaching on *iustitia civilis,*[37] showing how man is able to do good works in civil life—a view that was by no means in conflict with the teaching of Calvin or Beza.

Szegedi's effect on the Reformation in Hungary, however, is more comprehensive than this. By his subtle endeavor to emend the teachings of Bullinger (who was very popular in his days in Hungary) with Beza's most important teachings, Szegedi was instrumental in introducing Calvin and Calvinism to Hungary. By his ingenious eclecticism he did it in an irenic spirit, however, mediating between the two trends of the Helvetic Reformation represented by Bullinger's *Second Helvetic Confession* and the *Heidelberg Catechism,* which was written in Calvin's spirit. This was the unifying "gospel" for which the factions of the Reformation were yearning, and this was the secret of the enormous success of "the most scholarly Hungarian Reformer" both at home and abroad.[38]

### Gregory Szegedi (d. 1569)

The person of Gregory Szegedi offers an answer to three important questions: (1) The identity of the Hungarian student from Belényes, a correspondent and visitor to John Calvin in 1544;[39] (2) the puzzle of the great number of Hungarian students who, after their return from Wittenberg, became front-line leaders of the Helvetic Reformation; and (3) the problem of the origin of "Calvinism" in Hungary.

According to the eighteenth-century church historian, Peter Bod, Szegedi was the only Hungarian Reformer who, *before* his studies in Wittenberg (1556–57) visited John Calvin in Geneva (in 1544). Under Helvetic influence, he was instrumental in introducing psalm singing at the worship, was a contributor to the *Debrecen Confession* and, above all, was an erudite teacher and preacher of the Helvetic doctrine of the Lord's Supper in the spirit of the *Consensus Tigurinus* (1549). By all these features Gregory Szegedi became one of the first exponents, if not the very first one, of Calvinism in Hungary.[40]

Szegedi held the inconspicuous role of rector in Debrecen until 1556, when he went to Wittenberg for a study leave. Departing from Debrecen under not only Roman Catholic but also Lutheran pressure, he found refuge in the very citadel of Lutheranism. As a devout student of Melanchthon, he accepted the great teacher's mediating theology, often called Crypto-Calvinism.

As Hungarian students in Wittenberg were numerous, it is understandable that graduates of Wittenberg returned to Hungary not only as accomplished scholars of the Reformation, but also as its frontline leaders.[41] When we consider, however, that most of these graduates emerged from Wittenberg to become the "general staff" of the Helvetic Reformation in Hungary, the question arises, Who was the student with such dedication to, and such personal knowledge of, the Helvetic Reformers and churches that he was able to win many of his fellow students over to the Helvetic trend? It is M. Bucsay's conjecture, strongly supported by his elaborate research, that he was no one else but Gregory Szegedi alias Belényesi, who had corresponded with Calvin and visited him in Geneva.

This conjecture is supported by three pieces of evidence.[42] First, in his year in Wittenberg, Szegedi did not make a secret of his confessional standing, but in two printed letters of appreciation, he expressed his unfailing gratitude to his two patrons—Peter Petrovics, the great statesman, and Martin Kálmáncsehi Sánta, "plebanus" of Debrecen —both uncompromising exponents and defenders of the Helvetic trend. Second, in 1557, on his return trip to Debrecen, he stopped over in Eperjes and Kassa and, in Eperjes at the invitation of friends and in Kassa at the invitation of the city council, he preached several sermons on the Lord's Supper. In Eperjes he represented Melanchthon's views, but in Kassa he proved himself such an eloquent exponent of the Helvetic doctrine that the council extended a call to him. Third, even though because of Debrecen's objection he had to decline the call, within two months he sent to Kassa a promised fresh statement of the Helvetic doctrine that had just been accepted under his guidance by the Synod of Partium. It was the *Confession on the Lord's Supper (1557)*,[43] uniting Cistibiscia and Transcistibiscia in sound Helvetic faith.

In his Eperjes-Kassa episode Szegedi followed the Helvetic trend in regard to the Lord's Supper, thereby raising a storm among the Lutherans. He taught Christ's objective presence in the Supper but defined the mode of His presence as *ratione officii,* just as did Oecolampadius; Bucer; Calvin; and the "Hungarian Luther," Matthias Dévai Biro.[44] Szegedi's *officio* referred to Christ's role now on the Father's right hand, as the Head nourishing His spiritual body, the church, in which the believers unite with the Lord through the Holy Spirit's indwelling. This spiritual body of Christ is taken only by the believers. Such was the Helvetic view, expressed in the *Consensus Tigurinus*. Szegedi's Lutheran opponents, however, with considerable ill will, contrasted his teaching, not with the 1540 Augustana Variata, nor even with the Latin text of the 1530 Augustana, but with the 1530 German variation, which is far less compromising than the other two.[45]

The solemn Synod of "Christian teachers of all Hungary and Transylvania" in Marosvásárhely, Transylvania, in 1559, following the

*Propositiones de coena Domini disputandae in synodo Vasarheliensis,*
agreed on the *Common Christian Confession concerning the Lord's
Supper.* This very first statement of faith in the Magyar language is a
Zwingli-Bullingerian statement, but it is also Calvinistic when it deals
with the believer's participation in the sacrament. Gregory Szegedi's
doctrine appears here, but the influence of Szegedi Kis and the
craftsmanship of Peter Mélius are also detectable, the latter being the
key representative of the churches from Hungary at the Synod.[46] The
creed in German transcript was sent to Heidelberg, where it was approved and published by the faculty, a recognition of its Calvinistic
character.

The same Calvinistic heritage was codified in the *Confessio
Debreceniensis-Agrovalliensis* in 1562, of which again Gregory
Szegedi and Peter Mélius are considered joint authors, the latter having
the major role. The *Confessio* is in remarkable agreement with Calvin's
position, mostly in two closely related doctrines, Christology and the
Lord's Supper. Concerning Christ's presence in the Supper it sides
neither with Luther's objectivism of signs, Word, and occasion, nor
with Zwingli's subjectivism of faith, but builds a construction of the
"objectivism of the Holy Spirit through the Word." Concerning the
believer's uniting with Christ—"Christ in me and I in Christ"—the
Debrecen confession teaches union with the totality of Christ, yet limits
it to His spiritual benefits. This is in harmony with its Christology and,
not surprisingly, with Calvin's teaching on the *Communicatio
idiomatum utrius naturae ad personam!*[47] The Confession, however,
carries this Calvinistic principle beyond Calvin, in its doctrine of the
Lord's Supper.

After the publication of the Debrecen Confession, in 1563, Szegedi
received a call to Kolozsvár, Transylvania, but for some unknown reason, he declined it. In the same year he left Debrecen and held pastorates in Tokaj and later in Eger, but we are given no explanation for his
leaving Debrecen. Some historians suggest a reason: a possible conflict
between Szegedi, Debrecen's senior minister, and the lively, productive, and successful second minister, young Bishop Peter Mélius.

## PETER MÉLIUS JUHÁSZ (1536–72)

Peter Mélius, a son of lower nobility, was born in Horhi (a place no
longer inhabited) in Somogy county, Lower Transdanubia. His family
name, Juhász, means "Shepherd"; the name Mélius is derived from a
related Greek word. After elementary and secondary schooling in the
area, he most likely entered the newly established and rapidly growing
college of Tolna in 1553 or 1554 where he was won over from his early
Brentian-Lutheran conviction, to the Helvetic doctrines by the scholar
Stephen Szegedi Kis. They continued by correspondence after the latter

moved to Laskó and became bishop of Baranya in 1554.[48] Szegedi also changed the confessional loyalty of the Tolna school over to that of the Helvetic Reformation.

The next rector of the school, Paul Thuri Farkas, was a staunch adherent of Geneva.[49] Thus, even before his studies in Wittenberg in 1556–57, Mélius was strongly influenced by Helvetic doctrines. In 1557 his studies were suddenly interrupted when he was called home to combat the growing forces of Antitrinitarianism. Where he was between mid-1557 and mid-1558, however, before his call to Debrecen, remains a puzzle.[50]

Debrecen was a city of ranchers, stock merchants, and tradesmen. With a population of 15,000, it was Hungary's largest city in the after-Mohács era (1526). It was at Debrecen that the Helvetic Reformation under the ministry of Kálmáncsehi gained the upper hand from 1556 on. The twenty-two-year-old Mélius, a scholar of high reputation and extraordinary talents, set to work there in 1558. During his ministry of less than fifteen years, he published forty-four works, most of them extant. Twelve others remained unpublished. His works include six confessions of faith, five volumes of sermons, nineteen works on polemics, two catechisms, three devotional books, one hymnal, three theologies, seven Bible translations and expositions, one canon law, one work on botany and one collection of correspondence.[51] As second minister, under Gregory Szegedi as *plebanus,* he was elected bishop at the age of twenty-five by the district that in his short lifetime was enlarged by the Nagyvárad and the Szatmár areas and came to comprise practically all Transcistibiscia. Mélius was an impetuous preacher of the expository style, an earnest Bible scholar, an erudite theologian, an efficient organizer, and an indefatigable debater. His greatness, however, is in none of these qualities but in his deep sense of calling: "It is God's counsel, God's decree," he said, "that in Hungary, in Debrecen, the Word of God be preached. It is not by chance." Of himself he wrote, "I am a trumpet, a voice crying. I am speaking not of myself, but of God." Again: "I am obliged to preach, whether the world will strike me or persecute me; whether I live or die; but I have to teach even at the price of the loss of my life."[52] After a life spent mostly in fierce debates with the Antitrinitarians, he died at the age of thirty-six, in 1572.

About two hundred of Mélius's sermons are extant in five volumes. This is a relatively small number in comparison with the number of sermons he actually preached in his fifteen years of ministry. Although he never observed the classical rules of homiletics, yet through his faithful biblicism, solid theological grounding, educational purpose, and, above all, prophetic consciousness of his calling, he exerted an extensive influence. These qualities are reflected in his printed sermons too, penned after the actual delivery. Even in the printed text his impetuous nature shines through with the fire of the original pulpit presentation.

Mélius's volume on *Colossians* (1561) is verse-by-verse "expository preaching," in the style of the Reformation. The topical sermons on "Christ's mediatorial office" (1561) are rather dogmatic treatises, abundantly supported by Scriptures and enlivened by witty expository remarks. His *Hungarian Sermons* (1563) are expositions of the Epistle to the Romans, while his *Selected Sermons* (1563), to which is appended his *Agenda* (Book of Order), are for the holy days of the Christian year. The volume on *Revelation* (1568), reflecting the rapture of his mind, is the truest representation of his personality.[53]

God, for Mélius, is the living God whose being manifests itself in Christ both in creation and in redemption. Christ is the head, the plan, and the purpose of creation and salvation. The framework of His plan and action is predestination. We can grasp Christ and His benefits by faith worked in us by the Holy Spirit. His Christ-centered theology, very practically applied, shines through all his rumbling, passion-filled preaching, always leading the hearers to the quiet waters of God's love.

In his *Prayer Book* printed between his two *Dialogues,* Peter Mélius, the erudite theologian and the thundering preacher appears as the faithful shepherd of the flock of God. The book's unique importance is that it is the first prayer book in Hungarian for the people of the Reformed faith. It is a radical departure from traditional ways of prayer: a product of the author's creative mind. The prayers have a close affinity with the first dialogue related to real life. They are biblical prayers designed to strengthen the believers against lurking superstitions, enchantments, and surviving traditions of ancient folklore sanctioned by medieval religion. They are "uplifting, refreshing, edifying, heart-moving prayers."[54] Their tone is not the *mea culpa* of "miserable sinners" but rather the joy of the elect by the love and grace of God. They breathe the assurance of faith that leans on the covenant of God and adoption into His sonship. The desire of Mélius's heart was a peaceable and happy life, and he often offered prayers and taught others to pray for that.

Mélius's time and energy in a large part were consumed by theological controversies—first with the papists, then with the Lutherans, but mostly with the Antitrinitarians. Nineteen of his fifty works, quantitatively about half of his writings, were devoted to the latter.

Early in his ministry in a two-week debate in 1560 he defeated Thomas Arany, the foremost representative of the pre-Servetus type of Antitrinitarianism.[55] Then in the mid-1560s he supported the Cistibiscians in their struggle against Lukas Egri, who died in prison. Between 1566 and 1569, Mélius had five major debates in Gyulafehérvár, Debrecen, and Nagyvárad with two of his staunchest Antitrinitarian opponents—Francis Dávid (1520–79), who was first a Lutheran, then a Reformed, and finally an Antitrinitarian bishop in Translyvania, and George Blandrata, court physician and Dávid's *spiritus rector*. In addition, he had some minor debates with their followers in his own area until 1570.

The *Brevis Confessio Pastorum,* the Latin confession of the 1567 Constitutional Synod in Debrecen, with Mélius as principal writer, devotes half of its pages to the defense of the doctrine of the Trinity and the refutation of the "Servetus followers." The Hungarian creed of the same Synod also devotes nearly that much to the subject.[56]

Owing to his authoritative rule, the title "Pope Peter" was attached to Mélius's name, not without reason. The other title "Hungarian Calvin" traditionally assigned to Mélius, however, has proven to be a misnomer in the light of recent elaborate research. The historian Bishop Imre Révész showed, and studies in the 1960s and 1970s confirmed, that Mélius could not be considered an ideological representative of Calvin alone. His theology reflects the influence of Melanchthon and, through Stephen Szegedi Kis, of Musculus. Although it is evident that directly or indirectly he knew the teachings of Bullinger and Calvin, traces of his one-time Lutheran masters, Brenz and Flacius, are also detectable in the formal elements of his theology.

It is certain that Mélius did not become a servile imitator of any Reformer, at home or abroad. In the key doctrines he agrees with Calvin, in several others he resembles the teachings of various other theologians, but his deductions and presentations are quite different. Without subjecting himself to the exclusive authority of any one of the Reformers, he proved himself a wholehearted follower of the Helvetic Reformation, while at the same time upholding his independence.

Mélius's significance is not that he is an imitator of Calvin. Actually he was an eclectic theologian of the Helvetic Reformation, occasionally going beyond even that line of demarcation. He knew in detail the systems of contemporary theologians, but his independent mind did not tie him down to one authority or another. He maintained his freedom even against his former teachers, let alone his theological sources, and he allowed his doctrines to unfold according to the genius of his mind in the freedom of the Spirit. His historic significance is that with his theology, forged in the combat against Romanism, Lutherism, Antitrinitarianism, and radical sectarianism, he laid a foundation for future centuries for the *ecclesia militans,* his much loved Reformed church.[57]

## CONFESSIONAL STANDARDS

Confessional synods were frequent and important to the Helvetic Reformation in Hungary because of its several regional centers and shades of doctrinal difference.

## Confession Catholica or Debreceniensis, 1562

The first major confession of the Helvetic camp in Hungary was the product of Debrecen and appeared under three different names: *Confessio Catholica, Confessio Agrovalliensis,* and *Confessio Debreceniensis.*[58] Originally it was written for Debrecen in 1561; however, it first appeared in print under the name *Confessio Agrovalliensis* (Confession of Eger Valley) in 1562.

Eger was a small fort in Habsburg-dominated northeast Hungary. Eger had valiantly repelled a long siege by the Turks in 1552. A decade later its armed forces and the population of the city and the region were accused of treason and sedition against the Hapsburg king because of their evangelical faith. In response to the request of the Eger church, the leaders of the Debrecen church sent them their *Confessio Catholica* or *Confessio Debreceniensis,* just off the press, with a new cover bearing the title *Confessio Agrovalliensis.* The main body of the creed is written in the heavy and terse style of Mélius, while the letter of recommendation and several passages are in the lighter style of Gregory Szegedi.

"The entire regiment of cavalry and foot soldiery in the Eger Valley, and the noble and common inhabitants of the city of Eger" swore allegiance to this statement of faith declaring that they would abide by the "true and Catholic faith and doctrine" and that they would not allow their pastor to leave. The congregation of Eger swearing allegiance to God and uniting in their common faith as a church is the first clear example in Hungary of the "Reformed" concept of the church. They rejected the charges of conspiracy and sedition spread by their papist adversaries. They declared before the royal commissioners their determination to leave the fort if they were further pressed to dismiss their pastor to whom they swore allegiance. They then petitioned the king to permit them "to remain in the true and Catholic faith and doctrine and to keep their pastor who nourishes them with the clearest Word of God."

## The Confession of Tarcal-Torda, 1562–63

In 1562, the Synod of Tarcal, in spite of the Lutheran presence, accepted Beza's 1560 *"Confessio Christianae Fidei,"* a purely Calvinistic creed, with slight abbreviations and omissions.[59]

The Synod, by accepting Beza's Confession with a few emendations, was clearly Calvinistic in doctrine, especially on two cardinal issues: predestination and the Lord's Supper. The powerful landlord of the area, the Lutheran Gabriel Perényi, bitterly resented the Helvetic pronouncements of Tarcal. Paul Thuri, writer of the famous distich on Calvin's *Institutes*[60] bravely answered the charges, saying in regard to the Lord's Supper and the question of predestination that these are matters of faith in which they have to listen to God rather than men.

The same Confession was accepted in 1563 at the Synod of Torda, Transylvania, jointly held by the Cistibiscians and the Transylvanians and therefore it was given the title "Confession of Tarcal-Torda." The Synod of Gönc, again in Cistibiscia, confirmed the same Helvetic position in 1568. We may also add here that John Calvin's 1545 Catechism,[61] translated and published by Peter Mélius in 1563, was also accepted by the 1564 Synod of Tarcal.

## The Second Helvetic Confession[62]

The Second Helvetic Confession, an amplified version of the First Helvetic Confession (1536), was written by Heinrich Bullinger in 1562. It gained public recognition when Elector Frederick III of the Palatinate presented it to the Imperial Diet. The Second Confession was known prior to this in the Swiss Protestant Cantons, which, with the exception of Basel, unanimously accepted it as their own statement of faith and published it as such in 1566. The Helvetic Confession served as common ground, uniting various centers of the Reformation—in Switzerland, in the Palatinate, and in Lower Germany—in a covenant in their constitutional struggle to secure freedom of religion. In Hungary, the Confession filled a dire need and served the same goal. By the mid-1560s, Roman Catholic pressure declined and Lutheran zeal flagged. Antitrinitarianism, however, in its full vigor, was not only at the doorstep but within the threshold of Debrecen.

At the Constitutional Synod of Debrecen,[63] 1567, Peter Mélius and his co-workers gave a decisive blow to the Antitrinitarians. Their two confessions, *Brevis Confessio Pastorum* in Latin and *True Confession According to the Scripture* in Hungarian, were effective refutations of Antitrinitarianism and elaborate statements of the orthodox faith.[64] The Debrecen fathers, however, felt the need of still another creed covering the entire field of doctrine and conduct. In the unity of faith they wanted to express their cohesion with their brethren at home and also likeminded Christians abroad. The Second Helvetic Confession was accepted as such a common denominator at the Synod of Debrecen, 1567, for Transtibiscia and Cistibiscia. It is referred to in the *Canons of Hercegszőllős* (1576), in Danubia under Turkish rule, and in Stephen Pathai's work *On the Sacraments* (1592), in Habsburg-ruled Transdanubia. The Confession was translated into Hungarian by Peter Szenci Csene and published by Albert Szenci Molnár in Oppenheim in 1616. It appears in the historic name of the church in Hungary: "Reformed according to the Helvetic Confession."

## The Heidelberg Catechism

Traditionally, Zachariah Ursinus and Caspar Olevianus are considered coauthors of the Catechism.[65] Recent research confirmed Ursinus's role as the major one in authorship, but for the lectoring and final wording, a cooperative fellowship is recognized today, Thomas Erastus having had an equal share with Olevianus. Other members of the committee most likely were (1) professors and pastors Emanuel Tremellius, Pierre Boquinus, Diller, and Dathenus and (2) laymen Eheim, Zuleger, and Circler. According to recent research, the role of Frederick of the Palatinate is also seen in a new light. He claimed the title "father of the Catechism" and referred to it as "my Catechism." The idea, the planning, and the biblical undergirding are his contributions.[66]

Views on the source material have also been revised. Traditionally a number of other catechisms, works of the Reformers, and Ursinus's two outlines were considered the sources. Now it is known that Beza's shorter and larger Confession (1560), which served as a basis for the Tarcal-Torda Confession, also exercised an influence throughout the Heidelberg Catechism. It is important to recognize that Beza, Calvin's first and foremost co-worker, exerted such a vital influence in Hungary just about the same time that he did in the Palatinate. This discovery offers an interesting clue to the origin of Hungarian Calvinism. Through the centuries one hundred editions of the Catechism were published in Germany, one hundred in Holland, and almost two hundred in Hungary.[66]

It is interesting to trace the channels through which the Heidelberg Catechism found its way to Hungary. Its first trace is the letter of the Heidelberg professors to pastors in Kolozsvár and all brethren in Transylvania, written September 1, 1564. In the 1560s there were fierce debates on the Lord's Supper between the Lutheran and Helvetic camps. The Lutherans, guided by Bishop Matthias Hebler, made their pronouncement at the Synod of Medgyes, February 6, 1561, in *Brevis confessio de sacra coena Domini . . . Una cum iudicio quatuor Academiarum Germaniae. . . .*[67] They requested the opinion of Lutheran Academies in Germany. In July 1564 the Reformed pastors, in turn, requested the Heidelberg scholars to express their views. The Heidelberg response, *Epistola Professorum Theologiae Inclytae Academiae Heydelbergensis,* was published in 1565. In it the professors, under Boquinus as Dean at that time, expressed their solidarity, responsibility, and empathy with their Reformed brethren in warm terms. They did not consider more literary support necessary. They felt that Ursinus's already-published work on the sacraments and Boquinus's and Olevianus's on the Lord's Supper were sufficient. They deemed Hebler's writing "unworthy of a new response." The Catechism of their churches, the *Book of Order* of the Palatine churches, a *Defense of the Catechism,* and some literature on the Lord's Supper were enclosed. This was a weighty response and a helpful means of defense. On the other hand, in this bitter disagreement, as both camps dug in, it became evident that there was no more hope for their reconciliation. The rift became final. Lutherans hated the Reformed even more wholeheartedly than the papists did. It was in the midst of this fierce war over doctrines that the Catechism arrived. Yet it, as well as the letter from Heidelberg, breathes a deep desire for unity.

The *Catechismus Ecclesiarum Dei,* published in Kolozsvár, Transylvania in 1566, marks a unique episode in the history of the Heidelberg Catechism.[68] It was the first Latin edition of the catechism in Hungary with modifications acceptable to the Antitrinitarians. The latter, however, abused the compromise, much to the disappointment of the Helvetic Reformer, Peter Mélius. The Synod of Debrecen, 1567, on the other hand, violently opposed and ultimately rejected it. The first Hungarian translation of the Heidelberg Catechism was prepared by David Huszár and, with an appendix of a sizeable prayer book, was published in Pápa, Transdanubia, under the title *Summary of the Teaching of True Faith in Short Questions* (1577).[69]

There is no trace of acceptance of the Heidelberg Catechism at Debrecen as an official symbol of the church. The fathers of the Synod, however, indirectly affirmed their adherence to it by ordering, in Article 52 of the *Canon Book,* the teaching of the catechism in the congregations. After Debrecen 1567, the teaching of the Heidelberg Catechism was ordered by the Synod of Sók in 1619 in Upper Danubia, the Synod of Pápa, and that of Transylvania in the same year. In Cistibiscia the 1621 laws of Sárospatak College ordered its teaching and the Seniorate of Zemplén, meeting in Sátoraljaujhely, incorporated it in the ministers' ordination vows in 1630. The joint Synod of Cistibiscia and Transtibiscia required students leaving for and arriving from academies abroad to pledge allegiance to the "Heidelberg." Finally, the National Synod of Szatmárnémeti, 1646, under the influence of the Hungarian Puritans, accepted the Heidelberg Catechism, along with John Siderius's catechism. The direction of acceptance is noticeable: from the lower strata, the ministers and the people, to higher courts of the church.[70] In spite of the tremendous popularity and teaching of the book in church and school, its solemn acceptance by the General Synod as the official symbol of the Reformed Church in Hungary took place in Budapest only in 1928.

## The Confession of the Synod of Csenger, 1570

This Confession, which was Peter Mélius Juhász's elaborate final statement of the trinitarian doctrine and presents his clearly Calvinistic teaching on the Lord's Supper and of particular election, marks the climax of his struggle against Antitrinitarianism. It is his polemic and organizational masterpiece, in which he wrote, "We are in harmony with the Word of God and the Catholic doctors of the true Church." In support of this he presented Theodore Beza's recent letter, a complimentary appraisal of Mélius's three most recent Antitrinitarian works.[71]

This Confession, with other creeds of the Reformed churches abroad, was published in the *Syntagma confessionum;* unfortunately, however, under the erroneous title *Confessio Polonica.* Niemeyer also published it in his *Collectio confessionum.* Its full title is *Confessio vera ex Verbo Dei sumpta et in Synodo Czengerina uno consensu exhibita et declarata.*

## ORGANIZATION AND GOVERNMENT

Reformation in Hungary started at the congregational level. It was also supported by court preachers of the higher nobility, under the protection of great landlords such as Peter Petrovics and the Nádasdy and the Török families. It was, however, the personal zeal of its protagonists that mostly contributed to the rapid spread of the movement.

Congregations were soon united in "church counties," following the Roman Catholic pattern of dioceses.[72] Even though there was constant, sharp division between the two main Protestant denominations in doctrinal matters, the Helvetic element accepted the Lutheran system of organization and government. In the Helvetic churches the names "church county" and "diocese" reflect a Roman Catholic remnant, whereas *contubernium, fraternitas,* and *districtus* have a Lutheran derivation; their designations *tractus* and *seniorate* sound more original. The moderator or dean, of the Helvetic churches was considered *primus inter pares;* he was elected for life. His responsibility was to call meetings, prepare agendas, preside at the meetings, execute the decisions, and represent the seniorate. His task was also the examination, ordination, and deposition of ministers; canonical visitation; and the exercise of discipline.

Church counties *(tracti, seniorates)* were united in church districts, synods, dioceses, or superintendencies, comprising major areas of the land, under the leadership of the bishop or superintendent elected by the district churches. The Transtibiscian district came into existence at the joint meeting of the Debrecen-Nagyvárad and Szatmár area superintendencies in 1557. The Danubian district comprised the former Mid-Danubian and Baranya (1554) superintendiencies, i.e., the area between the Tisza and Lake Balaton. The Transdanubian district, after long decades as a joint Synod of Lutheran and Helvetic churches, began its independent existence as a Reformed Synod in 1595. In Cistibiscia, four church counties were the highest unit of self-government in loose federation and cooperation until 1735. At that time, they yielded to the ruling of the *Bodrogkeresztur Conventus* that they should elect their own bishop and organize themselves into a district.[73] The District of Transylvania was organized, after the decisive split with the Lutherans, at the Synod of Nagyenyed in 1564.

Church districts were the highest units of organization and government in the sixteenth century. Their task was training and ordaining ministers, making episcopal visits to the area churches *(generalis visitatio),* formulating confessions and canon laws, ruling in matrimonial cases, and representing the churches to the government.

The office of bishop (superintendent) was introduced at an early stage, in the 1550s, partly to fill the vacuum created by the absence of Roman Catholic bishops, partly to follow the Lutheran pattern, and partly to have an authorative representation to the secular authority: Hungarian, Hapsburg, or Turkish. The office was set up without any claim to apostolic succession, through appointment by the churches of the district. A bishop was to act only as a "first among equals." The theological authority of the office was John Calvin's letter to the king of Poland, in which he recommended the establishment of the office of archbishop who would be the chairman of the National Synod. Bishops were to be chosen on the basis of the judgment of the ministers, and after the election all parishes were to ratify the choice. It was this free election of the bishop that the papal church had allowed to fall into desuetude, Calvin concludes.[74]

The corporate principle, on the other hand, did not become a reality as far as the involvement of the laity was concerned. The Confession of Tarcal-Torda[75] soft-pedaled the passage in Beza's Confession regarding the matter of eldership, since the time was not ripe. In fact it did not become ripe until 1618, first in Transdanubia.[76] It was popularized by the Puritan Movement in the late 1630s, in the east and northeast. However, laymen were heavily involved in the life of the church as patrons, following the Lutheran pattern, and as city councilors, following the Geneva pattern.

Although the organization at the national level could not take place for centuries on account of the tripartition of the country, some of the partial synods attended by representatives of two, three, or sometimes only one church district gained the authority of national synods. Their resolutions were recognized nationwide and were historically honored. Such were the synods of Tarcal, Cistibiscia (1562), Torda, Transylvania (1563), Debrecen, Transtibiscia (1567), and Hercegszőlős in Danubia (1576).

Among the Canon Laws, the *Articuli majores* is one of the products of the Constitutional Synod of Debrecen held on February 25–26, 1567. It was published later that year under the title *Articuli ex verbo Dei et lege naturae compositi.* It is considered mostly the work of Peter Mélius Juhász. Its abbreviated form, *Articuli minores,* was edited and published in 1577 by George Gőnczi Kovács.[77]

The ecclesiastical constitution of the Danubian area, the *Canons of Hercegszőlős,* was approved and accepted by the Synod of Hercegszőlős in Lower Danubia on August 16–17, 1576. It was to replace the *Canons of Baranya,* which was a somewhat tentative document, and was a fully Helvetic exposition of it. Its Latin original consists of forty-seven articles, while the Hungarian translation consists of forty-six. *Baranya* in the 1550s and *Hercegszőlős* in the 1560s were authored by Stephen Szegedi Kis. The translation most likely was the work of Szegedi's disciple, Matthew Skaricza. The original was signed by the forty attending ministers. David Huszár published both the Latin original and the Hungarian translation in his print shop in Pápa in 1577. Because of their common origin and source material, the later *Sopron County Lutheran* (1598) and the *Pest County Reformed* (1628) Canons have much affinity with the Baranya and Hercegszőlős canons.

By the end of the sixteenth century over 90 percent of the population of Hungary, divided as it was, followed the Reformation, most of them the Helvetic trend.

### THE HUNGARIAN BIBLE

As Erasmus and the humanists abroad became roadbuilders of the Reformation, so did their Hungarian counterparts. Their biblical translations soon spread widely through the art of printing.

Benedict Komjáthi's *Epistles of St. Paul,* published in Crakow in 1533, opened the series. It was based on Erasmus's *Paraphrases.* This carefully written book is difficult to read. Gabriel Pesti Mizsér's *New Testament* (Vienna, 1536), based also on Erasmus, contains only the four Gospels. It is a truer and more compact translation than Komjáthi's. John Erdősi Sylvester's magnum opus was his *New Testament* (Sárvár, 1541). Although its language is difficult, Sylvester deserves credit for its dedication, "To the Magyar People," written in smoothly rolling distiches.[78]

Representatives of the Helvetic Reformation also translated several portions of the Bible. Stephen Bencédi Székely made a superb translation of the Psalms (Crakow, 1548). Peter Mélius Juhász translated from the original texts several major books of the Old Testament and the entire New Testament. Thomas Félegyházi, the most erudite theologian of the Helvetic persuasion, produced an excellent translation of the New Testament that was very popular in its posthumous edition published in Debrecen in 1586. The cooperative fellowship of Caspar Heltai published seven volumes of their translation of almost the entire Bible from 1551 to 1566. Because of the lack of unity in style and the changing confessional loyalty of the fellowship, however, it did not gain popularity.

The Károli Version, or Vizsoly Bible, published in 1590, was the first complete Hungarian Bible in print. "If God allow me to live so long that I will be able to publish this Bible, I will be ready to die and to go to Christ," said the godly old man, Caspar Károli, while he was strenuously working in his very last years to complete the translation of the entire Bible.[79]

Károli was born about 1530 in Nagykároly in northeast Hungary. Recent research just unearthed the information that he was a student of John Honterus's famous school in the Transylvanian Brassó. After Wittenberg (1556) he studied also in Switzerland and Strasbourg. Returning home in 1562, he received a call to Gönc, where he stayed for a lifetime of ministry. It was here also that he prepared the translation during his last decade.

The translation and publication of the Bible was Károli's major work and the crown of the Hungarian Reformation. He expressed his motivation for the sacred task in these words in the foreword: "Although God's Book is available for every nation in their own language, the Hungarian nation did not take care of this for a long time. . . . Considering, therefore, the deficiency and the future upbuilding of the Holy Mother Church in our nation, as well as our calling, I did not cease until I completed the translation of the entire Bible."[80]

Károli considered the sacred task of translating the Bible his spiritual vocation. At the beginning of the work he assembled the pastors of his seniorate for prayer, and they jointly prayed for the successful progress of the undertaking. As a cooperative fellowship they laid down the principles, distributed the tasks, and established the schedule.

It is evident from the text that the translation is the cooperative venture of several men. Károli himself says that "a few devout and scholarly brethren" helped him in his work. However, the New Testament seems to be the most consistent in principles and language, and we have every reason to believe that it was done by Károli alone. Some books of the Old Testament were translated by others, though he reserved for himself the task of revising and supervising, as well as directing the entire project. It is very likely that Matthias Thuri of Szántó; John Czeglédi of Vizsoly; Nicolaus, Károli's brother; and Emery Huszti, the second minister in Gönc, were his associates in the translation, while John Pelei, the local rector, may have been helpful in technical assistance.[81]

The printer of the Károli Bible, Bálint Mantskovit (d. 1597 in Vizsoly), himself a man of letters and of the Reformed faith, moved to Hungary in 1573. After examining three other locations he was attracted to Vizsoly in 1588 and contracted for printing the Bible. His printing shop was set up in a house provided by Sigismund Rákóczi, one of the anonymous sponsors, on the grounds of his mansion. New type faces and paper were purchased by the other patron, Stephen Báthori, supreme judge of the country. The printed pages were stored in a rear extension of the Vizsoly church, where in troublesome times the shop was also operated in hiding under the protection of the militia provided by the patrons.

The translator provides information in the foreword concerning the text the Károli Version is based on.[82] He gives a faithful account of the various translations he used in addition to the original Hebrew and Greek texts. First of all, he read and studied the Vulgate, and with his sharp, critical mind discovered several errors in it. "Therefore," he writes, "we did not bind ourselves to it, but we consulted devout, scholarly men and their translations besides the Greek translation of the seventy interpretors—Vatabulus, Münsterus, Pagninus, and Tremellius." Santes Pagninus was a Dominican. His first edition appeared in 1528 and enjoyed wide popularity. Francis Vatabulus was a famous professor of the College of France. The first edition of his translation was published in 1544. Sebastian Münsterus was first a Franciscan, then, after accepting the Reformation, he became a professor in Heidelberg and a highly esteemed Hebrew scholar. His Hebrew edition and its Latin translation were held in high regard. Emanuel Tremellius, a Jew by birth and a renowned Hebraist, became Calvin's ardent follower and, after many mishaps, also a professor in Heidelberg. He published first the Old Testament, then the entire Bible in Latin, with scholarly comments. That Károli did not use Luther's translation is more understandable than that he omitted Beza's excellent New Testament edition, the Latin translation of which he must have known, and which would have been available.

Károli mostly followed Tremellius's translation and comments. In addition to the other translators mentioned, he also used "many other interpreter doctors." Furthermore, he consulted those "who previously translated certain parts of the Bible," such as C. Heltai and Peter Mélius.

Through the centuries the Károli Version or Vizsoly Bible was published in 293 editions—25 of them without the year of publication. Since 1869, the British and Foreign Bible Society has been the publisher, and during World War II, the Hungarian Bible Society. Although a new translation of the Bible was prepared by the Hungarian Bible Council and published in 1975, the Károli Bible continues to remain the standard version in Hungarian.

In recognition of the first edition of the Károli Version or Vizsoly Bible (1590), a facsimile edition of it was published by the Hungarian-government-sponsored Europa Publisher in 1981.

## WORSHIP AND HYMNODY

The first hymns of the Reformation in Hungary were translations of medieval Latin hymns on the one hand and German hymns—some of them Luther's—on the other. The first printed hymnal, that of Stephen Gálszécsi (Crakow, 1536, extant only in fragments), contained three of Luther's hymns and about ten others of German origin. Hungarian Reformers themselves were very productive in writing Psalm paraphrases and hymns.

The worship service, like Luther's *Formula Missae,* did not differ much from the Roman mass, except that it was in the vernacular. Louis Szegedi, known as Kálmáncsehi's co-worker in the 1550s and renowned for his paraphrases of the Psalms in his Lutheran period (c. 1542), sang the mass in Hungarian.

These liturgies were preserved in handwritten *graduales,* of which the *Batthyány Codex* (about the mid-1550s) is the oldest. Printed graduales were those of Martin Kálmáncsehi Sánta and perhaps Stephen Beythe (both of these liturgies are now lost) and the first part of Gál Huszár's *Godly Hymns and Prayers* (Komjáti, 1574). The eight-hundred-page *Old Graduale* (1636), edited by the Transylvanian bishops John Keserui Dajka and Stephen Geleji Katona, was a grandiose but unsuccessful last attempt sponsored by Prince George Rákóczy I to salvage and revive the tradition.

The first hymnal, containing hymns for congregational singing, appeared in 1560 and was used along with the graduales. The hymns were grouped not according to the progression of the liturgy, but according to the history of salvation, the festival seasons, and other special occasions of worship. The first two hymnals of this type are evidence of the favorable attitude of the Helvetic Reformers to congregational singing.

Gál Huszár's *Godly Hymns and Psalms* (1560) was believed nonextant until the discovery of a copy in Stuttgart in 1975. It was compiled and printed in three phases: the first in Óvár, the second in Kassa where he was under house arrest, and the third soon after his escape to Debrecen. The Letter of Dedication was addressed to Mélius, in all probability to pave the editor's way to "the Calvinist Rome." Its sequence of hymns—psalm paraphrases and festival, confessional, and occasional hymns—must have been followed in the now nonextant "miniature hymnal" edited by Peter Mélius and Gregory Szegedi and printed very likely by Huszár in Debrecen in 1562. Both Huszár's 1560 hymnal and the 1562 Mélius-Szegedi hymnal were incorporated in the second half of Huszár's larger hymnal (Komjáti, 1574). Since, however, the latter does not contain the music of the former and smaller hymnal, the Stuttgart discovery with its forty-nine tunes is invaluable to Hungarian hymnody.[83]

Numerous revised and emended editions of the 1562 Debrecen hymnal followed in rapid succession. The *Várad Hymnal* published in Nagyvárad in 1566 by "L.F.," most likely Mélius's brother-in-law, followed the hymns-and-psalms order. The *Debrecen Hymnal* of 1569 reversed the order, and this has remained the standard order ever since. The series of the Debrecen-type hymnals was climaxed by George Gönci Kovacs's 1590 edition entitled *Christian Hymns,* the prototype that set the pattern of development through forty editions during subsequent centuries.

In the light of such abundance of hymn writing and hymnal production, it goes without saying that the Hungarian Reformers, radical as they were in theology and ecclesiastical traditions, did not follow the amusical order of Zurich or even the Genevan example of using only psalms in congregational singing. Mélius, himself a hymn-writer, was strongly opposed to the Zwinglian view of music and vehemently defended congregational singing.[84] The Synod of Erdöd II (1555) warned against unscriptural hymns but encouraged communal singing and praising God. The *Confession of Eger-Debrecen* (1562) deems ''hymns taken from the Scriptures'' necessary in the service of worship. The Synod of Debrecen (1567) considered the reasons for ''beautiful singing in the Christian church,'' among them being the fact that many people are converted by God through singing. Article 47 of the *Confession of Csenger* (1570) may have been directed partly against Romans and partly against radical enthusiasts when it states that scriptural hymns should be sung with understanding, spirit, and heart, and not shouted in meaningless language like that of the priests of Baal.[85]

The crown of Hungarian hymnody was the somewhat belated *Psalterium Ungaricum* (Herborn, 1607). It is the translation of the *Geneva Psalter* by the vagabond scholar of Hungarian Reformation, Albert Szenci Molnár.[86]

Szenci Molnár—under Reformed influences in Strasbourg (1593–96), through the inspiration of his friendship with Beza in Geneva and with the assistance of Clement Duboys in Frankfurt—translated the psalms in Altdorf in less than one hundred days. He published the psalter in Herborn (1607) and again in Hanau (1608), the latter edition being attached to the Vizsoly Bible, which he had revised. Since 1635, Szenci's psalter has always been published in one volume with the Debrecen-type hymnal, the psalter being placed following the hymns. After 1806, the psalter preceded the hymns, and the name of the book became *Zsoltár.*

Molnár's *Psalter* is a major feat in linguistics and poetry. With the exception of the playfully versatile poet Bálint Balassa (1554–94), there was no Hungarian poet comparable to Molnár during the sixteenth and seventeenth centuries. His translation of the ''verses of delicate French vocabulary'' into a language of long and difficult expressions was a remarkable achievement. His scholarly knowledge of the Bible, his theological and linguistic expertise, and his poetic genius are not sufficient explanations for his wonderful work; one must take into account the inspiration by the Holy Spirit. Molnár's wide popularity was brought about by the rise of Puritanism in and after the 1630s. Through its numerous editions, the *Psalter* became the most popular and very much loved book of the people.

The credit goes to Albert Szenci Molnár for bringing Calvin's *Geneva Psalter* into the life-stream of the Hungarian churches of the Reformation. By this and by the translation of Calvin's *Institutes* (Hanau, 1624), he bound the Reformed Church in Hungary inseparably to John Calvin and Geneva.

## SUMMARY

All through this study an endeavor was made to trace the sources and channels, contacts and results of the Helvetic Reformation in Hungary. The reader may have noticed the cautious use of terminology and the avoidance of the names Calvin and Calvinism, while other representatives of the Helvetic trend were constantly in the foreground.

Following the results of recent, elaborate research indicated in our introduction, we have to start our concluding remarks with a rather *negative statement* regarding Calvin's role in Hungary through most of the sixteenth century. Géza Kathona, one of the most prominent contemporary researchers states that John Calvin, in spite of his leading role among the Swiss Reformers, exerted little direct influence in Hungary before the last decades of the century and that even that influence was only through works of secondary importance and the mediation of Theodore Beza, his closest associate. "Even such influence became strengthened only in the last decades of the century," he says, "when the doctrinal structure of our Reformed church had already been formulated in its essential characteristics. Calvin's influence on the wider masses of people can be spoken of in our church only after 1624, when Albert Szenci Molnár, under Heidelberg's influence, published in Hungarian, Calvin's *Institutes* in Hanau." And again, "We cannot speak of the dominance of Calvinian doctrine during the sixteenth century in the Reformed Church in Hungary."

Negative evidences for the presence of Calvinism, however, are numerous. Article XI of the Law of 1548 banned Anabaptists and Sacramentarians from the land. The Diet of Transylvania also banned Sacramentarians in 1558 and 1559. That Calvin's name was well known in Hungary and Transylvania by 1550 is evident from George Draskovich's pamphlet against him (1551) and the report on his followers (1552), as well as from the three writings against Kálmáncsehi and Calvinism (1556 and 1557).

In the 1550s, when the Helvetic Reformation made its first conquest (1551–52) and established itself as of 1556, there were signs of Calvin's growing authority and reputation. Ambrosius Moibanus, a reformer in Breslau, in his letters of September 1, 1550, and March 24, 1552, assured Calvin that his works were received in Poland and in Hungary with great enthusiasm. On October 26, 1557, Gál Huszár, a Hungarian Reformer, reported to Heinrich Bullinger the wide popularity of Calvin's works in Hungary. About the same time, Paul Thuri Farkas, who had just returned from Wittenberg as an ardent adherent of John Calvin, wrote the renowned distich on the Institutes.

Francis Ferinus Kaprophontes, the second of Calvin's two Hungarian correspondents, on December 26, 1561, wrote Calvin from Wittenberg that Luther's work was brought to sublime perfection by him (Calvin), and the confidence of all Hungary was now in his authority and that of the Helvetic scholars. Peter Mélius Juhász's *Catechism,* published in Debrecen in 1562, refers to Calvin in its subtitle: "Compiled from the Holy Scripture and emended according to Johannes Calvinus' writing." Although this claim cannot be substantiated from the text except that the introductory questions resemble Calvin's 1542 Catechism and the *Institutes,* this inscription is a clear evidence of the high regard held for Calvin at that time in Hungary. Lastly, on May 1, 1568, three seniors of Cistibiscia—Caspar Károli, Michael Hevesi, and Gregory Szikszai—meeting in Gönc, jointly wrote to Theodore Beza, advising him that in Hungary the teachings of Calvin had been accepted in regard to predestination, free will, and the Lord's Supper.

All these testimonies support the assumption that Calvin was widely known in Hungary in the 1550s and 1560s and that his authority kept increasing.

Although Calvin's teachings do not dominate the Reformation movement in Hungary in these same decades, other substantial traces of their presence are detectable. The *"opera Calvini"* listed in Caspar Károli's estate are external signs that his teachings were present. More important is the information that, in preparation for their historic Synod of 1562, the Fathers of Tarcal used Calvin's *Admonitions to Westphal* in 1561. Calvin's *Geneva Catechism* of 1545, translated and published by Peter Mélius in 1563, was accepted by the Synod of Tarcal in 1564. There is a record of questionable repute that Calvin's *Optima ineundae concordiae* was presented as a representation of the Reformed doctrine on the Lord's Supper, at the Synod of Nagyenyed in Transylvania in 1564 by George Blandrata, the Antitrinitarian court physician, though the author was not identified.

More than formal importance is attached to representations of Calvinist doctrines by the three "giants" of the Reformation: Stephen Szegedi Kis, Gregory Szegedi, and Peter Mélius, whom we have already considered in detail.

Considering the doctrinal endowment of the Reformed Church in Hungary, we may conclude that at the time of the Reformation Calvin's teachings that were directly channeled to Hungary were on dual predestination by Stephen Szegedi Kis, Gregory Szegedi, and Peter Mélius Juhász in the *Confessio Debreceniensis-Agrovalliensis*; and on verbal inspiration and the Lord's Prayer by Szegedi Kis; on the Lord's Supper and the condition of souls after death in the *Confessio Debreceniensis-Agrovalliensis*; and on the nurture of the believer's soul in the Supper through his ascension to Christ by Francis Dávid. All other Reformed doctrines conquered the field of the Hungarian Reformation in the 1550s and 1560s through the mediation of Theodore Beza, Heinrich Bullinger, Wolfgang Musculus, Peter Vermigli Martyr, Martin Bucer, and the Heidelberg Catechism. Thus, while Calvin's genius is reflected in all these intermediaries, it is more accurate to consider the Reformation in Hungary, rather than in terms of Calvinism, as a reflection of the whole "Helvetic Reformation," which so eminently and eloquently represents the amalgamation of the spirit of Bullinger and Calvin.

# Calvin
# and the
# Church of England

*Philip Edgcumbe Hughes*

*Philip Edgcumbe Hughes is Professor Emeritus of Trinity Episcopal School for Ministry, Ambridge, Pennsylvania; Visiting Professor at Westminster Theological Seminary, Philadelphia; Associate Rector of St. John's Episcopal Church, Huntingdon Valley, Pennsylvania. He holds degrees from the University of Cape Town (B.A., M.A., D.Litt.), the University of London (B.D.), and the Australian College of Theology (Th.D.). His numerous works include commentaries on* Paul's Second Epistle to the Corinthians *and the* Epistle to the Hebrews, Theology of the English Reformers, Interpreting Prophecy, Creative Minds in Contemporary Theology, *and* The Register of the Company of Pastors of Geneva in the Time of Calvin. *A former editor of* The Churchman (London), *he is a member of the Renaissance Society of America, the American Society for Reformation Research, and Studiorum Novi Testamenti Societas.*

# 8

# Calvin
# and the
# Church of England

The English Reformation, however considerable its indebtedness to Luther, Calvin, and other Continental leaders might prove in the end to be, was not an import from Germany or Geneva, for it could boast its own indigenous line of communication reaching back by way of the Lollards to the fourteenth century and, in particular, to "the morning-star of the Reformation," John Wycliffe (1329–84). The distinctive protest against the errors and abuses of the papal church commonly associated with the reforming movement of the sixteenth century was no new thing in England. Foxe, when narrating the persecution of Lollards in the fifteenth century, offers this trenchant comment:

> If the knowledge and good-towardness of those good men had had the like liberty of time, with the help of like authority, as we have now, and had not been restrained, through the iniquity of time and tyranny of prelates, it had well appeared how old this doctrine would have been, which now they contemn and reject for the newness thereof; neither needed Bonner to have asked of Thomas Hawks, and such others, where their church was forty years ago, inasmuch as for forty years ago, and more, . . . was then found such plenty of the same profession and like doctrine which we now profess.

He adds that the records showed "such society and agreement of doctrine to be amongst them, that in their assertions and articles there was almost no difference: the doctrine of the one was the doctrine of all the others."[1]

The nature of their protest is plainly illustrated by the objections that were brought against them, complaining that they taught that "confession is not to be made unto a priest, but unto God only, because no priest hath any power to absolve a sinner from his sin''; that ''no priest hath power to make the body of Christ in the sacrament of the altar'' and that ''after the sacramental words there remaineth pure material bread as before''; that ''every true Christian man is a priest to God''; that ''it is lawful for priests to have wives''; that ''men ought not to go on pilgrimage''; that ''there is no honour to be given to the images of the crucifix, of our lady, or any other saint''; that ''the holy water, hallowed in the church by the priest, is not holier or of more virtue than other running or well water, because the Lord blessed all waters in their first creation''; that ''relics, as dead men's bones, ought neither to be worshipped nor digged out of their graves, nor set up in shrines''; that ''prayers made in all places are acceptable unto God''; that ''men ought not to pray to any saint, but only to God''; and that ''the catholic church is only the congregation of the elect.''[2]

Where there is still much misunderstanding, it needs to be stressed that the essence, equally with the origin, of the reforming movement in England had (to borrow the words of Professor Dickens) ''little in common with the old Tudor saga: Divorce, Reformation Parliament, Dissolutions, and Prayer Books.''[3] The Reformation, in England as elsewhere, was essentially an evangelical movement, demonstrating afresh that the gospel of Jesus Christ is the power of God effecting the salvation of all who believe (Rom. 1:16) and at the same time dynamically bringing the assurance that the message of Holy Scripture is the Word of God addressed to sinful men. The flame of saving faith was kindled in the heart of Thomas Bilney at Cambridge in 1519 as he was reading Erasmus's *Novum Testamentum*—Bilney whom God then used to bring Hugh Latimer to conversion and who, in 1531, was burned alive for publicly proclaiming the same gospel. On coming to Cambridge, William Tyndale, who while at Oxford had ''increased as well in the knowledge of tongues and other liberal arts, as especially in the knowledge of the Scriptures, whereunto his mind was singularly addicted,'' was the instrument of the conversion of the brilliant young scholar John Frith.[4]

It was these men and others whose lives had been transformed by the gospel that used to meet together in Cambridge at the White Horse Inn to study the Scriptures and to encourage each other in the faith, and who afterward went out to bear witness to and to die for their new-found faith. In the intensity of their experience of the grace of God we meet the true heart of that great movement of spiritual revival that we know as the Reformation.

These things were taking place while John Calvin was still a boy growing up in France. As the Reformation gathered momentum in Germany, Switzerland, and England, so also there developed a demonstrable unanimity of conviction between Luther, Calvin, and Cranmer regarding such cardinal doctrines as the sovereignty of God, the authority of Scripture, the depravity of man, and justification *sola gratia* and *sola fide*. The one area of serious disharmony was associated with the eucharistic dogmatism of Luther, to which neither the Swiss nor the English found it possible to consent. Both Calvin and Cranmer settled on a doctrine of receptionism that avoided the extremes of Luther's consubstantiation and the bare memorialism commonly connected with the name of Zwingli. The receptionist teaching is found in Wycliffe, who himself had found it in Augustine; but the eucharistic treatise of the ninth-century monk Ratramnus (Bertram), which was read in turn by Frith and Ridley, played an important part in persuading the English Reformers of the truth of this position.

Calvin's interest in the progress of the Reformation in England, as in other countries, was genuine, and he was always ready to do anything in his power to encourage his fellow Reformers in their work. He had no desire to impose on them a form of church structure other than that to which they were accustomed. Indeed, his horror of schism (see, for example, *Institutes* IV.i.9ff.) may well have caused him to view with some envy the possibility in England of reforming the church from the top down. His correspondence with the English leaders shows, as Professor Basil Hall has observed,

> that Calvin did not press the Genevan type of reform, rather he urged the principles of reformation in general terms; proposing the drawing up of a confession of faith, the practice of catechising, more frequent and abler preaching, and the discipline of morals.[5]

The French congregation in London, whom Calvin was concerned to supply with able pastors and who enjoyed the good will of the English authorities, was also an important link with England. During the Marian persecution, moreover, an English congregation, under the leadership of John Knox, flourished in Geneva, and it was in this city that William Whittingham (later to become Dean of York) and others of his compatriots worked on the production of the Geneva Bible, which was published in 1560.

The profound and sympathetic interest of the Genevan Reformer in the advancement of spiritual renewal in England is displayed in the letters he wrote to the leaders of church and state in that country. Our purpose in what follows is to give a survey of this correspondence, thus documenting from original sources the relationship between John Calvin and the Church of England.

Our starting point is the dedicatory epistle of Calvin's commentary on the Pastoral Epistles (June 1548) addressed to the Duke of Somerset, Protector of England and uncle of the young King Edward VI. The effusive and laudatory tone of the letter may be taken as characteristic of the age. What is of interest to us here is the manner in which, through this dedication, Calvin hoped to encourage the Protector to conduct affairs of state and instruct his royal nephew in accordance with the principles of biblical doctrine. The following extracts will serve to show the spirit in which Calvin wrote:

> The difficulties, so great and numerous, which you have experienced have not hindered you from making the restoration of religion your principal concern. This consideration is indeed no more worthy of a prince than it is beneficial to the state; for kingdoms enjoy secure prosperity and faithful guardianship when he, on whom they are founded and through whom they are preserved, the Son of God, presides over them. Accordingly, you could not have established the English state more beneficially than by overthrowing idols and setting up instead the pure worship of God; and this cannot come about unless the genuine teaching of godliness, which for too long has been suppressed by the sacrilegious tyranny of the Roman Antichrist, is restored by placing Christ on his throne. And to do this, which in any case is excellent, is all the more praiseworthy because today so few rulers are to be found who subject the honor of their high rank to the spiritual scepter of Christ. It is therefore an outstanding advantage to this most serene king to have such a person, closely related to him by family ties, as the guide of his boyhood. . . . As, under the auspices of your king, you strenuously expend your labor for the reform of the English Church, which, as is the case with almost the whole of Christendom, has been dreadfully corrupted by the appalling impiety of the Papacy, and for this purpose have the cooperation of many Timothys [a reference, apparently, to the ecclesiastical leaders such as Cranmer, Latimer, and Ridley], you could not organize your holy endeavors more effectively than by following the rule laid down by Paul. . . . May the Lord, in whose hand are the ends of the earth, long preserve the kingdom of England in safety and prosperity; may he adorn its most serene king with the spirit of leadership and shower on him all blessings; and may he enable you to persevere happily in your distinguished course, so that through you his renown may be extended ever more widely.[6]

Some four months later, on 22 October 1548, Calvin sent a long letter to the same correspondent. The previous year, encouraged by the commendations of Calvin, the English king and Archbishop Cranmer had welcomed the Italian exiles Peter Martyr Vermigli and Bernardino Ochino to their country, the former being appointed Regius Professor of Divinity at Oxford and the latter being granted a Prebend of Canterbury and a royal pension. The following year (1549) Martin Bucer accepted a similar invitation and became Regius Professor of Divinity at Cambridge. These appointments are eloquent of the mutual confidence and good will that prevailed between the Reformers in England and Calvin and others on the Continent. Meanwhile, however, Somerset had not been without his troubles, and in October 1549 the adversaries who had devised his downfall secured his imprisonment in the Tower of London. Though released in February 1550, those who wanted him completely removed from the scene succeeded in having him executed almost two years later. Aware of Somerset's reforming zeal and of the difficulties that beset him, Calvin took the opportunity to urge on him the value of perseverence in the good work to which he had set his hand. Writing as a fellow servant of the same Master, he incited him in the following terms:

> I have no other end in view, save only, that in following out yet more and more what you have begun, you may advance his honour, until you have established his kingdom in as great perfection as is to be looked for in the world. . . . We have all reason to be thankful to our God and Father, that he has been pleased to employ you in so excellent a work as that of setting up the purity and right order of his worship in England by your means, and establishing the doctrine of salvation that it may there be faithfully proclaimed to all those who shall consent to hear it; that he has vouchsafed you such firmness and constancy to persevere hitherto, in spite of so many trials and difficulties; that he has helped you with his mighty arm, in blessing all your counsels and your labours, to make them prosper. These are grounds of thankfulness which stir up all true believers to magnify his name.

Reminding Somerset of the ceaseless activity of Satan, especially where the truth of the gospel is advancing, Calvin appealed to him to consider attentively certain methods of reformation he wished to propose. The first proposal concerned the type of instruction in the faith that should be given to the people. ''I do not mean to pronounce what doctrine ought to have place,'' Calvin explains.

> Rather do I offer thanks to God for his goodness, that after having enlightened you in the pure knowledge of himself, he has given you wisdom and discretion to take measures that his pure truth may be preached. Praise be to God, you have not to learn what is the true faith of Christians, and the doctrine which they ought to hold, seeing that by your means the true purity of the faith has been restored. That is, that we hold God alone to be the sole Governor of our souls, that we hold his law to be the only rule and spiritual directory for our consciences, not serving him according to the foolish inventions of men. Also, that according to his nature he would be worshipped in spirit and in purity of heart. On the other hand, acknowledging that there is nothing but all wretchedness in ourselves, and that we are corrupt in all our feelings and affections, so that our souls are a very abyss of iniquity, utterly despairing of ourselves; and that, having exhausted every presumption of our own wisdom, or power of well-doing, we must have recourse to the fountain of every blessing, which is in Christ Jesus, accepting that which he confers on us, that is to say, the merit of his death and passion, that by this means we may be reconciled to God; that being washed in his blood, we may have no fear lest our spots prevent us from finding grace at the heavenly throne; that being assured that our sins are pardoned freely in virtue of his sacrifice, we may lean, yea rest, upon that for assurance of our salvation; that we may be

sanctified by his Spirit, and so consecrate ourselves to the obedience of the righteousness of God; that being strengthened by his grace, we may overcome Satan, the world, and the flesh; finally, that being members of his body, we may never doubt that God reckons us among the number of his children, and that we may confidently call upon him as *our* Father; that we may be careful to recognize and bear in mind this purpose in whatsoever is said or done in the Church, namely, that being separated from the world, we should rise to heaven with our Head and Saviour.

Recognizing the need for "preaching of a lively kind," and at the same time the necessity for the use, so long as there was a shortage of competent pastors, of approved written homilies by those who were ill equipped to preach, so that everywhere the people might be soundly instructed in biblical teaching, Calvin advocated the provision of "an explicit summary of the doctrine which all ought to preach" and a catechism or "common formula of instruction for little children and for ignorant persons, serving to make them familiar with sound doctrine, so that they may be able to discern the difference between it and the falsehood and corruptions which may be brought forward in opposition to it." Calvin expressed his conviction that "the Church of God will never preserve itself without a catechism, for it is like the seed to keep the good grain from dying out, and causing it to multiply from age to age." A catechism was in fact included in the first of the Edwardian prayer books, which was published during the following year (1549), and it continued to be a feature in every subsequent edition of the Book of Common Prayer.

Calvin's second proposal emphasized the importance of a total eradication of all unbiblical errors and distortions if a proper reform of the church was to be effectively achieved.

> Whatsoever mixtures men have brought in of their own devising have been just so many pollutions which turn us aside from the sanctified use of what God has bestowed for our salvation. Therefore, to lop off such abuses by halves will by no means restore things to a state of purity, for then we shall always have a dressed-up Christianity.

He "willingly acknowledged" that "we must observe moderation, and that overdoing is neither discreet nor useful," indeed, that forms of worship needed to be accommodated "to the condition and tastes of the people"; but always provided that satanic and antichristian corruptions were not admitted under that pretext.

> Wherefore [he urged] seeing that God has brought you so far, take order, I beseech you, that so without any exception he may approve you as a repairer of his temple, so that the times of the king your nephew may be compared to those of Josiah, and that you put all things in such condition, that he may only need to maintain the godly order which God shall have prepared for him by your means.

If only we remember that the reformation of His church is the work of God, we will wish to be guided in all things by Him rather than by our limited human understanding, lest we "bring that which is heavenly into subjection to what is earthly."

> I do not thus exclude the prudence which is so much needed [Calvin explained], to take all appropriate and right means, not falling into extremes either on the one side or upon the other, to gain over the whole world to God, if that were possible. But the wisdom of the Spirit, not that of the flesh, must overrule all; and having inquired at the mouth of the Lord, we must ask him to guide and lead us, rather than follow the bent of our own understanding.

Calvin's third proposal was a plea for the exercise of discipline, and especially for the curbing of indecency and blasphemy.

> The great and boundless licentiousness which I see everywhere throughout the world constrains me to beseech you that you would earnestly turn your attention to keeping men within the restraint of sound and wholesome discipline. That, above all, you would hold yourself charged, for the honour of God, to punish those crimes of which men have been in the habit of making no very great account. I speak of this because sometimes larcenies, assault, and extortions are more severely punished, because thereby men are wronged; whereas they will tolerate whoredom and adultery, drunkenness, and blaspheming of the name of God, as if these were things quite allowable, or at least of very small importance. . . . Scripture clearly points out to us that by reason of blasphemies a whole country is defiled. . . . When holy matrimony, which ought to be a lively image of the sacred union which we have with the Son of God, is polluted, and the covenant, which ought to stand more firm and indissoluble than any in this world, is disloyally rent asunder, if we do not lay to heart that sin against God, it is a token that our zeal for God is very low indeed. As for whoredom, it ought to be quite enough for us that St. Paul compares it to sacrilege, inasmuch as by its means the temples of God, which our bodies are, are profaned. Be it remembered also that whoremongers and drunkards are banished from the kingdom of God, on such terms that we are forbidden to converse with them, whence it clearly follows that they ought not to be endured in the Church.

The more tolerant and indulgent people are toward such excesses, the more certain is the judgment of God against them. Accordingly, Calvin appeals to Somerset in the following terms:

> Wherefore, to prevent his wrath, I entreat of you, Sir, to hold a tight rein, and to take order, that those who hear the doctrine of the Gospel approve their Christianity by a life of holiness. For as doctrine is the soul of the Church for quickening, so discipline and the correction of vices are like the nerves to sustain the body in a state of health and vigour. The duty of bishops and curates is to keep watch over that, to the end that the supper of the Lord may not be polluted by people of scandalous lives. But in the authority where God has set you the chief responsibility returns upon you, who have a special charge given you to set the others in motion, on purpose that every one

discharge himself of duty, and diligently look to it, that the order which shall have been established may be duly observed.

This letter displays very clearly the genuine concern of Calvin for the promotion of the evangelical cause in all countries and the wise and frank manner in which, without being immoderate or officious, he sought to encourage others who had set their hand to the reform of their church and nation. That his counsel to the Protector of England was not unappreciated is shown by the action of the Duchess of Somerset who sent him a ring as an expression of gratitude. Calvin, strangely enough, felt himself unfitted to convey his thanks directly to the Duchess, but did so by means of a letter, dated 17 June 1549, to her daughter, the Lady Anne Seymour, in the following terms:

As your mother, illustrious lady, lately presented me with a ring, as a token of her good will towards me, which I did not at all deserve, it would be exceedingly unbecoming in me not to show some sign of gratitude, by giving expression, at least, to my regard for her. But not being able to find language, again, in which to discharge this sort of duty, nothing seems fitter than that I should call you to my aid, noble lady, distinguished no less by your worth than by your descent. For as you will be, of all others, the most suitable negotiator with your mother, you will be glad to present this mark of respect to her, in virtue of your very great affection for her; and, particularly, as the address will not, or I am mistaken, be unpleasant to her. For I learn you have understood from her words that she is agreeably disposed towards me. Now, if my prayers be of any avail with you, I would particularly request of you not to take amiss the humble salutation offered, with all submission, by me to her, that she may, at least, understand that the gift of which I was held worthy was not bestowed upon one who knew not to be grateful.

Referring to Anne Seymour's own reputation for being well grounded in the doctrines of Christ, he exhorted her to persevere steadfastly in the course of the gospel. "Certainly," he continued,

among so many excellent gifts with which God has endowed and adorned you, this stands out unquestionably first, that he stretched out his hand to you in tender childhood, to lead you to his own Son, who is the author of eternal salvation and the fountain of all good. It becomes you to strive, with all the more zeal, to follow eagerly at his call. . . . May the Lord enrich you daily with his blessing, and may he be the constant guide of the whole course of your life.[7]

In the autumn of that year, the Duke of Somerset was imprisoned in the Tower of London, as I previously mentioned. It was after hearing that the Duke had been set at liberty that Calvin wrote to him again. The letter is undated but must have been written some time after 6 February 1550, the date of Somerset's release. In it Calvin expressed his joy that Somerset was once again a free man and his confidence that he would resume his labors for the establishment of Christ's gospel.

It is not I alone who rejoice at the good issue which God has given to your affliction, but all true believers who desire the advancement of the kingdom of our Lord Jesus Christ, forasmuch as they know the solicitude with which you have laboured for the re-establishing of the Gospel in all its purity in England, and that every kind of superstition might be abolished. And I do not doubt that you are prepared to persevere in the same course, in so far as you shall have the means.

Reminding him of the apostle Paul's admonition that "we have not to fight against flesh and blood, but against the hidden wiles of our spiritual enemy," Calvin appealed to him to concentrate his energies on the warfare with Satan and to show a spirit of forgiveness to his persecutors.

Wherefore let us not waste our energies upon men, but rather let us set ourselves against Satan to resist all his machinations against us, as there is no doubt whatever that he was the author of the evil which impended over you, in order that the course of the Gospel might thereby be hindered, and even that all should be brought to confusion. Therefore, Sir, forgetting and pardoning the faults of those whom you may conceive to have been your enemies, apply your whole mind to repel his malice who thus engaged them to their own destruction in setting themselves to seek your ruin. This magnanimity will not only be pleasing to God, but it will make you the more loved among men.

Whether or not he was influenced by this advice—which Calvin offered under the impulse of "the love I bear you and the care which I have for your honour and welfare"—Somerset behaved toward those who had harmed him in a manner that was both amiable and free from vindictiveness. Calvin exhorted him, further, to regard the sufferings he had endured as chastisement from the hand of a benevolent God intended for his blessing.

Your zeal to exalt the name of God, and to restore the purity of his Gospel, has been great. But you know, Sir, that in so great and worthy a cause, even when we have put forth all our strength, we come very far short of what is required. However, if God, in thus binding you to himself anew, has meant, in this way, to induce you to do better than ever, your duty is to strive to the uttermost and with all your energy, so that so holy a work as that which he has begun by you may be carried forward. I doubt not that you do so; but I am also confident that, knowing the affection which induces me to exhort you thereunto, you will receive all my solicitation with your wonted benignity. If the honour of God be thus esteemed by you above all else, he will assuredly watch over you and your whole household, to pour out his grace there more abundantly, and will make you know the value of his blessing. For that promise can never fail, "Those who honour me I will honour" [1 Sam. 2:30]. True it is that those who best do their duty are oftentimes troubled the most by many violent onsets. But this is quite enough for them, that God is at hand to succour and relieve them.

Calvin goes on to express his thankfulness because of the godliness of the young king, Edward VI, and his dedication to the task of promoting the evangelical faith throughout his kingdom.

> Now, although it is enough for you to look to God and to feel the assurance that your service is pleasing to him, nevertheless, Sir, it is a great comfort to you to see the king so well disposed that he prefers the restoration of the Church and of pure doctine to everything else, seeing it is a virtue greatly to be admired in him, and a peculiar blessing for the kingdom, that in a youth of such tender age the vanities of this world do not hinder the fear of God and true religion from ruling in his heart.[8]

On Whitsunday 1550 Martin Bucer, then at Cambridge, sent Calvin a letter in which, after describing the various hindrances to the progress of reform in England, he too spoke highly of the youthful monarch's zeal and perception in spiritual matters. Bucer pleaded:

> Redouble your prayers for the most serene king, who is making wonderful progress both in piety and learning. For you may easily perceive the danger in which he is placed, humanly speaking, when the papists are everywhere so furious, and when they see and know that the king is exerting all his power for the restoration of Christ's kingdom.

Bucer mentioned in particular the danger posed by the obdurate attachment to the papal religion of Edward's elder sister, Mary, who, as things turned out, all too soon would ascend the English throne and bring in a reign of terror for those who professed the Reformed faith.

That the king himself thought highly of Calvin and his labors is apparent from a letter dated 4 December of the same year (1550) written from London to Calvin by Francis Bourgoyne, who for a time had served as a minister in France. He told Calvin that

> our Josiah, the king of England, made most courteous inquiry of me concerning your health and ministry, to which when I had made such reply as in my judgment I considered worthy of you, he sufficiently declared both by his countenance and his words, that he takes a great interest in you and in everything belonging to you. Mention was incidentally made of the letter which you once sent to be delivered to his uncle, the then protector of the kingdom, and which he declared to have been exceedingly gratifying to him.

He urged on Calvin the advisability of sending the boy king "such a letter as would add spurs to a willing horse." "The king," he added, "supports and encourages pure religion and godly and learned men to the utmost of his power, and would effect much more if his age allowed him."[9]

No time was lost by Calvin in acting on this advice, for on Christmas Day, just three weeks later, he dedicated his commentary on Isaiah with a prefatory epistle addressed to "His Serene Highness, Edward the

Sixth, King of England, a truly Christian prince.'' The Reformer praised Edward for courageously taking his stand as a champion of the truth of the gospel and encouraged him to continue as he had begun.

> It may justly be regarded as no ordinary consolation [he wrote] amidst the present distresses of the Church that God has raised you up and endowed you with such excellent abilities and dispositions for defending the cause of godliness, and that you so diligently render that obedience to God in this matter which you know that he accepts and approves. For although the affairs of the kingdom are hitherto conducted by your counsellors, and although your Majesty's most illustrious uncle, the Duke of Somerset, and many others have religion so much at heart, that they labour diligently, as they ought to do, in establishing it; yet in your own exertions you go so far beyond them all as to make it very manifest that they receive no small excitement from the zeal which they observe in you. Not only are you celebrated for possessing a noble disposition and some seeds of virtues (which at so early an age is usually thought to be remarkable), but for a maturity of those virtues far beyond your years, which would be singularly admired, as well as praised, at a very advanced age. Your piety especially is so highly applauded that the prophet Isaiah, I am fully convinced, will have one that will regard him with as much reverence, now that he is dead, as Hezekiah did when he was alive.

Calvin instructed the king that ''when we repair the ruins of the Church we give our labours to the Lord, in obedience to his laws and injunctions'' and that ''yet the restoration of the Church is God's own work''; and he then continued:

> Nor is it without good reason that this is taught in every part of Scripture, and that it is so earnestly enforced by the prophet Isaiah. Remembering this doctrine, therefore, and relying on the assistance of God, let us not hesitate to undertake a work which is far beyond our own strength, and let no obstacle turn aside or discourage us, so as to abandon our undertaking. And here I expressly call upon you, most excellent King, or rather, God himself addresses you by the mouth of his servant Isaiah, charging you to proceed, to the utmost of your ability and power, in carrying forward the restoration of the Church, which has been so successfully begun in your kingdom.

He drew his attention to the fact that Isaiah calls kings ''the fostering fathers of the Church'' (Isa. 49:23) and also ''pronounces a woe on all kings and nations who refuse to give her their support,'' and then he urged him: ''You ought not to be turned aside from your purpose by any event, however calamitous.'' The letter concluded with this prayer:

> Farewell, most illustrious King! May the Lord prosper and preserve your Majesty for a long period, aid and guide you by his Holy Spirit, and bless you in all things! Amen.[10]

A month later, on 24 January 1551, Calvin followed up this missive by another dedicatory epistle, this time prefixed to his commentary on the Catholic Epistles. In it he gave vent to some severe strictures on the Council of Trent (whose sessions had commenced in 1545); but at the same time he expressed his willingness to attend a council, provided he and his fellow Reformers were not muzzled.

> Let them give us a council in which we shall be given free liberty to speak in defence of the cause of truth, and if we refuse to come to that and to give a reason for all that we have done, then they will justly charge us with contumacy. . . . They declare that it is not lawful to admit any one to their sittings except the anointed and the mitred. Then let them sit while we stand, provided we are heard declaring the truth.

After affirming his determination to devote himself as long as he had breath to the cause of scriptural and evangelical reform, Calvin ended his letter by addressing Edward in the following terms:

> To return to you, most illustrious King, you have here a small pledge, my Commentaries on the Catholic Epistles. . . . As interpreters of Scripture according to their ability supply weapons to fight against Antichrist, so you must also bear in mind that it is a duty which belongs to your Majesty, to vindicate from unworthy calumnies the true and genuine interpretation of Scripture, so that true religion may flourish. . . . Farewell, most noble King. May the Lord continue to preserve your Majesty in his faith as he has already begun, govern you and your counsellors with the Spirit of wisdom and fortitude, and keep your whole kingdom in safety and peace.[11]

The bearer of this letter, together with one for the Duke of Somerset, was Calvin's aristocratic colleague Nicolas Des Gallars, who later spent some time in England as pastor of the French church in London. The news he brought back from England of the favorable manner in which Calvin's communications were received at the royal court is described with elation by the Genevan Reformer in a letter addressed to Farel on 15 June 1551:

> Nicolas has at length returned from England, having been detained for eleven days by head winds, and afterwards tossed about by so severe a tempest that he scarcely escaped shipwreck. He reports that he was so kindly and affectionately received, that I have good reason to congratulate myself that my labour was spent to the best advantage. After having delivered my letter to the Duke of Somerset, and having said that he had another also for the King, the Duke himself undertook the duty of presenting it, and on the following day set out for the Court. If I am not deceived, the work not only greatly pleased the Royal Council, but also filled the King himself with extraordinary delight. The Archbishop of Canterbury informed me that I could do nothing more useful than to write to the King more frequently. This gave me more pleasure than if I had come to the possession of a great sum of money.

In a letter of 25 July in the same year to Somerset, Calvin declared his inability to thank the Duke sufficiently for the kindness with which he had received Des Gallars, for the trouble he had taken to present his commentaries in person to the king, and "for all the other proofs of the singular friendly affection which you have hitherto graciously shown me."[12]

It was at this time that Thomas Cranmer, Archbishop of Canterbury, who, as the extract from Calvin's letter to Farel given above indicates, had already communicated with Calvin encouraging his association with the English Reformation, was developing his grand scheme for the assembling of an ecumenical council of Reformed theologians. This council would not only be a counterblast to the Council of Trent then in process but also an occasion for resolving the controversy over eucharistic doctrine that was dividing the Lutherans from their fellow Evangelicals in Europe and England. In the spring of 1552 Cranmer sent off letters to the leading Continental Reformers proposing the calling of such an assembly. In his letter to Calvin, dated 20 March, he wrote as follows:

> As nothing tends more injuriously to the separation of the churches than heresies and disputes respecting the doctrines of religion, so nothing tends more effectually to unite the churches of God, and more powerfully to defend the fold of Christ, than the pure teaching of the Gospel and harmony of doctrine. Therefore I have often wished, and still continue to do so, that learned and godly men, who are eminent for erudition and judgment, might meet together in some place of safety, where by taking counsel together, and comparing their respective opinions, they might handle all the heads of ecclesiastical doctrine and hand down to posterity, under the weight of their authority, some work not only upon the subjects themselves but upon the forms of expressing them. Our adversaries are now holding their councils at Trent for the establishment of their errors; and shall we neglect to call together a godly synod, for the refutation of error and for restoring and propagating the truth? They are, as I am informed, making decrees respecting the worship of the host: therefore we ought to leave no stone unturned, not only that we may guard others against this idolatry, but also that we may ourselves come to an agreement upon the doctrine of this sacrament. It cannot escape your prudence, how exceedingly the Church of God has been injured by dissentions and varieties of opinion respecting this sacrament of unity; and though they are now in some measure removed, yet I could wish for an agreement in this doctrine, not only as regards the subject itself, but also with respect to the words and forms of expression.[13]

This letter shows that Cranmer's vision, like Calvin's, was not limited to one country or territory. Calvin's response to the Archbishop's proposal was enthusiastic:

> Most illustrious lord, you truly and wisely judge that in the present disturbed state of the Church no more suitable remedy can be adopted than the assembling together of godly and discreet men, well disciplined in the school of Christ, who shall openly profess their agreement in the doctrines of religion. . . . The Lord, indeed, as he has been wont to do from the beginning of

the world, is able wonderfully, and by means unknown to us, to preserve the truth from being rent in pieces by the dissensions of man. Nevertheless he would by no means have those persons inactive whom he himself has placed on the watch, since he has appointed them his ministers, by whose aid he may purify sound doctrine in the Church from all corruption, and transmit it entire to posterity. For yourself, most accomplished Archbishop, it is especially necessary, in proportion to your more exalted position, to bestow all your attention upon these matters, as you do. And I do not say this as though I considered it needful to spur you on afresh, who are not only outrunning us of your own free will, but are also of your own accord urgent in exhorting so happy and excellent a course of action.

Turning to the advance of the Reformation in England, Calvin continued in the following appreciative terms:

We hear indeed that the Gospel is making favourable progress in England. But I doubt not that you find it there also to be the case, what Paul experienced in his time, that when a door is opened to receive pure doctrine there forthwith arise many adversaries. But though I am aware of the number of champions you have at hand well qualified to confute the lies of Satan, yet such is the wickedness of those parties whose great business it is to create confusion, that the diligence of good men in this respect can never be deemed excessive or superfluous. I know, too, in the next place, that your care is not confined to England alone, but that you are at the same time regardful of the world at large. Then not only is to be admired the generous disposition of the most serene King, but also his rare piety in honouring with his favour the godly design of holding an assembly of this kind, and in offering a place of meeting within his realm. And I wish it could be effected, that grave and learned men from the principal churches might meet together at a place appointed, and, after diligent consideration of each article of faith, hand down to posterity a definite form of doctrine according to their united opinion. But this is also to be reckoned among the greatest evils of our time, that the churches are so estranged from each other that scarcely the common intercourse of society has place among them, much less that holy communion of the members of Christ, which all persons profess with their lips, though few sincerely honour it in their practice. . . .

The concluding section of this letter contains Calvin's celebrated declaration of his willingness to cross ten seas to attend such a congress:

As far as I am concerned, if I can be of any service, I shall not shrink from crossing ten seas, if need be, for that object. If the rendering of a helping hand to the kingdom of England were the only point at issue, that of itself would be a sufficient motive to me. But now, when the object sought after is an agreement of learned men, gravely considered and well framed according to the standard of Scripture, by which churches that would otherwise be far separated from each other may be made to unite, I do not consider it right for me to shrink from any labours or difficulties. . . . Farewell, most accomplished and sincerely revered Archbishop. May the Lord continue to guide you by his Spirit and give his blessing to your holy endeavours![14]

Further evidence of Calvin's deep interest in the advance of the Reformation in England is afforded by a letter dated 4 July dedicating yet another work to the English king (the third such in some two-and-a-half years). This was a small volume of four sermons on Psalm 87 that Calvin had written out with Edward VI particularly in mind. The letter is in effect a brief and friendly exhortation:

> You well know, Sire, what danger there is to kings and princes, lest the height to which they are elevated should dazzle their eyes and amuse them here below, causing them to forget the kingdom of heaven; and I doubt not but that God has warned you of this danger that he might preserve you from it, and that you will guard against it a hundred times better than those who experience it without being aware of it. Now in the Psalm before us is set forth the grandeur and dignity of the Church, which ought in such wise to draw over to itself both great and small, that all the riches and honours of the world cannot hold them back, nor keep them from aiming at this object, namely, to be enrolled among the people of God. It is a great thing to be a king, especially of such a country; yet I have no doubt but that you esteem it incomparably better to be a Christian. It is therefore an inestimable privilege that God has made you, Sire, a Christian king, to the end that you may act as his vicegerent in maintaining the kingdom of Jesus Christ in England. You see, then, that in acknowledging this especial benefit, which you have received from his infinite goodness, you ought to be very zealous in employing all your powers to his honour and service, affording an example to your subjects to do homage to this great King to whom your Majesty is not ashamed to subject yourself in all humility and reverence under the spiritual sceptre of his Gospel. . . . Sire, after having·most humbly commended myself to your grace, I implore our good God to fill you with the gifts of his Holy Spirit, to guide you in all wisdom and virtue, and to make you flourish and prosper to the glory of his name.[15]

Calvin perhaps did not fully appreciate the mammoth task that confronted the Reformers in England as they sought to reform the national church, which stretched far and wide throughout the whole land, compared with which (far-reaching though his concern and vision were) Calvin's operation in the city of Geneva and its environs was, despite the many problems and frustrations with which he had to contend, of a much more limited and therefore much more manageable nature. The handful of pastors required for the Genevan situation was nothing compared with the need for competent and responsible pastors in the many hundreds of parishes of the Church of England—a need that there was no hope of supplying except over a period of a number of years. The appointment of men like Peter Martyr and Martin Bucer as professors of divinity at the two English universities was designed by Cranmer to tackle this problem at its source, the training-ground itself of the future ministry. Meanwhile, though steps were taken to provide suitable pastors and to remove those who were unfit for their duties, the fact that the resources immediately available were meager meant that the situation could not be rapidly remedied. Calvin, as a letter from him to Cranmer in the middle of 1552 shows, was impatient to see more spectacular progress and actually charged the archbishop with dilatoriness. In fact, Cranmer and his colleagues were at this very time taking vigorous action for the advancement of reform. Calvin also deplored the way in which the revenues of the Church of England had been plundered; but this had taken place during the reign of Henry VIII, and Cranmer was in no way responsible for it, nor was there anything that he could do about it. The letter, however, is an expression of Calvin's profound solicitude for the promotion and establishment of the evangelical faith in as many countries as possible. "Difficulties so numerous and so trying as those against which you are contending," it concludes, "appear to me a sufficient excuse for the exhortations I have offered. Adieu, most distinguished and esteemed Archbishop. May the Lord long preserve you in safety; may he fill you more and more with the Spirit of wisdom and fortitude, and bless your labours! Amen."[16]

On 13 February 1553 Calvin wrote to Edward VI's preceptor, Sir John Cheke (the Duke of Somerset had been executed early in the preceding year), to inquire whether there was any way in which he could encourage the English king in the good course that he was following. He praised Cheke for the excellent instruction he had given the young monarch:

> This one reason is sufficient to win for you the favour of all good men, namely, that England has a king whom you have trained by your labour, not only possessing very superior talents, but also a maturity of moral excellence beyond his years, who is extending a hand to the suffering Church of God in these very sad times. . . . I have indeed particularly to request of you, whenever at any time you think that the most serene King could be cheered forward by my exhortations, to advise me thereon, and, according to circumstances, that you will not grudge me your opinion.[17]

The hopes of seeing the day of evangelical reform reach its high noon in England were dashed, temporarily at any rate, by the death of Edward on 6 July in that year (1553). So also were Cranmer's plans for convoking a congress of Reformed theologians. Numbers who were sympathetic to the Reformation found refuge on the Continent; but many who remained in England, including Archbishop Cranmer, suffered death by burning. Calvin, naturally, was deeply distressed at this turn of events. How far he may have sought to maintain some contact with the evangelical leaders who were under arrest and facing death and to inspirit them in their sufferings is difficult to say. We have a letter from him dated 13 November 1554 to Lord John Grey, who on 21 February of that year had been imprisoned in the Tower of London, and whose brother the Duke of Suffolk had been beheaded two days afterwards. Less than two weeks prior to his brother's death, his niece Lady Jane Grey had been executed. Lord John Grey had been released at the end of October. Calvin's letter is one of compassion and comfort:

> Though it cannot be, most noble sir, but that the misfortunes of your house, so distressing and deplored by all good men, must have inflicted a doubly severe wound upon yourself, and must even now occasion you the most lively sorrow, I am nevertheless assured that, as is befitting a Christian man, you have always stood firm and unmoved, and still continue to do so, under this excessive weight of trials. For though we sometimes perceive that godly minds, through the infirmity of the flesh, are grievously shaken even by lesser calamities, yet the faith that reposes upon Christ can never be entirely overthrown. Wherefore I have no doubt but that when you were carried away in that stormy tempest you had your anchor fixed in heaven, and that you bravely endured, and firmly sustained, the fury of those waves which might otherwise have overwhelmed you a hundred times. But something of more importance yet remains, that you should carry on the warfare of the cross even unto the end. . . . But though I congratulate the most illustrious duke your brother and your excellent niece, a lady whose example is worthy of everlasting remembrance, to both of whom it was given, even in death itself, to commit their triumphant souls into the hands and faithful keeping of God; yet in the midst of so many most distressing tidings it has always afforded me no common comfort to have heard that you have been snatched from the very jaws of death, and are still preserved to us in safety.

Calvin seems to have been unaware that Lord John Grey had suffered the loss of another brother, Lord Thomas Grey, also by execution (in April)—the executions were in consequence of the rebellion led by Sir Thomas Wyatt against Mary—and he seems also to have been prompted to put pen to paper in this instance by the desire to commend the two European Hebrew scholars Immanuel Tremellius and his son-in-law Anthony Chevalier, then in England and destitute of means, as worthy of his assistance.[18]

Sir John Cheke was one of those who escaped from England to the Continent and on 20 October 1555 he wrote to Calvin from Strasbourg concerning the tragic state of affairs under Mary in England:

> I pray that in this general confusion and overthrow the Lord may afford some aid and assistance to wretched England, wherein there are very many manifestations of his most heavy displeasure, and but very few of his goodness and mercy. For good men, and, what is yet more distressing, those who take the lead in learning and authority, by whose counsels and prudence many and important measures have been effected in the church, are not only brought in danger of their lives, but are actually under condemnation, and are daily expecting a death which, though desirable to themselves will yet be lamentable and disastrous to the church. These ought by their example and constancy not only to give encouragement to those of the present age, but to afford an eminent example to future generations. Among whom, Cranmer, Ridley, and

> Latimer, the bishops of Canterbury, London, and formerly of Worcester, having firmly and boldly persevered in the Christian doctrine they had embraced, and not allowing themselves to be led away from it by the terror of punishment, death, and the flames, are now condemned and degraded, as they call it; and are either, I understand, already burned, or are shortly to experience the power of the flames and the cruelty of their tyrants.

Ridley and Latimer had, in fact, been burned at Oxford four days prior to the writing of this letter. Cranmer's martyrdom took place on 21 March of the following year. Cheke affirmed his conviction that, whatever might be God's purpose in permitting "this slaughter of godly men," he would "effect it in such a way as that all things might tend to the good of his elect, whose support and protection he undertakes."[19]

The death of Mary in November 1558 and the accession of her sister Elizabeth meant the restoration of the Protestant faith in England. Calvin, whose writings together with those of other Reformed theologians had been placed under official prohibition during Mary's reign, lost little time in trying to exert his influence as a new day of evangelical opportunity dawned for the people of England. On 15 January, the date of Elizabeth's coronation, he sent her (as he had previously sent to Edward VI) a copy of his commentary on Isaiah, now completely revised, together with a letter dedicating the work to her. He explained the reason for this double dedication as follows:

> Although in making improvements in this commentary I have bestowed so much care and industry, most noble Queen, that it ought justly to be reckoned a new work, yet, as in the first edition it was dedicated to your brother King Edward, who, though a youth, greatly excelled the men of his age, and whom I wish to be held in remembrance by posterity, as he deserves, I had intended to make no change in that dedication. But since, amidst that wretched and lamentable dispersion of the Church and oppression of pure doctrine, which raged with prodigious violence for a short period, this book, together with the whole doctrine of true godliness, was banished from England for a time, but now, I trust, favoured by your happy reign, will be restored to its former privileges, I thought that there would be no impropriety if to the name of a most excellent king I should join your own name, which is regarded by all good men with not less esteem and satisfaction. Not only was an opportunity offered, but necessity appeared to demand, that I should obtain your full protection to this commentary, the banishment of which, I am aware, was beheld by a great number of your godly subjects with deep sorrow.

He took care to point out that his concern was not just for his own work but for the work of all worthy authors and for the advancement of biblical teaching under her patronage.

> Yet it is not so much my object to be favoured with your countenance in my personal labours as humbly to entreat, and by the sacred name of Christ to implore, not only that, through your kindness, all orthodox books may again

be welcomed and freely circulated in England, but that your chief care may be to promote religion, which has fallen into shameful neglect.

Reminding her of the remarkable manner in which God had brought her safely through the storms of the Marian period, he urged her to recognize that this was done

> for the express purpose that you should, with invincible determination and unshaken firmness of mind, acknowledge your obligation to your Protector and Redeemer, and, laying aside all other kinds of business, a vast number of which, I have no doubt, will crowd upon you at the commencement of your reign, labour to have his worship, which for a time was basely and disgracefully corrupted in that kingdom, restored to its former splendour.

Calvin exhorted her both to "cherish the flock which not long ago lay trembling and concealed" and to "gather the exiles who chose rather to part with the advantages of their native country than to remain in it so long as godliness was banished from it."

> This will be the crowning proof of your gratitude to God, and a sacrifice of most delightful savour, that the faithful worshippers of God, who, on account of their profession of the Gospel, were constrained to wander far and wide through distant countries, shall now, through your kindness, be restored to their native country. We, too, in whom that mournful spectacle awakened, as it ought to have done, the most poignant grief, have abundant cause for rejoicing, and for congratulating you, when, through the gracious exercise of your royal will, we see the way opened for the return of our brethren, not only to be at liberty to worship God in your Majesty's dominions, but to render assistance to others.[20]

Two weeks later, on 29 January 1559, Calvin took the step of writing to William Cecil (Lord Burleigh), whom Elizabeth had appointed her secretary of state—a post he had held also under Edward VI. Calvin had apparently been encouraged to initiate this correspondence by "some pious individuals" who had spoken highly of Cecil as a man of integrity, a promoter of the Reformed faith, and influential with the Queen. The English nobleman was urged by the Genevan Reformer not to be deterred by any "vexatious difficulties, struggles, or terrors" that might lie in his way:

> I doubt not indeed but obstacles are every now and then occurring, or that even dangers openly menace you, which would damp the resolution of the most courageous, did not God sustain them by the marvellous efficacy of his Spirit. But this is a cause above all others for the defence of which we are not permitted to shrink from any kind of labour. As long as the children of God were exposed to open and avowed slaughter, you yourself held your place along with the others. Now at last, when by the recent and unlooked-for blessing of God greater liberty has been restored to them, it behoves you to take heart, so that if hitherto you have been timid, you may now make up for your deficiency by the ardour of your zeal. Not that I am ignorant how much

mischief is sometimes produced by undue precipitation, and how many persons retard, by an inconsiderate and headlong zeal, what they strive to drag all at once to an issue. But on the other hand you are bound gravely to ponder that we are doing God's work when we assert the uncorrupted truth of his Gospel and all-holiness, and that so it should not be set about with slackness. From your position you can better ascertain how much of progress it will be expedient to make, and where it may be fitting to adopt a prudent moderation; still, however, remember that all delay, coloured by whatever specious pretexts, ought to be regarded by you with suspicion.

Calvin expressed his awareness of the danger of popular tumult being stirred up by ill-disposed noblemen; but his desire was that the Queen, to whom he had himself written, should pursue her course without deviation.

Nevertheless as her most excellent Majesty the Queen has been raised to the throne in a wonderful manner by the hand of God, she cannot otherwise testify her gratitude than by a prompt alacrity in shaking off all obstacles and overcoming by her magnanimity all impediments. But since it is scarcely possible that in so disturbed and confused a state of affairs she should not, in the beginning of her reign, be distracted, held in suspense by perplexities, and often forced to hold a vacillating course, I have taken the liberty of advising her that having once entered upon the right path she should unflinchingly persevere therein. Whether I have acted prudently in so doing, let others judge. If by your co-operation my admonitions shall bring forth fruit, I shall not repent of my advice.

This further admonition was then offered to Cecil:

And do you also, most illustrious sir, continually keep in mind that you have been exalted by Providence to the rank of dignity and favour which you now occupy, in order that you should give yourself entirely up to this task and strain every nerve for the promotion of this great work.[21]

It was a disappointment to Calvin to learn that the English Queen had received his communication with coldness and that Cecil had spoken of him without enthusiasm. With Elizabeth as an active protagonist of the Reformation not only would the prospects be bright for England but also the cause on the Continent would be greatly strengthened. With his statesmanlike perception Calvin was fully conscious of the issues that were at stake. Yet this measure of English disfavor was the consequence of the offense that had been occasioned by the appearance of John Knox's work entitled *The First Blast of the Trumpet against the Monstrous Regiment and Empire of Women* and Christopher Goodman's treatise on *The Obedience of Subjects* (both actually published during the latter part of Mary's reign). The fact that the provenance of these writings was from Geneva rebounded unfavorably upon Calvin, since it was assumed that they had his approval. Calvin hastened to explain that he had been in no way privy to their preparation, addressing himself to

William Cecil in a letter that is undated but which probably was written in the early spring of 1559.

> The messenger to whom I gave in charge my commentaries upon Isaiah to be presented to the most serene Queen brought me word that my homage was not kindly received by her Majesty, because she had been offended with me by reason of some writings published in this place. He also repeated to me, most illustrious sir, the substance of a conversation held by you, in which you seem to me more severe than was consistent with your courtesy, especially when you had been already assured by my letter how much I promised myself from your regard towards me. But though sufficient reasons prevent me from vindicating myself by a serious discussion, yet lest I should seem by my silence to confess in some measure the consciousness of having done wrong, I have thought it right to state, in few words, how the matter stands. Two years ago John Knox asked of me, in a private conversation, what I thought about the government of women. I candidly replied that, as it was a deviation from the original and proper order of nature, it was to be ranked, no less than slavery, among the punishments consequent upon the fall of man; but that there were occasionally women so endowed, that the singular good qualities which shone forth in them made it evident that they were raised up by divine authority; either that God designed by such examples to condemn the inactivity of men, or for the better setting forth of his own glory.

Calvin adduced the scriptural examples of Huldah and Deborah and also Isaiah's prophecy (49:23) that queens would be nursing mothers of the church. (He had cited these examples in his dedicatory epistle to Elizabeth.) Consequently, he entertained no subversive feelings toward Elizabeth, or any other ruler for that matter; moreover, he had been unaware of the existence of Knox's book until a year after its publication.

> I came at length to this conclusion, that since both by custom and public consent and long practice it has been established that realms and principalities may descend to females by hereditary right, it did not appear to me necessary to move the question, not only because the thing would be invidious, but because in my opinion it would not be lawful to unsettle governments which are ordained by the peculiar providence of God. I had no suspicion of the book, and for a whole year was ignorant of its publication. When I was informed of it by certain parties, I sufficiently showed my displeasure that such paradoxes should be published; but as the remedy was too late, I thought that the evil which could not now be corrected should rather be buried in oblivion than made a matter of agitation.

Although displeased to have been the victim of unjust accusations, Calvin assured Cecil of his respect and good will both toward him and toward the Queen:

> I am indeed exceedingly and undeservedly grieved, in proportion to my surprise, that the ravings of others, as if on a studied pretext, should be charged upon me, to prevent my book from being accepted. If the offered

present were not acceptable to the Queen, she might have rejected it by a single word, and it would have been more candid to have done so. This certainly would have been more agreeable to myself than to be burdened with false accusations, in addition to the ignominy of a repulse. However, I shall always reverence both the most serene Queen and shall not cease, most illustrious sir, to love and respect yourself also, for your most excellent disposition and your other virtues, although I had found you less friendly to me than I had hoped, and though you say nothing about mutual good will for the time to come. From this, however, I am unwilling to draw any unfavourable conclusion.[22]

This letter reveals a surprisingly nettled and touchy Calvin. Cecil, for his part, responded reassuringly in a letter of 22 June, saying that he was convinced that writings of that kind were displeasing to Calvin, and concluding his communication with ''Yours most affectionately and with the warmest zeal for the evangelical profession.'' But Calvin did not succeed in gaining the attention of Elizabeth as he had that of Edward. By nature independent and circumspect, the queen preferred to pursue her own course and to heed (when she did so) English rather than foreign voices. At the same time, however, Calvin was held in the greatest veneration by the ecclesiastical leaders of the Elizabethan period and in all essentials there was harmony between their theology and his. This is well illustrated by the amicable exchange of correspondence between the Bishop of London, Edmund Grindal (who had found refuge on the Continent during Mary's reign and who subsequently became in turn Archbishop of York and Archbishop of Canterbury) and Calvin in 1560. Grindal had written urging Calvin to send an able pastor to minister to the French congregation in London, which he wished to see securely established to the benefit of all. This was deeply appreciated by Calvin, as his letter sent to Grindal in May of that year shows:

Though you do not expect me to thank you for an office of piety performed by you for the Church of Christ, yet the case is different with regard to the protection you have deigned to afford to those of our countrymen who inhabit the principal city of your diocese. By your cares, they have had permission, through the indulgence of the Queen, not only to invoke God in purity but also to send over to us a demand for a faithful pastor. . . . And since you have not hesitated of your own free impulse to ask and entreat me to see that a fitting pastor should be selected for my countrymen, I have no need to recommend to your fidelity and protection the persons for whose salvation you are so solicitous. And assuredly as, in assisting them so liberally up to this moment, you have given a rare and singular proof of your pious zeal, so now you will of your constancy in continuing your good offices to the end.

The man selected for this position was Calvin's own well-trusted and loved lieutenant Nicolas Des Gallars. This selection in itself is adequate evidence of the importance attached by Calvin not only to the French church in London but also to his relationships with the Church of England and its leaders. Calvin took the opportunity also to encourage Grindal to strive to exercise his spiritual authority bestowed on him by God with the assistance, but without interference, of the Queen. (An astonishingly courageous letter relating to this very issue written by Grindal to Elizabeth when he was Archbishop of Canterbury would precipitate a crisis for him some years later on.) ''But,'' Calvin ended, ''as neither your wisdom stands in need of counsel nor your magnanimity of incitements, I shall only have recourse to prayers, and supplicate God, my most excellent and honoured sir, to govern you by his Spirit, sustain you by his power, and bless all your holy labours.''[23]

Des Gallars, who had been the carrier of this letter when proceeding to his new post, reported back to Calvin (on 30 June) regarding his meeting with Grindal, as follows:

I waited upon the bishop, by whom I was received very courteously. I presented to him, my father, your letter, which he read in my presence with an open and cheerful countenance, and forthwith briefly related to me its contents, expressing his thanks to you for having written to him in so friendly a manner, and also for reminding him of his duty. He then accosted the elders who had accompanied me to his residence, to some of whom my arrival was by no means agreeable, and exhorted them not to be ungrateful to God and you, since they had obtained more than they had dared to hope for; that they should follow my recommendations, and henceforth act in all circumstances by my advice, and show themselves friendly towards me, and admonish the whole church of their duty towards me. Then . . . he offered me his good offices, and that I might have familiar access to him as often as I wished.[24]

Two weeks previously, on 16 June 1560, Calvin had sent Des Gallars a letter that clearly displayed his attitude of esteem and confidence toward Grindal:

We have learned that certain persons of your congregation have made themselves busy in order to have the charge of superintendent, which was entrusted by the Queen and her council to the reverend father, the Bishop of London, transferred to another. If that is true, you must do your endeavour to check their importunate officiousness, for which there will be found no other motive than private cupidity. For the pretext which they bring forward, that it is uncertain what the character of his successor may turn out to be, is of no sort of importance to you, since the inspection over your churches has not been accorded to any Bishop of London whatsoever, but to this upright, faithful, and sincere protector of your liberty. Should any other equally fit be at your disposal, still, in my judgment, it would be better for you to make no change, because it is not advantageous for you to alienate from you the good will of the man who has embraced you with the warmest affection, who has undertaken to defend the repose of your church, whose activity and courage in procuring your tranquillity you have already experienced, and whose authority in a word, is more than ever necessary to you.[25]

In a letter to the Earl of Bedford (undated, but written at about the same time) Calvin expressed his concern lest Elizabeth should continue unmarried and thus, without heir, open the way for turmoil in church and state once she was removed from the scene:

> It is a matter of regret that your Queen does not consult the good of posterity, and give her mind to raise up a race of children to succeed her. For what will take place, think you, should she die without leaving any offspring? But transported by my anxiety and my love of country, I overstep the bounds which I had prescribed to myself. I could not, however, refrain from making a tacit allusion to the solicitude of those who wish a continual duration of good fortune to your nation. In the meantime, most illustrious sir, I rejoice that you are unwearied in your holy zeal for piety, and advancing the progress of the Church, and I pray God from the heart to preserve you more and more, enrich you with his gifts, and shield you with his protection.[26]

Finally, the affection of Grindal for Calvin and his anxiety lest the latter, through inattention to his health, should cause the church to be deprived of one whom it could ill afford to be without are movingly attested in a letter from London to Geneva dated 19 June 1563 (the year before Calvin's death):

> I grieve from my heart that at your age, and with so slender a frame, you have been attacked, as Des Gallars informs me, with a fit of the gout. I have no doubt but that you have contracted this disorder by excessive study and exertion. Henceforth, therefore, you must relax somewhat of your former labours and unseasonable lucubrations, lest, by not sparing yourself, you greatly increase your disease and become of less benefit to the Church. Think of [Gregory] Nazianzen, who, because he did not, when in advanced years, relax at all from that austerity which he practised in early life, was almost constantly obliged to keep his bed, and on that account was rendered less useful to the Church. As you and Bullinger are almost the only chief pillars remaining, we desire to enjoy you both . . . as long as possible.[27]

We see, then, that Calvin viewed the English Reformation with approval, sympathy, and understanding, impatient though he was at times that matters seemed to be moving more slowly than he would wish. He had a clear recognition that the success of the gospel in England, desirable as it was in itself, would not fail to help forward the success of the gospel on the Continent, and he was ever ready to help in the promotion of the evangelical cause in any way open to him. His influence, moreover, did not cease with his death, for through his writings he continued to instruct and inspirit the evangelical leaders of the Church of England as they applied themselves to the advancement of the cause of establishing biblical faith and worship throughout their country. Still today, more than four hundred years after Calvin's death, the attentive study of his *Institutes of the Christian Religion* can result only in immense benefit to those who are concerned for the progress of sound Christianity.

# The Puritan Modification of Calvin's Theology

## R. T. Kendall

*R. T. Kendall is the Minister of Westminster Chapel, London. He holds degrees from Trevecca Nazarene College (A.B.), Southern Baptist Theological Seminary (M.Div.), University of Louisville (M.A.), and Oxford University (D.Phil.). He is a native of Ashland, Kentucky, and is the first American to become the Minister of Westminster Chapel. He has served in the pastoral ministry in Florida and Indiana. Dr. Kendall is the author of* Calvin and English Calvinism to 1649 *(Oxford University Press),* Jonah: an Exposition *(Zondervan), and* Believing God *(Zondervan). He is editor of the monthly* Westminster Record. *He is a member of the Oxford and Cambridge Club.*

# 9

# The Puritan Modification of Calvin's Theology

One of the easiest things for an admirer of Calvin to do is to overestimate his direct influence in and upon England. While it is certainly possible to err by underestimating his influence, much that leads to the exaggeration of his influence is owing to the popular assumption that "Calvinism" is also Calvin. The term *Calvinism* to this day is largely used interchangeably with much predestinarian theology, and for this reason there is a temptation to superimpose the label of Calvinism on any English thinker, whether pre-Elizabethan or post-Elizabethan, if he believes in the doctrine of unconditional predestination. The truth is that the predestinarian theology that is embedded in English theology in the sixteenth century preceded Calvin's influence by a good number of years. When William Tyndale (1536) translated and plagiarized much of Luther's famous preface to the latter's commentary on the Epistle to the Romans, Calvin was but sixteen years old. Furthermore, Continental Reformers such as Peter Martyr (d. 1562), Martin Bucer (1491– 1551), and Henry Bullinger (1504–75) were making an incalculable impact on Englishmen such as Thomas Cranmer (1489–1556), John Bradford (1510–55), and John Hooper (d. 1555). All these men may be called predestinarian in their theology.

To put it another way, before Mary Tudor ("Bloody Mary") acceded to the throne in 1553, the name of Calvin, though known in England, was not revered nearly as much as those of Martyr, Bucer, or Bullinger. When Calvin wrote to Archbishop Cranmer in 1552 that he would "not be afraid to cross ten seas"[1] to help heal the bleeding wounds of the body of Christ, he no doubt endeared himself to the English brethren in a special way, but he was less influential than the others. In any case, Calvin's influence during this period was probably more eucharistic than predestinarian. While John Hooper claimed that Calvin's treatment of the Lord's Supper "displeased me exceedingly,"[2] the views of Cranmer and Nicholas Ridley (1500–55) were so much like Calvin's that it is hard to believe this likeness was simply coincidental.

During the reign of Mary Tudor (1553–58) about 800 people fled to the Continent,[3] about one-third of them going to Geneva. No fewer than 233 were members of the English church in Geneva, led by John Knox (c. 1514–72) and Christopher Goodman (fl. 1560).[4] In his funeral eulogy for Queen Mary in November 1558, John White, Bishop of Winchester, made this prediction: "I warn you, the wolves [will] be coming out of Geneva, and other places . . . full of pestilent doctrines, blasphemy, and heresy, to infect the people."[5]

These "wolves" did indeed return to England, bringing with them the Geneva Bible, a taste of Genevan reform, and a stronger biblical theology that they had learned within the shadow of John Calvin. How much they were directly influenced by Calvin in Geneva cannot be known. These exiles would have had to understand French if they heard Calvin preach in St. Peter's and would have needed a fluency in Latin if they heard him lecture to theological students. But the reformed atmosphere generally in Geneva during those days did not need translation. And such an atmosphere "spoiled" many of them so that they were determined to try to reproduce it in England once they began returning to their homeland in 1559. There is no doubt that the returning exiles paved the way for Calvin's deepening influence on the Church of England. John Foxe's *Acts and Monuments (Book of Martyrs)* kept alive the memory of the horrible persecutions that were suffered under Mary and thus further guaranteed that Roman Catholicism would not be revived in England. While the *via media* of Elizabeth I was hardly the kind of reform[6] these returning exiles and not a few others wanted, one may suspect that their influence restrained the nominally Protestant queen from leaning toward Roman practices more than she did. However, to the dismay of many, Elizabeth did not reform the church; she merely "swept the rubbish behind the door."[7] Those who objected to a church "but halfly reformed" were soon branded "puritans."[8]

The Geneva Bible (published in Geneva in 1560) became the family Bible of the English people, replacing the Great Bible (1540), always outselling the Bishop's Bible (1568), and, much later, outselling the Authorized Version (1611) for a generation.[9] The annotations of the Geneva Bible became the people's hermeneutic, for they learned "much of their biblical exegesis from these notes."[10] It was popular with the people but "distasteful to the Bishops."[11] The notes in the margins were read and accepted quite uncritically, much as some read the notes in the Scofield Reference Bible today. The Geneva Bible was the first English edition to introduce verse enumeration. It was dedicated to Queen Elizabeth, yet it never received royal or ecclesiastical authorization. Although Calvin himself had nothing directly to do with either the production or the annotations of the Geneva Bible, he must be credited for its existence and to a large extent its flavor. For there was no place but Geneva where such a Bible could have been produced.

Calvin's influence on England during the reign of Elizabeth, then, was strengthened by many of the returning exiles and made even more acceptable by the popularity of the Geneva Bible.

However, the attempts made toward reform during the reign of Elizabeth until around 1589 were preponderantly of an ecclesiological nature, not soteriological. The issues were largely confined to such matters as vestments, details of public worship, making the sign of the cross, the place of the eucharist in worship over against the place for preaching, and also church government. As for church government, certain men, such as Thomas Cartwright (1535–1603), pushed for a presbyterian form. That the influence of Geneva partly lay behind this ecclesiological emphasis is not to be denied, but to say that this emphasis perfectly mirrored Calvin's views or wishes is going too far. For one thing, the push for presbyterian ecclesiology in England was led by men who went beyond Calvin himself.

This matter of going beyond Calvin is actually what became known as Calvinism, at least in England. The one man more than any other who was the architectural mind for English Calvinism was Calvin's successor at Geneva, Theodore Beza (1519–1605). Beza perhaps would not have wanted his theology to be known as Calvinism, but his systematizing and logicalizing theology had the effect of perpetuating a phenomenon that bore Calvin's name but was hardly Calvin's purest thought.

Beza's theological effect was both ecclesiological and soteriological, going beyond Calvin in both realms. For example, the implicit presbyterianism in Calvin was made explicit and dogmatic by Beza. It was not uncommon for prominent nonpresbyterian churchmen to claim Calvin for support for the very stand they were taking. When John Whitgift (1530–1604), who became Archbishop of Canterbury in 1583, invoked the name of Calvin against those who pushed for a presbyterian ecclesiology, Cartwright merely replied that he did not believe something to be true merely because Calvin espoused it.[12]

However, it must be said that during the 1580s, when the presbyterians were making their assertion, there was no equating of Calvinism with any particular interpretation of ecclesiology. The term *Calvinism* came later and has been understood largely in terms of things soteriological, not with reference to the "classical" movement of that period. The point here is that Beza dogmatized the presbyterianism for which Calvin has gotten so much credit.

Why is this? The answer is that presbyterianism was popularly associated with Geneva, and the venerated Calvin remained the towering figure of that "holy city." Beza's subtle but definite alterations seemed not to matter to most people. Surely anyone so close to Calvin's side could not be much different from the master! And yet the intricacies of presbyterian polity were developed by Beza and mediated in England chiefly by Cartwright and Walter Travers (1548–1635). These two men sat at Beza's feet in 1571, and Cartwright himself taught in the Geneva Academy. Bishop Edwin Sandys (c. 1516–88) cited Cartwright as "the author of these novelties, and after Beza the first inventor."[13]

Calvin's name in the meantime became more and more appreciated in England. His writings particularly were well received. By 1600 no fewer than ninety of Calvin's works were published in England, including fifteen editions of the *Institutes of the Christian Religion*. The *Institutes* became standard theological reading for theological students at Oxford and Cambridge. The returning exiles sang the praises of Geneva, and the Geneva Bible sealed the name of Calvin in the hearts of many. Calvin's great reputation was becoming sufficiently trustworthy to let nearly anything coming out of Geneva receive almost uncritical acceptance in much of England. In a word, Calvin handed Beza to England on a silver platter.

And yet it must be said that Calvin's influence was both magnified and eclipsed by Theodore Beza. Beza's *Briefe and Pithie Summe of the Christian Faith* reached its sixth edition by 1589. *A Booke of Christian Questions and Answeares* went into five editions between 1572 and 1586. *A Briefe Declaration of the Chiefe Points of the Christian Religion Set Forth in a Table, The Treasvre of Trueth,* went into at least four editions by 1613. These three writings contain substantially all one needs to know about Beza's doctrine of salvation. One irony of this period is that perceptive men were able to disassociate Calvin from Beza's ecclesiology, but apparently not one from the Elizabethan reign came forward to make a similar observation with regard to Calvin and Beza's soteriology. Yet Beza went beyond Calvin in this as he did in the other. An even greater irony is that Beza's writings made the name of Calvin more popular than ever in England.

The explanation for this is quite simple: William Perkins (1558–1602). Perkins came up to Cambridge in 1577, enrolling as a pensioner at Christ's College. He received the B.A. in 1581, the M.A. in 1584, and was elected that year to a fellowship at Christ's College. Toward the end of 1584 he was appointed lecturer at the prestigious pulpit at Great St. Andrews. His sermons "were not so plain, but the piously learned did admire them; not so learned, but the plain did understand them." He "used to pronounce the word *Damn* with such an Emphasis, as left a dolefull Echo in his auditors ears a good while after."[14] Indeed, "the Scholar could heare no learneder, the Townsman no plainer Sermons."[15] Moreover, "all held Perkins for a prophet—I mean for a painful dispenser of God's will in his word."[16]

By the end of the sixteenth century Perkins had replaced both Calvin and Beza near the top of the English religious best-sellers. Some of these were already being translated into other languages. After his death, Perkins's works were printed in Switzerland, Germany, Holland, France, Bohemia, Ireland, and Hungary. In addition, there were translations in Spanish and Welsh published in London. Between 1600 and 1608 three one-volume editions of Perkins's collected works were issued. After 1608 the collected works constituted three folio volumes (totaling over twenty-five hundred pages), which reached eight printings by 1635, alongside repeated editions of other single treatises.

All of the treatises of Perkins are essentially soteriological in nature. Never once does he refer to elders, deacons, and church courts, which had been stressed by the proponents of presbyterianism. The reason for this seems to be that, as Elizabeth was effectively crushing the "classical" movement and other ecclesiological radicals by 1589, Perkins saw the handwriting on the wall. The ecclesiological enterprise went underground for the next several years. When it was to emerge later, the radical ecclesiologists were not merely Presbyterians and Separatists but also Independents. Both Separatists and Independents espoused a congregational type of church government, but the latter sought to make this work within the Church of England. In any case, Perkins stayed clear of things ecclesiological in his treatises and sermons.

In 1589 Perkins published his first major work, *A Treatise tending vnto a declaration whether a man be in the estate of damnation or in the estate of grace: and if he be in the first, how he may in time come out of it: if in the second, how he maie discerne it, and persevere in the same to the end.*[17] This treatise inaugurated a new era in English theology. *Whether a man* assumes a doctrine of faith, however refined or modified by his followers, which was given creedal sanction by the Westminster Assembly (1643–49).

Perkins's thesis was concerned with the nature of "saving" faith (which only God's elect have) as opposed to "temporary" faith (which the reprobate, or nonelect, may possess). The fundamental concern in the theology of Perkins centers on the question, How can one know he is elect and not reprobate? The doctrine of double predestination is an assumption in the writings of Perkins. Hence his doctrine of faith is developed in the context of the teaching that all men are eternally predestined to either election or reprobation, salvation or destruction, heaven or hell. In *Whether a man* Perkins begins with the unalterable decree of reprobation. Its comprehensive title is given as a warning to professing Christians to examine themselves lest they happen to possess but a temporary faith—a lofty position to which the reprobate, though doomed from the start, may attain. Perkins opens with "Certaine Propositions declaring how farre a man may goe in the profession of the Gospell, and yet be a wicked man and a Reprobate." Behind his reference to "how farre" a reprobate may go is his view that the nonelect may excel in the "certain fruites of the elect" and that this comes about by what he calls an "ineffectual calling."[18]

However, Perkins's treatment of the "ineffectual calling" was not given much detail until his *Magnum opus* appeared the following year: *Armilla Aurea,* which was translated as *A Golden Chaine* in 1591. All that Perkins had espoused in *Whether a man* was given detailed and systematic treatment in *A Golden Chaine,* which with its Latin original reached no fewer than seventeen editions by 1614 (apart from its inclusion in his *Workes*). It is on the title page of *A Golden Chaine* that Perkins discloses his indebtedness to Theodore Beza:

## A GOLDEN CHAINE:

or,

The Description of Theologie:

Containing the order of the causes of Salvation and Damnation, according to Gods word. A view whereof is to be seene in the Table annexed

Hereunto is adioyned the order which M. Theodore Beza used in comforting afflicted consciences.

The "Table annexed" is indeed "the order which M. Theodore Beza used." For Perkins embellished Beza's chart, which was a visual aid in the latter's *Briefe Declaration . . . Set Forth in a Table.* This "table," or chart, makes central a supralapsarian doctrine of predestination; indeed, the doctrine of double predestination is the most obvious feature of this fascinating chart and is the predominant theme of *A Golden Chaine.* Perkins's contribution to Beza's chart was merely making it more attractive and (possibly) more understandable.

Beza's chart contrasted (1) God's love for His elect with His hatred for the reprobate, (2) an effectual calling of the elect vis-à-vis an ineffectual calling of the nonelect, (3) a softening of the heart of the elect over against the hardening of the heart of the reprobate, (4) faith as opposed to ignorance, (5) justification and sanctification versus unrighteousness and pollution, and (6) the glorification of the elect as compared with the just damnation of the reprobate.[19]

Perkins's entire theological system is built on Beza's chart—the "golden chaine" of Romans 8:30. *Whether a man* begins with the assumption that the ineffectual calling of the nonelect is so powerful that the subject manifests all the appearances—to himself and others—of the elect: such as zeal, good works, and sanctification. The pastoral implications of this teaching are enormous. A sincere Christian could well fear he was but reprobate.

This doctrine, however, began not with Perkins or Beza but with John Calvin himself. But it is at this point one may see the subtleties between Calvin and Beza. Calvin pointed men to Christ alone if they doubted their election, whereas Beza pointed men to their sanctification. Perkins followed Beza's solution and also Beza's use of 2 Peter 1:10—"Give diligence to make your calling and election sure: for if ye do these things, ye shall never fall" (KJV). Beza and Perkins saw this verse as the formula by which people may prove to themselves that they have been the object of an *effectual* calling. Second Peter 1:10 became the biblical banner for English Calvinism. Perkins and his followers centered the assurance that is to be derived from this verse on the *conscience*. It is here one may quickly see the difference between Calvin and the Beza-Perkins tradition.

One may readily see the dilemma posed by trying to solve the problem of whether or not one is elected by examining his sanctification. If people may attain to sanctification by virtue of an *ineffectual* calling, how may they be sure that the sanctification they see in themselves comes from an *effectual* calling?

Calvin knew about this unsatisfactory way of dealing with the matter of assurance. And yet this basic reason for avoiding this way of handling 2 Peter 1:10 was not merely because of the obvious pitfall of continued anxiety. He pointed people to Christ for the same reason Beza could not do so: the matter of the "extent" of the atonement. Calvin pointed them directly to Christ because Christ died indiscriminately for all people. Beza could not point people directly to Christ because Christ did not die for all; Christ died only for the elect. If one is told that his only hope of being saved is that he is one of those for whom Christ died, there is the possibility that one would be trusting in Christ who did not die for him. Beza took the decree of election out of eternity and attached it to Jesus' death on the cross. In other words, the number of the elect and the number for whom Christ died are one and the same. One could get no more satisfaction from looking to Christ than he could in looking to the eternal decrees of God.

Beza knew this and worked out his theology with this in mind. He came up with this solution: we look inside ourselves. We cannot ascend to God's eternal counsel but we can see whether He is at work in us.

> Nowe when Sathan putteth us in doubte of our election, we maye not searche first the resolution in the eternall counsell of god whose majesty we cannot comprehende, but on the contrarye we must *beginne* at the sanctification which we feele in our selves . . . forasmuch as our sanctification from whence proceedeth good works, is a certaine effect of the effect or rather of Jesus Christ dwelling in us by faith (italics mine).[20]

The difference between Calvin and Beza on this is that Calvin made the object of faith and the ground of assurance the same thing (Christ's death), but Beza made a separation between the object of faith (Christ's death) and the ground of assurance (sanctification). For Beza one could not know he could look assuredly to Christ until he had sufficient assurance from his sanctification. But Calvin affirmed, "If Pighius asks how I know I am elect, I answer that Christ is more than a thousand testimonies to me."[21] Calvin could say this because of his conviction that Christ died for all.[22]

There was one more difference between Calvin and Beza that will bear our attention. Beza raised a question that Calvin regarded as speculative, namely, the order of decrees. Taking his cue from Romans 9 generally and Paul's discussion of the "lump" particularly,[23] Beza devised a system that later became known as supralapsarianism, a term that apparently emerged near the time of the Synod of Dort (1618–19). He raised the question whether the term *lump* means "the created and corrupted mankinde, whereout of God ordineth [*sic*] some to honour and some to dishonour" and concluded:

> There is no doute but God taketh both ye sorts out of the same lump, ordeining them to contrary endes. Yet too I say and playnely avouth, that Paule in the same similitude, mounteth up to the said soverain ordinance whereunto even the very creation of mankinde is submitted in order of causes, and therefore much less dooth the Apostle put the foreseene corruption of mankinde before it. For firste by the term Lump *(massae)*, there is manyfestly betokened a substance as yet unshapen *(materia adhuc rudis)*, and onely prepared to woorke uppon afterwarde. Againe in likening God to a Potter, and mankinde to a lumpe of clay whereof vessels are to bee made afterworde, out of all doubte the Apostle betokeneth the first creation of men. Furthermore hee should speake unproperly, to say, that vessels of wrath are made of that lumpe. For if that lump betokened men corrupted: then were they vessels of dishonour already, and the potter shoulde not bee saide to make them, other than such as they had them selves already.[24]

The nearest Calvin would come to this question was to say that men are chosen from a "corrupt mass."[25] But he said no more, neither did he explain how he arrived at this. Beza, on the other hand, claimed that both elect and reprobate are predestined from a mass "yet unshapen."

Supralapsarianism, then, is the position that the decrees of election and reprobation have chronological priority over the decree of both Creation and the Fall; predestination thus refers to the destinies of people not yet created, much less fallen.

It is at this stage that we may see more clearly why Beza's teaching became known as Calvinism. Not only had Perkins incorporated Beza's supralapsarianism into *A Golden Chaine,* but when he wrote *De Praedestinationis Modo et Ordine,*[26] he worked out this supralapsarianism in even more detail. Not only that; Perkins called it "the Calvinists doctrine."[27]

The fact that Perkins would call his system "the Calvinists doctrine" suggests (1) that he thinks his and Beza's views are those of Calvin and (2) that he has not read Calvin thoroughly or critically. Indeed, when Perkins quotes Calvin, it is always with approval; and he gives no hint that he sees any difference between Calvin and Beza or himself and Calvin. He freely admits to following Beza's scheme and he gives every reason for his readers to assume that both he and Beza are continuing the teaching of Calvin himself.

Perkins did not follow Beza only, however. There was a group of divines from Heidelberg whom Perkins also leaned on. The chief of these was Zacharias Ursinus (1534–83). In 1563 Ursinus and Kaspar Olevianus (1536–87) drew up the famous Heidelberg Catechism. Ursinus wrote a commentary on this catechism that was widely read in England, namely *The Summe of Christian Religion.*[28]

The theology contained in *The Summe* gave rise to what is now known as federal theology. This was a motif known as the covenant of works and the covenant of grace, although it emerged as "covenant of works" and "covenant of faith" in *The Summe.*[29] Ursinus presented this as an assumption, not an innovation. How widely this view was held is not known. It was not in Calvin; but it did cohere consistently with the thinking of Beza. In any case, Perkins borrowed this motif and it became an assumption in English Calvinism from Perkins onward.[30]

But there was one other expression Perkins may have borrowed from Ursinus: the "practical syllogism."[31] Ursinus centered faith in a "good conscience"[32] and claimed that the conscience is "nothing else" but "a Practicall Syllogisme" in the mind.[33] Perkins accepted this way of thinking and built his entire doctrine of faith on it, for it coalesced perfectly with Beza's scheme. Perkins used the practical syllogism in two ways: (1) to draw a conclusion from the fact of one's having believed and (2) to reflect on the appearances of sanctification in oneself and draw a conclusion. Perkins could state the hypothesis: "Every one that believes is the child of God." The test is: "But I doe beleeve." The conclusion follows: "Therefore I am the child of God."[34] Or he could state it this way:

> He that beleeves and repents, is Gods child.
> Thus saith the Gospell:
> But I beleeve in Christ and repent: at the least
>   I subject my will to the commaundment which
>   bids me repent & beleeve: I detest my
>   unbeleefe, & al my sinnes: and desire
>   the Lord to increase my faith.
> Therefore I am the child of God.[35]

In other words, the practical syllogism became the ground of assurance. Perkins did not point people to Christ but to this reflection of oneself. This later became known as the reflex act. It was an enterprise in subjectivism and introspection. Never did Perkins direct people to Christ before they satisfied the demands of the practical syllogism first. Perkins even equated the practical syllogism with the witness of the Spirit. But "if the testimonie of Gods spirit be not so powerful in the elect," then one looks for his assurance of election "by that other effect of the holy Ghost: namely, Sanctification."[36]

Perkins lists these "effects" of sanctification: (1) feeling bitterness of heart when we have offended God by sin, (2) striving against the flesh, (3) desiring God's grace earnestly, (4) considering that God's grace is a most precious jewel, (5) loving the ministers of God's Word, (6) calling upon God earnestly and with tears, (7) desiring Christ's second coming, (8) avoiding all occasions of sin, and (9) persevering in these effects "to the last gaspe of life." And yet if these effects are but "very feeble," we should not be dismayed; it means that God is testing us. For the absence of these effects does not mean that we are nonelect. For God "doeth oftentimes prefer those which did seeme to be most of all estranged from his favour."[37]

This emphasis on Christian piety may well be regarded as the consequence of Calvin's emphasis. For godly living, not at all unlike these "effects," is no less in Calvin—but with this critical difference: Calvin looked at these effects as flowing from assurance, not producing assurance. For "when the Christian looks at himself he can only have grounds for anxiety, indeed despair."[38] We should not seek assurance by "conjecture," for faith corresponds "to a simple and free promise"; hence "no place for doubting is left."[39] Therefore, to Calvin, faith itself is assuring because it looks to the free promise; Calvin knew nothing of a distinction between faith and assurance. It is faith, or assurance, that *produces* the sanctification that is to characterize God's elect. But never are they to look to their sanctification first. To the degree that our obedience *confirms* our adoption, "experimental knowledge" may give "subsidiary aid" to its "confirmation."[40] But such fruits can give comfort only a posteriori.[41] Love, then, may serve as an inferior aid, and a "prop to our faith."[42] But even in the context of this statement Calvin hastens to add that none should conclude from this that "we must look to our works for our assurance to be firm."[43]

Behind these assertions of Calvin lies his conviction that the seat of faith is the heart.[44] By "heart" he means the mind, not the will. The will is "effaced" in conversion.[45] By faith one is "convinced by a firm conviction,"[46] and such a conviction lies in a fully persuaded mind. The "heart" often means "the mind itself," says Calvin, "which is the intellectual faculty of the soul."[47]

It is at this stage that we may see how Perkins thought he was truly following Calvin. For Perkins insisted that the "seate of faith" is in the "mind of man, not the will." He thought this was true because faith "stands in a particular knowledge or persuasion, and there is no persuasion but in the mind."[48] But Perkins ought to have said that it is assurance, certainly not faith, that is seated in the mind. For he defines faith as "apprehending and applying Christ" to oneself.[49] It is the "applying" of Christ that precedes assurance. To Perkins there is no way whereby one may be assured by merely apprehending Christ. One is assured only when he is able to reflect that he has truly applied Christ. Such assurance, or persuasion, indeed is in the mind. But such "applying" is surely in the will. Thus the act of the will must transpire before the reflex act can occur in the mind. What Perkins ought to have said, then, is that faith is seated in the will, and assurance is seated in the mind.

But Perkins apparently was unable to grasp this. He was too involved in his own enterprise to look at Calvin, Beza, and Ursinus with objectivity. He did not realize that the doctrines of Beza and Ursinus were new wine that did not preserve well in Calvin's wineskin. The use of the practical syllogism by Perkins made a distinction between faith and assurance that he was unable to see.

Perkins's system, which seems so theocentric, becomes anthropocentric in its application. It requires a "descending into our owne hearts,"[50] the introspection Calvin warned against. The teaching of limited atonement is preponderantly the doctrine that forfeited faith as assurance in Perkins's thought. Since there is no way, apart from extraordinary revelation, that one can know he is one of those for whom Christ died, one must *do* certain things to infer his assurance.

Thomas Fuller says that Perkins reportedly died "in the conflict of a troubled conscience." This is "no wonder," he says, for God "seemingly leaves his saints when they leave the world, plunging them on their death-beds in deep temptations, and casting their souls, down to hell, to rebound the higher to heaven."[51]

Samuel Ward, who visited the dying Perkins, wrote in his diary: "God knows his death is likely to be an irrevocable loss and a great judgment to the university, seeing there is none to supply his place."[52]

On 25 October 1602 James Montagu preached the funeral sermon, using Joshua 1:2: "Moses my servant is dead."

When the bells tolled Perkins's death, Thomas Goodwin, who became a leading divine in the Westminster Assembly, was two years old. Goodwin came up to Cambridge in 1613 and later wrote that the town was filled "with the discourse of the power of Mr. Perkins' ministry."[53] John Cotton, however, secretly rejoiced over the death of Perkins. Perkins's sermons had deeply disturbed the eighteen-year-old Cotton, who was relieved to have Perkins out of the way. Cotton was later converted under the preaching of Richard Sibbes. Sibbes had been converted under Paul Baynes, Perkins's successor at St. Andrews.

Paul Baynes (d. 1617) never reached the heights of Perkins, in either popularity or influence. A number of his works were published but they do not make a significant contribution. There is one thing worthy of mention, however: Baynes shifted the problem of "how farre a reprobate may goe" to "how far an unbeleever may go."[54] Baynes is the first figure in the Perkins tradition who seems consciously to veer the anxious inquirer away from facing the awesome possibility of an ineffectual calling. Baynes's substitution of unbeliever for reprobate tends to take away the horror of being eternally lost.

Richard Sibbes (d. 1635), while clearly in the Perkins tradition, continued in the spirit of pastoral concern that is so obvious in Paul Baynes. "The heavenly Doctor Sibbes" was the warmest English preacher in the Beza-Perkins tradition. There is very little in Sibbes's preaching that would make one worry that he was a nonelect person with temporary faith. He therefore stressed the positive, that Christ will not "break the bruised reed."[55] "Art thou bruised? Be of good comfort, He calleth thee."[56]

While remaining in the Perkins tradition, Sibbes shifted the emphasis of faith from the understanding to the will. But Perkins himself should have done this.

> The main thing in religion is the will and affections, and when the will and affections are wrought on, the work is done in the matter of grace. And there is no other way to know whether the former work of the understanding and persuasion be effectual and to purpose or not, but this: to know whether the will choose and cleave to good things, and whether our affections joy and delight in them.[57]

It is not surprising then that Sibbes's doctrine of assurance is based on a "reflect act inbred in the soul."[58] This act of reflection is the second of a "double act of faith," an idea Sibbes developed in the light of his observation that many children of God wait a long time before they have assurance. The first act is relying on God and the promise, the second is "the reflect act, whereby, knowing we do this, we have assurance."

And one may have the first without the second.[59] This is virtually saying that one may have faith without assurance, a point that is implicit in Perkins's system but which Perkins himself did not grasp.

Sibbes's most famous convert was John Cotton (1584–1652). Cotton became a minister and fell right into the mold set by Perkins, only following through on some of Perkins's implications as Sibbes had done. Perkins had said that the work of conversion was to be distinguished as taking place between the "beginnings of preparation" and "beginnings of composition."[60] But he came short of following through on the implications of a doctrine of preparation for grace. Sibbes said simply that "all preparations are from God,"[61] a position any predestinarian would obviously maintain. But Cotton moved much further in the direction of preparation for grace in suggesting a preparation on man's part before regeneration. We must "prepare a way for Christ to come to us," Cotton claimed.[62] His favorite phrase in this connection was "fit for Christ": When we are "willing to be whatsoever he would have us to be," we are then "made fit for Christ to come into us."[63]

> If there be nothing in a mans heart, but hee is willing to bee guided in it, by the straight rule of Gods word, and hee aimes directly at the glory of God, and the comming of His Kingdom, and the doing of His will, then is all a mans crooked wayes laid aside, and the heart lyes so levell, then Christ will suddenly come into His temple. . . .[64]

Cotton underwent a radical change of mind between the time he preached his earlier sermons (as found in *Christ the Fountaine of Life*) and his arrival in America in 1633. But that matter cannot be dealt with here.[65] His sermons preached in England find him definitely in the tradition of Perkins, if carrying Perkins's implications closer to their logical conclusion.

Cotton's early ministry was far from barren, however. In 1611 he preached a sermon that he thought was very poor. He went to his room in a melancholy state. He heard a rap at his door. It was John Preston, who had just been converted by Cotton's sermon. Preston (d. 1628) earned the B.D. degree and became dean of Queen's at Cambridge. He is the first man in the Perkins tradition to gain royal favor; his close relationship with the Duke of Buckingham appears to have been responsible for his becoming Chaplain-in-ordinary to Prince Charles.

Preston was largely influenced by Cotton, but he was also a very close friend of Sibbes. Sibbes had a hand in publishing some of Preston's sermons.

Preston is the first man in this tradition since Perkins to make much of the covenant of works and covenant of grace. The covenant of works consists in this: "Doe this, and thou shalt live." The covenant of grace is, "Thou shalt beleeve" and shall "receive the gift of right-eousnesse."[66] The contribution of Preston to this tradition is chiefly in his making faith a disposition, and, in doing so, he comes very close to a preparation for grace before regeneration. Using circular reasoning, Preston claims that the Spirit must change our disposition and yet he stresses that there are things we must do before we can have the benefit of the covenant of grace.[67] He claims that the promise to Abraham was not grounded in the "particular act" of faith, "but that habit, that grace of faith, that beleeving disposition."[68]

Thus while he said that the condition of the new covenant is faith, its application stresses not faith but repentance: "The Condition that is required of us, as part of the Covenant, is the doing of this, the action, the performance of these things, it is to repent, to serve the Lord in newnesse of life."[69] "Thou maist know" that "thou art within the Covenant" like Abraham "because thy faith workes."[70] Assurance is actually the second of two acts of faith: (1) the "direct act," taking Christ, and (2) the "reflect act" by which "we know we have taken Christ."[71] The second act is "grounded upon our owne experi-ence."[72]

Preston, more than others we have examined thus far, tends to make repentance a form of preparation for faith. Such repentance, if found, assures. The consequence suggests an interest in godliness more than in God.[73]

But it was Thomas Hooker (1586–1647) who gave this tradition a fully developed teaching of preparation for faith prior to regeneration. This is most evident merely by citing the title of Hooker's treatise *The Vnbeleevers Preparing for Christ*. Giles Firmin (d. 1692) relates an interesting incident:

> When Mr. Hooker preached those Sermons about the Souls preparation for Christ, and Humiliation, my Father-in-Law, Mr. Nath. Ward, told him: Mr. Hooker, you make as good Christians before men are in Christ, as ever they are after; and wished: would I were but as good a Christian now, as you make men while they are but preparing for Christ.[74]

The whole of Hooker's theology may be summed up in these words: "Before the soule of a man can partake of the benefits of Christ, two things are required: First, that the soul bee prepared for Christ. Sec-ondly, that the soule bee implanted into Christ."[75] This preparation is "the fitting of a sinner for his being in Christ."[76] Hooker's view is that the natural man by virtue of common grace "is able to waite upon God in the meanes, so that he may be enabled to receive grace."[77] The details of Hooker's system are too intricate to go into here. But two observations are in order: (1) that Hooker's theology is the eventual product of the Beza-Perkins system whose doctrine of assurance required introspection from the start and (2) that one may see how far "Calvinism" has departed from Calvin.

There is one more figure that deserves some attention—William Ames (1576–1633). Ames was Perkins's most famous student, but unlike most of Perkins's followers, who stayed clear of ecclesiastical confrontations, Ames got into trouble with the hierarchy and fled to Holland. Shortly after arriving in Holland, he got involved with the Remonstrants—the ardent followers of Arminius (1560–1609). Arminius himself had read Perkins's *De Praedestinationis Modo et Ordine*. Arminius prepared an answer to Perkins in 1602 but did not publish it when he heard of Perkins's death the same year. However, the Remonstrants published Arminius's pamphlet in 1612, shortly after Ames arrived in Holland.

Arminius made some cogent criticisms of Perkins's treatise. In a word, Arminius claimed to hold to virtually the same doctrine of faith as Perkins. Ames appears to have profited from Arminius's criticisms, for he took up Perkins's case and refined the latter's theology in a way that made Perkins's theology more defensible. Ames maintained the basic predestinarianism of Perkins while making two significant shifts: (1) Ames dropped the notion of the ineffectual calling and (2) he placed the seat of faith in the will not the understanding. The scandalous doctrine of temporary faith had been swept under the carpet since Perkins's death anyway, and Ames gave this teaching a decent burial. By making faith an act of the will he simply said what Perkins ought to have said himself.[78]

The net result of Ames's teaching was this: by making faith an act of the will and dismissing the possibility that the nonelect can ever attain to sanctification, Ames put assurance of salvation within immediate reach of anyone who willed to be godly. The threat of temporary faith was gone. For "sanctification is a certain effect and signe" of election.[79] For sanctification "is, as it were, actuall election." Ames went on to say that this tenet serves to refute those who allow sanctification to be in those "that are not elect,"[80] an undoubted allusion to his mentor. Finally, Ames gave his weighty sanction to the separating of faith and assurance. This he systemized in his book *Marrow*.

In a sermon before the House of Commons in 1641, Edmund Calamy (1600–1666) urged Parliament not only to "root out Arminianism" but to settle the church's doctrine so "that there may be no shadow in it for an Arminian."[81] On 12 June 1643 Parliament called for "an Assembly of Learned, and Judicious Divines" to be consulted with by Parliament for the settling of the government and liturgy of the church, and "for the vindicating and clearing of the Doctrine of the Church of England from all false Calumnies and Aspersions."[82]

The historic Assembly of Divines convened in Westminster for the first time on 1 July 1643. When the 121 divines were chosen, there was a soteriological consensus among them; this was guaranteed by Parliament's careful selection. While there was ecclesiological diversity, there was soteriological unity. On 20 August 1644 the Assembly appointed a committee to join with the Scottish commissioners to draw up a Confession of Faith. Perhaps the most telling disclosure of the Assembly's *Minutes* as a whole is the apparently unquestioned acceptance of a distinction between faith and assurance, for "Faith" was one heading in the Confession, and "Certainty of Salvation" another.[83] This division between faith and assurance seems to have been accepted implicitly early on in the Assembly. There is no indication at all of any questioning of this significant division. Calvin's view that faith *is* assurance was thus rendered incapable of penetration into the Westminster documents from the start.

When the Westminster Confession stated that "infallible assurance doth not so belong to the essence of faith," it virtually sanctioned the trend that followed Perkins and which was refined by William Ames. The Westminster Documents read so much like Ames's *Marrow* in places that one cannot help but suspect the divines had *Marrow* at their fingertips when they deliberated. By separating faith and assurance, Westminster theology restated, without using the express language, what Perkins's followers came to call the direct act (faith) and the reflex act (assurance).

The theology of the Westminster Confession is universally regarded as Calvinistic. It is rather to be seen as the culmination of the Beza-Perkins tradition. Westminster theology will no doubt continue to be known as Calvinism as it was in the 1640s. But it is hardly the kind of theology that will let a person proclaim by a "direct" act that "Christ is better than a thousand testimonies to me."

# Calvinism's Contribution to Scotland

## J. D. Douglas

*J. D. Douglas is editor at large for* Christianity Today. *An air force veteran, he studied at Glasgow and St. Andrews universities and at Hartford Theological Seminary, Connecticut. He holds the degrees of M.A., B.D., S.T.M., Ph.D. He has been lecturer in ecclesiastical history at St. Andrews, Church of Scotland minister in Bute, and librarian of Tyndale House, Cambridge. He has written three books; edited several major works, including the* New Bible Dictionary *and the* New International Dictionary of the Christian Church; *and contributes regularly to various religious journals.*

# 10

# Calvinism's Contribution to Scotland

The Reformation came late to Scotland. When parliament abolished popery in the summer of 1560, Zwingli had been dead for twenty-nine years, Luther for fourteen, Henry VIII for thirteen; and Calvin's course had a mere four years to run. John Knox thus belonged to the second generation of Reformers who benefited from the thinking and experience of predecessors in the fight against Rome.

He and his colleagues, nevertheless, were confronted by a set of problems for which the Continental blueprints were not always applicable. Such is the vitality of Calvinism that it has flourished in different forms, countries, and circumstances. In Scotland it made an impact unparalleled elsewhere. To understand this calls for a look backwards in Scottish history to see how extraordinary evil was countered by extraordinary remedy.

### SCOTLAND BEFORE THE REFORMATION

During the turbulent two centuries that separated Robert Bruce and John Knox, Scotland was an ill-governed land. Used as a pawn in the perennial French-English conflict, it was also torn by civil war and local clan feuds; it was backward in civilization and offered scant security to life and property. Bedevilled latterly by a pathetic succession of child kings (whose average age on accession was no more than eight years) and by disputed regencies, the monarchy was weak, the nobility rebellious, the church corrupt.

Yet this unpromising region was here and there touched by the outreach of John Wycliffe and his missionary-evangelists concerned to spread knowledge of the Bible in a language people could understand. One such messenger, James Resby, wandered across the border from England to tell the Scots about the new-old gospel and paid with his life at Perth in 1408.

In 1433 Paul Crawar (Craw), a Bohemian physician, came to Scotland and settled in St. Andrews. Soon the town rang with Hussite teaching: the denial of transubstantiation, purgatory, and the efficacy of absolution. To bishop and clergy in the ecclesiastical capital this was monstrous, and Crawar too was consigned to the flames, a brass ball put in his mouth so that the people might not hear his last words.

In the same century emerged also a more indigenous movement when the Lollards of Kyle spread distinctively Protestant beliefs, especially in southwest Scotland. So alarmed were church and parliament that every St. Andrews graduate had to swear to guard the church against them. By the end of the century, nevertheless, the movement had touched the higher classes. They too began to inveigh against transubstantiation and purgatory, condemned the use of images, and scoffed at the pretensions of the pope, whose control of the Scots clergy had for many years been fitful and unsatisfactory.

These Lollards, who before Luther was born anticipated much of his teaching, affirmed also that every faithful man and woman was a priest. The simplicity and austerity of their doctrine were oddly appealing in a country that knew little of Renaissance glories and was somewhat remote when Continental scholars rediscovered the writings of antiquity and when that great humanist Erasmus poked fun at clerical claims. Even before the new learning spread from Germany and England, there was in Scotland an increasing spirit of hostility between churchmen and the rising middle class.

Then the awakening began in earnest. Copies of Tyndale's New Testament began to reach Scotland by way of the Low Countries. Lutheran literature came from Campvere through Aberdeen and Leith; and into Dundee sailed priests who had lived in Germany and brought home to Scotland hymns used by the German Reformers adapted to the tunes of Scottish ballads.

> This their tyranny notwithstanding [wrote Knox], the knowledge of God did wondrously increase within this realm, partly by reading, partly by brotherly conference, which in those dangerous days was used to the comfort of many; but chiefly by merchants and mariners who, frequenting other countries, heard the true doctrine affirmed, and the vanity of the papistical religion openly rebuked.[1]

In 1525 at the instigation of the church, which possessed at least half the nation's wealth and maintained its grip on the people through fear, ignorance, and superstition, an act was passed against those who introduced the offensive doctrines. The clergy was largely illiterate, preaching was almost unknown, parochial duties were neglected, revenues were squandered in worldliness, church buildings were sacked by the English or by rebels or allowed to fall into decay. For this in some cases Knox was later conveniently blamed. Bishop Robert Hall commented that many measured their distance from heaven by their distance from Rome.

## FIRST SCOTTISH PROTESTANT MARTYR

But the tide could not be stemmed. They burned for heresy an aristocratic young student at St. Andrews in 1528, but "the reek of Master Patrick Hamilton infected as many as it blew upon."[2] Alexander Alane (Alesius), who had tried to convince Hamilton of error, had himself been converted and narrowly escaped a similar fate. Many even in the universities began to "call in doubt what they had before held for a certain verity . . . and to espy the vanity of the received superstition."[3]

Despite strict legislation, Protestant views spread. In 1546 George Wishart, a humble, likeable scholar who on the Continent had learned much from Calvin and Zwingli, was burned at the stake in St. Andrews. First, though, he had sent away his bodyguard, a priest called John Knox, who was prepared to wield a huge two-handed sword in his master's defense. Wishart would have none of it. "Return to your bairns," he advised Knox, the tutor, "and God bless you. One is sufficient for one sacrifice."[4]

The following year, the church petitioned the Queen Regent, Mary of Guise/Lorraine, widow of James V, to enforce the laws against the "Lutherans," a term often used as a comprehensive name for Protestants, with whose "pestilential heresies the land was now infected, and who were now preaching openly."

## VICTORY IN SIGHT

But some of the more powerful nobles were in fact genuinely sympathetic to the cause of reform and attempted to bring about changes by constitutional means. In 1557 they signed the Common or Godly Band, a covenant that advocated the use in all parish churches of the Second Prayer Book of Edward VI and the exposition of Scripture "privately in quiet houses."

The year 1558 saw the last Protestant martyr in Scotland when eighty-two-year-old Walter Myln, parish priest of Lunan, died in the flames at St. Andrews. No rebel himself, Abbot Quintin Kennedy that same year lamented his church's corruption and told how vacant benefices were coveted by great men: "If they have a brother or son . . . nourished in vice all his days, he shall at once be mounted on a mule, with a sidegown and a round bonnet, and then it is a question whether he or his mule knows best to do his office. What wonder is it . . . the poor simple people, so dearly bought by the blood and death of Christ, miserably perish, the Kirk is slandered; God is dishonoured.''[5] In March 1559 the Provincial Council of the church met for the last time and offered so little so late that it showed merely how completely out of touch it was with the mounting spirit of the age.

Then John Knox came home. "When the tale of bricks is doubled,'' says the Hebrew proverb, "Moses comes." Now in his middle forties, Knox had been ordained priest some two decades before. Since his adherence to the martyred Wishart, he had been successively tutor, minister in St. Andrews, galley slave in French bondage, and chaplain to the English king Edward VI. When offered the bishopric of Rochester, however, he declined, prophesying "evil days to come."

During most of Mary Tudor's reign in England (1553–58), Knox was in exile, first in Frankfurt, then in Geneva. But his burning interest was Scotland, and we hear of him consulting Calvin and Bullinger about a subject's attitude toward "a magistrate who enforces idolatry and condemns true religion."

He came to Scotland for six months in August 1555 and in quaint but compelling language refers to the welcome he received and to "the fervent thirst of our brethren, night and day sobbing and groaning for the bread of life." Through his preaching many were won to the Reformed faith, after the manner of which he celebrated the Lord's Supper. He dissuaded people from attending Mass, and this abstention became the mark of a thoroughgoing Protestantism.

On his return to Geneva he left behind a "Wholesome Counsel," reminding heads of families that they were bishops and kings, and recommending the institution in private congregations of something like the early apostolic worship. Sentence of death was passed on him in his absence, but Knox was undaunted. When near the close of 1559 French intervention and the English Queen Elizabeth's fickleness put the cause in jeopardy, Knox in a memorable sermon exhorted his colleagues to "turn to the Eternal, our God . . . which, if we do unfeignedly . . . our dolour, confusion, and fear shall be turned into joy, honour, and boldness."[6]

So it happened. Victory was effectively secured in July 1560. The revolution was at an end—and it had been remarkably bloodless. John Knox's God had triumphed, the Auld Alliance with France was revoked, and the Scots gave unheard-of applause to the appearance of a friendly English army.

## THE SCOTS CONFESSION

Knox and his colleagues had neither the time nor the systematic discipline of mind to produce a statement of the Reformed faith. Under

Knox's guidance, therefore, they resorted to what Calvin had done. In four days, borrowing from the *Institutes* and from other Reformed as well as Lutheran statements, they produced the Scots Confession of 1560. Much of the material in the twenty-five vigorous chapters reflects teaching identifiable with that of Paul and Augustine.

This compilation of the six Johns—Knox, Spottiswoode, Row, Douglas, Winram, and Willock—saw the features of the true church as threefold:

1. The true preaching of the Word of God.
2. The right administration of the Sacraments.
3. Ecclesiastical discipline lawfully administered according to the Word of God.

The Confession renounced papal authority, forbade celebration of the Mass, implied acceptance of the historic creeds, set out the doctrine of Atonement and of justification by faith, and treated election (as earlier Calvinism had done) as a means of grace and as evidence of the "invincible power" of the Godhead in salvation.

Expressed in places less like a theological document than like a robust manifesto that reflected the contemporary climate, the Confession remained the basis of Church of Scotland teaching until the Westminster Confession of 1647. Even then the earlier document was often regarded as the purest expression of the Kirk's mind and heart; Edward Irving in the nineteenth century used to read it twice a year to his London congregation. Irving, a brilliant but unstable son of the Kirk, held that the Scots Confession was "the banner of the Church, in all her wrestlings and conflicts, the Westminster Confession but as the camp-colours which she hath used during her days of peace; the one for battle, the other for fair appearance and good order."[7]

## First Book of Discipline

How should a Reformed church best be governed? Originally composed in less than three weeks in May of 1560, but revised later, the first *Book of Discipline* is in some ways even more important than the Confession, for it has left a lasting mark on Scottish religion and life.

A practical and comprehensive work that drew much from Reformed churches abroad, the Book laid the foundation of Scotland's future on a basis of true religion. Hume Brown considered it "the most important document in Scottish history," embodying a scheme to which the term "Christian socialism" would not be inapplicable.[8]

The scheme outlined in the first *Book of Discipline* was incompatible with the very existence of the medieval church. A complete Presbyterian system did not emerge until 1581, but it was deeply rooted in the Scottish Reformation. The first *Book of Discipline* disposed of the hierarchical structure in church and society. Since the church is the people of God, every member had equal status in controlling the nation's religion.

The establishment of such equality necessarily called for the deliverance of the oppressed from both civil and ecclesiastical tyranny. "Stubborn and idle beggars" were discouraged, but the cause of the widow, the orphan, and the aged and impotent poor was to be warmly and compassionately espoused, and provision made for them from the church's resources.

Regarding equality, there was no contradiction in holding that God had bestowed special gifts on individuals for service in His church. This was not only Calvin's view, but it also found explicit warrant in Scripture. While realizing the shortage of "godly and learned men," the first Book of Discipline insisted on a high standard of educational qualifications for the ministry. It is a view from which modern Presbyterian churches have not departed.

The aim of all preaching was to be instructional and persuasive, unsentimental, unemotional, and uncontroversial except in dealing with the Roman Church. Scripture was to be expounded consecutively, so that people might know the complete teaching. The impact was to be assessed at weekly meetings for catechetical purposes. There were weekly exercises for ministers within reasonable distance for the discussion of Scripture doctrine. A moderator was to preside and check any tendency to invective and irrelevance. Herein was the germ of the presbytery.

The lofty scheme of having a school in every parish and equal opportunity for all to be educated to university level showed an intention to create and develop a thoroughly egalitarian Christian nation. It was not enough for "the godly magistrate to purge the Church of God from all superstition, and to set it at liberty from bondage of tyrants"—he had to ensure also that it would "abide in the same purity to the posterities following." Wisdom and learning were regarded as a more valuable legacy to posterity than earthly treasures.

The Word of God was to be the very life and soul of the Kirk, but godly conduct and discipline were also commended. The latter would ensure that those who lived evil lives were not numbered among God's children, that the bad would not infect the good, and that sinners would be brought to repentance and newness of life.

Capital crimes were punishable by both civil and spiritual authorities. Sins such as drunkenness, intemperance in any form, licentiousness, slander, and oppression of the poor were punishable by church courts. Discipline was to be administered with strict impartiality—which admirable feature doubtless contributed to the fact that the Book of Discipline, unlike the Scots Confession, was never ratified by parliament.

In planning the book, Knox had drawn on his acquaintance with the

*Ordonnances* of the Genevan Church under Calvin, the *Forma* used in
John Laski's German Church in London, and the French Reformed
Church's *Discipline* of 1557–59. At the very heart of everything was
the urgent need for preachers. It was a burden Knox carried to his
deathbed, for one of his last prayers was, "Lord, grant true pastors to
Thy Kirk." Pastors were needed because for Knox the Reformation did
not mean a few modest improvements in the Christian church. Rome
was not a defective form of Christianity; to Knox it was not Christianity
at all but the result of a cosmic swindle by which people had been
cheated once more, as in Eden, and lured into unconscious devil-
worship. It is a view still fiercely held in Scotland by at least one of the
smaller Presbyterian bodies.

## OPPOSITION GROWS

Trouble soon came. The ministers held that religion was inseparable
from government and that if true religion reigned, true politics would
follow. Most of the high-ranking nobility, however, having "greedily
gripped to the possessions of the kirk," were not of a mind to let them
go to benefit the ministers, the schools, and the poor. Thus were the
ministers betrayed by the self-seekers.

Two-thirds of the revenues remained in the hands of the former
owners, the remaining one-third divided between stipends for the Reformed pastors and the Crown. "Two parts freely given to the Devil,"
commented Knox, "and the third must be divided betwixt God and the
Devil."[9]

It did mean, nevertheless, that the ministers continued to be identified
in Scotland with the poor, sharing their lot and knowing their daily
difficulties and troubles. In 1843 disruption was to be traced in part to a
patronage system which, set up in 1712, appointed to parishes men who
might have nothing in common with their parishioners.

Andrew Lang has typically idiosyncratic views on the Reformation
establishment in Scotland. Calvinism, he suggests, was "the cheapest
system, entailing no expense on archbishops, bishops, deans, canons,
cathedrals, and other luxuries."[10] Perhaps, but Lang ignores the fact
that the contemporary Church of England continued to have both the
"luxuries" and the Calvinism.

The Reformers were not without their successes. The corollary of the
equality of all people before God was the accountability of all people
before God. There was no respect of persons. In 1563 the Lord Treas-
urer of Scotland did penance for immorality; in 1567 the Countess of
Argyll was forced to appear in sackcloth during service in the Chapel
Royal, Stirling, for having assisted at the Roman Catholic baptism of
the future James VI. Such humiliations did not endear the zealous
Reformers to the upper classes.

## The Godly Commonwealth

Following the Genevan model, both the Scots Confession and the first *Book of Discipline* had assumed church and state to be two parts of a Christian commonwealth, an idea originating in Augustine's *City of God*. What the authors evidently did not foresee was that such a theory was basically impracticable when the ruler was in opposition to the Kirk.

Calvin's system, intended for a single community, presented glaring difficulties when applied to a whole kingdom. The idea of the godly commonwealth was feasible in republican Geneva where Calvin himself had helped to formulate the civil code. It was fundamentally untenable when the sovereign was someone like Mary Queen of Scots, a nineteen-year-old unrepentant Catholic who joined battle with Knox soon after her arrival from France in 1561.

"Ye have taught people to receive another religion than their princes can allow," she protested, "and how can that doctrine be of God, seeing that God commands subjects to obey their princes?" A valid point, for did not the appropriated Genevan doctrine and Scripture itself hold that kings were "appointed for maintenance of true religion"?

Knox was forced to fall back on his more fundamental principle that "right religion took neither origin nor authority from worldly princes, but from the Eternal God alone."[11] In one sense Knox was on his own here, for Calvin's views (and Luther's even more) had not envisaged their application in circumstances such as those that obtained in Scotland.

It is part of Knox's greatness that he was not slavishly dependent on guidelines laid down by the pioneers. He was a man with an eye and with imagination, a man who could improvise. It is sometimes forgotten that he was remarkably well equipped to do so. Not only had he seen ordained service in the Church of Rome and the Church of England, but he had seen for himself the effect of the Reformation on Germany, France, and Switzerland.

Calvinism had given basic principles to Knox and his colleagues. These principles in turn gave the Scots the necessary justification for a rebellion in a way Lutheranism could not have done. Calvinism thus opened the door in Scotland for a religious movement with an ecclesiastical organization capable of functioning effectively in times of adversity, as well as in more favorable circumstances when the church was established and given due recognition by the state. Whereas in England there was anxiety about retaining the link with the past, Scotland reflected a different political situation that allowed for a more radical type of church organization.

In Scotland, nonetheless, the past was not rejected in one important particular: the Reformers maintained a doctrine of the church as high as that found in Rome itself. The Kirk was not merely the Church of Scotland, but the representative in Scotland of the church universal. It was the Roman hierarchy that had departed from this conception. Increasingly from the Reformation until 1690, the true Reformed voice in Scotland found it necessary to assert that Christ was the only Head of the Church—not the pope, nor the Crown.

It was thus no depreciation of Calvinism, but rather a declaration of it, when in 1644 the Scots commissioners at the Westminster Assembly asserted in a pamphlet: "To call us *Calvinians,* and the Reformed Churches *Calvinian Reformed Churches,* is to disgrace the true Churches of Christ, and to symbolise with the Papists, who call themselves the Catholic Church. . . . They who apprehend any danger in names (as there is a great deal of danger in them) ought not . . . to join with Papists in giving names of sects unto the Reformed Churches."[12] The same objection could be adduced against the twentieth-century Anglican publication that is given to referring to "the Presbyterian Church of Scotland."

To the Scots Reformers, there were not to be two churches: Protestant and Catholic. This was unthinkable; there was a consensus that for two churches to coexist in the same realm was as monstrous as the idea of having two states. There is still in Scotland the vision of the one church, and an uneasy conscience about disunity. Found in every denomination are those who will echo the old Highlander's exclamation when his minister referred to the church: "Church! We have only the splinters of a Church."

KNOX'S LITURGY

Another legacy from Geneva was the liturgical forms used by Knox's Genevan congregation. In 1562 and in 1564 the general assembly sanctioned and authorized the *Book of Common Order,* known by some as Knox's Liturgy, as a serviceable directory of worship in the Church of Scotland. This book, which had been in use even earlier in Scotland, incorporated also a metrical version of the Psalms.

After the assembly had appointed John Craig and others to revise the Genevan Psalm Book and adapt it to the Kirk's needs, the Old Scottish Psalter was published in 1565 and was widely in use until 1650. Every Sunday in some Scottish churches today can be heard Psalms 100 and 124, sung to tunes first heard in Calvin's Geneva.

In parishes the reader had to instruct the children in the rudiments "and specially in the catechism as we have it now translated in the Book of Common Order called the Order of Geneva." Every Sunday afternoon in every parish church and in the presence of their parents, the children had to repeat the answers to the questions, and the minister or reader had to explain both questions and answers, and apply the doctrines.

That this practice was long continued suggests how profound was Calvin's influence on Scottish thought. During the early 1950s I was invited on a Fast Day to examine the pupils of a Highland school in the Shorter Catechism and to deliver an appropriate address. The formalities having thus been observed, the children could then have the rest of the day off!

The *Book of Common Order* was officially still in force until Archbishop William Laud's misguided attempt seventy-five years later to interfere in Scottish liturgical practice. The attempt failed, and ministers were allowed to conduct services at their own discretion, but present-day forms are still essentially those that took shape under the influence of John Calvin.

After Calvin's death in 1564, the Genevan connection was maintained through Beza. A letter to Bullinger from Beza in 1566 enclosed "a specimen of the very extensive correspondence of Knox from which you will learn the entire condition of Scotland." Earlier that year, Beza through Knox had asked the Kirk to approve the Second Helvetic Confession, which major Calvinistic document had just been produced. Close ties with Beza continued long after Knox's death in 1572.

### EDUCATION AND LAITY

Knox went to the Bible for his inspiration, and because he found Calvin had been there before him, the Swiss Reformer became for the Scot "that singular instrument of God." From systematic study of the redemptive message came the Protestant creed. Rome had reason to be alarmed when people began to read or hear the Bible freely, for here was a source of spiritual strength directly available, and a dispeller of superstitions.

The seeds of an intellectual revolution were sown with the Reformers' zeal for education. They regarded education as vital, not only because the young are most susceptible to learning, but also because the new system demanded literacy for the reading of the Word of God. Not until 1696 did each Scottish parish in fact have its own school, but thereafter Scotland was equipped with what was claimed to be the finest educational system in Europe.

Despite the avarice of the nobility, which thwarted an imaginative program of university reform, the Reformers pressed on at that level also, and in the days of Andrew Melville (Knox's successor from 1574) students left Scotland to teach, not to be taught, in foreign universities.

Education, good government, morality and religion were bound up together in the Reformed outlook, and in all of this the laity were given opportunity for service. One of their number, John Erskine of Dun, was moderator of the general assembly as early as 1564 and held the post at least three more times. Perhaps no other church in the world has pioneered so much in its enlistment to key offices of the laity.

At his best the God-fearing Scottish elder, with a sound education and a concern for the spiritual conversion of his fellows, is a remarkable historical figure. He remained no less so when after about 1700 he could no longer effectively summon the aid of the civil magistrate in upholding his godly rule. The high ethical standards he set were reminiscent of Geneva, but these were seen to be inadequate in themselves. As Calvin had put it, "To lift our hands to heaven is nothing if our hearts remain below."

Many of the Reformed schemes were imaginative; some were centuries ahead of their time. Church representatives are still found on many national bodies; two of Scotland's nine regions at present have Presbyterian ministers at their head. A further fact, the significance of which is not always appreciated, is that the four Church of Scotland divinity colleges are also the faculties of divinity in the four ancient universities.

## CHURCH GOVERNMENT

John Knox, like Calvin, had no deep-rooted aversion to episcopacy as unscriptural. Under Andrew Melville a rigid presbyterian polity evolved, which is reflected in both the 1560 and 1578 Books of Discipline, because of church-state relations.[13] It might fairly be added, nonetheless, that for three centuries prior to the Reformation the conduct of Scotland's bishops had not endeared them to the country.

In the sixteenth century, the problem was thrown into sharp relief by Andrew Melville, often regarded as "the father of Presbyterianism." He regarded it as the most biblical form of church government, for it acknowledged the Bible as the seat of authority, not the king or the pope. It offered, moreover, an ordered and spiritual government of the church in a land that had seen much misgovernment. It is regrettable, however, if understandable, that overreaction drove some into holding to the divine right of presbytery, a theory indefensible though espoused in the following century by the redoubtable Samuel Rutherford. The Church of Scotland minister on ordination today is required to acknowledge only that his church's presbyterian government is "agreeable to the Word of God."

During the latter part of the sixteenth century, episcopacy was found by James VI to be useful in the promotion of his own political ends, not least as claimant to the English throne. His son pushed episcopacy further, under the influence of Archbishop William Laud, until the Scots rebelled—and told why they had done so in the National Covenant of 1638. Later, under Charles II and James VII, episcopacy was identified with the use of naked force and atrocities against nonconformity.

The English form of episcopacy comfortably allied itself with monarchy and allowed itself to be manipulated, but Scottish conditions were different. The problem of presbytery vs. episcopacy came to a head in the bitter campaign against the Covenanters after the Restoration of the monarchy in 1660. But it was Melville and his two-kingdom view that triumphed finally in Scotland; and the democratic institutions of the Western world have benefited because of that victory, for it was in Scotland that Presbyterianism vindicated its claim to be a practically effective form of polity in the circumstances of the modern centralized state.

## CALVINISM AND COVENANTERS

The seventeenth-century Covenanters in Scotland continued the Calvinistic emphasis on the sovereignty of God. The battle against Rome had been won, but a new battle had to be fought on the ground that "none but Christ reigns." Here was that Calvinism which, in Alexander Smellie's words, "teaches that the high decree and the regal sceptre and the majestic dominion of the Lord God Almighty extend to every thing that happens in the universe."[14]

In Covenanting eyes, the state commanded only a limited loyalty, for loyalty was conditional on morality; even kings could be deprived at the will of the people who had erected them. Asked if they thought the king's power was limited, the Covenanters rightly replied that no power but God's was unlimited. That thought, which long predated the Reformation, had been elaborated by George Buchanan, came to maturity under the strongly Calvinist Rutherford, became a thorn in the flesh after the Restoration to the tyrannical regimes of Charles II and James VII, and made a marked contribution to the toppling of the Stuart dynasty.

More than three centuries have passed since the signing of the National Covenant (1638) at Greyfriars, Edinburgh, but it remains true that nothing undermines the foundations of totalitarian power more successfully than a free Christian church that gets right its priorities in dealing with God and man.

Calvin had founded his religious system on the ground of truth rather than on liberty of conscience. If the Covenanters on occasion showed little pity or understanding toward those they considered willful enemies of the truth, then they were doing nothing that would not have been endorsed by Calvin or Knox. All were keenly aware of the great gulf fixed in this world and the next between those who are Christ's and those who are not.

Confronted by these seventeenth-century Scots Calvinists, we must ask why they were what they were; what motivated them; what sustained them through weary years; what gave them a ringing testimony when uncomprehending authority dragged them from the hills or pushed them up the scaffold steps. The answer is the same answer that would have been given had the same circumstances obtained in sixteenth-century Geneva: their confidence of being the elect of God.

Given that conviction, disaster came for "the punishment of former sins, and for future trial." Defeat prompted James Renwick's "We shall never ken better that God is our covenanted God than by this, that we are brought into captivity." Success or good fortune was the God-given assurance that above were the everlasting arms. Failure to take reprisals meant bringing themselves "under that curse of doing the work of the Lord deceitfully."[15]

The Covenanters tended to renounce all things for which they could find no scriptural warrant. As Knox had put it a century earlier, every man was to have "liberty to utter and declare his mind with knowledge to the comfort and edification of the Church." That, however, was heady wine that tended to raise up a class of "saints of God" who alone could interpret his will—and often such interpretation at their hands was devoid of the mercy that should ever be linked with the concept of a holy God's dealings with sinful men.

Nevertheless, it was their very perseverance in fighting for religious and political freedom that preserved a Kirk identifiable with that of the Reformers and that contributed to building up the national individuality and character. This aspect was very well appreciated by the Anglican historian J. A. Froude when he wrote:

> For more than half the seventeenth century, the battle had to be fought out in Scotland, which in reality was the battle between liberty and despotism; and where, except in an intense, burning conviction that they were maintaining God's cause against the devil, could the poor Scotch people have found the strength for the unequal struggle which was forced upon them? Toleration is a good thing in its place; but you cannot tolerate what will not tolerate you, and is trying to cut your throat. Enlightenment you cannot have enough of, but it must be the true enlightenment, which sees a thing in all its bearings. The Covenanters fought the fight and won the victory; and then, and not till then, came the David Humes with their political economies, and steam-engines, and railroads, and political institutions, and all the blessed or unblessed fruits of liberty.[16]

John Calvin himself was undeniably intolerant of theological opinions that differed from his own. It often led to the dissentient's being excluded from church membership or even to more drastic penalty. Calvin had his Servetus, and in 1696 the reestablished Church of Scotland, all danger past and in cold blood, made its own tragic blunder. Thomas Aikenhead, an Edinburgh divinity student, was executed on the testimony of a single witness for denying the divinity of Christ.

That sad blot on the Scottish church should be considered against the background of the bitter struggle during the latter seventeenth century to maintain the concept of the personal Christ and His headship, not merely His earthly life and example, but His spiritual presence in the world. The Calvinism that reminded people that it was a fearful thing to fall into the hands of the living God, exalted them again in the consciousness of their newborn liberty in Christ. And if God had really done something in Christ on which the salvation of the world depended, then, as James Denney put it, "it is a Christian duty to be intolerant of everything which ignores, denies, or explains it away."

## A Love of Controversial Divinity

Calvinistic theology fostered the argumentative and speculative turn of Scots genius. When in 1670 Archbishop Leighton sent a committee of conciliatory Episcopalians on a traveling mission through the Covenanting West, they found the people more than a match for them. As Bishop Gilbert Burnet put it:

> We were indeed amazed to see a poor commonalty, so capable of arguing upon points of government, and on the bounds to be set to the power of princes, in matters of religion: upon all these topics they had texts of Scripture at hand; and were ready with their answers, to any thing that was said to them. This measure of knowledge was spread even among the meanest of them, their cottagers, and their servants. . . . As soon as we were gone, a set of those hot preachers went round to all the places in which we had been, to defeat all the good we could hope to do. They told them, the devil was never so formidable as when he was transformed into an angel of light.[17]

There grew up a tendency for his fellows to assess a person, not according to the fruit of the Spirit he might evince, but according to whether he was "sound on the fundamentals." Not untypical was the woman who commented that her minister had given them a grand discourse, but she "couldna bide that trash o' duties at the hinner end o't."

Scottish theology at its best, of course, renounces such an outrageous distinction. In the true tradition of Calvin it has always held that the Word of God was not for speculation but for reformation of life. Knowledge of right doctrine and practice of piety were inseparably bound together. The country had outgrown its Scots Confession and its Book of Common Order, but basic principles were unaltered and unalterable.

## Calvinism Anti-aesthetic?

Both Calvin and Knox could be cheerful and humorous. Both had tender qualities undiscerned or ignored by those who dismiss them as sour fanatics. "For hard times," said Froude in a rectorial address at St. Andrews in 1871, "hard men are needed, and intellects which can pierce to the roots where truth and lies part company."

But hard men sometimes have other moods. Calvin, for example, once wrote, "The little singing birds are singing of God: the beasts cry unto Him: the elements are in awe of Him: the mountains echo His name. Waves and fountains glance at Him, grass and flowers laugh out to Him." And who shall say that the sovereignty of God is belittled by such description?

Knox too deserves better of modern Scotland than to be remembered as the purveyor of a joyless creed that inhibits innocent enjoyment and the tourist trade. This, after all, was the author of the sensitive and moving rubric that begins, "Be merciful unto me, O Lord, and call not into judgment my manifold sins; and chiefly those whereof the world is not able to accuse me."

In his writings Calvin approved the divinely given instinct of Jubal and declared that "all the arts come from God and are to be respected as Divine inventions." The arts, he held, are given for our comfort; music can be ennobling. Here was a constant reminder to man of a higher reality than a fallen world.

It would be idle to deny, however, a certain anti-aesthetic character in Presbyterian history. In Scotland during the sixteenth and seventeenth centuries, Christians were totally involved in building up or defending the Kirk. Certainly there is a notable absence of mysticism in Scottish literature over that period (and not too much since). One of the few exceptions—and one of the few seventeenth-century books still read today (another is Leighton's commentary on Peter)—is Samuel Rutherford's *Letters*. Yet even they testify to the times and to the abuse endured by the Covenanters for their testimony:

> I have borne scorn and hatred,
> I have borne wrong and shame,
> Earth's proud ones have reproached me
> For Christ's thrice blessed name;
> Where God His seal set fairest,
> They've stamped their foulest brand;
> But judgment shines like noonday
> In Immanuel's land.[18]

But this too was part of the divine plan. Thus Rutherford declared, "Christ hath a great design of free grace to these lands; but His wheels must move over mountains and rocks. He never wooed a bride on earth, but in blood, in fire, and in the wilderness." Usually the acknowledgment of God's sovereignty was expressed rather less poetically.

No account of Scottish religion is complete without a reminder of the physical characteristics of a land from which had to be wrung the bare necessities of life. To win a livelihood called for endurance and perseverance, and it was somehow fitting that the Scots should embrace a religious system with an austere code of worship and duty. Alas, this meant also that beauty was distrusted and leisure suspected, as it still is in some Scottish remnant churches.

This attitude lent itself to an inordinate emphasis on "the Law." Presbyterianism acquired a bare and unlovely image. Thus the eighteenth-century Charles Calder of Ferintosh, whose great preaching theme was the love of Christ, was condemned by some of his parishioners as "the piper of one tune." The best of Scots poetry that same century originated in or about heroes very different from Knox, Melville, and the Covenanters; some of it arose, indeed, out of the reaction to Presbyterian traditions. Even today in a Highland village the introduction of a gospel song into a Church of Scotland evening service will bring from more Calvinistic bodies the charge of turning worship into "a concert."

The view of Calvinism as harsh and unyielding was furthered by the most rigid interpretation both of the canons of the Synod of Dort (1618–19), which restated the doctrines of sin and grace over against the teaching of Arminius, and of the Westminster Confession. An "Act concerning Doctrine" passed by the general assembly in 1722 reflected the inflexibility and coldness of the Dutch theologians' influence in Scotland.

As the years passed, Scottish morality still tended to lag behind its theology. "A perverse caricature of Calvin's predestinarian theology was preached," says Geddes MacGregor, "and his lofty doctrine of the sovereignty of God turned into a picture of a very unamiable deity. Hell and the Last Judgment were among the most popular subjects in the pulpit, and some travelled thirty or forty miles to hear a sermon upon them by an outstanding preacher."[19] The Puritan influence encouraged also a legalistic view of the Sabbath, though the full effect of this does not seem to have been felt until well into the eighteenth century. Sabbatarianism is still strongest in the Scottish Highlands and Islands.

Gradually the Puritan tradition became associated more with the dissenting bodies who from 1733 crowded and complicated Scottish ecclesiastical life. By 1819 they constituted some 40 percent of the population of Glasgow. Yet, and this is a remarkable thing about the differences, even then there was little variation in doctrine: not until 1893 did Scotland know an ecclesiastical division caused chiefly through doctrinal disagreement.

Writing in the latter nineteenth century about his Skye parish, an Established Church minister reported that he had to contend with three other Presbyterian groups, each concerned to preserve the purity of its doctrine. The four did not worship or pray together. The preaching was joyless. There was a gloomy Sabbatarianism. "The music and dancing which welcomed the prodigal were banished from the home; and the Table of the Lord was unfurnished with guests."[20]

In such cases the people saw the sovereignty of God as something that prevented them as sinners from coming to His table. This attitude is one that has persisted to this day. Official figures published in 1977 show that the Free Church of Scotland, claiming the loyalty of 22,000 people, has no more than 5,500 in actual membership. The comparable figures for the even more Calvinistic Free Presbyterian Church are 6,694 and 781.[21]

A misuse of the inheritance from John Calvin of a high view of Word and sacrament long prevented the growing up of an evangelism not closely linked with Communion. The practice had not widely varied until near the end of the eighteenth century, with the ministry of Robert and James Haldane. Even afterwards, Presbyterian custom, particularly in the Highlands, continued to make the Communion season its main channel of evangelism.

In the eighteenth century we may note also that the Knoxian stress on education was carried forward with the planting of new schools where there was an imaginative approach to curricula, and with the reform and expansion of the universities, a work in which churchmen had the major role.

The Knoxian conviction of the crucial place of education, particularly religious education, was reactivated in the following century when Thomas Chalmers applied it in an age of industrial and social revolution. Chalmers saw it as the remedy for social ills. Character could achieve what legislation could not; the wretchedness of the few could be relieved by the kindness of the many.

In Chalmers's eyes, state charity was a bad thing; it was fitting that the undeserving poor should ''feel the weight of those severities which are intended by the God of Nature to follow in the train of idleness, improvidence and vice.''[22] One finds in Chalmers an oddly Malthusian strain, yet no churchman of his day showed greater concern for the poor. Here was a prominent evangelical with a highly developed social gospel, a farsighted churchman who looked back as well as forward, one who reminded his countrymen of the old Scots virtues inculcated by the Reformers: piety of life, diligence in work, good citizenship, and the sturdy belief that before God all people are equal.

Chalmers reflected the Calvinistic comprehensiveness that deals with the whole of life. As minister of St. John's, Glasgow, for example, he devised a remarkable poor-relief scheme. His ten thousand parishioners were divided into twenty-five subdivisions, each so organized that spiritual and material needs were fully catered for. In ameliorating the lot of the less-well-endowed classes, Chalmers's aim was ''not only that they might participate more largely in the physical enjoyments of life, but that, in exemption from oppressive toil, and with the command of dignified leisure, there might be full opportunity and scope for the development of their nobler faculties in the prosecution of all the higher objects of a rational and immortal existence.''[23]

## MORE THAN A THEOLOGICAL CREED

It has always surprised more thoughtful investigators to discover that a religious system evidently calculated to sink people into the deepest despair should instead have given moral impetus in the highest degree. As the English man of letters Viscount Morley put it, ''Those who were bound to suppose themselves moving in chains inexorably riveted, along a track ordained by an unseen will before time began, have yet exhibited an active courage, a resolute endurance, a cheerful self-restraint, an exulting self-sacrifice, that men count among the highest glories of the human conscience.''

Calvinism was more than a creed; it was a comprehensive philosophy that covered the whole of life. It was, for example, a Christian's quickened consciousness of responsibility to God and to other people everywhere, a concept that pervades the whole Reformed system of doctrine, which gave birth in Scotland to its now world-wide missionary enterprise. Calvin's writings lead on from the fundamental conception of divine sovereignty to the obligation on all Christian believers to make the gospel known. Those who took that gospel to other lands and those exiled by economic necessity alike found comfort in a basic Calvinistic tenet. This was expressed by the Highland poet Donald Matheson, who said that because the earth belongs to the Lord, His people are in their own country, whether they be in Carolina or any other land. This may well explain the Scottish tendency to settle in the far corners of the earth. Far from being a hindrance to missions, Calvinism has encouraged them; indeed the stronger the Calvinism, the more notable has been the dedication to missions. The generous giving for this purpose by the smaller bodies that have maintained a strong Calvinistic tradition is a reproach to the national Church of Scotland.[24]

## CALVIN AND CULTURE

Calvinism raised questions about the great mysteries of creation, providence, and redemption, and the Scottish mind developed an attachment to discussion of such matters. It was not uncommon for country laborers, their day's task done, to meet together to debate such high themes as predestination.

A nineteenth-century visitor to Scotland, the Protestant historian Merle d'Aubigné, wondered why the gospel had worked best in Scotland of all Reformed countries. His conclusion: ''Her attachment to sound doctrine,'' unimpeded by inordinate preoccupation with apocalyptic speculation. ''You can see,'' commented d'Aubigné, ''that the Christian spirit has been transfused into them, not from the weakened off-shoots of the Romans, but from a young, vigorous, and indigenous stock.''

Samuel Johnson had previously directed a rare tribute to the culture he had found during his famous visit to the western islands. ''I saw not one in the islands,'' he testified, ''whom I had reason to think either deficient in learning, or irregular in life, but found several with whom I could not converse without wishing, as my respect increased, that they had not been Presbyterians.''[25]

Calvinism has made a deep mark even on those who revolted from it. Some detest it, yet retain grudging admiration for it. The more famous have been in the literary field. One might think of Sir Walter Scott, Robert Louis Stevenson, Robert Burns, John Buchan, even David Hume. All of them, in one way or another, for better or for worse, were haunted by Calvinism, and in their writings returned to it again and again. One might say that if it did nothing for them spiritually it contributed to their material enrichment.

Perhaps we may see in that influence of Calvinism an odd link with Max Weber's attempted identification of the Protestant ethic with the spirit of capitalism. While that theory must remain what the Scots legal system calls ''not proven,'' it is unquestionable that Calvinism inculcated habits of diligence in daily work and high ethical standards in commercial interchange.

The most striking example of the lasting imprint of Calvinism on a Scottish writer is probably Thomas Carlyle. Not known for the robustness of his religious faith despite a pious upbringing, Carlyle wrote toward the end of his life: ''The older I grow, and I am now upon the brink of eternity, the more comes back to me the first sentence of the Catechism which I learned when a child, and the fuller and deeper its meaning becomes, 'What is the chief end of man? To glorify God and to enjoy Him for ever.' The ethical discipline of life is here regarded as obedience to the will of God in every sphere. That is fundamental to Calvinism.''[26]

## MODERN TENDENCIES

One might have imagined that the growth of the Moderate party in the Kirk, with its great stress on culture and good manners, would modify the Calvinistic influence and the vision of the godly commonwealth. One of the great Moderate leaders, William Robertson, indeed called John Knox ''barbarian,'' but not because of his theology. It was during the ascendancy of Moderatism in 1831 that John McLeod Campbell was deposed from the ministry for preaching the doctrine of universal atonement. Fifty years later, a very different general assembly, composed of Evangelicals, removed William Robertson Smith from his chair in the Free Church College for expressing views that undermined another Calvinistic cornerstone: belief in the inspiration of Scripture. The remnant Free Church would take the same action today, but the national Church of Scotland gives an honored place to professors and ministers much more radical than McLeod Campbell.

Scotland in many ways has moved far from the Calvinism of its forefathers, but it continues to haunt those who think to shrug it off. "My greatest enemy is still that old Presbyterian, John Knox," complained Lord Harewood, artistic director of the Edinburgh Festival in 1963, when the appearance on stage of a nineteen-year-old nude model caused outrage in the capital.

Two years later, the tradition of centuries was broken with the inauguration of a Sunday steamer service from the mainland to Skye—"the day sin came to the islands"—despite objections and demonstrations from the inhabitants. The same Calvinistic island saw the hand of God in the burning down of a local cafe that had installed a juke box. In another island a woman of strong religious convictions unsuccessfully instituted legal proceedings in trying to stop an electric cable passing above her land to give her neighbor the benefit of worldly television.

But there is a more serious aspect to this. In 1973 the people of Lewis, perhaps the most Calvinistic of all Hebridean islands, were confronted by a painful dilemma: a $15 million construction project that would bring much needed employment was threatened with cancellation unless Sunday work were permitted. "They don't only want two hundred acres of our land," lamented an islander, "they want part of our heritage as well."

The 1972 Church of Scotland yearbook listed in its 475 pages important anniversaries. These included the Queen Mother's birthday and Girl Guides' Thinking Day. It omitted to register the fact that it was also the four-hundredth anniversary of the death of John Knox.

The Scottish Education Department, heedless of the enormous and farsighted contribution made by the Reformer to education, ignored the quatercentenary completely. A speaker on the British Broadcasting Corporation, a body never afraid to ally itself with the spirit of the age, referred to "that tiresome old thunderer."

In St. Andrews, the old city with which Knox had such close links, the parish church did schedule a service in commemoration. Attended by town council, university court, presbytery, and distinguished guests from other churches and countries, the proceedings were raced through in forty minutes. There was something ironically apt when the city's provost, reading from Ezekiel, forgot the last verse prescribed—and left the dry bones with skin and sinew, but lifeless. One feels that Knox would have appreciated this with grim humor.

The Free Church of Scotland, however, gave honor to Knox by holding special meetings throughout the land. Its moderator that year warned that the quatercentenary might be used as an occasion for cheap jibes at the Reformer from "some of his fellow-countrymen who are mentally incapable of appreciating the ideals for which he gave his life, and morally insensitive to the degradation from which he lifted people and nation." It is true; the irreligious do not understand the religious. One need look only at the *Oxford Dictionary of Quotations:* there are some 2,450 references under William Shakespeare; not one under John Calvin.

Two significant events in recent years suggest that the Church of Scotland has not quite forgotten its past. One concerns St. Giles' in Edinburgh, that mother church of Presbyterianism in which Knox himself had ministered. Its minister, Harry Whitley, had fought for years to have a statue of John Knox brought from the church and erected outside in Parliament Square, where the metal inset that reportedly marked Knox's grave was usually obscured by the car of some legal pundit. Although this was technically church land under his control and jurisdiction, the minister found every possible obstruction put in his way. He was threatened with legal action by the lord provost and by the crown authorities.

Undaunted, he and some friends moved the statue to the square early one morning. He was summoned to city hall, told he had "no planning permission" for such an action, and ordered to remove the statue. In the best traditions of his famous predecessor, Whitley defied the establishment. The statue remained. Authority backed down. In 1965 a plaque was unveiled below the statue by a five-year-old thirteenth-generation descendant of Knox.[27]

Even in the national Kirk, however, Calvinism is still nominally acknowledged, as became evident in 1974. That was to be the year when, a majority of presbyteries having approved the proposal, the Westminster Confession was to be demoted from the status of "subordinate standard" to that of mere "historic document." But things did not go as planned by the liberal element that had been chipping away at the Confession for years. In what remains a mystery, a former moderator with legal training and few evangelical sympathies, unexpectedly rose to persuade the assembly to shelve the issue until a fuller statement of faith is forthcoming. Such a document has not yet been produced. The Kirk, which has invited Roman Catholic dignitaries to address its supreme court in recent years, is still officially committed to double predestination, strict Sabbatarianism, and identification of the pope as the Man of Sin.

# America's "Christian" Origins: Puritan New England as a Case Study

## George M. Marsden

*George M. Marsden is Professor of History at Calvin College, Grand Rapids, Michigan. He holds degrees from Haverford College (B.A.), Westminster Theological Seminary (B.D.), and Yale University (M.A., Ph.D.). He is author of* The Evangelical Mind and the New School Presbyterian Experience *(Yale, 1970),* Fundamentalism and American Culture *(Oxford, 1980), and coeditor (with Frank Roberts) of* A Christian View of History? *(Eerdmans, 1975).*

# 11

# America's "Christian" Origins: Puritan New England as a Case Study

One of the opinions most persistently and widely held in the American evangelical community and in many conservative Reformed circles is that America had essentially Christian origins from which lamentably it turned in the twentieth century. Recently, for instance, a version of this thesis has been given immense publicity in the film and book by Francis Schaeffer, *How Should We Then Live?* Schaeffer speaks repeatedly of a lost "Christian base" of Western Civilization, a "Christian Reformation base" of countries such as the United States, and of a "Christian consensus which gave us freedom within the biblical form."[1] The Moral Majority bases its programs on similar views. In whatever form such claims are made, they have to rest heavily on an appeal to the Puritan heritage as the most influential Reformation tradition shaping American culture. Logically it would be conceivable to argue for a laudable Christian foundation for American culture without appealing to the Puritan tradition. Yet if it were shown that the Puritans who settled America did not establish truly Christian dominant cultural principles that were in some important ways perpetuated, then a strong suspicion might be raised that the entire case for a now-lost Christian America rests on rather nebulous foundations.

The purpose of this chapter is to examine such general claims concerning an original "Christian" base for American culture by looking specifically at some of the cultural achievements of Puritan New England and the Puritan contributions to later American culture. The thesis

241

is that such claims should be severely qualified in the light of the ambiguous character of much of the Puritan cultural achievement and influence. This thesis in turn is based on a more theoretical argument questioning whether there are likely to be found any actual historical examples of truly Christian cultures. These conclusions finally, and more incidentally, raise some questions about various programs of present-day Calvinists for the "Christian transformation of culture."

The case of New England is especially intriguing and important because the Puritan leaders had a relatively free hand in shaping their culture according to clearly articulated rules, which they believed were uniquely and consistently Christian. As such they represent an uncommonly ideal "laboratory" in which to analyze the possibilities and pitfalls of a truly Christian culture. In the southern colonies, by contrast, major institutions such as representative government or Negro slavery evolved under circumstances motivated more by material ambition than by specifically Christian ideals. The Puritans, on the other hand, could hardly till a field without writing down a Christian rationale for their work. This explicitness and articulateness gave the Puritans a great advantage as shapers of culture. Much of what they said explicitly, other Protestants of the seventeenth century shared implicitly; but the Puritans' articulations gave the ideas distinct shape, both intellectually and institutionally. At least partially for such reasons Puritan conceptions long remained major influences in America. In the most influential American churches Puritan categories were commonplace until the mid-nineteenth century. Except for a number of remarkable southern politicians, almost every American thinker before World War I was either born in New England or educated there. As late as the early decades of the twentieth century many American literary figures were still wrestling with the vestiges of the Puritan heritage. And even more pervasive than such influences on American ideas was the Puritan impact on American values. While Puritanism could not claim to have single-handedly shaped the American conscience, it certainly helped define its most distinctive traits.

The wider community of scholars has long recognized the broad impact of Puritanism in shaping American culture. Symptomatic of the continuing interest in this theme is Sacvan Bercovitch's book *The Puritan Origins of the American Self* (New Haven, 1975), which has been remarkably popular for an academic publication. Bercovitch focuses his exposition on the Puritans' concept of their own identity. Based on their understanding of typologies in the history of God's people, they viewed New England's corporate mission as recapitulating the mission of the Old Testament nation of Israel. The related conclusion that America was chosen by God and destined to lead mankind has been traced by many historians to American Puritan concerns with the covenant and the millennium. The continuing American moral fervor has likewise commonly been traced to Puritan origins. And, growing from this, the connection between the "spirit of capitalism" and the Protestant ethic can readily be illustrated in a New England line of descent from Cotton Mather to Benjamin Franklin. In his notable *Religious History of the American People,* Sydney Ahlstrom emphasizes this formative Puritan culture, or, as he puts it, the "dominance of Puritanism in the American religious heritage":

> The future United States was settled and to a large degree shaped by those who brought with them a very special form of radical Protestantism which combined a strenuous moral precisionism, a deep commitment to evangelical experientialism, and a determination to make the state responsible for the support of these moral and religious ideas. The United States became, therefore, the land *par excellence* of revivalism, moral "legalism" and a "gospel" of work that was undergirded by the so-called Puritan Ethic.[2]

Yet, granting the view of Ahlstrom and other scholars that the Puritan influences on American life were indeed large, the issue remains to be settled as to whether the Puritans provided a truly Christian basis for American culture. The question is complicated by the fact that "Christian"—like "Puritan"—has a confusing variety of meanings. First, it can have a weak generic meaning as simply describing some connection with the Judeo-Christian heritage. Almost everything in Western culture from the late Roman Empire until about 1800 was "Christian" in this sense. Yet it is clear that there are many such "Christian cultural developments"—the Thirty Years' War and persecution of the Jews and the Waldensians, for instance—of which we would not approve.

A second common use of the term *Christian* and related terms refers to the presence of many individuals in a culture who were apparently Christians. A brief reflection indicates that the presence of Christians is no guarantee that the cultural activities they pursue warrant our approval. Many Christians today, for instance, disapprove of South African racial policies even though these are promoted by many apparently sincere Calvinist Christians. Throughout history many genuine Christians, even when they have been attempting to apply their Christian principles to guide their cultural activities, have turned out to have been drastically mistaken.

If we wish to talk about Christian cultural activities in an evaluative way, then, we will have to indicate that we have a third and more restricted meaning in mind. We will mean cultural phenomena produced by apparently Christian persons who not only are attempting to follow God's will but in fact succeed reasonably well in doing so. That is, although we do not expect perfection, we may expect that a "Christian" society in this sense would generally distinguish itself from most other societies in the commendability of both its ideals and its practices. Family, churches, and state would on the whole be properly formed. Justice and charity would normally be shown toward minorities and toward the poor and other unfortunate people. The society would be predominantly peaceful and law-abiding. Proper moral standards would generally prevail. Cultural activities such as learning, business, or the subduing of nature would be pursued basically in accord with God's will. In short, such a society would be a proper model for us to imitate.

## New England as a Test Case

Was Puritan New England such a model Christian culture? The Puritans thought of themselves as a "city on a hill" for the world to imitate. In fact, their culture did display many admirable features. Yet their achievements were flawed in some basic and most ironic ways. The corruption of the best often becomes the worst. And in this case, some of the best of Puritan principles were transformed for the worse in the actual historical setting. Most ironically, probably the principal factor turning the Puritan cultural achievement into a highly ambiguous one was the very concept that is the central theme of this chapter—the idea that one can create a truly Christian culture.

Viewed from a Reformed Christian perspective, the Puritans indeed seem to have started with many of the best of principles. The presupposition of Puritan thought was that the Triune God had revealed himself preeminently in Scripture. Scripture, then, through God's gracious illuminating work among the regenerate, was the only sure guide to God's truth. Everything that one did had therefore to be based on biblical principles. Although Scripture might not reveal everything one needed to know (reason must be a subordinate guide), Scripture touched on a great deal, and persons were to be guided by it wherever it spoke. Especially in the area of redemptive concerns, the Bible was a complete guide. Hence with respect to the church one was to do nothing that went beyond Scripture. This initially was the issue that separated Puritans from Anglicans in the late sixteenth century. Both accepted the authority of Scripture, yet Puritans saw the Bible as regulative on every subject on which it spoke, even to the wearing of wigs, for instance. With respect to the conduct of the church, the Puritans' fundamental principle was not only to do what was consistent with Scripture, but to do nothing that was not commanded by Scripture. Certainly the Puritans could not be faulted for neglect of the principle of *sola Scriptura*. Indeed, if they had a fault in this area, it was in sometimes pushing this good principle to an extreme.

Their essential theological principles must seem, from a Reformed Christian perspective, laudable also. Their theology was essentially in the tradition of Calvin, especially in emphasizing the sovereignty of

God, human inadequacy, dependence solely on God's grace, and the necessity of directing all of life toward the end of glorifying God.

With respect to expressions of basic motives, Puritan society accordingly appears especially commendable. Both publicly and privately God's sovereignty and the necessity of dependence on His will were widely recognized.

Furthermore the moral standards to which most of the population apparently subscribed appear to have been extremely high. God's law was intensely studied and in principle respected. Unquestionably the presence of such high ideals had some very positive cultural effects—in family life, respect for neighbors and their rights, concern for the poor, avoidance of ostentation, expressions of reverence for God's name, and the like. The line, of course, between morality arising out of genuine piety and that arising from formal legalism is a thin one, and no doubt the Puritans often transgressed into the latter, as their opponents were fond of pointing out. Nevertheless one could hardly doubt that the vigorous introduction of biblical moral standards had a generally commendable influence in their cultural life.

On this score, however, the Puritans themselves were the first to emphasize how far short of the standards they professed their actual practice fell. Their own very realistic accounts of the state of their society make clear that if moral practice is to be the gauge for whether a culture is "Christian" in a strict sense, even the Puritans are hardly a reliable model to imitate. This is so not only because of their frequent moral failures. Apparently they often simply drew implications concerning the Christian life from the proclivities of their age and movement more than from eternal principles. Their harsh attitudes toward outsiders, for instance, are hardly models that we should imitate.

While it would be impractical here to attempt to weigh the relative success or failure of each aspect of the Puritan experiment, in their central effort in culture building—that of establishing a civil government—we can see most sharply the difficulties of establishing a truly "Christian" society. In founding their government the Puritans started with the commendable principles just described. Regarding Massachusetts Bay, certainly the principal Puritan colony, John Winthrop, the first governor, had formulated a very precise social-political rationale even before his ship touched American shores. Starting with the premise that God's glory should be made manifest in human affairs, Winthrop outlined how those who love God should live. His summary was essentially in the Augustinian and biblical tradition. Those who glorified God should keep His law. With respect to social relationships it is "commaunded to love his neighbor as himself vpon this ground stands all the precepts of the morrall lawe, which concerns our dealings with men.''[3] Such a conception of the ideal for the relationships and attitudes of Christians seems, at the least, a good start.

The central problem, however, immediately presented itself when Winthrop, the civil governor, attempted to apply the summary of the law to the entire society of Massachusetts Bay. While in the "modell" he made the distinction between justice, which should be expected in any society, and mercy to be found in Christian associations, he clearly considered the entire Massachusetts society as such to be essentially Christian. In making this assumption Winthrop was, of course, only reflecting a point generally taken for granted since the latter days of the Roman Empire—that Western society was at least in principle, or at the very least in potential, Christian. Winthrop expressed this assumption in typically Puritan covenantal form, from which the Puritan conception of the American enterprise followed. The Old Testament clearly taught that God dealt with nations according to covenants, either explicit or implicit, the stipulations of which were God's law. Covenant-breaking nations were punished; covenant-keeping nations were blessed. The people of God, Israel in the Old Testament and the church in the New Testament age, stood of course in a special relationship to God. If they were constituted as a political entity, and here Israel seemed obviously the model to imitate, then they should make their social-political covenant explicit, following the examples in the Pentateuch. This is precisely what Winthrop and his fellow Puritans regarded themselves as doing. They were becoming a people of God with a political identity and so they stood in precisely the same relationship to God as did Old Testament Israel. Bercovitch explains this equation in terms of typology:

> Sacred history did not end, after all, with the Bible; it became the task of typology to define the course of the church ("spiritual Israel") and of the exemplary Christian life. In this view Christ, the "antitype," stood at the center of history, casting His shadow forward to the end of time as well as backward across the Old Testament. Every believer was a *typus* or *figura Christi,* and the church's peregrination, like that of old Israel, was at once recapitulative and adumbrative.[4]

Winthrop accordingly assumed that he could transfer the principles of nationhood found in ancient Israel to the Massachusetts Bay Company with no need for explanation. In the "Modell of Christian Charity" he accordingly based his argument that love summarizes the law of the land directly on the Old Testament covenant. "Thus stands the cause between God and us," he affirmed. "We are entered into Covenant with him for this worke. . . ." He went so far as to say that if God heard this company's prayers and "bring us in peace to the place wee desire [that is, if the ships make it safely to Massachusetts], then hath hee ratified his Covenant and sealed our Commissions [and] will expect a strict performance of the

Articles contained in it. . . . ." Quoting directly from Moses' farewell in Deuteronomy 30, Winthrop concluded with the promise of either blessings or curses dependent on the observance of the law:

> Beloved there is now sett before us life, and good, deathe and evill in that wee are Commaunded this day to love the Lord our God, and to love one another to walke in his wayes and to keepe his Commaundements and his Ordinances, and his lawes, and the Articles of our Covenant with him that we may live and be multiplyed . . . [or] perishe out of the good Land. . . .[5]

Here, before the main body of Puritans ever set foot on American shores, is compressed in Winthrop's thought the paradoxical character of almost the entire Puritan enterprise. They believed their vision for the transformation of human culture was grounded solely on the best principles drawn from Scripture. Yet their historical experience—a tradition of over a thousand years of living in "Christendom," a concept that classical Protestantism did not dispel—led them to interpret Scripture in an ultimately pretentious way that gave their own state and society the exalted status of a new Israel. Some of the results of this identification were laudable, such as the awareness of the necessity of dependence on God in human affairs, the recognition of the fact that states are ordained by God, and a clear affirmation of the rule of law. But these positive accomplishments were offset by more dubious practical consequences. Old Testament law was directly if not exclusively incorporated into the legal systems of New England. So we find in the Massachusetts "Body of Liberties" of 1641 that "if any man after legall conviction shall have or worship any other god, but the Lord God, he shall be put to death." The same penalty was prescribed, together with the corresponding Old Testament citations, for witchcraft, blasphemy, murder, sodomy, homosexuality, adultery, and kidnapping.[6] Such laws were not all without precedent in English Common Law and elsewhere, yet here the Old Testament texts were copied directly into the New England law books. The most notorious cases of a major miscarriage of justice in New England, the Salem witchcraft executions, although not as extensive as many similar incidents in Europe and resulting from a temporary social hysteria, nonetheless were based legally on the assumption that New England law should duplicate that of ancient Israel.

Although sincere efforts were made to keep church and state technically separate, in fact it was the state that established the church in the colonies, saw to it that only true religion was taught, required church attendance, banished dissenters, and even called synods. In Massachusetts Bay the voting franchise was limited to church members, with the corollary that only church members were eligible for public office. Behind all the practical confusion of church and state was the overriding presumption that New England was the New Israel.

Nowhere do the dangers of this assumption become more clear than in the Puritans' treatment of the Native Americans. Since the Puritans considered themselves God's chosen people, they concluded that they had the right to take the land from the heathen Indians. Again, they had explicitly biblical rationale for their policies. They regarded themselves as the new political Israel; but it was a case of mistaken identity. The result was worse than if they had made no attempt to find a Christian basis for politics. Ironically, they were using Christian rationale to justify their own pride and selfish interests.

The paradoxes in the "Christian" ideals of the main body of New England Puritans become more apparent when we contrast their formulations with those of the one person to challenge their crucial assumption regarding Israel and the church, Roger Williams. Williams too may be counted among those Calvinists who contributed to the American heritage, though among Calvinists themselves he represented a minority position. In his view of the church Williams in a sense was more puritan than the Puritans. Concerned above all else with preserving the purity of the church, he came to the conclusion that this could be accomplished only by the clear separation of the church from the state and society. Williams differed from the vast majority of Calvinists of his era in holding consistently that the church was an essentially spiritual entity made up of those bound together in pure love to God. This conception altered his view of the proper interpretation of the Old Testament and typology. In the prevailing Puritan view Christ was the antitype toward whom Old Testament history pointed and the principles of the Old Testament age were recapitulated in the church. Williams, on the other hand, though he saw that the Old Testament types were fulfilled in Christ, also held that the church was the spiritual antitype of Israel, rather than a type exactly equivalent to political Israel. So in reference to Old Testament Israel, Williams writes:

> The *Antitype* to this state I have proved to be the *Christian Church* which consequently hath been and is afflicted with spirituall *plagues, desolations, captivities,* for corrupting of the *Religion* which hath been revealed unto them.[7]

In Williams' view, then, even the church was prone to corruption as Israel had been, and surely the civil government did not stand closer to representing purely God's elect nation than did the church. Hence states, far from being potentially new Israels, were a further corrupting influence and had no business trying to enforce principles of true religion.

Thus perhaps we ought to credit Williams as the best exemplar or the truly positive Calvinist influence in American culture. His clear separation of church and state with the consequent toleration of religious dissent recommends him as a most attractive figure. So does his refusal to suppose that Englishmen by virtue of their covenant with God had acquired some special right to take land from the Native Americans. Yet it is surely ironic to have to present Williams as the chief evidence for the commendable influences of Calvinism on American culture. First, by almost anyone's standards he was something of an eccentric. Second, by the Puritans' own standards it was precisely for his stand on the relationship of Christianity to culture that Williams was despised by the vast majority of Puritans and their most direct heirs.

When we look then at the Puritans' efforts to establish the actual structures of a "Christian" society, our quest for finding laudable Christian origins in the American experience ends, lost in a maze of paradoxes. The principles with which they start seem good enough, and certainly there were many positive achievements. But every culture in history has some good laws and institutions mixed with some bad ones. Puritan New England does not seem to be unusually distinguished in this respect. Despite their strenuous efforts to apply good principles in building a model Christian society that would be a "City upon a Hill"[8] for the world to imitate, we are left uncertain that the city in question is the City of God.

## THE LONGER-RANGE IMPACT OF CALVINISM ON AMERICAN CULTURE: A CALVINISTIC ASSESSMENT

### American Principles of Government

Given such uneven foundations, it is not surprising that later America's secularized cultural edifice displays accentuations of the paradoxical traits. Secularization* certainly does not correct the fundamental design. Sometimes it may inadvertantly improve it, but such alterations are both accidental and haphazard. The unevenness remains, sometimes more spectacular or even grotesque.

Such conclusions apply to the subject of the long-range Puritan contributions to American principles of government—certainly the focal point for the persistent and popular arguments that America had laudable Christian foundations. The cornerstone in such conceptions is the Puritan emphasis on law, Rousas J. Rushdoony puts it this way:

---

*"Secularization" is an ambiguous term that legitimately might be used in a positive way. I have in mind, however, either or both of two things that are essentially negative: (1) a debasing of Christianity by a mixture of it with alien elements so that phenomena or ideals that are essentially unchristian come to be regarded as part of Christianity, or (2) a replacing of Christianity by a new "secular" religion, such as Marxism, nationalism, materialism, rationalism, existentialism, individualism, political liberalism or conservatism, etc.

But, basic to all colonial thought, was the ancient and Christian sense of the transcendence and majesty of law. According to John Calvin, "the law is a silent magistrate, and a magistrate a speaking law."[9]

Such principles had been explicit in the Puritan view of the covenant in which God's law was ordained above both the government and the people. The execution of Charles I in England in 1649 took for granted the centrality of this higher law. John Locke's formulations in the next generation were clearly a secularization of this fundamental concept. Natural law, ordained by the deity and discoverable by reason, reigned above monarchs. By 1776 such conceptions were so widely held in America that the archpropagandist of the Revolution, Thomas Paine, could claim them as common sense. Echoing the Puritan language, Paine suggested that a

day be solemnly set apart from proclaiming the charter; let it be brought forth, placed on the divine law, the Word of God; let a crown be placed thereon, by which the world may know that so far as we approve of monarchy, that in America the law is king.[10]

As Paine was well aware, this concept had a strongly Christian and Puritan lineage in America. In the terms we have defined, it would qualify as at least generically Christian, and to the extent that we might approve of the higher law idea we should give the Puritans and their heirs the credit for being among the chief promoters of it. Yet giving Puritans and other Calvinists credit for promoting such ideas is not equivalent to establishing that the concepts on which American government were based were essentially "Christian" in any strong, positive sense. Even in the weak generic sense there is some ambiguity in identifying the concept as essentially "Christian." After all, the concept has other roots as well—Greek, Roman, Anglo-Saxon, and (as the case of Paine makes clear) Enlightenment. To single out the "Christian" aspect is misleading, even though the Judeo-Christian tradition made an important and probably quite laudable contribution.

Suppose, however, that we examine the claim that is more central to our inquiry, that the basic principles on which the government of the United States was founded were Christian in the narrow, positive, evaluative sense. Furthermore, suppose we take as our standard for what is properly consistent with God's Word and will, a present-day Calvinist understanding. In other words, aside from the fact that there were some significant influences on the United States government that were generically Calvinist, we will be exploring the extent to which we can claim that the foundations of the government were *properly Calvinist*. The result of such an investigation is to find that at the very root of the eighteenth-century political theory on which the United States government was founded is a distinctly anti-Calvinistic view of human nature. Virtually all the prevailing political thought of the day in America was based on the assumption that the light of natural reason was strong enough to reveal the eternal principles of God's law to any unprejudiced right-thinking person. Depravity, it seemed, may have touched the wills of humans, but it was no longer considered to have blinded their intellects. So this position, which was at the basis of American theory of government, was indeed generically related to biblically founded higher law ideals, but it modified the distinctly Calvinistic version of this ideal at a crucial point.

In light of the view of human nature in the prevailing eighteenth-century epistemology, it is curiously paradoxical that one of the areas where there is some largely genuine Calvinist influence on the United States form of government is in the view of human nature reflected in the Constitution. This paradox cannot be resolved simply by the suggestion that the Declaration of Independence, based on optimistic natural law theory, represented a different and less properly Christian tradition of thought than the Constitution built around the assumption of human depravity. Eighteenth-century American political thinkers were in fact quite unified in their fundamental assumptions on this point. Persons as diverse, for instance, as Thomas Jefferson and John Witherspoon, to pick the most "Enlightened" and the most Calvinist of the major figures, agreed that humans naturally had essentially reliable innate abilities to apprehend the truth, both in the physical world and in the sphere of morality. Both Jefferson and Witherspoon were influenced on such points by the philosophers of the Scottish Enlightenment, such as Francis Hutcheson and Thomas Reid. It is true that James Madison, a student of Witherspoon, while sharing such an optimistic epistemology with the other founding fathers, had a stronger sense than did Jefferson of the tendency for the passions of self-interest or of factional interest to blind persons to the truth. The United States Constitution, shaped considerably by Madison, reflects this view. When in "Federalist #10" Madison describes a faction as citizens "who are united and actuated by some common impulse of passion, or of interest, adverse to the rights of other citizens,"[11] he is reflecting something of the Calvinist-Augustinian picture of the driving impulse in the civilizations of this world. Although some other traditions contributed to this picture, Puritanism probably had the most to do with giving it its prominence in American culture. Indeed in Western culture the Bible is probably the chief (though not the only) source of this account of human inadequacy. The Christian-Calvinist contribution then on this point is quite a positive one.

Nevertheless the same qualifications apply here as regarding the concepts of higher law. To say there is a Christian-Calvinist contribution to an idea is not to say that the secularized version of it is "Christian" in more than a generic sense. One of the most common forms of secularization is that of a properly Christian principle becoming mixed with a quite alien principle. The resulting amalgamation may well be no longer properly or consistently Christian, or it may be only weakly Christian. This was the case with the view of depravity in eighteenth-century American political theory. It was an attenuated view of depravity and in fact was doomed to a brief existence as the basis for a frankly secularized form of government. At least in the progressive and romantic atmosphere of nineteenth-century American culture, the dogma of the essential goodness and reliability of human perceptions soon obliterated the sense of the limitations of the human will. Whatever may have been the positive Christian contributions on this point, the fact remains that a quite anti-Calvinist view of human autonomy was a major factor at the center of early American political theory and very soon became a controlling idea.

These same qualifications in speaking of Puritan influences on the American concepts of higher law and human depravity are necessary when speaking of the Puritan contributions to democracy. There are simply too many other sources for it to be anything but confusing to speak of the development as basically "Christian," even in the generic sense. Nonetheless the evidence is clear that Puritanism was among the major forces that abetted the growth of democracy in America. Although the first settlers opposed democracy in principle on the ground that once God had ordained governors, the power of government resided with them and not with the people; they nevertheless did advocate representative government on the ground that originally it is "the People, in whom fundamentally all power lyes," even though they give this power away when they choose their representatives.[12] Puritan church government embodied the same representative principles. In either case there was a strong tendency, typical of Protestantism, to move away from simple authoritarianism toward democratizing the power base of society. Moreover, Puritanism was allied with the party of Parliament against the king and bishops. This anti-authoritarian tradition in the later seventeenth century merged into Whig politics and was carried on into the eighteenth century in the influential tradition of the "Commonwealth Men." These dissenting libertarian writers, arguing on the grounds of natural rights, morality, and Christianity, opposed both ecclesiastical and political tyranny and asserted the necessity of checking corrupt executive power by vigorously asserting the rights of the people. In America this merger of Whig and Puritan traditions was widely accepted as the self-evident political norm, both in New England and elsewhere. So, for example, we find so liberal a Congregationalist as John Adams beginning his attacks on British rule by a bitter denunciation of the "wicked confederacy between the two systems of tyranny," the canon and the feudal law.[13] Similarly, even the strictest Calvinists had by this time thoroughly accepted the standard eighteenth-century Lockean principles of representative government. There can be no doubt, then, that Puritanism made a major contribution to the growth of American democratic thought.

Yet as soon as we reach this conclusion, the usual ambiguities loom if we attempt to shift the ground to talking of the properly "Christian" foundations of American politics. In the development of American democratic theory, as in the cases of the previously mentioned issues of higher law and human depravity, the heart of the problem is the epistemological tendency of almost all eighteenth-century thought. The issue is most clear if we go back to the observation that even many of the strictest Calvinists in America accepted Lockean and eighteenth-century Whig "Commonwealth Men" tradition as political orthodoxy. The reason for their thorough acceptance of this essentially natural-law tradition was that they had lost any strong sense that reason for the Christian and the non-Christian will often point in different directions. Affirming rather the full validity of the honest conclusions of natural intellect, they could readily adopt the secularized political wisdom of the day as fully and properly "Christian." This identification of Whig politics as Christian in a positive evaluative sense was particularly plausible because the tradition was indeed Christian in the generic sense. The result was that at the time of the American Revolution there was no distinctly "Christian" line of political thought as opposed to secular political thought. Everything was Christian, and nothing was. Orthodox Calvinist American patriots accordingly shared a single political orthodoxy with the Thomas Paines, Thomas Jeffersons, and Ethan Allens of their day. Only when it came to narrowly restricted questions of "religion" did sharp differences appear.

This phenomenon of a lack of a distinctly "Christian" political thought, and yet a willingness to regard the contemporary secular political views as essentially Christian reveals a characteristic of the process of secularization that has been noted in other connections. When secularization begins to take place, it does not necessarily take the form of the contraction of areas that Christianity touches, but may very well involve the apparent expansion of such areas.[14] In this case the basis of the expansion is once again the apparently generous epistemological concession that allows the validity of unaided human reason and common sense. The result is a sort of Christian ideological imperialism in which Christian emblems are posted on the whole territory of the political thought of the day. Accordingly, when the American Revolution broke out, Calvinist clergy were among the first to identify the principles of the American cause with divine revelation. Typical of the abundant extravagant identification is that which came from a New England pulpit in 1777 informing the congregation that the Revolution was the cause of truth, against error and falsehood; the cause of righteousness against iniquity; the cause of the oppressed against the oppressor; the cause of pure and undefiled religion, against bigotry, superstition, and human invention. . . . In short, it is the cause of heaven against hell.[15]

Such sentiments bring us to the heart of the matter concerning America's "Christian" origins, for in fact in such rhetoric was born the notorious American civil religion. In this civil religion the state became the object of worship, yet the language used to describe the state was drawn from Scripture. More precisely, the redemptive-historical typology that the Puritans had applied to their own enterprise was now transferred to the secular American establishment. The same process that had blurred distinctions between Christian and non-Christian political theory in the eighteenth century allowed the obliteration in the minds of Americans of the distinction between sacred and secular history. So in American thought in the nineteenth century it became commonplace to refer to America as a land long hidden, but now revealed to be the stage on which the last act in the history of redemption would commence. As Lyman Beecher put it, in a context explicitly referring to the approach of the millennium:

But where could such a nation be found? It must be created for it had no existence upon the earth. Look now at the history of our fathers and behold what God hath wrought, . . . a powerful nation in full enjoyment of civil and religious liberty, where all the energies of men . . . find scope and excitement on purpose to show the world by experiment of what man is capable.[16]

Such rhetoric, which confused the United States both with ancient Israel and with the millennial kingdom, was a powerful ingredient in the growing American nationalism. The distortions involved became particularly apparent in time of war—especially in the Civil War, when Christianity became the chief rhetorical weapon in the campaign to save the political union. During that war the most popular song of the Union proclaimed that "His truth goes marching on," but secularized cultural factors called the tune and set the pace; Scripture supplied only the words.

## The Moral Influence of Calvinism

While American political developments taken as a whole may yield many "Christian" and Calvinist influences but not the conclusion that there was once a properly Christian America, there is at least one more major area where a case can be made for a version of such a conclusion. This is the area of general moral influence in helping to create a law-abiding citizenry with a strong conscience. Sidney Ahlstrom goes so far as to suggest that this was the principal contribution of Puritanism to American democracy in that "Puritanism almost created a new kind of 'civic person.' "[17] Although the exact connections are, of course, impossible to document definitively, it does appear that Americans were generally well disposed to obey the civil law, to play by the rules in the democratic process, and to bring their actions and those of others under moral review. These dispositions can be traced, at least in part, to the Puritan emphases on God's law as the fundamental basis of their society. Such emphases for the Puritans involved not only the idea that the government was subject to a higher law, but also that all citizens were obliged to keep God's law. The law, said Scripture, was a schoolmaster preparing persons for regeneration; hence it seemed a valuable service that the state could perform to require the entire citizenry to keep the law. Furthermore, since the terms of the covenant stipulated that the society would be blessed or cursed by God, depending on its obedience to the moral law, every citizen had a strong motive both to keep the law himself and to encourage his neighbors to do the same.

Since God's law was the schoolmaster for New England, and New England to a large extent was the schoolmaster for America, Americans in the Puritan tradition indeed seem to have had an unusually highly developed internalized sense of civic and moral responsibility. This generically "Puritan" conscience in fact still provides an important aspect of the explanation of the periodic eras of reform that shaped American political and social history. Such reforms seem typically to have had middle-class leadership that could not be explained in terms of self-interest of the class itself. The antislavery movement, for instance, had a strong Yankee leadership who saw the progress of the entire nation as retarded by the sins of its southern members. Similarly, although its expressions were in somewhat more secularized terms, the Progressive movement of the late nineteenth and early twentieth centuries must be explained at least in part in terms of the bad conscience of the otherwise comfortable middle class.

Such attitudes can be related to a general Puritan attitude toward culture, best summarized by the concept of "calling." As was true of Calvinists generally, Puritans emphasized that one's spiritual responsibilities were not confined to the church or devotional life. Rather, in every aspect of one's activities, even the very mundane, one was called to glorify God. Hence one's responsibilities to society—e.g., to participate in the political sphere and to see that justice was done—were part of one's spiritual vocation. Similarly one's work, whether pastoring actual sheep or God's people, was a sacred duty. Again, to the extent that these ideals reflected proper motives, we latter-day Calvinists would approve of them as properly Christian.

Ironically, however, Calvinists should probably take less pleasure than most other persons might concerning the longer-range impact of such Puritan ideals in shaping American culture. The sense of moral responsibility when it appears as an American trait appears so in a predominantly secularized form. That is, it is a moral sense detached from the gospel of grace. The irony involved is perhaps clearest with respect to the work ethic. The prototype of the typically American expression of this impulse is Benjamin Franklin. The morality has a Puritan lineage indeed; but its actual expression is a works righteousness detached from the gracious work of Christ. Similarly the moral and reform impulses in American society have in their secularized form the character of a religion of moralism. The nation, it is supposed, will save itself by its own works of righteousness; such moral fervor often becomes an end in itself. The clearest examples are found in the secularized versions of American Protestantism itself—such as Unitarianism and modernism—in which religion became morality. Calvinism indeed helped foster such traditions, but in their secularized versions the offspring of the Calvinist ethic turn out to be at best the works righteousness of Pelagianism or even of simple secular moralism.

Yet the defenders of a more positive view of Puritanism's contributions to American morality might point out that many American Christians never did bow the knee to the Baal of modernism, let alone Unitarianism, and that among the many conservative Protestants still found in America a healthy Protestant ethic still survives. In the late 1970s, after all, one-third of Americans reputedly claimed an experience of being born again. Yet American evangelicalism, at least since about 1870, provides little aid in our search for continuations of a truly positive Calvinist influence in American culture. Evangelicalism itself secularized in America and as it did some central aspects of the Calvinist ethical tradition were among the chief casualties. Modern evangelicalism and fundamentalism tended to shift the focus in Christianity from God's sovereignty to personal human experience. Typically the epitome of Christian experience was described in terms of a special act of consecration in which one gave up oneself (as in "laying all on the altar") and allowed Christ or the Holy Spirit to take over. Those who so consecrated themselves attained what they considered to be a life in which they enjoyed at least consistent victory over sin. The spiritual sensitivities, concern for holiness, and evangelistic zeal associated with this position certainly have often been admirable. Yet such perfectionist or semiperfectionist tendencies in American evangelicalism often involved the contraction of the areas that sanctification touched. The Christian life came to involve largely "spiritual" activities, especially personal devotions, witnessing about one's own experience, and the avoidance of select symptoms of worldliness. It tended also to be strongly individualistic, with relatively little sense of corporate callings or responsibilities.

A further crucial aspect of the puritan-Calvinist ethic was lost in this typically American evangelical ethic. Essential to the Puritan outlook, and certainly one of the great sources of virtue in their whole way of life, was a sense of the inability even of the Christian to serve God perfectly. The Puritan's life was hence characterized by continual self-examination and a strong sense of one's own worthlessness before the holiness of God. Such a sense of one's own limitations served as a continual reminder of the necessity to throw oneself entirely on God's grace. This sense of limitation was an essential aspect of the Puritan ethic and an important counter to the tendencies toward pretention in those who considered themselves to have been chosen by God. It applied even to their concept of the nation so that self-confidence was limited by recognition of unworthiness, as manifested in the immense Jeremiad literature lamenting the declines of Puritan societies. This sense of limitation before God was, however, an aspect of the Puritan ethic that could not easily be perpetuated in the process of secularization. Rather, as the emphasis in the culture generally shifted from God to humans, the sense of human limitation simply tended to disappear. This move away from the Calvinist view of human nature, almost completed by the mid–nineteenth century, soon transformed the ethic of most of Calvinism's evangelical heirs. Although American evangelicalism and fundamentalism preserved and proclaimed much of the gospel, they paradoxically acted as a force to counter one of the major positive influences of Calvinism on the moral ideals of Christians in America. Ironically, by this Calvinistic standard American evangelicalism itself became one of the sources of the destruction of positive Christian influences in America—a fact that evangelical spokespersons themselves so much lament.

## Why There Are No Christian Cultures

What is left, then, of the myth of America's "Christian" origins? On the positive side we find that the Puritans approached the task of culture building with some truly excellent principles and many apparently good motives. Christianity accordingly appears to have had positive influences on early New England culture. Such a claim, however, is considerably less than saying that the culture was essentially "Christian" in a strict sense or even that it has an essentially "Christian base."

The reason why the Puritans and all similar groups in history have failed to establish a "Christian culture" seems clear—although the advocates of "Christian culture" appear to ignore it. At the base of every human culture is a shared set of "religious" values that help hold the society together. These values are not simply those of the official organized religion of the culture (although usually such a religion strongly supports such value systems), but are those ideals or things that persons in a culture value most highly, are committed to, and would be willing to die for. Most of the traits of this central "religion" in a culture reflect directly the values that predominate in fallen human nature. So, for instance, one factor that we find universally as a major value holding cultures together is sinful pride. This pride might be manifested in any one of a number of ways; but among the most common have been tribalism, racism, nationalism, and pride in one's class or status. Each is a means of convincing a people that they are inherently superior to other peoples and hence can treat others as inferiors or even subhumans worthy of disdain or even abuse. Similarly, every human culture is held together by the simple shared values of selfish interests. Putting oneself and one's group first is in fact almost the premise on which human governments are based. Other widely held values found in almost every culture are materialism, love of power, and love of violence. While cultures may be held together also by other values—such as love or respect for elders, respect for law, love of virtue—most of the widely held values related to human nature turn out to be directly antithetical to Christianity.

What happens, then, when Christianity is introduced into such a culture on a large scale? First of all, if the "Christianization" is more than just a formality, many persons in the civilization may live lives radically transformed by God's grace. If this means that sin is eradicated in the lives of such saints who control the government, the society may be transformed into something that—except for some areas that might be missed due to blind spots, misinformation, prejudices of the age, and the like—is reasonably Christian in the narrowest sense. However, in no society of any considerable size has the overwhelming majority of citizens been radically committed Christians. Furthermore, even the greatest saints fail to overcome fully in this life such sins as pride and self-interest, and often even materialism, love of power, and love of violence. So a civilization, even if it contains many true Christians, will retain these nearly universal human traits. The introduction of Christianity will indeed improve the civilization, since many persons and some resulting cultural activities and institutions will be shaped by ideals more or less in conformity with God's will. So alongside the sinful tendencies at the core of a civilization may be other important positive tendencies to which Christianity has contributed. Hendrikus Berkhof, for instance, has argued that the coming of Christ has introduced into Western culture a new concept of the importance of the suffering and the oppressed. "An ordinary street scene, such as an ambulance stopping all traffic because *one* wounded man must be transported, is the result of the coming of the Kingdom." These and similar observations as to Christianity's impact on culture have considerable credibility. Yet it is important to emphasize, as Berkhof does, that these are the harbingers of the kingdom. "They are the crocuses in the winter of a fallen world."[18]

Christianity does on occasion transform aspects of culture; yet on any large scale or in the long run such transformation will be severely limited by other forces at the base of a society. The gains, although real, will almost always be ambiguous, since in many cases Christianity will be amalgamated with the various anti-Christian forces that distort the foundations of any society. Such ambiguities become particularly strong if the society comes to regard itself as more or less officially "Christian." In such cases the badge of Christianity will be superimposed on a culture that retains some essentially anti-Christian features.

Puritan culture, then, for all its merits, can hardly qualify as a model Christian culture for us to imitate. This by no means is to condemn the Puritans, for in many ways they present an attractive and successful example of applying Christianity to cultural activities. Yet just because of this degree of success, they are an excellent example of the inherent limits in attempting to establish a model Christian culture.

What can we say then about the positive "Christian" influences on culture other than that it does good for individuals? Certainly there are many broad, obviously good influences as when family lives are improved, charity is displayed, the poor are cared for, high moral standards are pursued, just laws are enacted, personal worth is properly valued, minorities and outsiders are regarded as persons in God's image—all because of more-or-less proper understandings of God's Word and will. Yet such influences do not result automatically from the presence of apparently sincere Christians in a culture. The equation between the number of Christians in a society and the positive cultural results is never a simple one. Often, in fact, the positive influences seem not to predominate. To resolve these apparent paradoxes it may be helpful to use the image of the salt of the earth. That is, Christianity acts as a retardant against the natural tendencies of cultures built on fallen human nature to fall into decay. Such Christian influences are not always obvious, but they may be crucial.

These observations have important implications not only for assessing Christian influences in the past but also for our own cultural task. Certainly if we speak, as many Calvinists do, of that transformation H. Richard Niebuhr described when he spoke of "Christ the transformer of culture," we must do so with a realistic view of the limited and often ambiguous nature of Christian accomplishments in these tasks in the past. We should be reminded also that we ourselves likely do not have the blueprints for establishing the kingdom of heaven on earth. We should recognize that we are no more careful students of God's will than were the Puritans and we are no more exempt from misreading that will than they were. The relationship between Christianity and culture is always reciprocal. The culture transforms the Christian at the same time the Christian transforms the culture. Hence as we assume our responsibilities for the "transformation of culture," we should do so with an equal appreciation for the view that Niebuhr describes as "Christ and culture in paradox."[19]

Yet the combination of these two views does not reduce the urgency or the necessity of our cultural task. If anything, we should use such obligations to apply our Christianity to all areas of life even more urgently. Yet as we do so, we should recognize that the positive effects of Christianity are basically those of mitigating the fundamentally distorted character of human cultural life. Although the principles of the kingdom are anticipated by Christian life in this age, anything even vaguely like the full-orbed reality of the kingdom in the progress of culture must await another age.

# The Scotch-Irish
# in America

## *C. Gregg Singer*

*C. Gregg Singer is professor of Church History and Systematic Theology at the Atlanta School of Biblical Studies. He holds the degrees of A.B. from Haverford College; A.M. and Ph.D. from the University of Pennsylvania. He has been chairman of the history departments at Salem College and Wheaton College; vice-president and chairman of the history department at Belhaven College; chairman of the history department at Catawba College before his retirement in 1977, at which time he assumed his present position. He has written* A Theological Interpretation of American History; John Calvin: His Roots and Fruits; Arnold Toynbee; A Critical Study; The Unholy Alliance; From Rationalism to Irrationality; A Christian Approach to Philosophy and History; South Carolina in the Confederation: 1781–1789, *and is coauthoring* The Church and the Sword *with Commander Russell Evans, USCG (Ret.).*

# 12

# The Scotch-Irish in America

Of all the ethnic and national groups who came to America during the colonial period, the Scotch-Irish were the most pervasive in their influence on the development of those colonies in which they settled. They were a major factor in the shaping of the character of American Presbyterianism. Not only were they the most numerous but their settlements were the most widespread, extending from Maine to Georgia by 1750.

Although the Scotch-Irish were sparse in numbers in much of New England, they gathered strength in New York and became a dominant voice in colonial life in Pennsylvania, New Jersey, Maryland, Virginia, and the Carolinas. The Puritans were confined to New England, for the most part; the Dutch were largely centered in New York, New Jersey, and Pennsylvania; the Swedes in the Delaware Valley; and the Quakers in Pennsylvania, New Jersey, and Delaware. Although the Germans rivaled the Scotch-Irish in their peregrinations, they were not as numerous and tended to concentrate in Pennsylvania, New York, New Jersey, the Valley of Virginia, and the Piedmont area of North and South Carolina. The Germans also represented differing strains of Protestant theology and practice. Many of the German groups were Pietistic in outlook and preferred to remain aloof from the main currents of colonial life. Thus the Germans were never able to attain the influence that the Scotch-Irish exercised in the colonial and early national periods of American history. In fact, over the colonies as a whole, the influence of the Scotch-Irish exceeded that of the Puritans, the Germans, the scattered French, and the more concentrated Dutch elements of colonial society; they very early rivaled the influence of the English. Within a very few years after the arrival of the Scotch-Irish in the colonies they became a force that the colonial governors could not ignore. By 1776 they were an important voice calling for independence from the mother country.

The Scotch-Irish played an even more important role in the shaping of the American Presbyterian tradition. They soon became, in a very real sense, the spirit and life of American Presbyterianism. It is very doubtful that Presbyterianism would have become the vital force that it has been in American Christianity if the Scotch-Irish had not arrived on these shores in sufficient numbers to capture the then-struggling Presbyterian establishment.

Their pervasive influence gained in Presbyterianism stems from the fact that Presbyterianism was the only religion these settlers knew. It has been said that if a Scotch-Irish settler was religious at all when he arrived in the colonies, he was a Presbyterian. The English settlers could be Anglican, Puritan, or Quaker, and the Germans could be Reformed, Lutheran, or Pietist; but the Scotch-Irish, as no other group in the colonies, were devoted to one theology and ecclesiastical polity, and this devotion gave them a high degree of unanimity of expression in their religious and political life.

However, the influence of the Scotch-Irish cannot be explained solely on such grounds. The blending of the Scotch and Irish character in Ulster had produced the sturdy stock that was needed to conquer the colonial frontier that, for most of them, would be their home upon arrival. The vast wilderness of the frontier had hardly been penetrated before their arrival and was waiting for them to subdue it. By contrast, the Puritans had been quite content to remain within the rather narrow confines of New England; the Dutch settled along the seaboard; the Quakers in eastern Pennsylvania, New Jersey, and Maryland; and the Roman Catholics in Maryland. The Germans, for the most part, preferred to remain aloof and thus maintain their cultural and religious distinctiveness. This they did to such an extent that their influence on the religious and political development of the colonies was rather weak.

## The Scotch-Irish: Why They Came

Historians generally agree that there were two basic causes for the prolonged migrations of the Scotch-Irish from Ulster in northern Ireland to the American colonies during the eighteenth century: the religio-political and the economic. The factors that lay behind this movement were by no means unique to the Scotch-Irish migration. The same basic causes had brought the Pilgrims to Plymouth and the Puritans to New England, the Germans to the Middle Colonies and the Huguenots to various settlements along the Atlantic seaboard. Religious persecution was clearly a factor in all of these migrations; economic distress, to varying degrees, also played a role.

Only the greatest urgency could have produced such a wholesale migration from Ireland to the New World as that undertaken by the Scotch-Irish. Economic factors undoubtedly entered into their urgency to leave, but by themselves they cannot be regarded as a satisfactory explanation for this mass movement. To so interpret such events in history would be a great error. Economic determinism is a widely held philosophy of history in academic circles in our day, but it leads to serious distortions in our interpretation of the past. In the eighteenth century religious motives were still a dominant force in the life of Europe. In the case of the Scotch-Irish they proved to be of singular significance, equalled only by the economic threat of the situation in Ireland, as a reason for their willingness to leave the homeland for frontier America. It is difficult for many modern historians to understand the compelling force of the desire for religious freedom as an explanation for such a migration, but the records leave no doubt as to the importance of this desire, which brightly burned in the Scotch-Irish hearts. That it was a factor of prime importance is borne out in their history when they established themselves in the colonies.

The roots of the migration are found in the efforts of James I of England to create a large settlement of Scotch Presbyterians in the County of Ulster in Northern Ireland. His purpose was to bring political order and stability to this part of his kingdom. His policy was commendable even if it seems to be beyond the comprehension of the twentieth-century mind in the light of the turmoil that actually resulted from his well-intentioned efforts. In fairness to James it must be kept in mind that Ulster had been the despair of the Tudor monarchs before him, and James believed that his rather unruly countrymen over whom he had reigned in Scotland might well prove to be the solution to his difficult problems in both countries. The quality of those chosen to fulfill this mission was of a high order. However, it is also true that the plan to grant these immigrants a farm for a period of twenty-one years lured a large number of adventurers to Ulster. When the Scotch immigrants arrived in Ireland, they encountered a series of crises—religious, political, and economic—that dimmed their enthusiasm for the venture, and they began to look longingly for another new home in the American colonies.

The Irish proved to be a serious cause of trouble for the Scotch in Ulster, but they were by no means the only cause for disillusionment. The religious situation in England under Charles I and Archbishop Laud produced a great deal of unrest since the Church of England was the Established Church in Ireland but not in Scotland. When the Stuart rulers of England sought to enforce the Act of Uniformity in Ireland, trouble ensued. In 1641 when the Irish arose against the Scotch-Irish, Cromwell used this turmoil as an excellent excuse for attempting to crush both the Catholics and the Presbyterians in that unhappy island.

If Cromwell fanned the flames of religious unrest and dissension in Ireland, the economic policies of Charles II added fuel to the flames. The policies of Charles were due, in part, to the fact that the Scotch-Irish had given a great impetus to the economic development of Ireland because of their expertise in weaving flax and linen goods.[1] In some areas of economic activity Ireland was becoming such a formidable rival of England that Charles II was forced by the English commercial interests to take appropriate action.

Thus the Navigation Act of 1663, famous in American history, prohibited the exportation of Irish goods to the American colonies, requiring that they first be shipped to English ports and then to the colonies. This act also prohibited the exportation of goods directly from the colonies to Ireland, although the "enumerated" articles might go to Ireland, after being imported into England. These restrictions proved to be a serious blow to the economic prosperity of Ireland.

Queen Anne intensified the dissatisfaction when she reopened the religious issue in 1703 with a requirement that all office holders in Ireland receive communion according to the practices of the Established Church. This prevented Presbyterians from holding public office. This discontent was brought to a head by the effects of a drought that lasted for four years.

One final factor lying behind these migrations and claiming an importance for the movement almost equal to religious and political factors in England under the Stuarts was the nature of the Scotch-Irish. They were a bold and adventurous people, willing to endure dangers and risk death for the religious and political convictions they cherished. The situation in Ulster, as difficult as it was, would hardly have caused such an exodus if the emigrants had not been willing and ready to make the sacrifices required for such a venture.

## THE MIGRATIONS

It has been estimated that between 1717 and 1775 over 250,000 Ulstermen came to the British colonies in North America. Four years of serious drought had set the stage for the first migration, which began in 1717 with the departure of about 5,000 for the new world. This first phase lasted for about two years. Between 1720 and 1725 very few felt compelled to leave Ireland.

Ireland was once again plagued with bad harvests, and the second wave of migration was set in motion in 1725. Such a loss in population occurred that Parliament viewed it with great concern. Improved economic conditions brought an end to this second migration about 1730. For about a decade there was but a small trickle of emigrating Scotch-Irish from Ulster to the colonies. Then in 1740–41 poor harvests brought a time of starvation to Ireland, resulting in the deaths of about 200,000 people. A renewed exodus to the colonies took place.

This migration was of such proportions that those arriving in Pennsylvania immediately began to make their way down the Cumberland and Shenandoah valleys to Virginia and the Carolina colonies. Propaganda from the colonies caused another wave of migration in 1754 and 1755, but this was brought to an end by the outbreak of the French and Indian Wars, which blunted the cutting edge of the reports from the colonies. Four more years of serious drought set off the last great migration, which began in 1771 and lasted until the commencement of hostilities in the War for Independence.[2]

Although it has been estimated that about 250,000 people came during the period from 1717 to 1775, the estimates vary greatly, even though the records of immigration for the period beginning about 1700 are much more accurate than they are for the seventeenth century.[3] In an address to the Scotch-Irish Congress in 1890, J. H. Bryson stated that one-third of the population of the colonies was Scotch-Irish in origin.[4] This estimate seems quite high, considering the estimate of 250,000 immigrants between 1717 and 1775. If Leyburn is correct in his estimate that the Scotch-Irish constituted about 15 percent of the population in 1790, this would mean that they numbered between 550,000 and 600,000 that year. The assertion that they constituted one-third of the population in 1776 also raises another question. How could the percentage decline that drastically in fifteen years (1775–90)? This is possible only if we accept the proposition that the rest of the population did increase while the number of Scotch-Irish either declined or remained stationary. This seems to be an untenable position.

The coming of peace to the colonies in 1783 did not bring any renewal of the migrations, and never again would the Scotch-Irish be able to claim such a strength in the total population of the country. However, their contributions to the national life would continue to be an important factor in the formation of an American culture because of their predominant influence in eighteenth-century colonial affairs.

The Scotch-Irish tended to settle on the frontiers of colonial America. By the time of the first migration most of the seaboard areas had already been settled. These more distant areas proved to be more congenial to the temperament of the Scotch-Irish. Their adventuresome spirits made them the first frontiersmen in American history. The southern coastal lands with their great plantations had little appeal to the Scotch-Irish; thus they looked to the more western regions of Virginia and the Carolinas for their new home.[5] By 1776 they were living in about 500 communities found in every colony, though they tended to be concentrated in a few colonies.[6] There were about 70 such settlements in New England (including those in Maine), 40 or 50 in New York, 50 or 60 in New Jersey, 130 in Pennsylvania and Delaware, over 100 in Virginia and Tennessee, 50 in North Carolina, and about 70 in South Carolina and Georgia, most of these being in South Carolina.

Of all the religious groups that came to this country during the colonial period the Scotch-Irish were the most diffused. It was this fact that brought William W. Sweet to the conclusion that by 1776 the Presbyterians were in the best position to become the greatest of the American churches.[7] His ensuing observation that they failed to take advantage of the opportunity afforded to them is open to serious question. In terms of sheer numbers of adherents, Sweet is probably correct in stating that other churches were greater. But do sheer number of members constitute a truly great church? Sweet seems to assume that this is the case. In terms of their later influence on the religions and political development of the American people his conclusion will hardly stand the test of historical verification. Although both the Methodists and the Baptists were far more numerous, they have not had the impact that the Presbyterians have achieved.

William Penn received the Scotch-Irish cordially in his colony, and they settled in the counties west of the Quaker settlements in large numbers. By the end of the century they had made their way from central Pennsylvania to the western section of that state and had spilled down the Cumberland Valley to Maryland, the Valley of Virginia and into the Carolinas. Penn's successors lost their enthusiasm for the fiery Scotch-Irish and by 1756 there was a great deal of friction between them and the ruling Quaker elements over the appropriation of money for the defense of the western frontiers against the Indians. The Scotch-Irish had little patience with the Quaker doctrine of nonresistance in view of the French use of the Indians against the frontiers of the colony. This conflict gave an added impetus to the move southward into Virginia and the Carolinas.

## THE IMPACT OF THE SCOTCH-IRISH
### ON AMERICAN PRESBYTERIANISM

The Scotch-Irish proved to be the determinative factor in framing the character of American Presbyterianism. Before their arrival the Presbyterians were not only few in number, but were scattered geographically and lacked cohesion and organization. Fifty years after the arrival of the Scotch-Irish the Presbyterian Church had become a national reality. Although the Puritans of New England shared their doctrinal heritage, they did not accept the Presbyterian form of government and had little influence outside of their own region. Puritanism was not destined to become a national church or a serious rival to Presbyterianism. By 1700 Puritanism was even beginning to lose its hold in New England's life and thought. As a result, Cotton Mather and other leaders of his generation began to look rather wistfully at the Presbyterian pattern of government as a means of bolstering the waning strength of their Puritan theological and ecclesiastical heritage. They took the first faltering steps in this direction when they adopted the Saybrook Platform. This approach was unacceptable to many in New England. As a result, it proved to be ineffective in stemming the tide of theological dissent arising within the Puritan community. It was equally ill adapted to creating a truly Presbyterian order in the Congregational churches.

The Scotch-Irish were fiercely loyal to Presbyterianism in the form in which they had inherited it from John Knox and his successors. This loyalty had been tested and strengthened by a century of intermittent persecution in Scotland and Ireland under the later Stuart rulers. This proved to be an excellent schoolmaster to prepare the Scotch-Irish for their life in the New World. They were conditioned to meet what lay ahead of them on the colonial frontier. They were disciplined in doctrine and trained in administering the affairs of their churches, and this gave them a distinct advantage as they sought a new life in the colonies and erected Presbyterian churches wherever they settled. Scotch-Irish-Presbyterianism was, in a very real sense, Puritanism restructured and adapted to a more pluralistic environment, no longer restricted to the narrow confines of Old or New England. Both its Calvinism and its presbyterial form of government provided the means by which it would become the dominant theological movement in American church history and also in the formation of the American national character.[8]

## THE GREAT AWAKENING

It was indeed providential that Presbyterianism gained a strong foothold in those decades that preceded the coming of the Great Awakening.[9] The first steps for the planting of the seed of Presbyterianism had been taken by Francis Makemie who came to Maryland and Virginia late in the seventeenth century and carried on an amazing evangelistic ministry. The first presbytery in America was formed in 1706, and Makemie was elected its first moderator.[10]

By 1735 the zeal of both the Puritans and the Presbyterians had subsided. Immorality had entered the ranks of the infant church, in both the ministry and laity. At least one scandalous case involving a minister had become well known. It is true, however, that it called forth fervent opposition, indicating that the zeal for Christian living had not disappeared from its ranks.[11]

It also seems that the heated controversy that soon engulfed the synod was, in part at least, the result of the desire of many ministers to restore

Presbyterianism to its original purity of life and thought. There is evidence that this zeal was being restored even before the Great Awakening. The formation of the synod in 1717 provided a hope for the best aspects of the great revival soon to come. The synod also provided an ecclesiastical home for the waves of immigrants coming from Ulster, the first of which would arrive that next year.[12]

The first event in the history of American Presbyterianism to play an important and a major role was the Subscription Controversy. This came to a head with the passage of the Subscription Act in the meeting of the synod in 1729.

This action was essentially an agreement that "all the ministers of this synod, or that shall hereafter be admitted to this synod, shall declare their agreement in and approbation of, the Confession of Faith with the Larger and Shorter Catechisms of the Assembly of Divines at Westminster, as being in all the necessary and essential articles, good forms of sound words and systems of Christian doctrine and do also adopt the said Confession and Catechisms as the confession of our faith."[13] This Adopting Act also called on the presbyteries to see to it that they would not admit any candidate to the ministry who did not subscribe to all the essential and necessary articles of the Confession or the Catechisms. It further provided that if any minister of the synod could not accept any article deemed by the presbytery to be necessary and essential, the presbytery was to declare him incapable of continuing as a member of that body.[14]

The passage of this Act was a notable victory for the Scotch-Irish and a defeat for the English and Puritan elements in the synod. It also determined the future of American Presbyterianism for the next 250 years.[15]

Although the controversy aroused by the passage of the Act continued and the Presbyteries of Newcastle and Donegal, strongholds of Scotch-Irish strength, demanded an even stronger act of subscription than that accepted in 1729, the Adopting Act remained unchanged as the doctrinal basis of the Presbyterian Church until the acceptance of a new creed in 1967. But its passage soon aroused discontent among those ministers who represented the more moderate New England elements in Presbyterianism. These held to the great essentials of the faith but they objected strongly to making these essentials a requirement for ordination through subscription.

Just what turn this controversy would have taken eventually is difficult to determine and Trinterud is probably correct in his conclusion that the emergence of the Great Awakening in Presbyterianism ultimately destroyed the delicate balance that existed between the two groups.[16] His further insistence, however, that the coming of the Great Awakening revitalized both the doctrine and the ethics of Presbyterianism in the colonies is open to serious question.[17]

Having its origins in the preaching of Jonathan Edwards of Stockbridge, Massachusetts, and receiving an added impetus from the evangelistic efforts of George Whitefield, the Great Awakening proved to be a powerful stimulus to Presbyterianism and propelled the church to new spiritual heights. In spite of the fact that it resulted in a temporary ecclesiastical division within the church, it can hardly be denied that it brought a new evangelistic zeal in its wake and opened up new opportunities for the preaching of the gospel in the colonies. At the same time it also made it possible for the Scotch-Irish to assume a leadership and influence within its ranks—an influence they did not relinquish until after the reunion of 1869. Some historians of the church would argue that this early Scotch-Irish passion for conservatism in theology and passion for missionary activity did not diminish until well into the twentieth century.

The Great Awakening, which had such a powerful but rather short-lived influence on the religious life of New England, had an equally powerful but more prolonged effect on Presbyterianism and its future development. Its most immediate result was felt in the Synods of New York and Philadelphia, which had been created in 1717.[18] The principal figure in the revival and resulting schism was William Tennent, who had been educated in Ireland and had been ordained in the Anglican church. Coming to this country in 1716, he applied for admission to the Synod of Philadelphia.[19] He began his pastoral activities in a church near Philadelphia in 1721. With his four sons he soon became a vital and even controversial force in colonial Presbyterianism, though he did not take an active part in the subscription controversy. He and his eldest son, Gilbert, signed the subscription to the Westminster Standards as required by the action taken in 1729.[20]

It would seem that at this period in their ministerial careers in matters relating to doctrine they stood rather close to the party in the synod that desired a strict interpretation of, and adherence to, the Westminster Standards. John Tennent, another son, signed the subscription in Newcastle Presbytery this same year. Trinterud insists, however, that the Tennents were definitely English Puritans in spirit and that the continuing controversy over the meaning of the Subscription Act of 1729 furnished the fertile soil for the growth of the Great Awakening among the Presbyterians in the Middle Colonies. He further maintains that in the intervening decades between 1720 and 1741 the leaders of what can be loosely called the Tennent Group had passed into the hands of Gilbert Tennent, who had begun his ministry in the Newcastle Presbytery, which was strongly subscriptionist in its theological stance.[21] The Tennents, accordingly, in this period dissociated themselves from the strict subscriptionist element.

There is no doubt that in his second missionary tour of the colonies Whitefield exercised a strong influence wherever he went. He brought powerful messages in many Presbyterian churches in and around Philadelphia. He came to know Gilbert Tennent, whom he met at the Log College founded in 1726. This experience, along with his previous contacts with Theodore Frelinghuysen, a minister of a Dutch Reformed Congregation in New Brunswick, New Jersey, made a deep impression on Gilbert Tennent. However, one should not place too much stress on the influence of these two men on Tennent. Rumblings of future controversy were already heard in the meeting of the Synod in 1734, before Tennent had met Whitefield or Frelinghuysen. At this meeting Tennent introduced an overture requesting the synod to exercise greater care in admitting candidates for the ministry, particularly inquiring "into the evidence of the grace of God in them, as well as their other necessary qualifications."[22]

In these overtures Tennent was not asking the synod to relax its vigilance over the orthodoxy of its candidates for the ministry. They apparently aroused little opposition or debate and the synod called on the presbyteries "to take special care not to admit into the sacred office loose, careless and irreligious persons but to particularly inquire into the conversations, conduct and behavior of such as offer themselves to the ministry. . . ."[23]

Although the seeds of his full-grown evangelical pietism had been sown by his father, there is little doubt that the later contacts that Gilbert Tennent had with Theodore Frelinghuysen and George Whitefield brought them to fruition. Tennent was not satisfied with the way the presbyteries applied the request of the synod of 1734, and the records for the period indicate that all was not well with the conduct of the ministry of the synod.

Tennent soon became involved in a controversy with the Presbytery of Philadelphia over the installation of David Cowell, a Harvard-trained New Englander, as pastor of the church at Trenton, New Jersey.[24] Tennent became convinced that too many unworthy men were being admitted to the ministry. He also harbored the suspicion that the subscriptionist group in the synod was unwilling to accept as members those ministers who were graduates of the Log College. On March 8, 1740, Gilbert Tennent preached at Nottingham, Pennsylvania, one of the most influential sermons in colonial Presbyterian history. His sermon, "On the Dangers of an Unconverted Ministry," proved to be the clarion call that brought the issue into clear focus at the meeting of the synod in 1741. He was responsible, more than any other Presbyterian leader of the day, for bringing the issue to the point that resulted in a schism between the New Side and the Old Side parties. The schism soon pitted the Tennents against the Scotch-Irish party in the church. Although the problems of the ministry were the immediate cause, the subscription issue seems to have lain at the heart of the division. The Scotch element was strongly in favor of the Subscription Act of 1729 and was strongly opposed to the revivalist techniques of the New Side, of which the Tennents had emerged as the leaders.

The Old Side, firmly in control of the synod meeting in 1741, expelled the New Brunswick Presbytery. This presbytery had been the center of the New Side strength and also of much of the agitation for a pietistic or "converted" ministry. But it was not a doctrinal matter, and the action of the synod of 1734 seems to indicate that the Old Side was as much in favor of a more careful policy for admitting new members to the Presbyterian ministry as was the New Side. There is no evidence that Gilbert Tennent was any less attached to the Westminster Standards than were the members of the Old Side.

Seen in retrospect, the gulf between the two groups was not as great as they imagined. After the death of Jonathan Dickinson both the leaders of the more moderate element in the Old Side Party and Gilbert Tennent fell heirs to the task of reuniting the groups, and this was accomplished in 1758. In this reunion both groups acknowledged their complete loyalty to the Westminster Standards.[25] What then was the cause of the rupture? It seems to have been caused by the apprehensions raised in the subscriptionist ministry by the techniques of the revivalist preachers of the New Side. The New Side had been guilty of some excesses in its services, and Gilbert Tennent admitted this. It is also true that the synod had been lax in its ordination policy before 1741 and that it had not always disciplined its members who were guilty of serious irregularities in their conduct. The life and witness of the church had been marred by more than one scandal, and Gilbert Tennent had cause to issue a warning against the dangers of an unconverted ministry.

The sovereign God brought forth much good out of this division among the saints in colonial America. A much firmer unity emerged, much stronger than it had been at the time of the division. The records indicate that the ministry was purified and there was much less discussion of scandal and laxity. The church was now ready for the task that would shortly confront it with the outbreak of hostilities between England and the colonies. In this now firmly united church the Scotch-Irish would have a very strong voice, even as they would play a major role in the military conflict that would soon arise.

Trinterud's evaluation of the impact of the Great Awakening on American Presbyterianism is interesting and suggestive, if not entirely convincing:

> In the welding together of the Log College presbyteries and the New York Presbytery, the genius of an American Presbyterianism had been forged. It was a union of the second and third generation of New England Puritan

presbyteries and a group of young Scotch Irish Presbyterians who through
William Tennent, Sr. had become imbued with the piety and views of English Puritanism.[26]

If this is the case, why was the subscription controversy hardly mentioned during the act of reunion and afterward? It seems that if New
England views had prevailed, there would have been a much stronger
outcry against the Act of 1729. There is no doubt that a much stronger
Presbyterianism emerged as a result of this action, but it is much less
certain that the resulting Presbyterianism was as much of a fusion as
Trinterud states. The reply of the synod at its 1734 meeting to the
overtures offered by Gilbert Tennent breathed a warm spirit of evangelical concern and piety and it was a reply that could easily have been
written by the adherents of the Log College movement.[27] No doubt
George Whitefield, Theodore Frelinghuysen, and Jonathan Edwards
inspired the Tennents and the Log College group and renewed their zeal
for the preaching of the gospel in a warm manner. Through these men
New England Puritanism, to a degree, entered into the stream of American Presbyterianism, but the main current in this broadening stream was
composed of the Scotch-Irish, who added a warmth and fervor of their
own.

One of the most beneficial results of the emergence of the New Side
was the intensification of a missionary zeal and the spread of the church
into the valley of Virginia and the Piedmont area of the Carolina colonies. The later Scotch-Irish migrations to the colonies brought these
immigrants in large numbers to the areas of Pennsylvania lying to the
west of the German settlements. From this region, they made their way
down through Maryland into Virginia and finally into the Carolinas,
where they found large tracts of land available to them.

Because they were Scotch-Irish they constituted a tremendous
missionary challenge to the Old Side church, but the Synod of Philadelphia was unable to take advantage of the opportunity this afforded
because of its failure to create a seminary for the training of the ministers necessary for such a venture. Thus it remained for the New Side,
with its Log College, to evangelize these restless spirits on the recently
settled frontier. The New Side promptly accepted the challenge.

One of these pioneers in evangelizing and bringing the Great Awakening to the South was Samuel Davies, often regarded as the greatest
pulpit orator of the eighteenth century.[28] More than a few congregations
existing in North Carolina and Virginia today owe their origin to the
pioneer work of this great man and his colleagues. They not only faced
the dangers of pioneer existence but also the determined opposition of
the clergy of the established Church of England, who regarded these
itinerant preachers with alarm. However, the established church made
little effort in either colony to win over these new settlers and organize

them into congregations. Episcopalian polity was an unsuitable vehicle for such expansion in eighteenth-century America.

By the end of the century Pennsylvania was a Presbyterian, and therefore a Scotch-Irish, stronghold. Scotch-Irish Presbyterianism was very strong in Virginia in Hanover and the Shenandoah Valley, but was quite weak in the Tidewater areas of the colony. This pattern held true for North Carolina to a lesser extent and was clearly discernible in South Carolina. In 1759 Presbyterianism was stronger in New York, Pennsylvania, and New Jersey than all the other denominations combined. This was still the case as late as 1775, but its leadership was being challenged by the rising strength of the Baptists and it would soon meet another formidable rival in the appearance of the Methodist movement on a large scale.

The Presbyterian form of government, with its emphasis on a well-trained ministry and its stately form of worship, was much less adaptable to a trans-Allegheny frontier than that of the Methodists and Baptists, whose missionary activities were not hampered by the allegedly rigid requirements of Presbyterian doctrine, education, and polity. The Baptists and Methodists had developed both a theology and a polity more suited to the demands of the democratic life of the frontier than was the Calvinistic theology of Scotch-Irish Presbyterianism. In neither theology nor polity was the Presbyterianism of the day democratic in its outlook, whereas the Baptist polity and the Methodist theology had a strong emotional appeal for the frontier settlers. This appeal became evident in the Kentucky and Tennessee revivals that broke out at the turn of the century and proved to be a turning point in Protestant history in America. These revivals gave the Methodist and Baptist churches a numerical superiority in American Protestantism that they have never lost.

The realization of the need for some elasticity in structure led the Presbyterian General Assembly of 1801 to enter into a cooperative plan with the Congregational churches of New England in the hope that such an arrangement would advance the evangelization of the West, particularly the Old Northwest (Ohio, Indiana, Illinois, Michigan, and Wisconsin). This well-intentioned plan of an ecumenical cooperation proved much less beneficial to the advance of Presbyterianism in this region than it was for Congregationalism, whose polity was much more adaptable to the needs of a frontier society. It also proved to be quite harmful to Presbyterianism itself. It provided an avenue through which the New England theology entered into Presbyterianism. Known more particularly as the New Haven theology, it represented a modified Calvinism, which proved to be very close to Arminianism. Its chief exponent, Nathaniel Taylor, elected to the chair of didactic theology at Yale in 1822, preached a sermon in 1828 in which he rejected the doctrine of original sin in the sense that "man inherits any disposition or tendency to sin, which is the cause of sin." As a necessary consequence of this basic assumption, Taylor was led to define sin as man's own act "by which he freely chooses some other object as his chief good rather than God."[29] Hence, man must be free to turn to God before he is regenerated by the Holy Spirit.

Taylor's emphasis on the freedom of the will necessarily led to further deviations from the teachings of the Scriptures and the Westminster Standards. Representatives of this New England theology rejected not only the Presbyterian doctrine of original sin but also unconditional election and the substitutionary view of the Atonement. They replaced these doctrines with a governmental theory of the Atonement, which was similar to that of the seventeenth-century Dutch scholar Hugo Grotius.

Charles G. Finney brought this New England theology to its logical conclusion when he declared that conversion is the sinner's act. He admitted that the Holy Spirit and the minister in the pulpit play a limited role in the spiritual transformation of the sinner, but the sinner is the principal agent in his redemption.[30]

This theology received a wide reception in the Presbyterian churches of New England, and its effects caused more concern within the church than that aroused by any preceding doctrinal crisis in its history in this country. The alarm was thoroughly justified, for this Arminian teaching threatened the historic theology and mission of Presbyterianism.

The situation came to a head in 1838 when Albert Barnes, pastor of the First Presbyterian Church in Philadelphia, was charged with heresy for preaching this New Haven theology. Although he was acquitted by the General Assembly of 1836, the issues raised by the trial were far from being settled. His acquittal actually gave a new momentum to the controversy, which threatened the unity of the church once again. The acquittal came from the hands of a general assembly that was heavily dominated by the New School party. This fact became even more evident in the case involving Dr. Lyman Beecher, a Congregational minister, who had been called to the pulpit of the Second Presbyterian Church in Cincinnati. He was accused by Dr. Joseph Wilson, a leading member of the Old School group, of leaning toward this New England theology also. However, the acquittal of Albert Barnes caused the case to be dropped, and it was not brought before this General Assembly of 1838.

The action of this Assembly convinced the Old School leaders that the Presbyterian church should withdraw from all cooperative efforts with the Congregationalists, which had developed out of the Plan of Union of 1801. The first efforts to bring a halt to these cooperative efforts actually began during the 1835 meeting of the Assembly when the Old School leadership called a special meeting of its members who were in attendance. This meeting issued the "Act of Testimony," which called for the restoration of the Presbyterian Church to its former purity of doctrine. In order to accomplish this aim, the document also called for a meeting of concerned ministers and elders prior to the meeting of the Assembly in 1836, with the New School element firmly in control of the proceedings. The Old School members were convinced that the time had arrived for a separation to take place between the two groups within the church. While the 1836 General Assembly was still in session, another meeting was held and plans were laid for a separation.

The details of this separation lie outside the scope of this study, but a study of the documents makes it quite clear that the strength of the Old School lay in those sections of the church where the Scotch-Irish were the predominant influence.[31] This influence was still quite strong in Virginia, the Carolinas, eastern Tennessee, and much of Georgia and Alabama as a result of migrations from the Old South into these areas.[32]

The formation of the Old School Presbyterian Church in 1837 may well be regarded as the last great triumph of the Scotch-Irish in the continuing struggle to preserve the doctrinal purity of American Presbyterianism. For the same reason, the reunion of 1869 may justly be called the end of the dominant influence of the Scotch-Irish in the resulting denomination, which took the name Presbyterian Church in the United States of America, popularly known as the Northern Presbyterian Church.[33] It should also be noted that this Scotch-Irish influence continued to play an important role in the history of the Presbyterian Church in the United States, popularly known as the Southern Presbyterian Church, until well into the twentieth century.

Some leaders within Presbyterianism have argued that the absence of the Old School element, quite strong in the southern church, from the union of 1869, had the effect of preventing the Old School element in the northern church from preserving to a greater extent the orthodox testimony of that body. This was a favorite theme of those leaders who had worked through the years so resolutely and, even until the present day (1982), so unsuccessfully, for a union between the two denominations. It is true that the reunion between the Old and New Schools in the North in 1869 left unsettled the basic issues that had caused the division in 1837.[34] It is very doubtful that the southern church, numerically smaller than the northern, could have so swelled the ranks of the Old School group in the North that it would have been able to achieve a union on the basis of an Old School theology, or that it would have been able to become a dominant force in the northern church after the reunion had taken place.

The division of 1837 and the unsatisfactory basis of reunion in 1869 cast doubt on the Trinterud thesis that the reunion of 1758 between the

Old and New Side groups made it possible for the Scotch-Irish to become the formative element in the development of American Presbyterianism. This was true before the emergence of the New England theology after 1801, but his position becomes difficult to defend in the light of the nature of the division of 1837. This separation was basically the result of a division of theological outlook between the New England elements and the Scotch-Irish, for the latter were Old School while the New England, or Congregational group, adopted the New England theology of Nathaniel Taylor and his associates. A much stronger case can be made for the continuing strong influence of the Scotch-Irish in the life of the Southern Presbyterian Church. However, this began to wane about 1935. In the past forty years it has become little more than a whisper in that communion. It gains what influence it may have today from the impact and achievement of individual leaders who are Scotch-Irish in descent and in theology, rather than from the Scotch-Irish as a composite element in the life of the church.

## The Scotch-Irish and the Struggle for Religious Liberty

Since the great emigration of Scotch-Irish began in 1717, these settlers came to colonies where religious policies were already established. Except in Pennsylvania, Delaware, and Rhode Island, churches were already established by law and their respective charters or by the fact that the groups settling within their borders had already created established churches. Even in Pennsylvania the Scotch-Irish began to suffer from a form of political discrimination after 1750 at the hands of the provincial assembly, which was controlled by the Quakers of the three eastern counties.

The lack of freedom of worship was most characteristic of those colonies in which the Church of England had become established, though freedom of worship was not common even in New England. The Scotch-Irish had settled in relatively large numbers in those colonies where the Church of England was established. For this reason they soon proved to be a serious challenge to the continued Anglican control of the religious life.

Although the early skirmishes for religious freedom took place in New York and Virginia soon after the Scotch-Irish had settled in these colonies, the most important struggles took place in Virginia after the Peace of 1783.[35] The winning of the war and the achievement of independence provided an impetus toward disestablishment, but even in the light of these developments the Anglican church was most unwilling to surrender its favored position, which it possessed not only by law but by wealth and social prestige.

Because of the increasing number of Baptists and Methodists in the more western part of Virginia after 1793, there was a rising demand for freedom of worship and for the disestablishment of the Anglican church, which had become the Episcopal church soon after the Treaty of 1783. The demand for religious freedom could no longer be ignored, for it was now receiving an additional impetus from more secular groups who had no great zeal for either the Presbyterian or Baptist churches and who also deeply disliked being compelled by law to support any Christian group financially. These people were determined to be free of all religious impediments. To achieve their goal they were willing to join forces with the other groups. Some, like Thomas Jefferson, felt that the legal establishment of any religious group was contrary to the philosophy of the Declaration of Independence and the democratic way of life that Jefferson had dreamed of for the new nation. It should be emphasized that the efforts of philosopher-statesmen like Jefferson and Madison followed the efforts of dissenting ministers and were not the primary factor in the granting of toleration. The initial impetus came from Christian ministers, largely Presbyterian and Baptist.

In 1776, during the war, the Scotch-Irish Presbyterians of Augusta County and Hanover Presbytery sent earnest protests to the Virginia Assembly against the additional financial burden imposed on dissenters because of the financial support required from them for the support of the Anglican church. The various petitions placed before the Assembly paved the way for the prolonged conflict that broke out in 1780. The issue came to a head with the appearance of James Madison's *Memorial and Remonstrance,* in which he argued with his usual insight and skill to the effect that religion must be free from intrusion by the state and society at large.

This document found much support from Virginia Presbyterians, who adopted a statement drawn up by William Graham of Liberty Hall Academy. The statement declared that the purpose of civil government is to secure the temporal liberty and property of mankind and "to protect them in the free exercise of their religion."[36]

In December 1785 Madison proposed in the Virginia legislature that Jefferson's bill of 1779 be enacted into law. The proposal was accepted and the Scotch-Irish Presbyterians of Virginia won their most notable legislative victory in American history.

## THE SCOTCH-IRISH PRESBYTERIAN COMMUNITY

The development of Presbyterianism in colonial America is largely the story of the transformation of the Scotch-Irish intellectually and socially as they became Americanized. This process of Americanization, by the very nature of the case, was a process of Americanization for American Presbyterianism at the same time. By 1783 the Scotch-Irish were the dominant element in American Presbyterianism; to deal with the one is necessarily to deal with the other.

Yet these two developments were not entirely synonymous. Presbyterianism in the colonial era had lost its hold on thousands of the Scotch-Irish who had advanced into the far reaches of the frontier. This loss was not the result of any rebellion against their religious heritage for the sake of which they had come to the New World. The fact that they had settled on the frontier made it very difficult for the churches of the older established regions to meet the demands of an established corporate life in widely separated congregational units. It was accomplished to a degree, but there was no consistent pattern of organized congregations.

The problem was accentuated by the lack of ministers to travel in these more remote areas and to pastor congregations where they were established.[37] As a result, in many frontier settlements the Scotch-Irish lacked the necessary pastoral leadership and teaching. Although some help was obtained from the Scottish universities, the aid was merely a trickle in comparison to the urgent need throughout the colonies.[38] This lack of adequate ministry was the principal reason for the founding of the Log College by William Tennent in 1726 and for the schism of 1741. The Log College was opposed by those pastors who feared that such a ministerial school would result in lower standards for the church. These fears were not unfounded, though they were exaggerated at that time.

The basic issue confronting the church was just how much, and how far, it should go in meeting the challenge of the frontier environment and changing its traditions of education and doctrinal teaching accordingly. The question of evangelism did enter the picture, but it was not this issue, per se, that lay behind the schism. The basic issue was whether the church should modify its educational standards sufficiently to provide a greater number of ministers for meeting the needs of the frontier than could otherwise be obtained from Scotland. Tennent's Log College proved to be a very effective institution for solving the problem. In its short span of life of twenty years it produced an amazing number of very able ministers of the gospel, and these men proclaimed the gospel far and wide, from Pennsylvania to the Carolinas.

Even though both the New and Old groups tended to move away from those forms of worship and religious life that they had brought with them from Ireland, there is no reason to assume that they were any less Presbyterian in doctrine. They did not intend to forfeit their Calvinistic doctrinal heritage to the needs of a frontier society. The Scotch-Irish in America remained strict Calvinists. The records of individual congregations, as well as those of the presbyteries, indicate that they had a general requirement for all young people to memorize the Shorter Catechism, while the Larger Catechism was to be a part of the curriculum of study. Many members were trained in the Westminster Confession of

Faith. Of all the religious groups in the colonies outside of New England, the Scotch-Irish were probably the most strict in the observance of Sunday. It was a day set apart for the worship of God and for resting from all labor except that which was absolutely necessary. Even the cooking of Sunday's meals was done on Saturday so that every member of the family could be free to devote Sunday to private and public worship.

The morning worship service was frequently three hours in length and the sermons were at least one hour in length, and often much longer. After an interlude for the noon meal the congregation would reassemble in the church for another three-hour service, with another sermon of the morning's length. The only kind of hymns sung were the psalms, as the people considered them the only suitable type for worship. In the stricter congregations, Rouse's metrical version of the psalms was used, while others felt that the hymns and psalms of Isaac Watts were also suitable. But the general use of the hymns of Watts did not come about without a struggle. In the colonial period no musical instruments were allowed in the Presbyterian churches, even for the support of congregational singing. More often than not, the hymns were "lined out" and a tuning fork was used to determine the key in which they were to be sung. Pianos and organs did not come into general use until well into the nineteenth century.

Scotch-Irish Presbyterianism was characterized by its control over the lives of its members and covenant children. "They were the Puritans of the middle and southern colonies."[39] All violations of the observance of Sunday, the use of profanity, immorality, fighting, and disturbances were proper reasons for church discipline. The records of colonial sessions reveal how far and how often the church felt it necessary to involve itself in the lives of its members. Particularly on the frontier the church was the only effective agency for maintaining discipline. Its Scotch-Irish members were a highly individualistic group, frequently inclined to an excessive manifestation of this individualism if left to themselves. As unwelcome as it would be today, even in Presbyterian congregations, it was this discipline that toughened the fiber of the Scotch-Irish and made Presbyterianism a force within American Christianity and the nation, far beyond what its numerical strength would warrant, even long after it had ceased to claim a large proportion of the people of the nation within its membership. Behind this spiritual authority and leadership lay the strength given to it by a well-trained ministry, for which the Scotch-Irish have stood since 1726, when William Tennent founded his Log College.

If the rigid structure of Presbyterianism made it less adaptable to meeting the religious needs of the frontier, it also gave to the church an organizational structure that was not only thoroughly biblical in its origin, but was well adapted for safeguarding the purity of its doctrine and the strength of its leadership for carrying out its biblically assigned mandate.

## THE SCOTCH-IRISH IN NATIONAL AFFAIRS

To measure the influence of the Scotch-Irish in national affairs is a much more difficult task than evaluating their role in the forging of American Presbyterianism. The records of Congress, of our courts, and even of the presidency very seldom self-consciously reveal the role that the Scotch-Irish played in the political, economic, and social life of the nation. We can enumerate presidents, members of the cabinets, Congress, and the courts who, to varying degrees, have represented their Scotch-Irish ancestry and theological heritage. But to do so is to fall far short of presenting the total impact of this people on national development.

In the first place, not all of the Scotch-Irish accepted or were deeply influenced by their heritage. As time elapsed, they lost sight of what they had originally possessed and fell by the wayside. They tended to adopt causes and political allegiances that were a far cry from their historical traditions. It would be of little value in such a study to name those individuals who were guilty of desertion. The task of measuring Scotch-Irish influence has been difficult also because there have been large numbers of people, neither Scotch-Irish in ancestry nor Presbyterian in theology, who, under common grace, have been committed to the political, economic, and social views generally attributed to Presbyterian theology and ecclesiastical policy. To enumerate these would be utterly impossible.

## THEIR POLITICAL INFLUENCE

The Scotch-Irish gave the first indication of their later political influence in their early demand for religious liberty in New York and Virginia. The coming of the War of Independence, however, gave them a much broader scope for the exercise of their political beliefs. Having come to the colonies because of their dislike of English policy toward them in Ulster, a great majority of them eagerly embraced the cause of the colonists in the struggle for independence.[40] In this conflict they played a leading role in both the political and the military aspects of the war. In Pennsylvania the Scotch-Irish had become quite discontented with the Quaker control of the colony during the French and Indian Wars and were particularly dissatisfied with the unequal representation accorded to the western counties by the Quakers in control of the general assembly. They joined in an even more active protest in North Carolina against what they felt to be the unjust policies of taxation and representation imposed on them by Governor Tryon and the general assembly of that colony. They provided the nucleus of the revolting forces who opposed Tryon after the Battle of Alamance in 1771.

When war with England began in 1775, the way had already been prepared for their support of the colonial cause. In 1775 the Synod of Philadelphia and New York addressed a pastoral letter asking Presbyterian ministers and laity to support the resolutions of the Continental Congress expressing opposition to the English colonial policy. A copy of this letter was sent to the assembly or provincial congress of all of the thirteen colonies.[41]

The role of the Scotch-Irish Presbyterians in these eventful years was not limited to the actions of presbyteries or synods as important as they undoubtedly were. Many individuals assumed positions of prominence not only in the halls of the Continental Congress but also on the major battlefields of the war. In the first Continental Congress of 1774 Robert R. Livingston of New York, John Dickinson of Pennsylvania, Patrick Henry of Virginia, and John and Edward Rutledge of South Carolina were quite influential and continued to exercise leadership throughout the conflict in various capacities.

In the Constitutional Convention of 1787 the Scotch-Irish played a major, perhaps a dominant, role. Alexander Hamilton, James Wilson, John Dickinson, and John Rutledge were prominent in their efforts to bring the work of the convention to a successful conclusion. George Bancroft, a leading nineteenth-century historian, declared that John Rutledge was the foremost statesman south of Virginia. The influence of the Scotch-Irish, however, did not come to an end with the adoption of the Constitution. In Washington's first cabinet they were represented by Alexander Hamilton, Secretary of the Treasury, and Henry Knox, Secretary of War. Four members of the first Supreme Court were also of Scotch-Irish descent: James Wilson, John Blair, James Iredell, and John Rutledge.

After 1800 the influence of the Scotch-Irish in national affairs began to wane. As they made their way westward they became less concentrated and their impact on American life was diminished accordingly. The new migrations from Europe also hastened this process of declining influence.

After 1775 the migrations from Ulster virtually ceased, and after 1800 the new waves came from England, Roman Catholic Ireland, Scandinavia, and Germany. The rise of the Methodist and Baptist churches, already noted, increased at a much faster pace than did Presbyterianism, which was now no longer the major factor in terms of numbers of theological influence in Protestantism. Calvinism was being overshadowed by the rise of the Arminian and even semi-Pelagian groups within American Protestantism.

These factors did not suddenly terminate the influence of Scotch-Irish

Presbyterians in the political life of the nation. Their continuing influence can be seen in the emergence of those political leaders who, to a greater or lesser extent, shared the theological and political convictions of their eighteenth-century forebears. Such presidents as Andrew Jackson and James K. Polk reflected their heritage. Many scholars insist that Woodrow Wilson was the most famous exponent of this heritage in twentieth-century American political life. Wilson may have been the last such influential voice of Scotch-Irish Presbyterianism in American life.

## EDUCATION AMONG THE SCOTCH-IRISH

The Scotch-Irish insistence on an educated ministry has had an enduring impact on American education extending far beyond the confines of Presbyterianism as such. Yet Presbyterianism has reflected this passion for education and has made an incalculable contribution to the educational development in the nation. Beginning with the founding of the Log College in 1726 and continuing with the founding of the College of New Jersey twenty years later, Presbyterianism inaugurated a noble tradition in American educational affairs. The College of New Jersey (later to become Princeton University) wielded a mighty influence for over a century and a half in behalf of the defense and extension of Scotch-Irish Presbyterianism. Through Princeton Seminary this influence became closely identified with the Old School theology, and the seminary became the citadel claiming a host of able defenders of the faith, beginning with the Hodges until the death of B. B. Warfield in 1921.

However, the school in New Jersey was not the only monument to this zeal for education. In many of the colonies academies were established, such as Liberty Hall in Virginia by William Graham, now Washington and Lee University. Virginia Presbyterians also established Hampden Sydney College in 1776. Although many of these schools have lost their Presbyterian identity and have deserted the faith that gave them birth and so long nurtured them, we should not close our eyes to the fact that these institutions played a very important role in the formation of the American character and provided a great many leaders for both church and nation over the years.

## THE SCOTCH-IRISH IN THE ECONOMIC LIFE OF THE NATION

During the eighteenth century the vast majority of the Scotch-Irish Presbyterians settled on the colonial frontier and thus most engaged in agriculture. A few of them, like the Livingstons of New York, became large landholders, while some, like James Iredell of North Carolina and the Rutledges of South Carolina, were able to combine their activities on the plantation with their legal activities and careers in public office, but these were the exception rather than the rule.

The agricultural pattern established during the eighteenth century held true for the first half of the nineteenth century also. Gradually many of the farmers left the farm and entered into the industrial life of the nation. One of the first to become a leader in the emerging financial and industrial life of the republic was Cyrus McCormick, famous for his introduction of the reaper, which revolutionized American agriculture.

It is doubtful, however, that as a group the Scotch-Irish had as great an impact on industrial and financial development as they did on the political realm. Even their political influence had been largely dissipated by 1850, except as it rose to power in individual leaders. And even then it is doubtful that it can be claimed that these men could be regarded as representatives of the Scotch-Irish heritage of the eighteenth century, except in a very general way.

In no way did the economic activities of the Scotch-Irish during the eighteenth or early nineteenth centuries lend any credence to the Weber-Troeltsch thesis that has become so popular in our own day. There is no evidence that their Calvinism produced modern capitalism in this country or that they ever believed that economic success was to be regarded as proof that they were of the elect.[42]

In all of their activities—agricultural, political, economic, social, and educational—they held steadfastly to their belief that man's chief end is "to glorify God and to enjoy Him forever." This great conviction was their enduring contribution to the life of America and to them we owe a great debt of gratitude.

# Dutch Calvinism in America

## John H. Bratt

*John H. Bratt is Professor Emeritus of Religion and Theology at Calvin College in Grand Rapids, Michigan. He holds degrees from Calvin Theological Seminary (Th.B.), Columbia Seminary (Th.M.), Harvard Divinity School (S.T.M.), and Union Theological Seminary (Th.D.). He taught in the Religion Department at Calvin College for thirty-five years. He has written* New Testament Guide *(Eerdmans, 1946, rev. ed. 1961),* Springboards for Discussion I *(Baker, 1970),* Springboards for Discussion II *(Baker, 1974), and* The Final Curtain *(Baker, 1977); and he has edited* The Rise and Development of Calvinism *(Eerdmans, 1959) and* The Heritage of John Calvin *(Eerdmans, 1973).*

# 13

# Dutch Calvinism in America

Entering the Netherlands through the writings of John Calvin that were smuggled in under the eagle eye of the Spanish overlords, through students who had studied in Geneva (including such luminaries as the musical composer Dathenus and Bogermann of Synod of Dort fame), and through Huguenots who came up from France, Calvinism took strong hold in the Lowlands in the mid-1500s. Lutheranism, Zwinglianism, and Anabaptism preceded it on the Dutch scene, but the cohesiveness of Calvinism, its genius for organization, and its devotion to spiritual and political freedom propelled it into a position of leadership. Eeningenburg says that

> Calvinism provided the kind of evangelical religion able to steel the nerves of a persecuted and hunted people. Its emphasis on the absolute sovereignty of God and the doing of His will at all costs, was precisely what this dread hour in the Netherlands required.[1]

And because of its strategic role in the fight for freedom and the breaking of the shackles of Spain, virtually accomplished at the Pacification of Ghent (1576), the Calvinist *Hervormde Kerk* became the state church, and Calvinism or the Reformed faith became the official religion of the Netherlands. That meant privileges and prerogatives and a heyday for Calvinism that reached its highwater mark in the historic Synod of Dort (1618–19).[2]

The seventeenth century was the glorious era in Dutch history. Inheriting a vast colonial empire from the Spaniards and the Portuguese, Holland became an economic and political power to be reckoned with.

Industry, fishing, shipbuilding, and cloth manufacture flourished. Cultural life was enriched and enriching—in painting there was Hals, Vermeer, and Rembrandt; in literature Cats, Hooft, Huygens, Vondel, and Revius; in the sciences van Leeuwenhoek, Boerhaave, and Swammerdam; in philosophy Spinoza; and in international jurisprudence Grotius the "father of international law." And it was in the early part of this *Golden Age* that Dutch Calvinism had its beginning on American soil.

## FIRST BEGINNINGS

The enterprise was a phase of Dutch mercantilism and colonialism. By 1620 various trading posts sponsored by the Dutch West Indies Company, a brainchild of William Usselinx in 1609 to match the high-dividend-producing Dutch East Indies Company, dotted the Hudson River and had established a thriving business in pelts and furs. The center of this bustling business activity was New Amsterdam, rechristened New York under the English occupation in 1664. But even though the commercial motif loomed large in this new enterprise and the Dutch West Indies Company was not religiously oriented,[3] religion of the Calvinistic brand was destined to play a significant role. It is true that the original charter of 1621 provided only for civil powers and commercial rights, but this was rectified in 1623 by the inclusion of this article:

> Within their territory they shall only worship according to the True Reformed Religion . . . and by a good Christian life they shall try to attract the Indians and other blind persons to the Kingdom of God and his Word, without however committing any religious persecution. . . .[4]

It is apparent from the last clause that even though public worship was permitted only for the Dutch Reformed Church, private worship for others (there were also Lutherans, Catholics, Anabaptists, and English Puritans in the colony at a very early date) was permitted in their homes, and this restricted liberty gave the people what was called "freedom of conscience."

As for the exercise of religion, at first a few laymen called *ziektebezoekers* (visitors of the sick) gave spiritual ministration. In 1628, however, the first ordained preacher, Dominie* Jonas Michaelius, a University of Leiden graduate with some missionary and chaplaincy experience, came over and organized the Dutch Reformed Church, setting up a Presbyterian form of church government. The group adopted the three doctrinal standards of the Synod of Dort—the Belgic Confession, the Heidelberg Catechism, and the Canons of Dort. They formalized membership and, with a beginning congregation of fifty

---

*Dominie* is a Dutch Reformed title meaning "pastor" or "minister."

communicants, established the first "pure" deposit of Calvinism (Calvinistic doctrine and Presbyterian polity) on the American scene. Five years later the Dutch Reformed communities erected two churches. They also began token mission work among the Algonquin Indians, even though Michaelius was very skeptical of its value. The American Dutch churches were attached to Classis Amsterdam, one of the classes in the Synod of North Holland.

In contrast with the Puritans, who settled New England with strong religious motivation, this colony in the New Netherlands grew very slowly (in 1646 the population was barely one thousand) and its early history was beset with many problems. One of the problems was tension in church-state relations. In keeping with Calvin's ideal of integration and his contention that the church should serve as the conscience of the state and the state should promote the true religion—in this case the Dutch Reformed—the church made forthright deliverances on civil and political affairs. And it did not hesitate to engage in censorious judgment and to rebuke the company leaders publicly on occasion. Dominie Michaelius called Director-General Minuit "a slippery man, who under the treacherous mask of honesty, is a compound of all iniquity and wickedness." Likewise Dominie Bogardus, who came over in 1631, called Minuit's successor, Wouter von Twiller, "weak, colorless and corrupt . . . a child of the devil . . . whose only qualification was that he had married the niece of Van Renssalaer and twice visited New Netherlands on a cattleboat."[5] The directors-general retaliated in similar invective and disrupted church services by scheduling target practice in the church yard while services were going on. Collusion of church and state under God is a noble ideal but, as history has so frequently illustrated, it is one that often breaks down under the harshness of concrete realities and results in a collision instead.

A second problem was the sparseness of colonists. By 1626 New Amsterdam had 200 inhabitants and by 1628 only 270. When England took over the colony in 1664—without much objection from the Dutch because the latter were not happy with their arrangement with the Dutch West Indies Company and the terms of surrender were very lenient—the population of New Netherlands, of which perhaps 75 percent were Dutch, was 8,000, distributed in some 33 towns and villages and the surrounding farming areas.[6] Nine of the chartered towns had elementary schools, and New Amsterdam had a Latin school; in all of them the Scriptures and the Heidelberg Catechism held a prominent place. No doubt the population remained small because the colony was primarily commercially oriented, the people were afraid of the Indians, and living conditions were satisfactory in the homeland (as Arnold Mulder says, "The comfortable do not emigrate"). After 1664 Dutch immigration virtually ceased.

One of the measures taken to promote immigration was the *patroon* system. An arrangement was made whereby a recruiter who brought over fifty families in the span of four years was given a landed estate of some proportions and the title of patroon, which carried with it semifeudal powers, and he in turn was obligated to promote the worship of God in conformity with the "Christian Reformed" religion and to provide a minister and a school teacher. Six of these patroonships were set up, but only one of them, Rennsaelerswijk near Albany, proved to be moderately successful. Furthermore, this arrangement created a new problem, that of the autonomy of the church of Jesus Christ. Could the minister, subject as he was to the patroon, speak prophetically and give supreme loyalty to his heavenly Lord or was he subject first of all to his "feudal" lord?

A third problem was the chronic shortage of preachers for the colony. From 1631 to 1645 there was but one minister in residence, Dominie Bogardus. In 1664 when the transfer to English rule occurred, there were 13 churches with 6 pastors, but soon thereafter three of these pastors left for the Netherlands, New Jersey, and South Carolina, respectively, leaving three elderly ministers—ages 62, 70, and 72—responsible for the spiritual care of the Dutch churches. The shortages persisted. In 1700 there were 23 churches and only 6 ministers; in 1721 there were 40 churches and 13 ministers; in 1740 the disparity was 65 and 20; in 1772 it was 100 and 41; and in 1792, when full independence was secured for the American Dutch church, there were 116 churches and 40 ministers.[7]

One of the main reasons for these shortages was dependence on the Netherlands for supplying preachers and for training and ordaining candidates for the ministry. Dutch ministers in Holland, with some rare exceptions, were not eager to serve in the American colonies. In addition, Classis Amsterdam was jealous of its prerogatives and, unlike the Puritans who set up Harvard College eight years after the founding of the colony so that "an illiterate ministry would not be left to the churches," insisted that candidates for the ministry in the Dutch Reformed Church in America secure their training and receive their ordination in Holland. As a consequence, spiritual life suffered and the moral tone of the colony, where there was considerable drinking, dishonesty, and licentiousness, was affected accordingly.

Agitation for an American classis was present relatively early. Dominie Polhemius at Long Island proposed in 1662 an association of ministers for intercommunication and mutual counsel. Little came of it, but in 1737 the progressive, evangelistically minded elements in the church, consisting of twelve of the sixty-four congregations and nine of the twenty-one ministers, proposed a *Coetus,* an association of elders and ministers to meet annually to consider, determine, give sentence upon and settle all matters and dissensions that occur, or which are brought before us for action, for being on the ground we are in the best position to judge upon them and to check and smother them in their very beginnings.[8]

The expressed goal was the maintenance of church order. And although these leaders professed continued loyalty to Classis Amsterdam and subservience to it, the powers of this incipient classis gradually broadened. It even ordained nine or ten men in the course of its history and kept up agitation for domestic training of its own ministers, either with a special chair at King's College or Princeton or in a seminary of its own. Abetting the movement was the translation of the liturgy, the psalms, and hymns into English in 1745; the initiation of English services by a Scotsman, A. Laialie, in 1763, an act that precipitated some lawsuits and rioting; and the securing of a charter for a liberal arts college in 1770, taking the name of Queen's College.[9]

Opposed to the *Coetus* party was the *Conferentie* contingent—highly conservative, doctrinally oriented men who insisted on the use of only the Dutch language in order to preserve orthodoxy[10] and who wanted to retain strong ties with the mother country. They looked with deep suspicion on the actions of the *Coetus* men and regarded the avowal of loyalty to the Netherlands Reformed Church on the part of the latter simply a "smokescreen." Bitter internal strife ensued. The church split in 1755 and was not reunited until 1772.

The reconciler of the two hostile parties was John H. Livingston, a Yale graduate, who was the last candidate from America to be sent to Holland for theological training and who holds the distinction of being the "Father of the Reformed Church in America." Returning in 1770, this noble and irenic ecclesiastical statesman made it his first goal to reunite the fighting segments. A Plan of Union was drafted in 1771 and submitted to a committee of four *Coetus* men, four *Conferentie* men, and four neutrals. After some vigorous discussion, they adopted the Plan and sent it on to their respective conventions and to the various congregations for ratification.[11] Although its signers pledged adherence to the constitution of the Netherlands Reformed Church, it called for a General Body in America with power to ordain, adding the *proviso* that the names of those examined and ordained would be reported to the Netherlands church. Provision was made for appeals to Classis Amsterdam and to the Synod of North Holland. It also agreed that a professor of divinity from Holland should instruct young men for the ministry here in addition to pastoring a church. The "apprentice" system was not operative for long, however, since very shortly afterward a theological department was attached to Queen's College and Livingston was made both president of the college and professor of theology.

A fourth problem was the threat of the establishment of episcopacy in the colony. When the takeover occurred in 1664 and the English flag was unfurled above New Amsterdam (New York), the population was overwhelmingly Dutch, and the English, by the *Duke's Laws,* promised the Dutch the free exercise of their religion so long as they did not disturb the peace. But after a brief episode of regained Dutch independence (1672–74), the English governors became more arbitrary and more assertive. And in 1686 the *Test Act,* first proposed in 1673 and promoted by some zealous Episcopalians, was passed to the effect that everyone must take an oath of allegiance to the king of England, everyone must take the sacraments according to the Church of England, and the Book of Common Prayer must be read in all the churches on Sundays and holy days. This looked suspiciously like the establishment of the Church of England in the colonies, and the Dutch protested vehemently. Conditions eased with the accession of a Dutch Protestant, William III, to the throne of England in 1689, and in 1696 the congregation in New York received a charter guaranteeing them the right to their church property and the "liberty of worshipping God according to the constitutions and directions of the Reformed Church in Holland, approved and established by the national Synod of Dordt."[12] Other Dutch churches throughout New York and New Jersey sought the same privileges and they too received charters of freedom.

A fifth problem was that of "dead orthodoxy" and a decline of religious fervor. Not only did rationalistic ideas generated by Newtonian science and Lockean philosophy threaten the church but formalism, traditionalism, and intellectualism struck in the latter part of the seventeenth and the early part of the eighteenth centuries. The time was ripe for the waves of revivalism that swept over America in the 1700s. In the Dutch colonies the forerunner was Dominie W. Berthorf (1656–1727), ordained by Classis Middleburg in the Netherlands. His preaching here was marked by emotional warmth and an emphasis on a conversion experience. The main figure in the revival, however, was Dominie J. F. Frelinghuyzen, who was called in 1720 to the Raritan valley in New Jersey. Son of a Reformed minister and deeply influenced by Dutch pietism, he found religion in the New York and New Jersey areas at a low ebb. There was coldness and formalism, a lack of discipline, much doctrinal precision but little evidence of spiritual life. Frelinghuyzen strove mightily to remedy the situation. He startled his hearers, accustomed as they were to long, dry, doctrinal disquisitions, with emotion-packed sermons marked by a sense of urgency and a call to repentance. He used the English language in order to lure back the young people, many of whom had drifted away. Directing his thrusts at the individual conscience, he stressed self-appraisal and the need of personal, conscious experience of the grace of God. As a result of the infusion of Pietism into the Dutch Reformed Church, there was a spiritual awakening of considerable dimensions and the creation of many new churches. The establishment of these congregations compounded the problem of the lack of adequate spiritual leadership, and Frelinghuyzen added his voice to those who pleaded for an American classis and ecclesiastical independence. After Frelinghuyzen's death in 1761, that agitation was carried on by Dominie Jacob Hardenburgh and as a consequence the charter of Queens College, mentioned above, called for

> study in the learned languages, and in the liberal arts, and in the philosophical sciences; also that it may be a school of the prophets in which young Levites and Nazarites may be prepared to enter upon the sacred ministerial office.[13]

Because of the revival the church grew at least one-third, and by the outbreak of the Revolution the Dutch Reformed Church had one hundred churches, forty-one ministers, and seventy thousand members. It was the seventh largest denomination in America.

It is to be expected that the long period of ethnic isolation promoted by retention of the Dutch language and ecclesiastical dependence on Holland would do little to enable the Dutch Reformed to make progress in the realization of the Calvinistic ideal of *Christ transforming culture*. It did little more than retain theological Calvinism. The Dutch made no such impact on the world of letters and played no such part in the creation of American literature as did, for instance, the New England Puritans. It is true that Walt Whitman and Herman Melville did have some Dutch blood in their veins and Washington Irving engaged in some journalism with his caricatures of the Dutch in his *Knickerbocker Papers* but the Dutch came into American letters more as subjects than as authors and offered a theme for imaginative American writers.

Since the scene of the fighting during the Revolutionary War was on the territory of the Dutch Reformed Church, the latter had to take some stand on the issue. Some attempted to maintain neutrality—a difficult stance to take since many buildings were damaged and much of the land was ravaged. Others, for personal safety and preservation of property, sided with the Loyalists, but the vast majority were Patriots, in hearty sympathy with the cause of freedom. Thousands of the Dutch fought in the Revolutionary Army, and the Albany area contributed three generals, of whom the best known is General Philip Schuyler, to the patriot cause. The *Coetus* party in the church stood for political as well as ecclesiastical freedom. The churches rallied in support of the American revolutionaries. Her pulpits "rang with stirring appeals which roused the patriotic ardor and inspired the martial courage of the people."[14] In 1775 and 1778, attributing the war to the sins of the people, the synods of the Dutch Reformed Church set aside a "specific day of solemn humiliation, with fasting and prayer, for the forgiveness of sins and the averting of deserved miseries."[15] And in 1780 the synod did not hesitate to assert that this was a "just and necessary"[16] war. Participation in the war, increasing Americanization, the breakdown of isolationism, and developing educational patterns put the Dutch Church in America, which severed its official ties with Classis Amsterdam in 1792, in a much better position to make an impact on the American world.

For some 180 years after the English occupation of New Amsterdam in 1664, emigration from the Netherlands to America was at a virtual standstill. It was revived in the nineteenth century when what is known as the *Great Migration* occurred. Between 1840 and the outbreak of the Civil War some 20,000 Netherlanders settled in America. There was a temporary lull during that conflict, but once the war ceased, immigration went on apace, some 55,000 coming over in the decade of the 1880s.

As is true in many migrations, there were both religious and economic motivating factors, in this case the former being primary. The eighteenth century had been a calamitous one for the Netherlands as far as the Calvinistic Christian faith was concerned. The winds of the French Revolution blew hard and strong, and rationalism, humanism, and mysticism sought to displace the orthodox faith. The Calvinists were reduced to a "faithful remnant," who, encouraged by a coterie of godly preachers who tried to stem the tide, met in "conventicles" in an effort to keep the faith alive.

Then, in 1816, an event of far-reaching significance occurred. King William I, welcomed back from exile, reorganized the Dutch State Church (Hervormde Kerk) in the interests of centralization. Synods, classes, and consistories were placed under the jurisdiction of a cabinet post, the *Ministry of Internal Affairs*. It was a transition from a state-favored church to a state-dominated church, and the crown rights of Jesus Christ as head of the church were in jeopardy.

Reaction to this assumption of control of the church by the state and to the liberal theology that was being propagated in the universities and proclaimed in the churches took the form, first, of vigorous protests on the part of Calvinistic preachers and their followers, and then, when that proved ineffective, secession by compulsion from the state church. It was known as the Secession *(Afscheiding)* of 1834. And it was the adherents of this seceding movement that accounted for the next influx of Dutch Calvinists into America.

## IMMIGRATION FOLLOWING THE *AFSCHEIDING*

The Secession of 1834 had been preceded by an evangelical revival in Geneva, which, through exchange students and evangelical writings, spread to the Netherlands. That led to the *Dutch Reveil,* an attempt to revive the Dutch church. Its leaders, notably Bilderdijk and Da Costa, issued warnings, pamphleteered against the liberal theology, attempted to reform from within, and by their efforts not only furnished inspiration for the Secession but gave impetus to the rise of the *Scholte Club* at the University of Leiden. This club consisted of a group of concerned young seminarians who were destined to play a leading role in the Afscheiding movement.

The pioneer leader of the secession was Hendrik De Cock, a University of Groningen graduate. De Cock had received a liberal theological training but was converted in his third charge, at Ulrum. His reading of the Bible, Calvin's *Institutes,* the Canons of Dort with their emphasis on the sovereignty of grace, and Pietistic writers such as Vader Brakel, as well as hearing the constant emphasis of a day laborer in his congregation, Klaas Kuipenga, on the need of regeneration and on the fact of total depravity led to De Cock's change of heart. His conversion meant revitalized preaching, which attracted hundreds to his service. But when he republished the Canons of Dort, baptized children of members of other congregations, criticized the hymns in the liturgical song book of the state church (192 hymns had been introduced in 1807, many of them doctrinally unsound), and issued a pamphlet calling many of his fellow ministers "wolves in sheep's clothing," he was suspended from the ministry of the state church on grounds of insubordination and disturbance of the peace. Thereupon De Cock (then only thirty-three years old) and 144 members of his congregation withdrew and drew up an *Act of Separation* in which (1) they refused to fellowship with members in the state church unless and until it returned to the faith, and (2) they invited to their fellowship all who loved the Reformed faith. That meant the beginning of a new ecclesiastical body, the *Old Netherlands Reformed Church.* Subsequent secessions—those by Scholte in North Brabant, Van Velzen in Friesland, Brummelkamp in Gelderland, et al. —augmented the new denomination and within a half year they numbered sixteen congregations.

In 1836 the Old Netherlands Reformed Church held its first synod. It adopted the doctrinal standards of the Synod of Dort, ordained A. C. Van Raalte (who had been refused ordination in the state church because he had refused to agree to carry out all of their legislative acts), and requested the government for legal status. They appealed to the Constitution of 1814, which guaranteed freedom of religion. The government, however, interpreted that article to apply only to those churches in existence in 1814 and proceeded to apply an article in the old Napoleonic Code, which forbade unauthorized assemblies of twenty or more people. The Seceders, on grounds of conscience, refused to obey that prohibition. As a consequence persecution set in. The Seceders were arrested, fined, and imprisoned, and soldiers were billeted in their homes. And although persecution virtually ceased with the abdication of William I in 1840, discrimination continued, and the economic situation worsened—taxes were high, there was much unemployment in the 40s, and there was a potato blight. In addition, the "fever of emigration" (Dosker) had caught hold. The Seceders therefore decided to emigrate. They considered several possibilities: Surinam, Indonesia, South Africa, Java, and America, finally opting for America. Immigration societies were formed in order to screen applicants and finalize plans. The *Great Migration* was under way.

One distinctive feature of this second influx of Dutch Calvinism on the American scene was the studied effort and scrupulous attention given to the spiritual well-being of the colonists. Religious leadership was deemed indispensable. During an attack of typhus fever when emigration was in the air, Van Raalte felt a strong call to accompany the colonists and asked, "Who will be their Moses, their Aaron? If no teacher, if no instructor accompanies them, will they not soon have to become a prey to atheism. . . ?"[17] Many a Dutch minister felt constrained to accompany his congregation, or a part of it, to America; for example C. Vander Meulen went to Zeeland, Michigan; M. Ypma to Vriesland, Michigan; and H. P. Scholte to Pella, Iowa. Scholte said on this score:

> Those who leave will be able to hear the Gospel in their native tongue during the first few years at least, and may thus receive the spiritual sustenance which will confirm them in the faith, kindle them in love (and) warn them against the cravings of the flesh that militate against the Spirit.[18]

The "cradle" settlements were Holland, Michigan, under the leadership of Dominie A. C. Van Raalte, and its offshoots, Overisel, Noordeloos, Vriesland, et al., which constituted "De Kolonie," and Pella, Iowa, under the leadership of Dominie H. P. Scholte, an independent who preferred to go it alone, but whose colony, after his death, affiliated with the Christian Reformed Church. Other Dutch Calvinistic settlements were made in Illinois and Wisconsin. Many colonists joined the Reformed Church in America; others of them joined the Christian Reformed Church, which came into being by 1857 by separation from the Reformed Church in America.

The *Afscheiding* movement was essentially a recovering of theological or doctrinal Calvinism, vitally necessary in this point of history. It was a return to the basic tenets of the faith, truths of the Bible that had evaporated or had become diluted under the blasts of the French Revolution. As such it reflects the "doctrinalist-pietistic" wing of the Reformed tradition. As the sermons of Van Raalte indicate, the lordship of Christ was limited in the main to matters of personal salvation; kingdom service, to the institutional church; and the sovereignty of God, to submission to the will of God in one's personal Christian life.[19] It was in a sense an "unfinished Reformation." The broader perspectives of the "sovereignty-of-God principle" remained to be developed. It is true there was something of that larger vision in Groen van Prinsterer, the founder of the *Antirevolutionaire* political clubs, but he remained in the Netherlands and passed on the torch to Abraham Kuyper. Little was done in America at this stage to lay the claims of Christ on all of life and reality.

There were at least four factors that limited the *Afgescheidene* involvement in American culture at this stage. One was the mystical, pietistic strain, which was particularly strong in the emigrating Zeelanders but present in some measure in many immigrants of this period. That strain was nurtured in the conventicle movement that preceded the Secession of 1834—a movement that spawned the "ecclesiola in ecclesia," where the religiously concerned sought an antidote to cold, rationalistic preaching and fed their souls on prayer, Bible study, and the "old writers" such as Hellenbroek, Brakel, and Lodenstyn. Although this pietistic spirit was wholesome in that it had no pantheistic overtones, it did create a temperament and a frame of mind that were not conducive to a vital cultural concern or development of a world-and-life view.

Second, it must be remembered that the primary motives of the Dutch immigrants in coming to America were conservation of religious values and economic betterment. These people wanted particularly the freedom to exercise their faith without restraint, the liberty to train their children in a Christian way, and the opportunity to make a decent living for their families. What impact on America they envisaged, according to their expressed aims of immigration, was restricted to the spread of the gospel and the saving of souls. Although it was not necessarily outside their purview, they had no expressed intention of laying any cultural claim on their adopted world.

Third, an inferiority complex marked the *Afscheiding* colonists, a trait not uncommon to immigrant groups. Most of them were of peasant stock and of meager means. Of one emigrating group of 2,300 only 300 were in comfortable financial circumstances. The greater number of them were farmers. Agriculture is no inherent enemy of culture but a cultural lag is inevitable when virtually all of one's waking hours must be devoted to uprooting tree stumps and wresting a livelihood from the soil. In Michigan particularly, life was a veritable struggle for existence, and Van Raalte, who did have some hopes and ideals of impact, was immersed in the harsh realities of survival.

Fourth, there was a deliberate attempt to maintain homogeneity, and that called for isolation and segregation. The grand objective in emigrating was the planting of solidly Christian communities, which Van Raalte called *brandings-punten* ("torches") to serve as radiating centers of the gospel. Christian commitment was the first prerequisite for membership in the emigrating societies. And even though some immigrants went to settled communities, yet by their clannishness they constructed for themselves self-imposed ghettoes. *Holland Hill* in Milwaukee and the *Groninger Buurt* in Grand Rapids are cases in point. There was distrust and suspicion of things American, the fear of contamination, and a quest for security—all of which drew them together.

As a consequence the *Afscheiding* colonists gave to many Americans an impression of aloofness and isolationism not unlike that of the Amish. That impression, however, was hardly accurate. There was a measure of penetration and assimilation, cautious though it was. The only two university-trained leaders, Van Raalte and Scholte, urged the colonists to become citizens of the new land at their earliest opportunity. One day in 1848 the county clerk from Grand Haven came to "De Kolonie" and conferred citizenship on four hundred people at reduced rates. They discovered that naturalization papers, like other commodities in this country, were cheaper by the dozen. Van Raalte and Scholte laid the groundwork for later cultural involvement by promoting higher education. Scholte was instrumental in setting up Central College in Pella, and Van Raalte established Hope Academy, later Hope College.[20] Van Raalte's express purpose, as he said, was "to deliver this people and their confession from irrelevance." The colonists were urged to run for public office at the local level, to give their allegiance to one of the major political parties, and to keep abreast of current affairs through its own community newspapers. Holland had its *De Hollander* from 1850 and its *De Grondwet* from 1860; Sheboygan, its *Nieuwsbode;* and Pella, its *Weekblad* and *Gazaette*.

Most of the colonists in Michigan affiliated with the Democratic party at first. Why they did so is not easy to determine. It may be that to their mind this party best expressed the ideals of Jefferson and Jackson with which they were sympathetic, but it is more likely that they did so because the Democrats, more than the Whigs, favored ease of obtaining citizenship. Wisconsin immigrants also were Democratic at first, but they swung over in large numbers in 1854 to the newly formed Republican party when *De Nieuwsbode* asserted vigorously that any vote for the Democratic nominees, Pierce and Scott, was a vote for injustice and sin. In Iowa, Scholte was critical of all the parties and reluctantly joined the Democratic party, which to him was the best of a bad lot. He broke with it in 1859, however, because of his disappointment with the Buchanan administration, and joined the Republican ranks. In the election of 1860, Lincoln carried Illinois and Wisconsin, while Douglas, a Democrat, eked out a narrow victory in Michigan and Iowa.

The two major social issues that agitated America in this period of our history were prohibition and slavery. Except for a few isolated pro-prohibition pockets, the Dutchmen in America were predominately anti-prohibition. And when the issue appeared on the ballot in 1853, prohibition was resoundingly defeated in Michigan, Wisconsin, and Iowa. The colonists considered it too sweeping in character, since it would also have forbidden wine at the Lord's Supper, and they had a strong feeling that prohibition supporters were misusing Scripture in support of their cause.

With respect to slavery, the colonists were unanimously agreed that it was an unmitigated evil. They differed, however, in their views as to the solution of the problem. In Michigan, where the philanthropic sentiments of the *Reveil* were strong and where Stowe's *Uncle Tom's Cabin* was widely read, abolition sentiment, promoted by such leaders as Van Raalte and Vandermeulen, was strong, and some of the people were active in the Underground Railroad. In Iowa the situation was different. Scholte regarded slavery as a sectional issue, one that the states must solve. He was a warm admirer of Henry Clay, the "Great Compromiser." Scholte felt that the Omnibus Bill of 1850 and the Kansas-Nebraska Bill of 1854 had real merit and he forwarded his own compromise proposals, which were acclaimed by some news analysts as "by far the most candid and luminous survey of the vexed slavery question that had yet appeared."[21] Lucas does not hesitate to assert that "in the momentous year of 1860, the Hollanders were as acutely interested in the political issues before the country as were the Americans of native ancestry."[22]

As is apparent from the above, a notable exception to the early pattern of relative isolation or cautious penetration of the American scene was Hendrik Pieter Scholte, founder of Pella, Iowa. He had acumen of mind, a good command of American history, and a ready voice and pen. He became immediately active on the American political scene. Within a year after the founding of Pella he addressed a petition to the Iowa legislature asking that a township be organized and that the newcomers, who had declared their intention of seeking citizenship, be permitted to vote and run for public office. The petition was granted and Scholte himself was elected justice of the peace and school inspector in the first election.

He was also active in national politics. In 1856 he and J. C. Breckinridge, the Democratic candidate for vice-president, hit the campaign trail. They held several political rallies in Michigan, trying to stem the movement there from the Democrats to the Republicans. Of course he met with criticism, and many told him to stay within narrowly religious boundaries. But he had a broader kingdom vision. As already noted, in 1859 he deserted the Democrats and joined the Republicans. In this party too he was very active. In 1860, at the Republican state convention in Des Moines, he was named as delegate to the National Republican convention in Chicago. He was an ardent admirer of Lincoln, became his personal friend, and attended the Lincoln inaugural in 1861. He was one Dutchman in this period who entered the national political and social scene. But he was an exception to the rule. The others were characterized by relative isolationism, or, at best, by a cautious penetration of American culture.

Back in the Netherlands in the second half of the nineteenth century there was a new surge of French Revolution–inspired liberalism in the state church. With the University of Utrecht as feeding center, humanism, rationalism, and ethicalism flooded the Hervormde Kerk. There was open denial of the deity of Christ, His miracles, His substitutionary atonement, His physical resurrection, and His coming again. The Forms of Unity were dropped, the state church lost its creedal character, and candidates for the ministry were simply asked to promise ''to promote the interests of the kingdom of God.''

The leader of the conservative wing that protested this emasculation of the faith was a spiritual and intellectual giant, Abraham Kuyper. He was a good theologian, a gifted journalist, and a conscientious politician who became Prime Minister of the Netherlands from 1901 to 1905. He had his theological training at the University of Leiden and graduated as a modernist but was converted to the historic faith in his first charge at Beesd. Again, as with De Cock, it was his reading of the Bible, his study of Calvin's *Institutes* and the Confessions, and the admonitions of one of his parishioners that were instrumental in his change of heart. When he assumed a second ministerial charge at Utrecht, the ideal of Christ as transformer of culture took hold of him, and he set himself to the goal of revitalizing Calvinism. A meeting with Groen von Prinsterer, the pioneer of the Antirevolutionary political party, fired his enthusiasm and reinforced his aims. And when the basic tenets of the faith were being repudiated far and wide, against Kuyper's vigorous protest, he and his followers were forced out, and the *Doleantie,* the second nineteenth-century secession from the state church, occurred. The new church, bearing the name *De Nederduits Gereformeerde Kerken,* held its first Congress in 1887 and already by that date had 10,000 members. It was this new movement that was responsible for the third flow of Dutch Calvinists to America.

### IMMIGRATION FOLLOWING THE *DOLEANTIE*

Kuyper, who led in this new recovery of theological Calvinism and the development of cultural Calvinism, encapsulated his convictions and his goals in his inaugural as president of the Free University, which he helped to found in 1882 as an institution free of both church and state, when he said, ''There is not an inch of reality of which Christ does not say, *It is Mine.''* He elaborated his views in his three-volume work *Pro Rege*. Christian liberty to him meant that the Christian has not only the freedom but also the responsibility to enter all areas of life and lay Christ's claims on them. He sought to make concrete the principle that he found to be central in Scripture—the sovereignty of God.

As far as theology is concerned, with a few exceptions such as membership in the Covenant of Grace and the destiny of children of unbelievers who die in infancy, Kuyper reproduced the views of John Calvin. In his confrontation of the culture of the day, he developed, in opposition to the liberal individualism of the Thorbeck School, the positions of Christian socialism, an organic view of society in which man's social concern for his fellow man finds expression; the perspective of the sovereignty of the various spheres of society under God, out of which arose parent-society, rather than parochial, schools; the belief that missions is the responsibility of the church, rather than a joint effort of church and state as in Geneva; the position that church and state should be separate, in contrast to Genevan integrationism, and yet which allocated such definite duties of the state toward religion as restraining blasphemy, maintaining the Lord's Day, and honoring the name of God in the constitution; and the principle of the antithesis, leading to the formation of specifically Christian organizations.

After 1870 there was renewed emigration to America. Religious persecution was no longer a factor, but economic conditions in the Netherlands—low wages, high unemployment, the liberal land policy of the United States government as reflected in the Homestead Act of 1862, and once again the "fever of emigration"—led thousands to emigrate. In the decade of the 1880s some 53,000 left the Netherlands to come to America.

There was a new surge of emigration after World War II. Again the emigration was prompted by economic difficulties, the "bad taste" of the recent occupation by the Germans, fear of World War III, overpopulation so that housing was at a premium and jobs were hard to get, and the encouragement of relatives and friends in America. Many of the immigrants settled in Canada as well as in the United States. Some of them joined the Reformed Church in America; most of them affiliated with the Christian Reformed Church in the USA and the Canadian Christian Reformed Church.

The new and salutary emphasis of these new waves of immigrants was on a Christianity that was not merely soteriological but also cosmological—a cultural Calvinism that sought to lay the claims of Jesus Christ as Lord over all areas of life. Idealism ran high. The people were inspired to aggressive effort by the fact that in the Netherlands Calvinism had become a religious, social, political, and scientific force to be reckoned with and they assumed that the time was now ripe to make a calculated, frontal assault on the culture of America.

As the *Afscheiding* and *Doleantie* traditions merged and intermingled in the American "melting pot," tensions developed because of two sets of opposing viewpoints. The first set was *penetrationism* versus *isolationism,* and the second, *permeationism* versus *organizationism.*

In the first set, there was the "mind of impact" arrayed against the "mind of conservation" or the "mind of involvement" opposed to the "mind of detachment." The first tended toward more communication between itself and the environment and more immersion into the American scene, while the other looked askance at closeness of contact, feared the loss of basic values, and adopted as its slogan, "In our isolation is our strength." Men like Henry Beets and Watson Groen represented the first position; men like Klaas Schoolland and J. Van Lonkhuyzen, the second position.

That tension was reflected in periodicals emanating from the Reformed community in America during this period. Representing the progressive point of view were two periodicals. One was *De Gereformeerde Amerikaan,* born in 1897 and expiring in 1916. The editors opposed the transplanting of Dutch patterns to the United States and contended that one could remain solidly Reformed even while becoming thoroughly Americanized. Of similar complexion was *Religion and Culture,* launched in 1919 under the editorship of E. J. Tuuk. It sought to apply the Calvinistic principles to every sphere of life.

Representing the conservative point of view was *The Witness,* a periodical that had its birth about the same time as that of *Religion and Culture.* It took on itself the responsibility of pointing out and warning against the dangers attendant upon exposure to the American environment. The *Reformed Herald,* which came into being a little later, presented the same viewpoint, stressing the need of isolationism if the Reformed faith was not to lose its distinctiveness. But their efforts were short-lived. The Kuyperian emphasis on assault and impact won the day.

The question of the proper mode of impact gave rise to new tensions because another set of opposing viewpoints—those of the *permeationists* and the *organizationalists.* Granted that the time was ripe for Calvinism to make its impact, how could such impact best be achieved? By individual Christians acting as a "leaven" and a "light" in existing organizations and running for public office as candidates of either of the two major political parties? Or by Christians banding together and forming separate, antithetical organizations? The latter was apparently effective in the Netherlands; would not the same be true in America? Christian day schools were already a viable antithetical organization in America; why not continue along that line and do the same in politics, labor, journalism, and the like?

There were a few abortive attempts. In 1903 a political study society bearing the Latin title *Fas et Jus* was formed. It had as its objective the eventual creation of a Christian political party. Led by Johannes Groen and Klaas Schoolland, men of rare vision, it drew up a constitution having at its core the principle of sovereignty of God in political affairs. This small but idealistic group met regularly, studied political principles in the Reformed frame of reference, leaned heavily on Kuyper's basic ideas, and after ten years of study deemed the time ripe for the formation of a Christian political party. B. K. Kuiper was appointed chairman of a drafting committee that was instructed to draw up the constitutional basis for such a party. That was in 1913. The next year, however, World War I broke out, international affairs took precedence, and the project was stillborn. The post-mortem judgment was that the movement was too philosophical and too theological for the average American, who was pragmatic in his political concepts and activities. In the 1960s a revival of this idealism found expression in the formation of the National Association for Christian Political Action (NACPA—now Association for Public Justice [APJ]) by Calvinists from Canada and the United States. It meets regularly to discuss political issues in the light of the Word of God, publishes an occasional position paper (e.g., on abortion), and cherishes the hope that eventually it may become a Christian political party. It publicizes its views in the *APJ Report,* a periodical that appears bimonthly, and it finds support for its organizationalistic stance in a Canadian periodical, the *Calvinist Contact,* as well as in a monthly in the United States, the *Christian Reformed Outlook,* formerly the *Torch and Trumpet.*

A second abortive effort was the attempt to produce a Christian newspaper. In 1920, six weeks after the death of Abraham Kuyper, who had served for many years as editor of *De Standaard,* a Christian paper in the Netherlands, J. C. Monsma, a Christian Reformed clergyman, came out with the first issue of the *American Daily Standard,* published in Grand Rapids, Michigan. It first hit the streets on the day before Christmas, its cover page carrying a picture of Christ and, in bold print, the nativity story from Luke 2. In its lead editorial the editor disclaimed the idea that the press must simply be descriptive and mirror life as it is, but asserted instead that it must give spiritual, moral, and intellectual leadership. He expressed the staff's intention of "applying the principles of Protestant Christianity to the public issues of modern times." "Nothing will be allowed to go to press," he added, "which, in our judgment, is incompatible with the TRUTH whose birth we now commemorate." The paper lasted two months and then foundered on the shoals of "limited circulation, lack of finances, and inexperienced management."[23]

The only other area besides education in which a measure of organizational success was achieved was that of labor. The *Christian Labor Association* was formed in 1930 for the express purpose of exercising

justice in labor issues and problems in accordance with Christian principles. It has become fairly strong in Canada and is strongly represented
in Reformed communities in the United States.

The permeationists, led by such men as Henry Stob and Eugene
Oosterhaven, voicing their convictions in such periodicals as the *Reformed Journal* and the *Reformed Review,* advanced the thesis that the
question of separate, antithetical organizations is not a matter of principle but one of Christian strategy. They asserted that there is no biblical
demand for them, that the proof texts usually advanced (e.g., Matt.
12:30; 1 Cor. 15:33; 2 Cor. 6:17) apply to the individual and his relationship with the world and cannot be extended to cover Christian
organizations without doing violence to the Scriptures. It comes down
to the utilization of the best means for advancing the kingdom of God.
With respect to children of Christian parents, it is highly essential that
their education be of one piece and that God be acknowledged in the
school as well as in the home and church, and in view of their pliability
and impressionism it is the part of wisdom to train them in separate
Christian schools. As to Christian labor unions, they may be effective in
certain areas and there they should be established; in other areas, e.g.,
in large cities, they could exert little or no power and their establishment
would be impracticable. The better way is to promote Christian candidates for all public offices on the local, state, and national levels; to
encourage Christians to be articulate and let their voices be heard in the
so-called neutral or secular organizations; to engage in Christian lobby-
ing; and, in general, to seek to exert a positive Christian influence in all
spheres in which we live and walk. The goal of Christ, the transformer
of culture, must always be kept in mind; we must work unceasingly to
get recognition of the sovereignty of God over all of reality; and we
must be indefatigable in our efforts to lay the claims of Christ on all
spheres of life.

That ideal of pristine Calvinism was cherished both in the *initial*
entry and in the *Afgescheidene* influx of Calvinism on the American
scene but, due to the factors referred to above, it found but little implementation, and it was the tradition of theologically sound Calvinism
that was carried forward on foreign soil. With the surge of Kuyperian
Calvinism in the nineteenth and twentieth centuries, that ideal bids fair
to come to far greater fruition with the *Doleantie* influence on American
life and culture.

# Calvin's Influence
# in Canada

## W. Stanford Reid

*W. Stanford Reid is Emeritus Professor of History, University of Guelph, Guelph, Ontario. He holds degrees from McGill University, Montreal (B.A., M.A.), Westminster Theological Seminary, Philadelphia (Th.B., Th.M.), The University of Pennsylvania, Philadelphia (Ph.D.), Wheaton College, Wheaton, Illinois (L.H.D.Hon.), and The Presbyterian College, Montreal, Quebec (D.D.Hon.). He has served in the pastoral ministry in Montreal and as a member of the Arts Faculty at McGill University, Montreal. Dr. Reid has contributed articles to* Church History, Fides et Historia, The Scottish Historical Review, The Canadian Historical Review, Speculum, Christianity Today, The Presbyterian Record, *and many other periodicals. He has authored or edited some ten books on the Protestant Reformation and on Canadian history. He is a member of the American Society of Church History, the Canadian Society of Church History, the Scottish Historical Society, the Conference on Faith and History, the Scottish Church History Society, and the Royal Historical Society.*

# 14

# Calvin's Influence
# in Canada

It may come as something of surprise to many people to hear that the followers of John Calvin were among the earliest Europeans to visit Canada in the opening years of modern history. Some have maintained that Jacques Cartier may at least have come from a Huguenot family, if he was not himself a Protestant. But it is certain that Admiral Coligny, one of the leaders of *la religion pretendu Reformé,* as the Roman Catholics called it, advocated to the French king in the 1560s that he allow the French Calvinists to migrate to New France, where they could have freedom of religion and at the same time be an outpost of French power. This was refused, but the French Calvinists continued to show much interest in the new colonies that were being set up in what is now Quebec.

There was more than interest involved, however, for it was the Huguenot merchants of Dieppe, La Rochelle, and other coast ports who were prepared to venture their money to establish the colony, and their ships to do the trading. Although there is considerable discussion as to whether Samuel de Champlain was a Huguenot, his name seems to indicate that he probably came from a Protestant family. Moreover, one of the families, the De Monts, who worked with him in the establishment of the settlement at Porte Royale on the Bay of Fundy, was undoubtedly Protestant. Moreover, after the founding of the city of Quebec in 1608 a considerable number of Calvinists moved into the area, and the first seigneury granted by the French crown was bestowed on one of the Caens, a Huguenot from Dieppe. We are also told that the

Roman Catholic governors used to complain that the Protestants attracted the attention of the Indians, who listened to them as they sang their psalms while sailing up the St. Lawrence, and then used that contact as a means of presenting to them the Protestant version of the Christian religion. The French Calvinists in this way played an important role in the beginnings of the country.[1]

Yet not all went smoothly, for the Roman Catholic missionary orders were not happy that Protestants in the New World were able to benefit from the freedom forbidden them at home. It was not surprising, therefore, that when the Society of Jesus and Cardinal Richelieu decided that New France should be a bastion of Roman Catholic orthodoxy, the Huguenots were banned from the country. This took place in 1633, and from that time on Cardinal Richelieu sought to bring only good Catholics to the colony and to have only Roman Catholics invest in its fur trade and other developments. He tried to organize various companies such as the Company of New France, known as the Company of the One Hundred Associates, and other groups, but never with any great success. The French authorities found it necessary, therefore, to allow Protestant merchants of La Rochelle to continue trading with the colony, although they were not permitted to own land or spend the winter there. When Quebec finally fell to the British forces in 1760, a thanksgiving service was held by the troops in one of the Roman Catholic churches in the city, and it was attended by a number of French Protestant merchants who were there on business. Thus, from its early foundation to the British conquest, Calvinism has been part of Canada's cultural tradition.[2]

In 1713, by the Treaty of Utrecht what is now Nova Scotia fell into British hands, and shortly thereafter the British brought into the area almost three thousand French- and German-speaking Protestant refugees from the wars in the Rhineland. A good many of these were of Reformed persuasion. Then in 1758 when the first meeting of the Nova Scotia legislature took place, an act was passed declaring the Church of England to be the established church but at the same time providing freedom of conscience to "Calvinists, Lutherans, Quakers," and all other Protestant denominations. This provision in the act immediately proved attractive to a good many different groups. New England settlers, many of Scotch-Irish background; Ulstermen directly from Ireland; Scots, both Highlanders and Lowlanders, all obtained land and established themselves as colonists.[3] Of all these a considerable proportion were Calvinistic in their theological beliefs.

Under the designation of "Calvinists" we find a number of groups, and the most obvious among these were the Presbyterians and Congregationalists who came from the New England area. In 1764 the Presbyterians from New Hampshire petitioned the presbytery of New

Brunswick, New Jersey, for a minister, with the result that the following year the Rev. James Lyon came to Nova Scotia, serving first in Halifax and then in Onslow and Truro. The Congregationalists who were in the colony seem to have cooperated heartily with the Presbyterians, as their basic doctrines were the same. Thus when the sixty German-speaking families in Lunenburg, who had withdrawn from the Church of England, wished to have their own minister and had failed to obtain one from Philadelphia, they asked that one of their own number, Brun Romkes Comingo, a forty-six-year-old fisherman without any academic training, be ordained. The question was, who would examine and ordain him? To meet this contingency two Congregationalist ministers along with Lyon and Murdoch, another Presbyterian, founded a presbytery and after duly examining Comingo ordained him to the ministry. In defending this action the presbytery stated that they were in no way being sectarian, for the Lunenburgers had been brought up in "the Calvinistic Presbyterian Religion" and therefore their call to Comingo was to be sustained.[4]

The second Presbyterian minister in this action, James Murdoch, represented another strain of Calvinism, namely that which came directly from the British Isles. Before Murdoch's arrival two men, David Smith and Daniel Cock, both from the Associate (Burgher) Synod, had arrived in Nova Scotia, Smith settling among the Ulstermen around Londonderry, and Cock in Truro. At the same time the General Associate Synod (Anti-burgher) had sent out the Irish-born James Murdoch, who became the minister of the Halifax Dissenting Church. These men, after the American Revolution, were joined by a considerable contingent of loyalist Highlanders who came from North Carolina and whose pastor was Rev. John Bethune. Bethune later moved to Montreal, where he founded the first Presbyterian church, St. Gabriel Street Church. But while the dissenting Presbyterian churches in Scotland and Ireland were anxious to minister to the colonists, the Church of Scotland did not display much interest in them until the beginning of the nineteenth century, and then it tended to adopt an attitude of exclusiveness that hindered cooperation between the members of the Church of Scotland and their fellow Presbyterians.[5] One of the reasons for this may well have been the Church of Scotland's rather lukewarm Calvinism, which did not stimulate it to any great evangelistic effort.

Although the Presbyterians were generally Calvinistic, there were other groups who equaled or even surpassed them in adherence to Reformed doctrines and practices. Most important and numerous of these were the Baptists. Although some of the English Baptists had accepted Arminian teachings, the larger majority held to Reformed teachings as expressed in a modified version of the Westminster Confession. This group, known as Particular Baptists in England, received the name of

Regular Baptists in America, while the Arminians were known as Free Will Baptists. Very early in the history of Nova Scotia a number of Baptists came over from New England, but the expansion of the Baptist churches was largely due to the evangelistic work of Henry Alline of Falmouth, Nova Scotia (1748–84). The Regular Baptists were centered around Sackville, and the Free Will Baptists in Carleton County. After the American Revolution a number of loyalist Baptists settled in the area around Wolfville, most of these being Regular Baptists. When a number of members withdrew from the Church of England in Halifax, they founded the Granville Street Baptist Church, which was again predominantly Regular, and out of this group eventually came Acadia College, established at Wolfville.[6]

As for the Church of England, it is rather difficult to determine what its actual position was. The fact, however, that the first bishop of Nova Scotia, appointed in 1787, was the Rev. Charles Inglis of Scotch-Irish origin might well indicate that he came of a Calvinistic background, at least as Calvinistic as the Thirty-nine Articles. This would seem to be confirmed by the fact that he was appointed largely in order to bring as many of the Presbyterians as possible into the established church, and that before his elevation to the episcopate, he frequently occupied the pulpit of the Halifax Dissenting Church when the minister was sick. In this he was imitated by two other Anglican clergymen in the city.[7] It seems, therefore, that generally speaking at this time the Church of England in Nova Scotia was dominated by the Low Church element, which was prepared to follow the church's Reformed tradition.

In the Canadas, now Quebec and Ontario, the development ecclesiastically was like that of Nova Scotia and the other Atlantic colonies. With the cession of New France to Great Britain by the French in 1763, the land was opened up to an influx of settlers, and those who held to a Calvinistic theology were among the most active in taking up land or doing business in the new colony. One of the first things the British government did was to settle some of its regiments on the land, and among those so placed were the Murray (42nd) and the Frazer (78th) Highlanders, of whom a good many were Presbyterians.[8] A considerable number were established at Murray Bay on the north shore of the St. Lawrence River. After the American Revolutionary War others received grants in Upper Canada around what is now the city of Perth, which became a center of Presbyterian influence throughout the area.[9]

From 1763, however, civilian settlers were moving into Lower Canada in considerable numbers. Although some settled in Quebec City, many more moved on up the St. Lawrence to establish themselves in Montreal. Here, as mentioned above, Bethune founded St. Gabriel Street Church as a congregation of the Church of Scotland. It was not long after this that Scots began to move out into the rural areas. Some settled in the areas north of Montreal in Ste. Thérèse and St. Eustache, and in the late forties a whole colony of Scotch-Irish forced out of Ireland by the potato famine, settled in the northern part of the Seigneury of Mille Isles, west of St. Jerome. To the south of Quebec City, in the Eastern Townships close to the United States border, another influx of Scots took place, most of them also being Presbyterians. They settled in an area bounded by a line drawn south from the city of Quebec to the American frontier and westward as far as the St. Lawrence River.[10] Here Presbyterianism was a predominant element in the ecclesiastical structure.

In Upper Canada, apart from the soldiers settled around Perth, the earliest Presbyterians were Americans and United Empire Loyalists who soon after 1770 began to settle the Niagara Peninsula and also crossed Lake Ontario to establish residence in York (Toronto). This early colonization of the southern part of modern Ontario was soon followed by Scots and Scotch-Irish who came into the country in large numbers via the St. Lawrence River. Both civilians and demobilized soldiers obtained grants of land up the Ottawa River and then spread back into the area that came to be known as Glengarry. Some later left Glengarry to cross the Ottawa and move up into the Laurentian Mountains on the Lower Canada or Quebec side, where they established Gaelic-speaking communities, which were strongly Presbyterian. Southwest Upper Canada extending west from York also had large numbers of Scottish settlers.[11] The Canada Company, whose first secretary was John Galt, the Scottish novelist, brought in many settlers, and the first church established in Guelph, one of the main centers, was St. Andrews Presbyterian Church in connection with the Church of Scotland.[12] Other Scots settled in Colonel Talbot's colony near Chatham. Likewise other Scots found land in Lanark and Renfrew counties west of Ottawa. In all these areas the Presbyterians formed a large, if not dominant, element in the population.

The Baptists constituted almost as large an element. They came principally from the United States, however, where a number of missionary societies were organized to carry the gospel into Canada among the new settlers. Although they set up a few churches in the southern part of Lower Canada, their chief work was done in Upper Canada, their bridgehead being the Niagara peninsula. Gradually their churches spread into the area around York from where, after 1820, they carried on active missionary propaganda. They were further aided by the advent of Baptists from England, who tended to restrain some of the extravagances of the frontier type of religion. At the same time Scots who had come under the influence of the Haldane brothers began to settle in Lower Canada north of Montreal and also to move into eastern Upper

Canada. The larger part of these Baptist groups was strongly Reformed in outlook. Generally speaking they held to the views of the Philadelphia Confession of Faith of 1742, which in turn was based on the seventeenth-century confession of the Particular Baptists. They took advantage of the act of 1798, which, like that of 1758 in Nova Scotia, permitted marriages to be performed by "ministers of the Church of Scotland, Lutherans and Calvinists," claiming that they came under the provision for Calvinists.[13]

The Church of England in the Canadas was in a somewhat different position from that in the Atlantic colonies. While the Low Church tradition dominated in the eastern colonies, the High Church tradition of the old-fashioned Laudian type tended to predominate in the Canadas. Undoubtedly there were some clergy who were Low Church Calvinists, but church leaders such as Bishop Mountain and particularly Bishop Strachan had little time or use for a Calvinistic theology.[14] Furthermore, they were determined to maintain the Church of England's position as the established church, with all the perquisites, including endowments, pertaining to it. The outcome of this situation was a struggle that lasted into the 1850s.

Although the Church of Scotland leaders in Canada had agreed in 1840 to a kind of coestablishment with the Church of England and had received some of the endowments originally bestowed on the Anglicans, this did not end the problem. For one thing, in 1843 the Church of Scotland suffered a secession from its ranks of almost one-third of its membership with the formation of the Free Church, which refused to accept government control of the church. This body was Reformed in its theological position in opposition to the prevailing "moderatism" of the established church. Quite a number of the congregations in Canada followed the Free Kirk example by organizing a Free Kirk in both the Atlantic colonies and the Canadas, and this church took a stand against establishment.[15] In this antiestablishmentarian position, the Free Kirk received support from the Baptists and from the Methodists. The result was that by 1854 it was quite apparent that church establishment was not suitable for the freer atmosphere of the colonies, and this concept was finally put to rest.[16]

While the conflict over establishment in the Canadas had been going on, as in the Atlantic colonies, other Presbyterian churches from Scotland had been making religious inroads. The Associate or Secession churches had established congregations, and when in 1847 the United Presbyterian Church was organized in Scotland as a result of the union of the United Secession Church and the Relief Church, their colonial offshoots also united. This in a sense began the movement toward Presbyterian union in Canada—a movement that was further strengthened by political confederation of all the British North American colonies, except Newfoundland, in 1867. As a result, in 1875 almost all Presbyterians joined in forming the Presbyterian Church in Canada.[17]

Similarly, although the Baptists held firmly to a congregational polity, they found that to accomplish much either in Canada or beyond its borders, they needed some form of cooperative organization. Therefore they began to organize associations for cooperative work. In 1800 nine Regular Baptist congregations met at Lower Granville, Nova Scotia, to organize the Nova Scotia Baptist Association, and by 1846 this had expanded into the Baptist Convention of Nova Scotia, New Brunswick, and Prince Edward Island. Meanwhile the Free Will Baptists had also been expanding, and in 1906 the two groups came together to form the Maritime United Baptist Convention, on a compromise theological basis. In the Canadas much the same type of development took place from 1802 on, with the Baptist Convention of Ontario and Quebec being established in 1888. About the same time Baptist conventions were organized in Manitoba, the Northwest Territories, and British Columbia, resulting in the Baptist Union of Western Canada in 1919.[18]

The question then arises as to how far both the Presbyterian and the Baptist unions were Calvinistic in their theological positions. In the case of the Presbyterians, although at the time of the union the Westminster Confession of Faith was accepted as the theological foundation of the church, there were many who came into the church, particularly from the Church of Scotland and the United Presbyterian Church, who were hardly very Calvinistic. On the other hand theologians such as Donald Harvey MacVicar, principal of the Presbyterian College, Montreal, were outspoken in their support of the Calvinistic position. MacVicar had continued differences with George M. Grant, principal of Queen's University, who tended toward Arminianism and the social gospel.[19] The result ever since has been a very mixed type of theological position in the Presbyterian Church in Canada. The same could be said for the Baptists, who, while not being "liberals" in their theology to any great extent, have often tended to move in the direction of an Arminian fundamentalism. Thus from the beginning of the present century, the Reformed witness of both churches has been considerably weakened.

The position of the two churches theologically is indicated by two major battles that took place within their borders. In the case of the Presbyterians it was the controversy over church union. Early in the present century it was proposed by some of the Presbyterians that there should be a union between the Methodists, Congregationalists, and their own denomination. Two votes were taken among the Presbyterians on the issue in 1912 and 1915. Although the ballots showed a majority in favor of union, they also indicated that this favorable attitude to union was declining. After World War I the push toward union increased, and finally an act of Parliament was passed creating the United Church of Canada with a statement of belief called the Twenty Articles, which avoided most of the points of difference between Presbyterians and Methodists. On June 10, 1925 the United Church came into existence with virtually all the Methodists and Congregationalists, and 75 percent of the ministers and 65 percent of the members of the Presbyterian Church in Canada.[20] It is now the largest of the Protestant denominations in Canada, but one that has very little, if any, Calvinistic position.

The minority Presbyterian Church continued. On its reorganization through the influence of Ephraim Scott, its first moderator and a strong Calvinist, it reaffirmed its adherence to the Westminster Standards. However, many in its ranks such as W. W. Bryden, later principal of Knox College, felt that this was a mistake. Bryden's position was close to that of Karl Barth, although as a result of his influence a number of his students took up the study of Calvin, eventually becoming thoroughly Reformed in their theological position. Many others in the church were more or less indifferent to theological questions, and gradually certain activities formerly considered important, such as the training of children in the Westminster Shorter Catechism, were dropped. Others, who were positively opposed to the Reformed position, have sought to introduce a new confession in line with neoorthodox or even more humanistic interpretations of Christian doctrine. So far such attempts have not succeeded. There is still a minority, which is perhaps growing, among both ministers and laity, who are turning to a revival of Reformed doctrine within the church. Some who are committed to the Calvinistic position have not "tarried for any" but have left the church and joined other denominations such as the Reformed Presbyterian Church (Evangelical Synod).[21]

The Baptists' conflict was not a matter of external influence so much as an internal problem. During the early part of the century, as in almost all other denominations, there had been a decline of the evangelical and particularly the Reformed element in the Baptist congregations. For this T. T. Shields of Jarvis Street Baptist Church laid the blame largely on MacMaster College, the Baptist theological training institution then located in Toronto. The result was a defection of a group of Baptist congregations from the Ontario and Quebec Convention, to form the Regular Baptist Church, followed by a withdrawal in 1930 of a number of Shield's followers from his organization to form the Federation of Independent Baptist Churches. Then in 1955 the bulk of the Regular Baptists left Shield's group to form with the Federation of Independent Baptist Churches the Fellowship of Evangelical Baptist Churches. It seems that the two breakaways from the Regular Baptists was to a considerable extent the result of personality conflicts with Shields. The continuing Regular Baptist Church is strongly Calvinistic in outlook, whereas the Fellowship Baptists could be perhaps classed more as evangelicals than Calvinists.[22]

The Presbyterians and the Baptists, however, were not the only denominations that had doctrinal problems. With the growth of the High Church movement in Canada, the Church of England also had its conflicts. Those who opposed the Anglo-Catholic tendencies, however, never classed themselves as Calvinists, although they might hold firmly to the Thirty-nine Articles. They wished to hold the denomination of "Low Church evangelicals." A number, however, did maintain a Reformed stance in doctrinal matters. It was out of this division that Wycliffe College in Toronto and the Diocesan College in Montreal were set up in the 1870s in opposition to the High Church colleges of Trinity in Toronto and Bishop's in Lennoxville, Quebec. But one can hardly think in terms of a strong Reformed witness by the Anglican Church in Canada, except for a small minority.[23]

While the established churches in Canada with a Reformed background have tended to move away from a strictly Reformed position, if not formally, at least in actuality, since World War II, another Calvinistic element has come into Canadian society. This is that of the large group of Dutch immigrants who began to arrive in 1945, reaching a peak in 1952, with more than 21,000 in that year and with a total close to 200,000. While perhaps one-third to one-half are Roman Catholics, the Protestant portion is usually Calvinistic. The dominant group is the Christian Reformed Church, which according to the 1971 census had over 83,000 members and adherents and is very insistent on its Calvinistic confession.[24] Holding to a similar position are two smaller denominations: the Canadian Reformed Church and the Free Reformed Church of North America. The Reformed Church of America does not seem to lay quite the same stress on the maintenance of doctrinal standards as do the others, although it is officially committed to the Calvinistic position.

As one looks at Canadian society, one can see that it has had deep Calvinistic roots. Whether one thinks of the Huguenots, the Scottish Presbyterians, the American Baptists, or the Dutch Calvinists, the population has had a very considerable admixture of people coming from the Reformed tradition. Those who have come to Canada from a Reformed background have brought with them their traditions and their beliefs, which have played an important part in both their thinking and their acting. They in turn have had an impact on the society in which they have lived, as one may see by looking at certain aspects of that society.

One of the important areas in which those with a Calvinistic tradition have been active is education. With a vital theological interest, there has been an impulsion to reading not only the Bible but also theological works generally. This in turn has led to the reading of other types of literature. And the important aspect of this tendency is that it has been fostered in the home. Added to this there has been theological discussion in the family, coupled with the memorizing of both biblical passages and the Westminster Shorter Catechism or the Heidelberg Catechism. Robert Louis Stevenson expresses the matter very well when he compares the English boy with the Scottish boy:

> Sabbath observance makes a series of grim, perhaps serviceable, pauses in the tenor of Scottish boyhood—days of great stillness and solitude for the rebellious mind, when in the dearth of books and play, in the intervals of studying the Shorter Catechism, the intellect and senses play upon and test each other. . . . About the very cradle of the Scot there goes a hum of metaphysical divinity; and the whole of two divergent systems [the Anglican and Presbyterian] is summed up, not merely speciously in the first questions of the rival catechisms, the English tritely inquiring, "What is your name?" the Scottish striking at the very roots of life with, "What is the chief end of man?" and answering nobly, if obscurely, "To glorify God and enjoy him forever." I do not wish to make an idol of the Shorter Catechism; but the fact of such a question being asked opens to us Scots a field of speculation; and the fact that it is asked of all of us, from the peer to the ploughboy, binds us more nearly together.[25]

And what Stevenson has said about the Calvinistic training of the Scottish boy could apply equally well to the Dutch child who was made to wrestle with the Heidelberg Catechism.

This tradition and practice of home training comes to the present writer's mind as he thinks of the account his father used to give of his training in the family home in the Eastern Townships of Quebec. On Sunday, besides the church service, which everyone attended, the evening would be spent with the children reciting one-half of the Shorter Catechism one Sunday and the other half the next. Then a sermon of some prominent minister, perhaps Spurgeon or MacLaren, would be read, and all would be concluded with family prayers. But the other days of the week were also days of work, both physical and intellectual. Whether at school or behind the plough or working with the scythe during the day, in the evening everyone was supposed to spend time reading, and the literature was not comic books. Before my father had reached the age of eighteen he had gone through such works as Bunyan's *Pilgrim's Progress*, Baxter's *Saints' Rest*, Alleine's *Alarm to the Unconverted*, Law's *Call to a Devout and Holy Life*, Doddridge's *Rise and Progress of Religion in the Soul*, Hetherington's *History of the Church of Scotland*, Lennie's *Grammar*, and similar works. He had also read a considerable number of Scott's novels, but gave them up, as he felt that they took his mind off the more important things of life.

The Calvinist drive to obtain an education is shown in the history of my father's family as a whole. The eldest boy went to Montreal, where he obtained his B.A. at McGill University and his B.D. at the Presbyterian College. He then went to Great Britain and Europe where he studied in Edinburgh, then Berlin, and later, after spending a year traveling around Europe and the Near East, enrolled at Harvard, where he obtained his M.A., finally returning home to become minister of a Presbyterian church in Montreal. Two of his three brothers also became Presbyterian ministers. One of his sisters studied medicine and became one of the first women psychiatrists in the United States, and two others became school teachers.

This entire Scottish Presbyterian community, where everyone was raised on oatmeal porridge and the Shorter Catechism, generally followed the same pattern. It has been reckoned that from it came over one hundred school teachers, some thirty-five nurses, twenty-five ministers, between ten and fifteen doctors, and seven lawyers. While some of the succeeding generations have gone into business, as one traces the lines down to the present day, the tendency to enter the learned professions is still strong, for although the Calvinism has, sad to say, weakened greatly, the majority of the present adult generation are either university professors, school teachers, doctors, lawyers, or scientists.

This community was by no means unique in its attitude toward education, for one finds that among Calvinistic groups—Presbyterian, Baptist, or Dutch Reformed—the same general pattern has been followed. As new arrivals were able to obtain enough funds to support the rising generations in gaining a sound education, they have been willing to make sacrifices for this purpose. It is also noteworthy that most of the English-language universities in Canada, from Dalhousie in Halifax to the University of Manitoba, were founded by Scots, most of whom had come out of Calvinistic backgrounds, even if they were not prepared to accept Reformed teaching themselves. With the secularization of most of these institutions, however, the new wave of Dutch immigrants has commenced a repeat of the process by founding Christian schools and, more recently, organizing at least two Christian liberal-arts colleges, one in Ontario and one in Alberta. Added to this, for some years the Association for Reformed Scientific Studies has had its Institute for Christian Studies in Toronto, committed to a Reformed stance in its basic philosophical presuppositions. Thus Calvinism in Canada has had a major influence on educational development.

Calvinistic influence extends beyond education, however, for the Calvinist is not usually an ivory-tower person. Most of the immigrants who came to the country in its earlier days eventually became farmers, and in their honest toil they honored the Lord. Others found a place in the business world, where they displayed their Calvinistic sense of responsibility and calling. Most of those of the next generation went into the professions or into business. One gets an indication of the Calvinist's diligence, honesty, sense of responsibility, and sense of calling from the comments made by Pierre Berton in his book, *The National Dream,* in which he quotes from an address delivered by Lord Mount Stephen, one of the founders of the Canadian Pacific Railway, who came from Aberdeen:

> Any success I may have had in life is due in great measure to the somewhat Spartan training I received during my Aberdeen apprenticeship, in which I entered as a boy of 15. . . . It was impressed upon me from my earliest years by one of the best mothers that ever lived that I must aim at being a thorough master of the work by which I had to get my living; and to be that I must concentrate my whole energies on my work, whatever that might be, to the exclusion of every other thing. I soon discovered that if I ever accomplished anything in life it would be by pursuing my object with a persistent determination to attain it. I had neither the training nor the talents to accomplish anything without hard work, and fortunately I knew it.

Berton then adds:

> It was this hard ethic, so forcefully expressed by Stephen, that explains the dominance of the Scot in pioneer Canada. . . . For the Scots it was work, save and study; study, save and work. The Irish outnumbered them as they did the English, but the Scots ran the country. . . . Though they formed only one-fifteenth of the population they controlled the fur trade, the great banking and financial houses, the major educational institutions, and to a considerable degree, the government.[26]

Some may, of course, feel that this does not necessarily prove anything about Calvinism. One must remember, however, that the Flemings, the MacDonalds, the Allans, and others from Scotland had usually been brought up in a warmly Calvinistic environment. This is brought out in a recollection of the writer's father who knew Donald Smith, Lord Strathcona, a cousin of Lord Mount Stephen. When Strathcona was Canadian high commissioner to London, he told my father of how, when he became a factor in Labrador for the Hudson Bay Company, he decided that church services should be held on Sunday for the factory staff and for the Indians and Metis in the area. He had announced, therefore, that a service would be held and that to everyone who came he would give a glass of whiskey. On Sunday morning he had a full attendance, but somewhat naively he gave them the drink before the service, whereupon they all left. One such experience was enough, however, and thereafter the whiskey was handed out after service! A little later he decided that it would perhaps be more appropriate to give a loaf of bread. When asked what sermons he had used, for he conducted the service himself, he said that he had brought some of the sermons of T. De Witt Talmadge with him, but a little later he obtained a volume of Spurgeon's sermons, which he found very good! What the Indians thought of them he did not say. But this does give a picture of the type of men many of the Scottish pioneers were and the abiding influence of the Calvinistic Presbyterian origins.

When we look beyond the professions and business to such fields as politics, we find that much the same type of influence prevailed. In the early nineteenth century, there were men like William Lyon Mackenzie, "the old rebel," who was one of the founders of Knox Presbyterian Church, Toronto, one of the newly organized Free Kirk congregations, and George Brown, editor of the Toronto *Globe,* who was active in politics in the 1850s and 60s. There were also many others who made a clear profession of a Reformed theological conviction, while some, like Lord Mount Stephen, stressed the Calvinistic background from which they had come.

Thus, although we cannot say that all Scots or Dutch, all Presbyterians, Baptists, or even Christian Reformed members were or are thoroughly Calvinistic in their thinking, yet the fact remains that many, indeed most of them, have come out of homes and backgrounds in which the Reformed element has been very strong. In some, perhaps many, cases they have turned away from any explicit acceptance of the Calvinistic position, regarding Calvin as a very austere and harsh character and followers of his, such as John Knox, as unattractive protagonists of Christianity. Nevertheless, in many cases they have inherited the moral stance of the Calvinist and are continuing to express it in their daily work. Perhaps the words of Donald Gordon, a Scot and a Presbyterian, who held many high positions in both government and business during the 1940s and 50s, make this plain:

> For my part, I see nothing old-fashioned about such virtues as honesty and truthfulness, a keen sense of public duty, and an obligation to do the right thing simply because it is the right thing to do. Moreover, I believe that the importance of integrity and good faith in the business world cannot be overstated; and it would confound many a cynic to know how often our hard-headed bankers look upon the integrity of management as the best and surest collateral of all.[27]

One must always remember, however, that while the Calvinistic influences in Canada today may not be as overt as in earlier generations, and therefore are more indirect, there are still many, not only within the Dutch immigrant community but also among the Scottish element in both the Baptist and the Presbyterian churches and to a lesser extent among the English element in the Anglican Church of Canada, who hold to a Calvinistic position. They still exercise an influence within Canadian society, though at times it may not be thought to be all that powerful or effective. And there are signs in various quarters that a revitalization of Calvinism is beginning to take place.

# The Impact of Calvinism on Australasia

## Alexander Barkley

*Alexander Barkley is Professor Emeritus at the Reformed Theological College, Geelong, Australia. He holds degrees from the University of Dublin (M.A.); Reformed Presbyterian Theological Seminary, Pittsburgh (Dip.Th.); and Central School of Religion, London (D.D.). He has served in the pastoral ministry in Belfast, Northern Ireland, and Geelong, Australia, and as Professor of Church History and Missiology and Principal of the Reformed Theological College, Geelong. Dr. Barkley has written articles for* Vox Reformata *and* Trowel and Sword *and is President of the Tyndale Fellowship of Australia. He is a life member of the Association for a Christian University and also of the governing Council of the Australian Institute of Biblical Archaeology.*

# 15

# The Impact of Calvinism on Australasia

Unlike the white colonial settlers of North America, the early settlers in Australia and New Zealand were not of Puritan vintage. There was no religious crisis in Europe to precipitate a mass movement of the population to Australia for the purpose of escaping religious persecution. Actually the first British colony in Australia was established in New South Wales in 1788, eighteen years after its discovery by Captain Cook. This was a settlement for convicts. For more than half a century Australia became the dumping ground for undesirable individuals sentenced by judges throughout the British Isles. Even though these convicts were not all hardened criminals, the early white population of Australia was not a soil very favorable to Christianity. It is not, therefore, easy to assess the impact of Christianity in general, and of Calvinism in particular, on the colonial developments in Australia.

To a greater extent than in North America, where greater European influences prevailed, the religious denominations corresponded to those in the British Isles. Protestantism was represented largely by the Church of England, Methodists, and Presbyterians. Calvinistic influences were largely channeled through the Evangelical Anglicans and the Scottish Presbyterians. With the development of the Baptist churches there were significant pockets of Calvinistic influence that had a leavening effect on the development of church-state relations.

The first chaplains appointed for the spiritual oversight of the early settlers were naturally from the Church of England, as the Church of

England was the state church in the mother country. However, it is important to note that both Richard Johnson, who accompanied the First Fleet, and Samuel Marsden, who arrived later, were evangelicals.[1] Largely responsible for the appointment of Johnson was the Eclectic Society, an interdenominational group of Evangelicals formed for the investigation of religious truth. The appointment of Marsden was influenced by the Elland Society, a group of Anglican Evangelicals who supported promising young men seeking university education with a view to ordination.[2] Another important product of the Evangelical movement was the Church Missionary Society formed in 1799. The Evangelicals accepted the Thirty-nine Articles as an almost perfect summary of the faith. Some were extreme Calvinists.[3] Many young men, including Samuel Marsden, sat at the feet of the saintly Charles Simeon, who for over fifty years molded the lives of a multitude of Cambridge graduates.

These pioneer Anglican chaplains preached the gospel of God's sovereign grace in Christ. In the colony of New South Wales both bond and free were taught the principles of the Evangelicals. They endeavored to raise the standard of Christian ethics in a community with little respect for law and order. Marsden was interested in farming and grazing. He imported and experimented with new crops, plants, and livestock. Some of these experiments had far-reaching consequences in the economic development of Australia.[4]

The greater impact of Calvinism was, however, to emanate from the Scottish Presbyterians. The number of convicts from Scotland was relatively small compared with the aggregate from England and Ireland.[5] However it was the Scottish free settlers who were to spearhead the planting of the more comprehensive brand of Calvinism in Australia.

It is remarkable that the laws against sedition in Scotland were responsible for the transportation of five men who propagated the teachings of the Enlightenment on politics. In the words of C. M. H. Clark there was brought about in Australia "the association between men whose minds were steeped in Calvinist traditions and men whose minds were fashioned by the teachings of the enlightenment."[6] This was to set the stage for the struggle that the minority forces of Calvinism had to face in Australia. The battle was waged on three main fronts—politics, church, and education.

Politically one might say there is not much evidence of any significant impact. Among the early Scottish settlers in the 1820s the outstanding leader was John Dunmore Lang, who was born in Greenock and educated in Glasgow. Lang's theological inclinations had been molded under the ministry of Dr. Chalmers. In addition to his church activities Lang became involved in politics. Although he had been ordained in the Established Church of Scotland, he gradually came to accept Voluntaryism in Australia. This meant coming into conflict with the government and also with Bishop Broughton, who sought permanent endowment of the Church of England as the Established Church in Australia. Lectures were given on the "impolicy and injustice of Religious Establishments." Lang based his political principles on the Bible. He held that there were three main principles of republican government "in operation under Divine sanction and appointment in the commonwealth of ancient Israel."[7] These principles were universal (male) suffrage, perfect political equality, and popular election. He argued successfully for a free and united Australia consisting of separate states with social and political justice for all. He never became a member of a political party but voted on each occasion according to conscience for the policy and not the person.

The political developments in Australia were much more influenced by the Enlightenment and the philosophy of natural rights than by any evangelical force. Political liberalism was a massive movement that left its mark not only in all the countries of Western Europe and in America but also in Australia and New Zealand.

With the evangelical influence in the Anglican church and the Scottish plantation of Presbyterianism, the prospects for Calvinism were reasonably propitious. The unsettled situation in the Church of Scotland in the first half of the nineteenth century actuated families to move to the colonies. In 1832 the first presbytery was formed, and this was the seed from which the tree of Presbyterianism was to grow throughout the Eastern states of Australia.[8] Lang figured prominently in the settlement of families and organization of the church. He was a fervent, eloquent, and powerful preacher. He traveled widely throughout the country, forming preaching stations with a view to the settlement of ministers. Several visits were made to the home country to bring out migrants and secure the services of ministers and teachers.

However, the development of the Presbyterian church was not to be undisturbed. Divisions occurred, and the secessions in Scotland had their counterparts in Australia. The Disruption in Scotland in 1843 had very significant repercussions in Australia, and a very potent Free Church influence was widespread in most states. When union eventually took place, there emerged a Presbyterian church in each of the states, with a smaller body, the Presbyterian Church of Eastern Australia, remaining separate and maintaining the standards as interpreted in the Disruption documents.

The Presbyterian churches in their constitution accepted as subordinate standards the Westminster Confession of Faith, the Larger and Shorter Catechisms, the Directory for Public Worship, the Form of Presbyterian Church Government agreed on by the Assembly of Divines at Westminster. Theological halls were established in Melbourne and

Sydney and later in Brisbane. The training of students for the ministry was placed under the supervision of scholars and theologians who were faithful to the doctrinal standards of the church. Outstanding among such were Adam Cairns,[9] who came to Australia from the Free Church of Scotland, and John L. Rentoul, who came from the Presbyterian Church of Ireland.[10]

The census taken in 1861 showed that about 16 percent of the population belonged to the Presbyterian church and smaller churches adhering to the Westminster standards. There was a growing concern for expansion as the population of the country increased. Attention was given to the plight of neglected children. Conflict with the state arose through concern for the observance of Sunday and the use of Scripture in the state schools.

Perhaps it was in the realm of education that Presbyterianism made its greatest impact in Australia during the second half of the nineteenth century. In true Calvinistic fashion there was concern for the education of children. John Knox sought to erect an educational ladder that stretched from every parish to the university, a ladder to which every member of the parish should have access. That spirit prevailed among the Scottish settlers and their descendants on Australia. The oldest Presbyterian church building in Australia, Ebenezer, near Portland Head on the Hawkesbury river, bears silent tribute to the faith and aspirations of the pioneers. This building was originally divided into two, one part being the school and the other the place of worship.[11] Schools were established in all states, and the standard of education was high. It was the ideal of the church to fill the land with day schools staffed by teachers of godly character, with the Bible as part of the regular curriculum.[12] When the denominational system of education was eventually displaced in large measure by state control, education throughout Australia became "free, compulsory and secular." Under the secular clause, the Bible was forbidden entry into the schools, and all lessons that savored of the Christian faith were removed from textbooks.

Although all the denominations became involved in a battle with the state governments, the result was not very satisfactory. The teaching of Scripture was eventually allowed during school hours. No uniform arrangement, however, applied in all states. The program for Scripture teaching in schools has been watered down to such an extent as to be almost worthless. In some respects this was the commencement of decline in the influence of Calvinism in Australia. Church-controlled schools were still retained but received no financial support from the government. This made education in a nonsecular environment somewhat expensive.

The philosophy of humanism has been a growing force from the first settlement of the country. When it gained control of the education system, not only in schools but also in universities, then a very strong and well-prepared Christian philosophy of education would have been required to offer resistance. Divided opinions were widespread, and no Australian Kuyper appeared on the horizon to utter a prophetic warning and lay the foundation for a solid biblical approach to education.

Toward the end of the nineteenth century the winds of change that had been blowing from the mainland of Europe were beginning to reach Australia. It was only a very gentle breeze at first, but it was to increase to devastating strength in the present century. The name associated with this new trend was that of Charles Strong, who was inducted in 1879 as minister of the Scots Church in Melbourne. Aeneas Macdonald, referring to what became known as the Strong case, writes:

> Throughout the Presbyterian world at that time the old sturdy Calvinism still held the field as a true and sufficient expression of the evangelical faith. But criticism was coming in around its flanks. Especially were men trained by Edward Caird in Glasgow bringing into the Church of Scotland a new attitude of mind distinctly disturbing to those of orthodox habits of thought. The Higher Criticism was also troubling the waters in Scotland, though in Victoria it had no apparent share in what happened.[13]

Strong was an attractive preacher and displayed an open-minded, modern attitude to doctrine. In the public press the doctrine of the Atonement was under discussion. In a letter, Strong presented the doctrine in such a way as to omit the personality of Christ as well as His atoning life and sacrifice. This sparked off debates in church courts and a torrent of correspondence unparalleled in Australia. So great was the interest aroused that an important Melbourne daily paper, the *Argus,* published the whole of the Westminster Confession in three installments. At a congregational meeting in Scots Church an elder, who was a lawyer, made an attack on the Confession of Faith. Strong became involved in other controversial matters. He presided at a meeting in Scots Church where Justice Higinbotham gave an address on "The Relation Between Religion and Science," in which creeds were denounced as "the most insidious enemies of the religion of Christ." The minister of Scots Church was charged with heresy and failure to implement his ordination vows before the General Assembly of the church. He was invited to appear before the Assembly and disown his complicity with erroneous teaching and affirm his faith in the true deity of Christ, the propitiatory character of His suffering and death, and the reality of His resurrection. Strong did not appear but, while the Assembly was meeting, he embarked on a ship and returned to Scotland. The Assembly declared him no longer a minister of the Victorian church.[14]

While the Strong case made it clear that historic Calvinism was by no means a dead issue in Australia, it also revealed a significant trend in the theological climate. In 1882 a Declaratory Act was adopted setting out how the Confession of Faith was to be understood regarding the divine decrees, the salvation of infants dying in infancy, the dealing of God with pagans, and the creation of the world in six days.[15] The Declaratory Act was introduced by conservative theologians, not to weaken the Confession of Faith, but to make its use more meaningful in the church.

Organic federal union between the Presbyterian churches in the Australian colonies took place in 1901 when the first General Assembly of the Presbyterian Church of Australia was constituted. The supreme standard was the Word of God contained in the Scriptures of the Old and New Testaments. The subordinate standard was the Westminster Confession of Faith read in the light of a declaratory statement. Although designed to remove some difficulties in order to make subscription on the part of officebearers more meaningful, the declaratory statement somewhat toned down the Calvinism of the Westminster standards. It could be argued that the essential doctrines were not affected and that liberty was granted only in nonessentials. Severe criticisms have been leveled against the declaratory statement. It has been condemned as bearing the taint of Arminian and Pelagian error. By some it has been regarded as a compendium of all the heresies. However , there are two objections that cannot easily be bypassed. One is the ambiguity of its terms and the other is the power that section 5 places in the hands of the General Assembly.[16] (Section V states: "That liberty of opinion is allowed on matters in the Subordinate Standard not essential to the doctrine taught, the Church guarding against the abuse of this liberty to the injury of its unity and peace"). The strong Calvinistic witness of the church was somewhat devitalized as a result of the weakening of the foundations. Instead of maintaining a warfare against the militant forces of humanism, materialism, and atheism, the Presbyterian church became a prey to the blighting attacks of liberalism. Where the blame lies is not easy to assess.

The change in the spiritual and theological climate of Presbyterianism was evidenced in the appointment of Samuel Angus as Professor of New Testament and Historical Theology in St. Andrew's College, Sydney, in 1914. Angus was a brilliant classical scholar. He was born into a solid Presbyterian family near Ballymena in Northern Ireland in days when the Bible and Shorter Catechism were taught in the home. He was educated at the Royal University of Ireland, Princeton University, the Theological Seminary, Marburg, and the universities of Berlin and Edinburgh. For twenty-nine years he taught young men entering the ministry of the Presbyterian Church of Australia. During the last ten years of his life he was the center of a prolonged controversy in the courts of the church. The views of Angus were expressed in his volume "Truth and Tradition," which was specially prepared for the heresy case in the Presbyterian Assembly. On the doctrine of the Trinity he made this astounding statement: "This is not one of the matters regarded as vital to the Christian faith by our Church, and on which, therefore liberty of opinion is allowed. The Presbyterian Church of Australia has no doctrine of the Trinity which it declares to be valid or vital."[17] He boldly rejected the doctrine of the Trinity, the deity of Christ, the sacrificial nature of His death as an atonement for sin, and His bodily resurrection. Publicity was given to the controversy in the press. Sermons were preached and pamphlets were written, but no action was taken by the church.

The decline of Calvinism in Australia was also seen in the development of the ecumenical movement in general and church union in particular. From the time of federal union of Presbyterian churches there was lively controversy on the policy of seeking union with the Methodist and Congregational churches. This union was effected in June 1977, and the Uniting Church in Australia emerged. As one might naturally expect, the basis of union is to a large degree inclusive. The Uniting Church expresses her willingness to learn "from the witness of reformation fathers as expressed in various ways in the Scots Confession of Faith (1560), the Heidelberg Catechism (1563), the Westminster Confession of Faith (1647), and the Savoy Declaration (1658). In like manner she will listen to the preaching of John Wesley in his Forty-Four Sermons (1793)."[18] This is the only reference to Calvinism in the eighteen articles constituting the basis of union.

Not everyone in Presbyterian circles was in favor of union. A considerable minority refused to enter the union, and so the Presbyterian church continues on the basis of the federal union of 1901. There is a revival of interest in the Calvinistic heritage, and under the guiding hand of men like Principal Robert Swanton in Melbourne and Principal Harold Whitney in Brisbane the seed of sound Reformed theology is being planted, which, under the blessing of our sovereign Lord, will contribute to a future harvest.

Although the Anglican church was planted in Australia by Evangelicals, the first bishop, William Grant Broughton, was a High Churchman with sympathy for the Tractarians.[19] He was not antagonistic to the Evangelicals but he had a task of great magnitude in organizing the expansion and government of the church in a vast area. Broughton's successor was Frederic Barker. As a disciple of Charles Simeon he was a devout Evangelical and he left his mark on the Sydney diocese and in many other areas of the church.

Bishop Barker was responsible for the establishment of Moore College in 1856, and for over a century this institution has made an impact for biblical and Reformation truth that is impossible to assess. Thomas C. Hammond was appointed principal in 1936 and for seventeen years he was a burning and shining light in an age when Australia was under the dark clouds brought about by liberalism in most of the theological schools.[20] By voice and pen Hammond raised the standard for the Reformed faith. Among his publications one of the best known is "In Understanding Be Men." This was published by I.V.F. and has passed through four editions with numerous reprints. Hammond exercised a far-reaching ministry among the students in Australian universities. He was not afraid to challenge the modernists, humanists, and atheistic philosophers.

Angus came from Northern Ireland and Hammond from the south of Ireland. Both were gifted with massive intellects, a goodly measure of Irish wit, and genial personalities. But what a contrast in their influence in both church and society!

Associated with Hammond in Moore College were men who are still active in the same ministry. Canon Marcus L. Loane succeeded him as principal. He is now Sir Marcus Loane and is Archbishop of Sydney. He is a stalwart for the heritage of the Reformation. In his volume on *Pioneers of the Reformation in England* he places himself in the tradition of some of the great Puritans who were graduates of Cambridge University, valiant in fight, and who loved not their lives unto death. In his recent volume *Hewn From the Rock,* Sir Marcus Loane provides a fine summary of the great contribution made by the Evangelicals in the Church of England in the development of a culture that could be characterized as Australian.

The present principal of Moore College, David Broughton Knox, stands in the same tradition as his precursors. He and Bishop Donald Robinson made available the campus of Moore College for the meeting of the Reformed Ecumenical Synod in 1972. They also participated in some of the discussions.

Despite the efforts of the High Church authorities in England, Melbourne's first Anglican bishop was Charles Perry. He came to Victoria in 1848 and for twenty-nine years exercised an effective ministry as an Evangelical with deeply rooted convictions. He took up the cudgels for the authority of the Bible when it was attacked by scientists. He was a strong opponent of Tractarianism. He became involved in the controversy with the government regarding control of education, holding that parents were responsible for the education of their children, not the state nor the church.

Ridley College, Melbourne, founded in 1910, has been noted for evangelical scholarship in connection with the Anglican Church. Canon Leon Morris, a former principal of Ridley, is widely known for his scholarship. He was largely responsible for the founding of the Tyndale Fellowship, which seeks to promote the study of biblical theology on a scholarly basis.

In the "Red Book Case" we have an example of the influence of the

Evangelicals in the Anglican church. In 1943 the bishop of Bathurst authorized for use in his diocese a devotional manual entitled "The Holy Eucharist," commonly referred to as the "Red Book." Objection was raised against the doctrinal teaching and ritualistic practices authorized in this manual. Legal action was taken in the civil courts. The judgment was that in the "Red Book" there was a departure from the laws and order of service set out in the Book of Common Prayer of 1662. This was illegal, and a decree was issued restraining the bishop from using or authorizing any liturgy for Holy Communion other than that of the Prayer Book of 1662. The charge of heresy was withdrawn. The appeal to the High Court was dismissed but the decree was somewhat modified. This left the door open for similar departures from the Book of Common Prayer.[21] Since 1962 the Church of England in Australia no longer has legal links with the ecclesiastical laws of England and is a self-governing church with an approved constitution.

Though a minority throughout the history of the Church of England in Australia, the Evangelicals have exercised a very significant influence in the areas of education, evangelism, and the moral standards in society.

In addition to the moderate Calvinism maintained by the Evangelicals in the larger denominations, there have been smaller churches and organizations that have stood for a more undiluted expression of the Reformed teaching.

The Presbyterian Church of Eastern Australia requires an unqualified subscription to the Westminster Confession on the part of officebearers. Though relatively small in numbers, they publish a monthly magazine and issue synodical reports calling the nation back to the ways of the Lord.[22]

The Reformed Presbyterian Church has also been in existence since 1858, when migrants from Ireland and Scotland felt compelled to maintain a separate existence. Though the church is very small, it has maintained a positive witness for Calvinism in pamphlets and lectures. A minister of this church, the Rev. W. R. McEwen, owns and publishes a monthly paper, "Evangelical Action," in which a pungent apology is maintained for the integrity of the Bible. In letters to some of the leading daily newspapers and in TV programs, he has contended for biblical standards in the face of such legislation as the abolition of capital punishment and the easing of the pathway to divorce.

Because of the liberal trends in the Presbyterian church before union took place, two ministers also led a secession that resulted in the formation of the Presbyterian Reformed Church.

In 1961 the Reformed Evangelical Church came into existence in Tasmania. This new church consists of former members of the Baptist church, who had come to accept Reformed theology through reading publications such as those made available by the Banner of Truth Trust.

This body is now known as the Evangelical Presbyterian Church.[23]

It is to be regretted that all these small churches holding the Westminster standards are not more united. There has been much turmoil, and perhaps the enthusiasm of those who have more recently discovered the rich heritage of Calvinistic theology has led to judgments and misunderstandings that will gradually be overcome in the years ahead. In the midst of tensions the terms *Calvinism* and *Arminianism* can become rather loaded, and the splitting of theological hairs can create unnecessary confusion.

A new dimension came into the ecclesiastical scene with the influx of new settlers from the Netherlands in the years subsequent to World War II. Those who belonged to the Gereformeerde Kerken and other Reformed churches found it difficult to accept the theological climate prevalent in the Presbyterian church. Liturgical convictions made assimilation into the Presbyterian Church of Eastern Australia impossible. The result was the formation of the Reformed Churches of Australia.

In the providence of God the great theological schools of Westminster Seminary, Philadelphia, and the Free University of Amsterdam were brought together in Australia. Cultural problems and misunderstandings were inevitable in the early stages. The great Scottish theologian, James Denney, wrote in 1900, "If you want to think well of Calvinism avoid the Dutch. There is far more of an inferior mathematical kind of metaphysics than of religious conviction in their Calvinism." However, Denney would probably have modified his criticism as the theological works of Kuyper and Bavinck became known in the English-speaking world. Australia has been enriched with the new interest in theology aroused by the spiritual sons of Kuyper in the Reformed Churches.

In 1954 the synod of the Reformed Churches decided to support the formation of an Association for Higher Education on a Calvinistic Basis (later the Association for a Christian University, ACU). From this association there came into existence the Reformed Theological College at Geelong, Victoria. The design was to blend the two theological streams, Westminster and Amsterdam, in this institution. The first members of faculty were Alexander Barkley of the Reformed Presbyterian Church, who became principal, and John A. Schep of the Reformed Churches. Klaas Runia joined the college staff in 1957 and for fifteen years exercised a wide ministry in Australia and New Zealand. Gerard Van Groningen, a member of the faculty for thirteen years, was a graduate of Westminster Seminary, and R. O. Zorn, the present principal, is also a graduate of Westminster. T. L. Wilkinson was formerly a member of the Presbyterian Church of Australia. We are grateful to the Lord for Westminster Seminary and for the help received both directly and indirectly from this institution. It is an honor for me to be included among those contributing to this volume and in this way to express a small token of our esteem for the ministry of Paul Woolley of Westminster.

The ACU has been expanding its program and now includes philosophy and Christian education in addition to theology. The majority of ministers in the Reformed Churches of Australia and New Zealand are graduates of the Reformed Theological College. There are also graduates serving in the Presbyterian Church, the Presbyterian Church of Eastern Australia, the Reformed Presbyterian Church, and the Free Reformed Church.

With the establishment of Reformed Churches there also arose the movement for parent-controlled Christian schools. Several schools are now operating, and an increasing number of Christians are coming to see the necessity for such education in the face of the humanism of the state system. However, the impact so far is only on a small percentage of the population.

In addition to the ACU, there has been the development of the Foundation for Christian Scholarship in Australia and the corresponding body in New Zealand known as the Foundation for Christian Studies. By means of lectures, seminars, and publications the FCS seeks to make an impact on students and teachers in the secular universities and colleges of advanced education.

With the growth of nationalism in Australia and the development of what might be termed Australian culture, there is need for the promotion of a Calvinism that is somewhat detached from its ethnic background. To speak of Westminster theology and Dutch theology is quite irrelevant to the situation that has to be faced in Australia. The content must remain essentially the same but it must be adapted to the culture of the nation and presented without foreign tags.

## New Zealand

Like those in Australia, the white colonial settlers in New Zealand were chiefly from the British Isles. There was intense loyalty to the throne, and the pattern of church development was largely determined by the ecclesiastical structures in the mother country. Unlike Australia, New Zealand was not a penal colony. An effort was made to plan the colonization. The chief architect in this project was Edward Gibbon Wakefield. His program was designed to encourage men and women of excellent character to become colonists. He had studied the influence of religion on the pioneer settlements in North America and he came to the conclusion that a similar policy could be followed in New Zealand.[24]

The Wakefield plan was only partially carried out in certain areas of the country and particularly in the south island. One important settlement was developed around the Church of England. The initial company of colonists founded the city of Christchurch and the name of Canterbury was given to the area. A similar settlement was established in the Otago area farther south by colonists from Scotland.

On the whole the church exercised a considerable influence in the early occupation of New Zealand by white settlers. As in Australia, the Anglicans, the Presbyterians, and the Roman Catholics were the main denominational bodies involved.

The first Anglican bishop of New Zealand was George Augustus Selwyn. He possessed outstanding intellectual gifts, and his leadership of the church was renowned for efficiency, courage, and tenacity. He was a close personal friend of Bishop Broughton of Australia, and his High Church sympathies brought him into conflict with the evangelical position of the Church Missionary Society. Under the leadership of Selwyn the Church of England experienced rapid growth.[25] The pattern, however, has followed the High Church emphasis, and from this source it is futile to expect any sympathy for Calvinism.

The main impact of Calvinism in New Zealand stemmed from Scottish Presbyterianism. The first Presbyterian minister, John Macfarlane, sailed from Glasgow in 1839 with a company of immigrants. They settled in Wellington. In 1843 a minister of the Church of Scotland, the Rev. W. Comrie, began services in Auckland. An important and influential pioneer minister was David Bruce, brother of A. B. Bruce, a professor at the Free Church College, Glasgow. He promoted the cause of church extension, and as churches came into existence with the growth of population, the Presbyterian Church of New Zealand was organized. The ministers of the church included men from the Free Church of Scotland, the Irish Presbyterian Church, the Church of Scotland, the United Presbyterian Church of Scotland, the English Presbyterian Church, and those trained in the colony. The first Assembly met in 1862.[26]

A separate Presbyterian church came into existence in the Otago area. This became known as the Presbyterian Church of Otago and Southland. It started with the settlement of members of the Free Church of Scotland who arrived in 1847. From the start these immigrants aimed at a spiritual as well as a material occupancy of the land. They believed they were founding a colony that would become a model Christian state. Originally the name of the settlement was to be New Edinburgh, but it was altered to Dunedin, an old Celtic designation of Edinburgh. The first minister to arrive in this colony was Thomas Burns, who was a nephew of the famous Scottish bard.[27]

For half a century this church exercised a powerful influence in the development of the southern half of New Zealand's south island. The members gave direction and tone to the social, educational, and religious life, which was in large measure under their guidance and control.

Both the Presbyterian Church of New Zealand and the Presbyterian Church of Otago and Southland exercised a widespread influence in education during the second half of the nineteenth century. Schools were established, and carefully selected teachers were brought out from Scotland. In most of the more populous centers there were first-class schools under the superintendence of Presbyterian influence.

The two churches agreed to establish the Divinity Hall in Dunedin where students could prepare for entering the ministry. Here the Reformed theology was taught, and for many years Dunedin was to exercise a wholesome influence in theological circles in Australasia.

The union of the two churches took place in 1901. As in Australia, the adoption of the Westminster Confession was qualified with a declaratory statement. In his volume "Will Presbyterianism Survive in New Zealand?" J. W. Deenick regards 1901 as "a decisive year in the history of New Zealand Presbyterianism." He contends that from that year the Presbyterian church of New Zealand ceased to represent the historic Reformed faith in that country. The declaratory statement, however well intended, did leave a loophole whereby liberalism could be introduced without running counter to conscience.[28]

The first indication of the more casual attitude of the church to the Reformed standards was evidenced in the proposal for union with the Methodists and Congregationalists in 1917. Two doughty defenders of the historic Presbyterian confession position arose in the persons of Kennedy Elliott and Thomas Miller. The "Twelve Reasons" why there should be no union of the churches were drawn up by Miller and sent to every Presbyterian church in New Zealand. Miller was an antagonist of union every time the issue appeared. He was a stalwart for the truth, and his two sons, J. Graham Miller and Robert S. Miller followed in their father's footsteps. They entered the ministry and earnestly contended for the faith both in New Zealand and later in Australia. Church union has not yet taken place; perhaps the situation in Australia will prove a warning to the enthusiasts in New Zealand.

The controversy arising from the proposal to unite with other churches whose doctrinal position is not Reformed has clearly indicated a departure from the doctrines set forth in the Westminster Confession. In 1967 the negotiations for church union included the Anglican, Presbyterian, Methodist, Congregational, and Church of Christ denominations. The result of this combination would be a church run by bishops, and doctrinal issues would be reduced to a minimum. To meet the conditions for union, modification of the doctrinal basis is always imperative. Already there has been such a general departure from their moorings on the part of all the churches concerned that union would seem to be the natural course to follow.

The Theological Hall, Knox College, continued for a number of years to be a center from which the seed of the Reformed faith was scattered abroad. In due course the tares of liberalism appeared. This was tolerated by the church and reached its culminating point when Principal

L. G. Geering could deny the fundamental doctrines of the faith with impunity.[29] So outrageous were Geering's denials of the faith that even the Roman Catholic newspaper "Zealandia," in an editorial, commented that he had forfeited his right to teach.

The flood of liberalism was not allowed to take its course without strong opposition. In 1950 a number of faithful ministers, elders, and members of the Presbyterian church were convinced that a stand should be taken. Accordingly the Westminster Fellowship was formed "to conserve the distinctive Reformed testimony of the Presbyterian Church of New Zealand as a daughter of the Scottish church, and so of the Calvinistic Reformation." "Members are wholehearted in receiving the Bible as the written Word of God, and cordial in their acceptance of the Westminster Confession of Faith and Catechisms as finely embodying the substance of the Biblical and Reformed Faith."

To implement the purpose envisaged, the Westminster Fellowship launched the publication of a journal entitled *The Evangelical Presbyterian*. At first it was published quarterly and later bi-monthly. The articles published were not only critical of the teaching of scholars like Bultmann, Geering, and others, but the Westminster Confession was presented as the biblical doctrine of the church. Among the names in the editorial board we find those of A. G. Gunn, J. Balchin, C. L. Gosling, J. Graham Miller, and R. S. Miller. The magazine attained a fairly wide circulation not only in New Zealand but also in Australia. It was like cold water to many a thirsty soul in churches where prophetic preaching had ceased.

*The Evangelical Presbyterian* had a wider range of interest than the *Reformed Theological Review,* which was started in Australia in 1941. The immediate aim of the latter was "a scholarly exposition, defence and propagation of the Reformed Faith, regarded as the purest expression of Historic Christianity." That aim was somewhat modified in subsequent years. In addition to the regular magazine the Westminster Fellowship was largely responsible for the publication and dissemination of a considerable number of booklets of an apologetic nature. Titles such as *Our Presbyterian Faith, The Authority of the Bible, After Death—What?, The Importance of the Reformation for the Discussion between the Churches* are indicative of the weapons used in the battle for the truth.

The Westminster Fellowship was involved in the "Geering Case" when it came before the Presbyterian Assembly. The decision taken, however, was disappointing, and compromise preserved a peace that is far from wholesome.

Three years after the commencement of the Westminster Fellowship a new denomination raised aloft a banner for Calvinism in New Zealand. This was brought about by the influx of new settlers from the Netherlands. As in Australia, these immigrants did not come to their new country with the intention of starting a church. They left their homeland because the situation was not too promising in Europe and there were prospects of better conditions in the young and more thinly populated countries in the Antipodes. However, they were disappointed with the preaching and teaching in many of the Presbyterian churches. They discovered that many ministers did not accept the Bible as the infallible Word of God, and there was disregard for the authority of the confessional standards of the church. They saw no alternative but to form a church that would be faithful to the Reformation heritage.

Accordingly they published a manifesto in 1953, stating the reason for establishing the Reformed churches. This was by no means a popular course, and there was much criticism. The pioneer leader in the establishment of these churches was J. W. Deenick. In 1954 there were nine congregations located in the larger centers of population. After twenty-three years there are now fourteen congregations and three presbyteries. The majority of the ministers are graduates of the Reformed Theological College, Geelong, Australia. The New Zealand churches support the college on the same basis as the Reformed churches of Australia.

The passionate zeal of the Reformed churches in New Zealand and Australia to spread abroad the imperishable truths discovered at the Reformation was seen in the formation of the Reformed Presbyterian Publishing House. It was decided to publish a monthly magazine, and the name chosen was *Trowel and Sword*. This was the reversal of the name chosen by C. H. Spurgeon for the magazine he edited. On the front cover of the first issue in October 1954 the symbols consisted of a wall in the process of construction, a sword and a trowel, and a foundation stone with this text: "The God of Heaven, He will prosper us, therefore we His servants, will arise and build—Neh. 2:20." There was also a picture of John Calvin.

The editors were John F. H. Vander Bom of Australia and J. W. Deenick of New Zealand. The first issues were published in New Zealand, but later the publishing house was transferred to Australia.

The objective of this magazine was indicated by Vander Bom in the leading editorial. He wrote:

> We do not intend a theological magazine, but a popular paper for the Reformed family, talking in a kindhearted tone about things in every sphere of life, home, science, labour unions and housework, church and schools and missions, politics and television, and indeed everything without exception, which comes under the aspect of our Christian responsibility and the authority of God's Word.[30]

No one would claim that in the twenty-four years since *Trowel and Sword* was first issued this lofty ideal has been reached. There is always the danger that such a magazine becomes obsessed with theological vagaries and leaves the ordinary people untouched. The original objective of *Trowel and Sword* must not become part of buried history.

The Reformed churches of Australasia have now become part of the ecclesiastical edifice. They are open to the theological changes that are rocking the churches in the Netherlands. They have seen the devastating effects of continental theology in Scotland and subsequently in Australia and New Zealand. To ignore the warnings of history will simply mean a repetition of the mistakes and failures of the past.

## THE NEW HEBRIDES

Any survey of the impact of Calvinism in the Antipodes would be incomplete without a reference to missions. Samuel Marsden not only was involved in introducing the Christian faith to Australia but also assisted in its spread to other areas in the South Seas. He inaugurated the first Christian mission to the Maoris of New Zealand. He conducted the first Christian worship in New Zealand. In 1838 the Church Missionary Society had a staff of thirty-five missionaries and fifty-one schools in New Zealand.[31]

In Australia the aborigines constituted a very difficult problem. Their tribal organization and social structures stood in marked contrast to the political and social structures of the whites. The blacks were cruelly treated by some whites. They were demoralized by the white man's vices. The Tasmanian aborigines disappeared completely. In mainland Australia the aboriginal population declined.

Little was attempted in churches holding the Reformed position to reach the aborigines in the nineteenth century. A few mission stations were started, chiefly in Queensland, but it was not until after the federation of the Presbyterian churches that the work among the aborigines was coordinated. This work has proved very difficult, and no sensational statistics can be offered by any church or missionary society working among aborigines.[32]

During the years when Australia and New Zealand were developing from colonial settlements toward self-government and nationhood, great missionary activities were going on in the South Pacific islands. The area where the greatest impact of Calvinism can be discerned was that of the New Hebrides. This group of islands lies about one thousand miles north of New Zealand and sixteen hundred miles east of Queensland. The first attempt to introduce the gospel was made in 1838 by the well-known missionary John Williams, who lost his life in the effort.[33]

The first Presbyterian church that attempted missionary operation in the New Hebrides was that of Nova Scotia. Their missionary, John Geddie, settled in Aneiteum, the southernmost island in the group, in 1848. We are indebted to Robert S. Miller for providing a detailed and fascinating account of the ministry of John Geddie in his volume *Misi Gete,* published in 1975 by the Presbyterian Church of Tasmania. Perhaps the greatest tribute to this pioneer missionary and planter of churches is the concluding words on a plaque in the church at Anelgauhat, Aneiteum: "When he landed in 1848 there were no Christians here, and when he left in 1872 there were no heathens."[34]

In 1852 he was joined by John Inglis and his wife from the Reformed Presbyterian Church of Scotland. Christians from Aneiteum pioneered the work in other islands and some of them paid for their devotion with their lives.

One of the best known and most distinguished missionaries to the New Hebrides was John G. Paton, who also came from the Reformed Presbyterian Church of Scotland. He first attempted work on the island of Tanna but was forced to leave after four years by the hostility of the natives. With support from the Presbyterian Church of Victoria, Paton made a fresh start on the island of Aniwa. Here he had the joy of seeing the whole island eventually accepting the Christian faith.

In 1869 the Presbyterian Church of New Zealand sent its first missionary to the New Hebrides. He was William Watt, and he was followed in 1870 by Peter Milne. Milne was assigned to the island of Nguna, and after twenty-five years the people there had become Christians. By 1914, in addition to Aneiteum, Erromanga, Nguna, and Aniwa, the Christian church was planted in five other islands—Futuna, Efate, Tongoa, Epi, and Paama.

When the majority of the Reformed Presbyterian Synod in Scotland decided to unite with the Free Church of Scotland, the missionaries in the New Hebrides threw in their lot with the majority. John Paton became a missionary of the Presbyterian Church of Victoria. Toward the end of the nineteenth century, missionaries were supported by the Presbyterian churches in Australia and New Zealand, the Free Church of Scotland and the Presbyterian Church in Canada.[35]

A solid foundation was laid by faithful missionaries for the young church in the New Hebrides. The gospel of God's sovereign grace in Christ was proclaimed, and a wonderful harvest was the result. The early pioneers were followed by missionaries who brought the same gospel. The church that was formed had a widespread influence on the cultural developments throughout the islands in the group. Schools were established, and the Bible was translated into the languages spoken on the different islands. Medical facilities were made available and hospitals were erected. The Tangoa Training Institute was established for theological education. This institute was closed in 1970 and replaced by the Presbyterian Bible College of the New Hebrides. The first principal of this college was J. Graham Miller (1971–73).

In 1948 the Presbyterian Church of the New Hebrides became fully autonomous. According to the constitution, the church receives "the Scriptures of the Old and New Testaments which contain the Word of God as its Supreme Rule of faith and life; believes the basic doctrines of the Christian faith founded on the Scriptures; and understands and teaches these doctrines by the guiding principles of the Protestant Reformation." Provision is made for the ministry, eldership, government, and discipline according to the general pattern for Reformed and Presbyterian churches. The communicant members number about 8,600 in a Christian community of about 30,000. This is the first self-governing church in Melanesia.

Politically the New Hebrides have been under the joint control of the United Kingdom and France. They have now attained self government and the new state is known as Vanuatu. A strong and active self-governing church has been like leaven in the political scene and must continue to have far-reaching influence.

The golden age of Calvinism in the vast continental area of Australia, New Zealand, and the South Pacific islands belonged to the nineteenth century. With the exception of the New Hebrides, there has been decline in the twentieth century. A pertinent question naturally arises, Is there a future for Calvinism in this part of the world? If we allow the failures of the past and the magnitude of the present task to determine the answer, then we might hesitate before giving an answer in the affirmative. We can appreciate what perplexed the mind of the prophet Ezekiel when in the valley of dry bones he was confronted with the question, "Can these bones live?"

Instead of trying to answer the question with pious expressions of hope, we should seriously endeavor to assess what our task is and what Calvinism demands of its adherents. If it is still the intention to plant some special brand of Calvinism such as Scottish or Dutch, there is no guarantee of success. If we see Calvinism as a living faith, there is much ground for optimism.

The keynote of Calvinism is belief in a sovereign God who is building His church. The command of Christ still stands: "Make disciples of all nations." That command was prefixed by the claim "All authority in heaven and on earth has been given to me." It is in obedience to this Lord that we must face the future. In this way we can claim the promises of God, which are assured in Christ. Calvin kept in view the triumph of the cause of God. Shortly before his death, when he was saying farewell to the pastors of Geneva, he gave a word of encouragement, "Take courage and strengthen yourselves, for God will use this church and will maintain it; I assure you that God will keep it."[36] The future could be in no better hands.

# Calvinism
# in South Africa

## Gideon Thom

*Gideon Thom is head of the Department of Ecclesiastical History and Missiology at the University of Fort Hare, Alice, South Africa. He graduated from the University of the Free State (B.A.) and the Stellenbosch Theological Seminary (Cand. Theol.) and is at present working toward a Ph.D. As an ordained minister in the Dutch Reformed Church (NGK), he served as pastor in various Xhosa-speaking churches in the Trans-Ciskei and Ciskei. Mr. Thom is the author of a catechism in the Xhosa language and he contributes to* Missionalia *and the* Journal of Theology for Southern Africa. *He is a member of the South African Missiological Society.*

# 16

# Calvinism
# in South Africa

For many years the strength of the Calvinistic apologetic lay in the quality of the lives of its professors, not only of individuals such as Calvin, Knox, de Coligny, and numerous others, but also of communities.[1] Because of the common-sense appeal of this apologetic, the weak points in Calvinistic practice were attacked without mercy. The death of Servetus, Quaker martyrs in New England, Presbyterians defending slavery—all received more than their fair share of criticism. Of all the "public failures" of the Reformed faith, the association of South African Calvinists with the racial policies of their country seems to be the most heinous of all. It is an embarrassment to the Reformed in other countries, and to the non-Calvinist it seems to confirm "natural tendencies" of doctrines such as predestination and total depravity.[2]

In his book *The Puritans in Africa,* W. A. de Klerk draws attention to the "irony of South African history."[3] There are indeed numerous (and humorous) paradoxes that could be pointed out, but in a sense de Klerk reinforces the "irony." He finds the roots of the Afrikaner "will to power" in the popular parallel between Afrikaner and Puritan and the (assumed) supralapsarianism of Dort, using the theories of Weber and Tawney in the process.[4] Now both friend and foe have accepted the assumption that Calvinism was indeed the cause of racial discrimination in South Africa, while direct historical evidence for this assumption is not easy to find.[5]

I am not suggesting that the influence of Calvinism can be isolated so as to "prove" that all the bad things were caused by other factors and all the good things by Calvinism. Life and history is certainly too complex for such a "laboratory test." And, in spite of the traditional apologetic, Calvinists do not claim perfection.[6] But as Calvinism is at the same time a very personal and a very public faith, it is possible to pinpoint its influence at certain stages in history.

It may not be superfluous to insist on a definition of Calvinism when one considers its wider influence. The English Calvinistic tradition seems to emphasize soteriology. The Scots tradition emphatically includes the freedom of the church in its own organization and in relation to the state. Abraham Kuyper made use of a wider cultural definition and even included Wesleyan Arminianism.[7] John T. McNeill claims Woodrow Wilson for Calvinism and ascribes especially his concern for the underprivileged and the small nations to the influence of Calvinism.[8] General Jan C. Smuts was not a Calvinist, yet he and General Louis Botha believed that the treaty of Versailles was unjust toward the Germans.[9] Both of them had a Dutch Reformed upbringing. Should we not include in the definition moral integrity, honest industry, and compassion for the oppressed shown by people who grew up in Calvinistic homes without making an open avowal of Calvinism? But there are pitfalls. Not everyone born or baptized in a Reformed church can be described as a Calvinist. Personal knowledge and commitment have always been treated with the utmost seriousness by the Reformed churches. It seems as if we must be satisfied with the more modest definition, even though this may mean that we may not be able to claim some of the legitimate "fruits of Calvinism." By Calvinism I mean that branch of the orthodox Christian church that emphasizes the freedom of God's grace in salvation[10] and the freedom of God's church in society.[11] Under the second aspect one should not forget the traditional Calvinistic view that society itself (including the state) must be brought to obedience to the living God.

## GLIMPSES OF CALVINISM
### IN THE HISTORY OF SOUTH AFRICA

In South Africa the direct influence of Calvin through his own writings was indeed small. The *Institutes* and his commentaries and sermons have not yet been translated into Afrikaans to any great extent.[12] English and Dutch translations have been available, however. The general decline of Calvinism in the nineteenth century affected all the South African churches more or less, with the exception of the Reformed Church (GKSA), which was founded partly under the influence of the "Afscheiding" in the Netherlands in 1834. Although the Dutch Reformed Church did not forsake its Confessions, the person of Luther received as much attention as Calvin.[13] In the 1930s however, interest in Calvin grew widely, and since then a number of doctoral studies have been carried out by South African scholars on some aspect of Calvin's writings.[14]

## The Dutch Reformed Church (NGK)

Calvinism was brought to South Africa in 1652 when the Dutch East India Company opened a station at the Cape to provide their ships with fresh food and water. In the seventeenth century the relationship between the Dutch church and the people was very close.[15] In South Africa this characteristic was reinforced by various factors in the following centuries. The company charter provided for the establishment of schools and churches for the benefit of the employees and for non-Christians in the population. When Jan van Riebeeck arrived, he prayed for the extension of "our true reformed religion" among the inhabitants of the new country.[16] The close relationship between church and company served as an inhibiting factor in the development of the church at the Cape.[17]

The "religious needs" of the inhabitants were not neglected (the first resident minister was appointed in 1665, but he died soon afterwards), but oft-quoted parallels with Puritan settlements of America are unduly favorable to the situation at the Cape.[18] The settlement was first and foremost a trade venture. The officials and settlers were not always of the best type. The middle-class Dutch did not find the Cape very attractive, and many a German soldier came to the Cape to seek his fortune.[19] The ministers came and went at frequent intervals, and few of them could be compared favorably with the men who accompanied the Puritans to America.[20]

The only group who settled at the Cape for religious reasons was the French Huguenots who arrived between 1688 and 1700. They made a real contribution to piety and agriculture and, according to J. du Plessis, also in respect to relations with the indigenous clans.[21] They were, however, not allowed to constitute their own congregation initially, and their language rights were curtailed. The result was that their contribution to the religious life was not what it could have been.[22]

A substantial number of Germans were assimilated by the earlier colonists during the first century of the settlement, as were also a minority of baptized slaves. Although organized missionary work was not undertaken, a number of the original inhabitants (Khoi-San) were baptized and assimilated by the white population.[23] As the farmers moved slowly into the vast interior of Africa and were in daily contact with pagan tribes and individuals, it is remarkable that they did not drift into paganism themselves. The Dutch authorized version of the Bible with explanatory notes, the Heidelberg Catechism, and the periodic ministrations of visiting ministers, preserved the Christian faith among them. Together with these aids, regular family worship and the writings of the Dutch Calvinistic Pietists played an important role. The writings of á Brakel, Smijtegelt, Hellenbroek, and others kept the Reformed doctrines of human depravity and salvation by grace alone, as well as a distinctly puritan ethic, alive in the hearts and homes of many deep into the nineteenth century.[24]

During the eighteenth century the Dutch church was influenced by insipid supernaturalism and Erastianism.[25] These influenced especially the population in Cape Town, which came to be known as "Little Paris." Toward the end of the eighteenth century, however, a few able ministers labored in Cape Town. Of them the saintly Helperus Ritzema van Lier, who was a friend of the famous English Calvinist John Newton, was the most outstanding.[26] Unfortunately his fruitful ministry was terminated by his early death in 1793. He and M. C. Vos of Tulbagh also began to arouse the Cape church to a concern for the salvation of the slave and colored populations. Several buildings were erected for the purposes of ministering to them the Word of life. The widow Mathilda Smit, who subsequently assisted Dr. van der Kemp at Bethelsdorp, 450 miles from Cape Town, was a convert of van Lier. This small-scale revival enabled van der Kemp to organize the South African Missionary Society shortly after his arrival in 1799.[27] In 1818 the South African Bible Society was also formed.

In 1795 the Cape fell into the hands of the British, but the church remained the official state-supported church. As a result of the perpetual need for ministers some missionaries of the London Missionary Society accepted positions in the Cape church. The British governor had ambitious plans to prohibit the use of Dutch as the official language and decided to recruit Scots ministers and teachers for the Cape.[28] Among the first to arrive was Andrew Murray from Aberdeen, father of the famous author and preacher of the same name. Those who came were mostly from the Evangelical (as opposed to Moderate) party in the Kirk of Scotland. They did not succeed in Anglicizing the Dutch population, but they strengthened the Evangelical and Reformed tradition in the Cape church. This became especially apparent in the subsequent struggle against Erastianism and rationalism. On the very day of his induction at Tulbagh, Robert Shand voiced his objection against state control. It was said that Shand read only two books, the Bible and the *Institutes* of Calvin. His strong Sabbatarian views, however, remind one more of Westminster than of Geneva.[29]

The severance of the link with the church in the Netherlands enabled the Cape church to develop independently, and its first Synod met in 1824. However, the church was still fettered by state control. The Scots ministers cooperated with the local leaders in their struggle to free the church. In 1843 the church was "disestablished" by law, although the state still supported certain ministers. And the fact that it was disestablished by civil law left an Erastian loophole.[30]

In 1836 the famous Great Trek took place from the eastern districts to the present-day Natal, Transvaal, and Orange Free State. The main reason for the trek was "too much and too little government." The Cape authorities could not protect the eastern population from the cattle-stealing foraging of the adventurous Xhosa tribes and they would not allow the frontiersmen to retrieve the cattle themselves. The frequently changing policy of the British colonial office was influenced by the unpopular Calvinist of the London Missionary Society John Philip.[31] He was unpopular with the colonists because he had plenty of sympathy for the blacks but was not always fair to the colonists—British and Afrikaans. Even the Methodist missionaries did not like his political role.[32] Philip's controversial views and the "mixed marriages" of van der Kemp and James Read gave the Afrikaners a permanent aversion to the missionaries of the LMS. The pioneers did not appreciate the fact that it was Philip's Calvinism that stimulated his interest in social and political matters.[33]

When the pioneers arrived in Natal, missionaries of the American Board were just trying to settle there to evangelize the turbulent Zulu nation. Francis Owen of the Church Missionary Society was stationed at the headquarters of Dingane, king of the Zulus. Pieter Retief, one of the leaders of the pioneers or Trekkers made a treaty with Dingane to obtain a large tract of land in central Natal for Trekker occupation. Even though he knew the customs of the black nations fairly well at that stage, Retief apparently did not realize that occupation did not mean private ownership in the Black point of view, but only a kind of conditional vassaldom. But Dingane had no intention of allowing them to occupy the land. Venable, of the American Board, warned Retief, but to no avail, and eventually Retief and his followers were massacred while Owen and his family watched the scene with incredulous horror.[34] In the following days Dingane's fast-moving men almost succeeded in wiping out all the Trekkers at Weenen ("place of weeping").

Some months later a commando under the leadership of Andries Pretorius set out to punish Dingane for breaking the treaty. Pretorius and the spiritual leader of the commando, Charl Cilliers, were both previously members of the Church at Graaff Reinet where Andrew Murray, Sr., was their pastor. On the initiative of Cilliers, they made a covenant with God, promising to keep the day of battle as an annual day of thanksgiving if God would give them the victory. Although this covenant fell far short of that of the Scottish Covenanters, who promised unconditional dedication to upholding the Reformed faith in Scotland, it is possible that the covenant idea derived from the Scots tradition, via Murray.[35] In His providence God gave them victory on that beautiful but terrible day (December 16, 1838). This day is annually commemorated as a day of thanksgiving by many South African Christians, but others consider it a racial commemoration.[36]

In spite of the initial opposition of the Cape church to the Trek, these experiences served to strengthen the relation between church and nation. The indigenous character and spiritual resources of the church were further augmented by four factors: (1) the opening of a theological seminary at Stellenbosch, (2) the struggle against rationalism in the Cape church, (3) the revival during the 1860s and the subsequent missionary movement, and (4) the Anglo-Boer War.

Because of the strong influence of rationalism in the Dutch universities, the Cape Synod decided to open its own seminary. Failing to attract men from the Netherlands, N. J. Hofmeyr and John Murray were eventually called to the seminary. Under these two able and God-fearing theologians, the seminary was instrumental in unifying the church in the general biblical and experimental character of its preaching, its evangelical character, and its aim to preach Christ to the whole of South Africa. An indigenous Calvinism, under the gracious work of the Holy Spirit, saved the people of South Africa from the spiritual destitution that would have resulted from European rationalism and African paganism.

The Seminary was opened in 1859. In the meantime young ministers who had studied in the Netherlands brought liberal theology back with them. In the sixties the Synod decided to exclude two of them from the ministry on charges of heresy.[37] Both the firmness of the Synod and its prayerful dependence on the Head of the Church in its disciplining activity was remarkable. The struggle continued in the press and the Supreme Court and from pulpit and platform for some time, but the learning and manifest piety of the defenders of the faith secured the victory, with the help and mercy of God.[38]

As a student, Andrew Murray listened to William Chalmers Burns, and in the Netherlands South African students had contact with the Reveil. As reports of the mid-century revivals in Britain and America were received, ministers and people started to pray for a visitation of God's grace. At Paarl the venerable G. W. A. van der Lingen prayed unceasingly. On Pentecost Sunday in 1861 God visited his congregation in a remarkable way, and many were awakened.[39] Also in other places God poured out His Spirit. Many saw for the first time the reality of their sinfulness and the sufficiency of the work of Christ for sinners. The revival touched young and old, black and white. Ever since that time the NGK has held prayer meetings between Ascension Day and Pentecost. Faith was revived, and the mission of the church received a stimulus, not only within the borders of South Africa but also beyond, into Botswana, Zimbabwe, Zambia, Malawi, and eventually even to Nigeria.

Although the Anglo-Boer war (1899–1902) brought terrible destruction of life and property,[40] it also brought spiritual renewal in its wake.

As spiritual renewal is not a natural result of war, it can only be ascribed to sovereign grace. There were revivals in the POW camps on the islands of St. Helena, Sri Lanka, and the Bermudas. Many young men dedicated their lives to the Lord. The Christian character of the officers (although there were exceptions) played an important role in setting the tone of conduct among the men. Some of the commandos were simply congregations in the veld (with or without their pastors). Leaders like Generals Koos de La Rey and C. R. de Wet were remarkable combinations of manly soldier and faithful Christian. Not only the well-known President Paul Kruger, but also President M. T. Steyn of the Orange Free State, were outstanding Christians. The influence of Christian leaders was equally beneficial during the reconstruction after the war. The farming industry, homes, schools, and even churches had been destroyed. The nation needed faith and hope and love. The fact that South Africa did not become a country of continual bloodshed between Afrikaner and Englishman must solely be ascribed to the grace of God, who enabled men and women to forgive. Although certain congregations were divided on the problem of the collaborators, the church supported the physical and spiritual reconstruction. Private schools were erected to counteract the influence of English and nonconfessional education and the relation between people and church was further confirmed.[41]

An important characteristic of this close relationship was the strong influence of ''lay'' leaders, partly as a result of a shortage of ministers, but no doubt also because of the importance of elders and deacons in the Reformed churches. That this lay Calvinism had its theological weaknesses no one will deny. But it is also possible that the remarkable absence of extremism (or ''fanaticism'') traditional among the Afrikaans people may be attributed to this patriarchal leadership, in combination with faithful and able ministers.

In this century, the Afrikaner struggled against various forces to maintain his cultural, political, and racial identity, as well as to insure his economic survival. The three most prominent leaders during this century—J. B. M. Hertzog, D. F. Malan, and H. F. Verwoerd—cannot be described as Calvinists, yet the relationship between church and the Afrikaner people became dangerously close. The Afrikaner felt that he could not face the future without the support of the church, but by the sixties many wanted the church to be *their* church. If the maintenance of the freedom of the church in society is part and parcel of Calvinism (as was suggested in the definition), then the NGK came very close to denying its Calvinistic character in 1962. At the General Assembly of that year proposals criticizing the racial policies of the government were rejected because of what appears to have been a sense of loyalty to the government.[42] The proposals themselves were not shown to be contradictory to Scripture.[43] But "councils may err" and the total life and witness of the church make such a judgment premature. Angus Holland's suggestion that the Afrikaner lives spiritually in a pre-1914 world may indeed be the most charitable explanation.[44] The church was disestablished, but in the minds of the majority the close relationship between church and people, going back to the seventeenth century, could not be destroyed.

## The Reformed Church in South Africa (GKSA)

In many ways the history of the GKSA parallels the history of the NGK, but its dinctinctive contribution to the preservation and expansion of Calvinism merits special attention.

Some time after the Great Trek, the church in the Transvaal was organized separately from the Cape church, eventually to form a third denomination, the NHK.[45] In 1859 the GKSA seceded from the Transvaal church, and subsequently congregations were also organized in the Cape. One of the main reasons for the secession was the introduction of the so-called evangelical hymns from the Netherlands.[46] Ironically, some of these hymns were decidedly nonevangelical. Not only did the Cape and Transvaal churches accept these without proper scrutiny, but the members who objected to them were treated in a high-handed manner. Because of a shortage of ministers in the Transvaal, the Christian Reformed Church in the Netherlands sent Dirk Postma to offer assistance to the Transvaal church. His arrival and his sympathy with the conservatives precipitated a secession that had been coming to a head over a period of years.[47]

There can be little doubt that this connection with "real Dutch Calvinism" was to the advantage of the church in South Africa. Apart from a special interest in Calvin, the main contribution of the GKSA was to Christian education. The Potchefstroom University for Christian Higher Education was modeled after the Free University of Amsterdam and has made a tremendous contribution to Christian education and Christian scholarship in South Africa and beyond its borders. By virtue of its smaller numbers and more distinct confessional character, the GKSA is less a church of the people than the NGK, yet it is still remarkably so. President Paul Kruger was a founding member of the GKSA.

## English Reformed Churches

Apart from LMS and Scottish missionaries, English-speaking Calvinists have been lamentably few in South Africa. The tercentenary of Calvin's death was commemorated in Cape Town with a lecture on Calvin by the Congregationalist minister William Thompson.[48] Spurgeon's sermons were widely read (also in Dutch translations) and various (English) Baptist churches were Calvinistic in doctrine around the turn of the century. During the 1950s Victor Thomas and L. G. Thomas, Calvinistic Baptists, arrived from England, and since that time there has been a revival of Calvinism among English-speaking South Africans, with a growing influence through the Evangelical and Reformed Fellowship. Although their emphasis is mainly on soteriology, the Koinonia Declaration of 1977, issued in cooperation with Afrikaans-speaking Calvinists, was a dramatic expression of this revival in terms of social and political problems.

## Calvinism in Black Churches

Toward the end of the nineteenth century Hodge's *Systematic Theology* was still used at Lovedale Seminary by T. D. Philip, son of John Philip.[49] In a general sense, the traditional Reformed influence is still present in the Presbyterian and Congregational churches. Black churches in communion with the NGK and GKSA are more directly under the influence of Calvinism, but on the whole Calvinism presently has little influence on the black churches. This may be ascribed to the general decline of Calvinism that coincided with the second half of the "Great Century" of missions, the preponderance of Methodist influence in the South African missions, the absence of an influential evangelical group in the Anglican church (The Church of the Province of South Africa), and the popular association of Calvinism with racial discrimination since 1948.

THE INFLUENCE OF
CALVINISM IN SOUTH AFRICA

In spite of their numbers, the influence of Reformed Christians in South Africa often lacks that concentration and effectiveness that their numbers would lead one to expect.[50] One reason for this is the characteristic of the Afrikaans-speaking Calvinists that they tend to think in terms of the whole nation and the whole country. Their history explains this tendency in part, but it must also be remembered that South Africa is a developing nation. In spite of the international character of Calvinism, Calvinists were always patriots in the best sense of the word.[51] This is very apparent in the support of South African Calvinists for a general Christian education for all population groups. It also helps to explain to some extent their support for a racial policy that endeavored to solve the problems of all the groups in the country. But a widely diffused influence is of necessity a weak influence, and it may even become a distorted influence. It also put a terrible strain on human and financial resources. After a few observations on the influence of Calvinism on education and politics, I wish to draw attention to its influence on missions and finally on the influence of Calvinism on race relations in South Africa.

## Education

The majority of older schools and universities were started or strongly supported by Calvinists. The oldest South African university for blacks, namely the University of Fort Hare, founded in 1916, developed out of Lovedale College, which was founded in 1841 by Scots Calvinists. The universities of Stellenbosch, the Free State, and Potchefstroom were founded by Calvinists but only that at Potchefstroom is still a Reformed University. South African Calvinists do not have any free Christian schools or high schools. Numerous Calvinist educationalists are to be found, however, in the schools and in the universities. Black education in particular received (and still receives) considerable support from men and women of the Reformed churches, both at high school and at university level. It may be, however, that the more élitist approach of confining their influence to Christian schools would have been a better policy in the long run. The Christian National Schools that were begun after the Anglo-Boer War were not supported long after the Dutch language regained its position in the state schools. Lovedale was the first multiracial school in South Africa, but white student numbers dwindled toward the end of the nineteenth century. As South African Calvinists supported the proliferation of "Christian" state schools for all groups (excepting of course Muslim and Hindu groups), they did not face the question of multiracial Christian schools since the "phasing out" of Lovedale. In theological education the Reformed churches retained the initiative, and a majority of the members of theological research societies belong to the Reformed churches. Reformed scholars also played a major role in the translation of the Scriptures into local languages, such as Afrikaans, Xhosa, Sotho, Venda, Tswana, and Shona.

## Politics

The first real political party in South Africa, the Afrikaner Bond, was the brain-child of an admirer of Abraham Kuyper, the erratic S. J. du Toit. It was cofounded by J. H. Hofmeyr.[52] For many years the Bond was able to attract the support of Afrikaans and English, with the exception of the rank imperialists.[53] For a short honeymoon it also had the support of educated blacks, led by Tengo Jabavu, who was trained at Lovedale.[54] The roots of both the original South African Party and the National Party of General Hertzog can be traced back to the Afrikaner Bond. Although Calvinists supported these parties, they cannot be described as Christian political parties, as was the Anti-Revolutionary Party of the Netherlands.

The fact that the Afrikaners of the Northern Cape did not rise in general rebellion during the War (1899–1902) may be ascribed to their respect for law and order.[55] Paul Kruger resisted anarchy in the Transvaal on the basis of the Constitution, in spite of the fact that the Constitution of the time limited the rights of those who belonged to the GKSA.[56] But against these must be balanced the rebellion of 1914,[57] as well as Kruger's unwise refusal to extend the political rights of the "Uitlanders" in the Transvaal. As I have already noted the general benevolent influence of Christian leaders during the reconstruction, which was perhaps the flood-tide of Christian influence on the nation, we may summarize by saying that the influence of Calvinism on politics was always present but seldom dominant.[58]

CALVINISM AND MISSIONS:
THE TRIUMPH OF GRACE

It was noted that the Cape church was again aroused to see the spiritual need of the slaves and other colored people with the revival of Calvinism in the time of H. R. van Lier. The arrival of J. T. van der Kemp in 1799, however, brought South Africa fully within the orbit of the modern missionary movement. It is of interest to note that William Carey proposed that the first world missionary conference should be held at the Cape in 1810. When the famous Henry Martyn visited the Cape in 1806, van der Kemp presented him with a Syriac New Testament.[59]

Van der Kemp is chiefly remembered for his work among the Khoi-San (Hottentots) but he has acquired a notoriety seldom equaled for his marriage to the daughter of a freed slave woman and for his prejudice in favor of the colored population. The poor physical condition of his station at Bethelsdorp, compared to that of the Moravians at Genadendal, was also criticized severely in his own time. His love for the colored population and his ideas of equality are usually ascribed to the influence of J. J. Rousseau's doctrine of the "noble savage."[60] To make the confusion complete, opposition to van der Kemp from the side of the whites has often been ascribed to their "Calvinism."[61]

Van der Kemp's training and the soil, climate, and size of Bethelsdorp make comparisons with Genadendal unfair, yet his eccentricity is not to be denied. His frank nonconformity no doubt gave offense, even in the Netherlands.[62] Even a sympathetic historian acknowledged that his ideas of equality derived from his preconversion days.[63] Certainly ideas of equality are not enough to make a Deist into a humble preacher of the Cross.[64]

From the study of Enklaar it is clear that van der Kemp was soteriologically a Calvinist.[65] In the foreword to his commentary on Romans he wrote that he "never denied the justice of God in imputing the sin of Adam to his posterity, not even in the blackest darkness of my Deistic unbelief."[66] His other writings and his teaching showed that his motivation was his "unexpected conversion on the 4th July 1791 through the everlasting mercy of the Lord Jesus Christ towards me a miserable sinner,'' as he said in the same foreword. He was a sinner saved by undeserved grace.

The idea that his critics were motivated by Calvinism is equally generally believed and equally without hard evidence. The uprising in Graaff Reinet in 1795 against Maynier (who was a disciple of Rousseau!) was at least partly a result of the ideas of the French Revolution,[67] and the uprising at Slagtersnek in 1815 was anything but a ''Puritan revolution.''[68] Slagtersnek showed the possibility and reality of the spiritual destitution from which Calvinism kept the majority of the colonists.[69]

Van der Kemp was the first to preach the gospel to the Xhosa nation of South Africa. Because of friction between the colony and the Xhosas, van der Kemp was not able to stay much longer than a year, and he subsequently settled at Bethelsdorp. Unknown to him, his preaching bore remarkable fruit. The first Xhosa Christian, Ntsikana, listened to van der Kemp as a young man. Some years later he experienced a ''sudden conversion'' while on his way to a traditional dance.[70] Ntsikana's preaching and especially his unique hymns laid the foundation of Christianity among the Xhosa people. Some of Ntsikana's converts had also heard the gospel for the first time from the lips of van der Kemp. Ntsikana's own conversion and his references to God's sovereignty in creation and salvation in his hymns emphasize the power of God's grace.[71] He spoke of God as the great ''Hunter of souls.''

The planting of the church among the Xhosa proceeded further under the ministry of Scottish Calvinists, mainly of the Glasgow Missionary Society. The first converts were baptized in 1823. The majority of them had been led to Christ by Ntsikana, who died in 1820. Attempts were made to reduce the Xhosa language to writing, and Ross brought out a printing press in 1823. One of the stations started by the Scots missionaries was named Lovedale, in honor of John Love, secretary of the Glasgow Society.

To this Scottish Calvinistic mission also belongs the honor (in the providence of God) of giving to the church the first tribal African to receive Protestant ordination, Tiyo Soga.[72] Soga's father had been appointed by his king, Ngqika (or Gaika), to listen to the preaching of Ntsikana, and in this way this polygamous family came into contact with the gospel. From Lovedale, in 1846 Tiyo was taken to Scotland by William Govan when the outbreak of the ''War of the Axe'' made all normal work impossible. In Glasgow Tiyo was baptized in 1848 and after a few more years at home and back again to Glasgow he was ordained as a minister of the United Presbyterian Church in the John Street Church on 23 December 1856. Soga's subsequent work as a minister of the gospel, hymn-writer, and Bible-translator set the seal of God on his ministry. It was also a monument to the dedication, faith, and faithfulness of the first generation of missionaries, so often criticized but so seldom imitated. Soga died in 1871 at the early age of 42, and it was only toward the end of the century that the next generation of black ministers (among them John Knox Bokwe) came on the scene.

It is beyond the scope of this chapter to discuss the decline of ministerial training, the lowering of the status of the black minister, and the numerous subsequent secessions for which churches in Africa became notorious. It should be noted, however, that the decline of Calvinism and the rise of Darwinism, with its emphasis on gradualism, coincided with the decline of ministerial training in South Africa (and not only in South Africa). Tiyo Soga's conversion and training, as well as his fruitful ministry, belied the doctrine of gradualism. God's call and gifts are not given according to race, but according to grace.[73]

And yet, race is not totally irrelevant. When the Livingstonia mission of the Free Church was started in Malawi, James Stewart was accompanied by four black Christians from Lovedale who were related to the Angoni of Malawi. The Angoni, as well as the Abambo who stayed among the Xhosa, were descendants of refugees from Zululand who had fled the wrath of the great Tshaka about 1834. In the providence of God, evangelists from the Xhosa church were able to assist in the planting of the church in Central Africa.[74]

I have already noted the American Calvinists who started the American Zulu Mission in Natal. Robert Moffat of the LMS was instrumental in the conversion of several chiefs and the planting of the church among the Tswana people. He also translated the Bible into Tswana. His son-in-law, David Livingstone, and others before and after him, preached the gospel in Botswana and Zimbabwe in spite of terrible hardships suffered among the Makololo and Matabele.[75] French Calvinists planted the church in Lesothe.[76]

In 1857 the Cape Synod decided to start mission work among unevangelized tribes in the Transvaal. The descendants of Coenraad de Buys, who had married a black woman, also asked for a missionary.[77] This work expanded eventually to Botswana among the Bakgatla in 1877. In 1889 T. C. B. Vlok and A. C. Murray went out to settle in central Malawi, in cooperation with the Scottish missions, where God abundantly blessed the preaching of the gospel. In 1891 A. A. Louw started a mission in Zimbabwe near the headquarters of a chief named Mugabe. In 1899, only months before the outbreak of the Anglo-Boer War, the Synod of the NGK in the Orange Free State started a mission among unevangelized tribes in the Eastern districts of Zambia. The existence of Reformed churches in these places, with schools, hospitals, and theological colleges witnesses to the fact that the grace of God triumphed over racial prejudice.

The foundation of the Commando Auxiliary Missionary Society is noteworthy. The Germiston Commando, under General C. F. Beyers, came into contact with unevangelized tribes in Northern Transvaal. They were accompanied by Rev. A. P. Kriel who subsequently founded the Langlaagte Orphanages. The men were so touched by the people's ignorance of the gospel that they covenanted with God and each other (on 10 October 1900) that they would support a missionary among these people as soon as possible after the war.[78] This support enabled the church to send out a missionary in 1904. About the same time, a missionary, J. de Klerk, was sent out to Sri Lanka to preach the gospel in the country where many POW's had found their Savior during wartime.

Although home missions among the colored and black populations (especially in the Cape Province and in the Free State) prospered considerably, the Cape Synod of 1857 accommodated color prejudice. The white members of the congregation at Stockenström were allowed to gather in a separate building. At most other places colored members also had, for all practical purposes, separate services. The Synod allowed these separate places of worship "because of the weakness of some." Two of these "colored" congregations remained in the Cape Synod when all those who wished were invited in 1881 to constitute their own synod. These eventually developed into the vigorous N. G. Sendingkerk, with larger or smaller congregations in almost every town and village of the Cape Province. The relationship between the NGK and the "Sendingkerk" has not been satisfactorily settled. There seems to be no reason why there should be two separate synods.

Given the natural tendency of the human heart and the color prejudice that was already a "way of life" in South Africa, the fact that the local churches did mission work at all must be ascribed to God's grace.[79] It is altogether to the glory of God's grace that men came forward to preach the gospel to the "coloreds," that they persisted in the face of innumerable obstacles, and that God blessed their labors. Common sense may also deduce that the relations between the races were not so bad as is commonly believed. But even if this is true, the honor for that does not belong to man but to God.

## Calvinism and Racialism:
### The Trial of Grace

Professor C. W. de Kiewiet affirms that the racial prejudice of the white colonists was "reinforced by the version of Calvinism which withholds the full grace of God from the natives."[80] W. A. de Klerk also accuses the "supra-lapsarianism of Dort" and triumphalistic puritanism.[81] The evidence seems to be the fact that the NGK was a Reformed church (and not Lutheran or Methodist) and the fact that

Afrikaners tended to see a close parallel between themselves and ancient Israel at certain stages of their history. The following considerations have to be kept in mind when it is asserted that Calvinism caused or strengthened racial discrimination:

1. Racial discrimination and prejudice is a universal phenomenon where differences based on race, culture, and religion coincide.

2. The belief of being in some sense a nation with a God-given purpose was likewise not restricted to Calvinistic nations. Imperial Russia developed a "sense of destiny" without Calvinism.

3. For a people of one book (i.e., the Bible) it is the most natural thing in the world to draw parallels between themselves and Israel. This phenomenon also occurred among other tribes in Africa (e.g., Biafra in 1967) and Asia. The people themselves, moreover, very seldom take the parallel as literally as outsiders suppose.[82] Somehow only the critics are entitled to use symbolic language.

4. I have already suggested that South African Calvinism was weak compared, for example, to English and American Puritanism and Scots and Dutch Calvinism. Its influence has therefore been overrated.

5. It is not quite clear what de Kiewiet means by "the version of Calvinism which withholds the full grace of God to the natives," but W. A. de Klerk assumes that supralapsarianism played a role in the formation of the character of the Afrikaner.[83] Yet it would be difficult to find a Reformed confession with less emphasis on the doctrine of election than the Heidelberg Catechism, the main source book of South African Calvinism. "Reprobation" is not even mentioned. The same is true of the Belgic Confession.[84] And although Bogermann, who commanded the Remonstrants to leave the meeting of the Synod of Dort, was a supralapsarian, it is generally acknowledged that the famous Canons are infralapsarian.[85]

6. Although Calvinistic theologians did not approve of the marriages of van der Kemp and James Read, it would be difficult to find one of them who approved of racial discrimination. The attitude of van Lier and Philip has already been noted. The French missionary E. Casalis was shocked when he found that the descendants of the Huguenots did not approve of the presence of blacks in the church.[86] William Robertson was successful in keeping his colored converts in the church, in spite of opposition.[87] The Cape Synod agreed reluctantly to allow white members at Stockenström to withdraw, obviously as a temporary measure.[88] Dirk Postma of the GKSA had an uphill struggle to convince some of his members of their wrong attitude toward blacks, but he persisted.[89]

7. Regarding the present century, I have noted that the three most influential leaders of Afrikanerdom, with all their great qualities of leadership and integrity, cannot be described as Calvinists. Because

D. F. Malan was formerly a minister of the NGK, his espousal of "apartheid" was seen as the final argument in support of the fact that Calvinism caused racial discrimination. There can be little doubt that Malan wanted to be a Christian politician and that he believed that the Christian religion should play a decisive role in this country. Theologically, however, he was much closer to the Christian socialists than to traditional Calvinism.[90] The fact that he came to office as Prime Minister shortly after World War II also earned him the accusation of being a Nazi. Yet it so happened that he stoutly opposed any suggestion of national-socialism as being a possible ally of Afrikanerdom during the war time.[91] Ironically, and sad to say, there was some sympathy with national-socialism in South Africa during the thirties, even in Reformed circles.

In spite of evidence that tends to disprove a direct causal relationship between Calvinism and racial discrimination, some Calvinist support of South African racial policies has to be considered. Attention will also be drawn to Calvinist criticism of these policies.

### Calvinist support of apartheid

Apartheid, or separate development, may be defined as a policy of segregation based on racial, linguistic, and cultural differences, aimed at the eventual separation of the population into independent or interdependent states by making use of residential, educational, political, and a limited socio-economic differentiation. South Africans distinguish between "petty apartheid," indicating personal and social discrimination, and "big apartheid," which indicates the agricultural, industrial, and educational development of the black territories of South Africa.

*Qualified support.* Eric Walker called Philip "a convinced segregationist" because of the fact that he wanted the blacks (and the whites) to have security of tenure of their lands.[92] His belief in equality did not force him to accept the idea of total assimilation of one group by the other. In the sense that apartheid was an attempt to provide (rather belatedly) for this territorial and associated cultural integrity, it had the support of numerous Calvinists.

From the black side no less a person than Tiyo Soga was deeply concerned about the maintenance of this cultural and territorial integrity. Donovan Williams calls Soga the "father of black nationalism in South Africa" for this reason.[93] Soga was first and foremost a minister of the gospel. He gave up his life in incessant labors for the salvation of his people, and it would be an injury to his memory to suggest that he had a divided loyalty. Soga was married to a Scottish lady (Janet Burnside) and he abhorred racial discrimination, but he could not accept the idea that the Xhosa people should be culturally assimilated with the British, because he loved the history, traditions, language, and institutions of his people.[94] Insofar as apartheid advocates the retention, and even the expansion, of a people's territory, it seems to be related to the liberal Calvinism of such as Woodrow Wilson. At the very least it is not incompatible with Calvinism on this issue and as such has been supported by modern Calvinists.

The problem of cultural integrity is not equally clear-cut. Cultural particularism went hand in hand with the Reformation, at least concerning the use of the vernacular in worship and Bible translation. Calvinistic missionaries, from John Eliot and William Carey onward, were always among the first to use the vernacular languages and to translate the Scriptures into them. In spite of the remarkable theological unity of Calvinism, it stimulated more Confessions of Faith than the more state-oriented Lutheranism. But the intellectual and spiritual unity of Calvinism is equally important. In spite of their variety, it is their unity that makes these Confessions recognizable as Reformed documents.

Calvinists accepted the cultural pluralism implied in the doctrine of apartheid. But the latent paganism in every culture has not received sufficient attention in the Calvinistic support for "cultural apartheid." Calvinists welcomed the proliferation of state schools for each cultural group, but the Christian basis of the cultural school has not yet been satisfactorily defined. Qualified support for apartheid, however, is shifting from emphasizing the diversity to emphasizing the unity of Christian cultural expression.

*"Scholastic" support.* South African Calvinism received a major setback when certain scholars ostensibly succeeded in using the concept of sphere sovereignty to justify the legally enforced and systematic separation of races.[95] The result was that the majority of ministers in sympathy with Kuyper and Dooyeweerd were effectively silenced where they were most urgently needed, namely in a courageous and constructive criticism of apartheid. With a misguided sense of loyalty some even entered the lists in defense of apartheid.[96]

But this defense was bound to be "scholastic" in the sense that it could not afford to face the facts about hardship and injustices caused by the application of the policy. Or, if they were faced, they were always ascribed to "human weakness" in the imperfect application of a good policy. It was seldom suggested that the character of the theory might be the reason for its wrong application. A theory based on the impeccable authority of Kuyper could not be wrong!

And here W. A. de Klerk was correct in pointing out that Calvinism contributed to apartheid, although, as he also pointed out, this was not a valid use of Calvinism,[97] not even a valid application of Kuyperian Calvinism. True Calvinism, seeking the glory of God, cannot make a human policy into an ideology. Unfortunately people who call themselves Calvinists can do that. And when apartheid was propagated as being "for the salvation of the white man in South Africa," a policy became a messianic ideology.

## Calvinist criticism of apartheid

In 1955 B. B. Keet, professor of Systematic Theology at Stellenbosch (and a former student of Herman Bavinck), warned against the negative and divisive tendencies of apartheid in his book *Suid Afrika Waarheen?*[98] He also warned that its impracticability made it a false dream. His was a prophetic voice, based on sound "biblical common sense," but it made little headway against the rising tide. Also, at Potchefstroom, a few academics warned against the danger of making human traditions more important than the Word of God. A decade later the periodical *Woord en Daad* continued this "Potchefstroom tradition" of constructive criticism. In the sixties, C. F. Beyers Naude came out strongly with a rejection of apartheid, eventually at great personal sacrifice. Individual ministers never stopped preaching the duty of love toward the black neighbor.

From the English side, Presbyterian ministers with a new interest in Calvin rejected apartheid *in toto*. Douglas Bax saw the roots of apartheid partly in the traditional Calvinistic doctrine of common grace.[99] The most significant criticism was the Koinonia Declaration.[100] This document calls on the white Christians of South Africa to oppose all tendencies of the state to abuse its God-given power. It also criticizes the tendency among pastors, black and white, to identify the political aspirations of a certain group with the kingdom of God. The fact that black Calvinists were also involved was a hopeful sign. If grace is to triumph over race, all races must be included in the vision. Yet, although this document recognizes ethnic and cultural differences, it refuses to make them decisive. But in spite of its moderation the declaration was too specific and pointed in its criticism for the "scholastic" defenders of the "traditional way of life."

### CONCLUSION

The strength of Calvinism in South Africa has been overrated by friend and foe. In spite of the fact that the first political party was co-founded by a Calvinist, Calvinism very seldom played a decisive role in South African politics. When the traditional limited and patriarchal apartheid was forged into a policy with messianic overtones, Calvinist support was more in evidence than Calvinistic criticism. This was unworthy and untypical of historical Calvinism, but can partly be explained by the good aspects in the policy of separate development. The present government policies of moving away from discrimination and of favoring constitutional renewal are to be welcomed, but Calvinists must bear their specific witness to the kingdom of God and continue to live in faith, hope, and love in South Africa.

But South Africa is part of Africa. If Warfield is correct in saying that Calvinism is "the more modern and specific title of Augustinianism"[101] then Calvinism was indigenous to Africa. In the strange providence of God, this African theology was absent from Africa for more than a millennium. When Tiyo Soga was ordained, Africa was still largely an unknown continent. In the following year (1857) appeared Livingstone's "Missionary Travels and Researches," which sparked a greater interest in the expansion of the church in Africa. When Soga returned to Africa in 1857, he prayed: "God, Lord of Truth, fulfil now Your promise and let all nations of the world obtain salvation. Rule, Lord Jesus, rule, for peace comes only through You. Because of our confusion the country is being destroyed. Look in mercy on our land and forgive our sins. . . ."[102] *Forgive, rule, fulfill Your promise. . . .* The church in South Africa cannot afford to neglect this prayer of the black Calvinist Tiyo, the son of Soga.

# Epilogue

In conclusion the authors of the various chapters of this book hope that they have presented a clear picture of the influence of Calvin and Calvinism in the Western world. Much more could have been said by way of additional detail and the consideration of problems that have arisen over the past four centuries. But they trust that in this short form readers, whether Calvinists or not, will find information that will give them a broad perspective on the influence of one of the world's great Christians—a perspective that may even change their views of Calvin and the system of biblical theology he set forth.

As one attempts to summarize the influence of Calvin and Calvinism set forth in this work, one cannot but recognize that it was both biblical and practical. Also one is enabled to see how Calvinism influenced the development of the culture of the Western world. At the same time, however, those chapters that have brought the story down to the present day reveal that Calvinism has lost much of its appeal and influence because of the growing acceptance of secular humanism in the world. Yet there is always a note of hope, for repeatedly these chapters close by pointing out that a revival of Calvinism seems to be taking place in the Western world despite all apparent tendencies to the contrary.

In this work we have sought to honor Professor Paul Woolley, who has taught the history of Calvinism for many years. But we have also sought to explain what Calvinism is and its practical effects in history since the sixteenth century. Most important of all, however, we trust that this work will stimulate Christians to greater perseverance and diligence in their work as Christians to "the glory of God alone."

*SOLI DEO GLORIA*

# Notes

## Chapter 1

[1] Writing in the 1930s, the outstanding Austrian Calvin scholar Josef Bohatec reported that the more recent Calvin scholarship had been attempting to determine what characterizes the Calvinistic world of thought as it relates to church, state, and society: "Geht das Interesse der neueren Forschung darauf aus, die Eigenart der calvinischen, auf die kirchliche, staatliche und soziale Wirklichkeit sich beziehenden Gedankenwelt zu bestimmen." Josef Bohatec, *Calvin's Lehre von Staat und Kirche: mit besonderen Berüchtsichtigung des Organismusgedankens* (Breslau: Marcus, 1937), p. xiii.

[2] Ed. Baum et al., *Corpus Reformatorum: Ioannis Calvini Opera quae Supersunt Omnia,* 7, 516. (Hereinafter referred to as Calvin, *Opera.)*

[3] Josef Bohatec has explored in great detail Calvin's relationship to the French humanism of his time, more particularly to that of the acknowledged leader of the French Renaissance, Guillaume Budé. Josef Bohatec, *Budé und Calvin; Studien zur Gedankenwelt des französischen Frühhumanismus* (Graz: Hermann Böhlaus, 1950). (Hereinafter referred to as *Budé und Calvin.)*

[4] Calvin, *Opera,* 7, 516. Cf. Bohatec, *Budé und Calvin,* p. 121.

[5] Ibid., 34, 304; 31, 94. Cf. Bohatec, *Budé und Calvin,* p. 264.

[6] Ibid., 33, 577. Cf. Bohatec, *Budé und Calvin,* p. 264.

[7] Ibid., 40, 554. Cf. Bohatec, *Budé und Calvin,* pp. 270–80.

[8] Ford Lewis Battles and André Malan Hugo, *Calvin's Commentary on Seneca's De Clementia: With Introduction, Translation and Notes* (Leiden: Brill, 1969).

[9] Bohatec, *Budé und Calvin,* pp. 467, 470.

[10] Bohatec comes out boldly with the assertion "Calvin was a humanist" *("Calvin war Humanist").* Ibid., p. 472. He takes pains, however, to define carefully what he means here by "humanism" and to distinguish Calvin's humanism both from that of the Renaissance and from that of ancient culture. Cf., in particular, ibid., pp. 472–83.

[11] Cf. ibid., pp. 127–41.

[12] Ibid., p. 479.

[13] Ibid., p. 265.

[14] Calvin, *Opera,* 39, 251. Cf. Bohatec, *Budé und Calvin,* p. 254.

[15] Wilhelm Risse, *Die Logik der Neuzeit.* I: *1500–1640.* (Stuttgart-Bad Cannstadt: Friedrich Fromann, 1964), p. 81.

[16] Ibid., pp. 82, 106, 120.

[17] Calvin's idea of the law of nature, unlike that of the Stoics, does not rest on a conception of a universal cosmic reason but is inextricably bound up with the biblical doctrine of creation and the created order of things. Thus Calvin has a place for the doctrine of God's "common" or "preserving" grace. Bohatec discusses extensively Calvin's view of the law of nature, relating it to the doctrine of creation and showing Calvin's use of the doctrine of common grace.

Cf. Josef Bohatec, *Calvin und das Recht* (Graz: Hermann Böhlaus, 1934), pp. 22–24, and passim.

[18]Calvin, *Institutes,* I.1.1. Cf. Bohatec, *Budé und Calvin,* p. 243.

[19]According to Calvin, Bohatec writes, man in his state of nature willingly subjected himself to the rational norms. Bohatec, *Budé und Calvin,* p. 352.

[20]Calvin's idea of the *humanum,* in contrast to an idea of human autonomy, is manifest in his view that human freedom is not license but a freedom in obedience to God's law. "Die wahre Freiheit ist nicht Ungebundenheit, sondern Freiheit im Gehorsam, Freiheit unter dem Gesetz." Ibid., pp. 473–74.

[21]Léon Wencelius, *L'esthétique de Calvin* (Paris: Société d'Edition 'Les Belles Lettres', n.d.), p. 30.

[22]Wencelius closely associates Calvin's idea of beauty with order. In every description of beauty is found the notion of order. "La notion d'ordre se retrouve à chaque description de beauté. Tout chose belle est ordonnée en elle-même." Ibid., p. 46. "La création révèle Dieu . . . grâce à sa beauté, c'est-à-dire grâce à son ordre merveilleux." Ibid., p. 40; cf. p. 34.

[23]Bohatec, *Calvins Lehre von Staat und Kirche,* pp. 638–39.

[24]Calvin, *Opera,* 2, 252. Bohatec, *Calvins Lehre,* p. 640.

[25]Bohatec, *Calvins Lehre,* p. 636.

[26]"Der Beruf ist gehorsame Antwort auf den göttlichen Ruf." Ibid., p. 644.

[27]Ibid., p. 647.

[28]Ibid.

[29]Bohatec is especially interested in showing that Calvin's idea of calling is intimately connected with this organismic view. "Die Eigenart des calvinischen Berufsgedankens wurzelt in seiner Einordnung in das Organismussystem." Ibid., p. 646.

[30]Calvin, *Opera,* 28, 148.

[31]Ibid., 52, 276. Cf. Bohatec, *Calvins Lehre,* p. 652.

[32]Bohatec, *Calvins Lehre,* p. 653.

[33]Ibid., pp. 169, 171.

[34]Ibid., p. 12.

[35]Ibid., p. 37.

[36]Ibid., p. 38.

[37]Bohatec, *Calvin und das Recht,* p. 126.

[38]Ibid., pp. 97, 101, 106, 122, 127.

[39]Ibid., pp. 98f.

[40]For Calvin, says Bohatec, natural law, which is virtually identical with the moral law, serves as the *ratio* of all written laws. Ibid., p. 97. ". . . das Natturrecht Regel, Ziel und Grenze der positiven Gesetze ist." Ibid., p. 101; cf. p. 106.

[41]"Sphere-Sovereignty" *(Souvereiniteit in eigen kring)* is the title of the famous address delivered by Abraham Kuyper at the opening on October 20, 1880, of the Free University of Amsterdam, 3rd ed. (Kampen: Kok, 1930). Cf. Abraham Kuyper, *Lectures on Calvinism,* (Grand Rapids, Eerdmans, 1931, 1943).

[42]Bohatec, *Budé und Calvin,* p. 284.

[43]Calvin, *Opera,* 39, 588. Cf. Bohatec, *Budé und Calvin,* p. 282.

[44]Ibid., p. 298.

45Bohatec, *Calvin und das Recht,* p. 121; cf. pp. 211ff.

46Cf. Wencelius, *L'esthétique de Calvin,* pp. 225ff.

47Cf. Bohatec, *Budé und Calvin,* pp. 300ff.

48Ibid., p. 263.

49Cf. André Biéler, *La pensée économique et sociale de Calvin* (Geneva: Georg, 1961), pp. 74ff., and passim.

## Chapter 2

1Cf. W. B. Bowsky, *The Black Death: A Turning Point in History?* (New York: Holt, Rinehart & Winston, 1971), passim; P. Burke, ed., *Economy and Society in Early Modern Europe* (London: Routledge, 1972), pp. 43ff.; F. Mauro, *Le XVI e Siècle Européen, Aspects Économiques* (Paris: Presses Universitaire de France, 1966), part 2.

2Ibid., pp. 326ff.; C. M. Cipolla, *Before the Industrial Revolution* (London: Methuen, 1976), pp. 139ff.; P. Smith, *The Social Background of the Reformation* (New York: Collier, 1962), pp. 15ff.

3A. J. Slavin, ed., *The "New Monarchies" and Representative Assemblies* (Lexington, Mass.: Heath, 1964), passim; H. Pirenne et al., *La Fin du Moyren Age* (Paris: Presses Universitaire de France, 1931), pp. 30ff.; M. P. Gilmore, *The World of Humanism* (New York: Harper & Row, 1952), pp. 100ff.

4Ibid., pp. 182ff.; J. R. Hale, *Renaissance Europe 1480–1520* (London: Fontana, 1971), pp. 275ff.; D. Hay, *The Italian Renaissance in Its Historical Background* (Cambridge: Cambridge University Press, 1968), pp. 102ff.

5J. Bonneret, "Ésquisse de la vie des routes au XVI e siècle" *Révue des Questions Historiques* (1931), CXV, 1ff. This book gives a good picture of the increasing facility for traveling in Europe in the late fifteenth and early sixteenth centuries. See also Hale, *Renaissance Europe,* pp. 283ff.; G. R. Potter, ed., *New Cambridge Modern History* (Cambridge: Cambridge University Press, 1957), pp. 95ff.

6P. Chaunu, *Les Temps des Réformes* (Paris: Fayard, 1975), pp. 314ff.; Gilmore, *World of Humanism,* pp. 186ff.

7H. G. Koenigsberger and G. L. Mosse, *Europe in the Sixteenth Century* (London: Longman, 1968), pp. 21ff.; Mauro, *Aspect Économiques,* pp. 138ff.; Cipolla, *Before the Industrial Revolution,* pp. 231ff.

8Cf. P. Jeannin, *Les Marchands au XVI e Siècle* (Paris: de Sevil, 1957) passim; Smith, *Social Background,* pp. 69ff.

9H. J. Cohn, ed., *Government in Reformation Europe, 1520–1560* (New York: Harper & Row, 1970), passim; M. L. Bush, *Renaissance, Reformation and the Outer World* (London: Copp Clark, 1967), pp. 26ff.; H. Lapeyre, *Les Monarchies Européenes du XVI e Siècle* (Paris: Presses Universitaire de France, 1967), pp. 59ff.; G. R. Elton, ed., *New Cambridge Modern History* (Cambridge: Cambridge University Press, 1958), 2:438ff.

10Ibid., 1:334ff.; Lapeyre, *Les Monarchies Européenes,* pp. 130ff.

11Smith, *Social Background,* pp. 109ff.; M. Spinka, *Christian Thought From Erasmus to Berdyaev* (Englewood Cliffs, N.J.: Prentice-Hall, 1962), pp. 1ff.; N. E. Fehl, *Science and Culture* (Hong Kong: Chinese University, 1965), pp. 273ff.

[12]W. S. Reid, ed., *The Reformation: Revival or Revolution?* (New York: Holt, Rinehart & Winston, 1968), pp. 18ff.; J. Atkinson, *Martin Luther and the Birth of Protestantism* (Gretna, La.: Pelican, 1968), pp. 182ff.; C. L. Manschreck, *Melanchthon, the Quiet Reformer* (New York: Abingdon, 1958), pp. 82ff.

[13]J. Rilliet, *Zwingle le Troisième Homme de la Réforme* (Paris: Fayard, 1959); G. R. Potter, *Zwingli* (Cambridge: Cambridge University Press, 1976); G. W. Bromiley's "General Introduction" to the Library of Christian Classics' volume: *Zwingli and Bullinger* (Philadelphia: Westminster, 1953). All of these works give accurate pictures of the work of Zwingli.

[14]Andre Bouvier, *Henri Bullinger, le successeur de Zwingli* (Neuchâtel: Delachaux & Niéstlé, 1940). This book gives a detailed discussion of Bullinger's influence on the Reformation. Cf. also U. Gabler and E. Zsindeley, eds., *Bullinger–Tagung 1975* (Zurich: Institute fur Schweizerische Reformationsgeschichte, 1977).

[15]Henri Naef, *Les Origines de la Réforme à Genève* (Geneva: Jullien, 1968), II, 161ff.; W. Monter, *Calvin's Geneva* (New York: Wiley, 1967), pp. 29ff.

[16]There have been many lives of Calvin ranging from that of E. Doumergue, *Jean Calvin. Les hommes et les choses do son temps* (Lausanne: Bridel, 1899–1927), 7 vols; to the most recent one-volume biography by T. H. L. Parker, *John Calvin* (London: Dent, 1975).

[17]J. Murray, *Calvin on Scripture and Divine Sovereignty* (Grand Rapids: Baker, 1960), pp. 11ff.; A. D. R. Polman, "Calvin on the Inspiration of Scripture," in *John Calvin, Contemporary Prophet*, ed. J. T. Hoogstra (Grand Rapids: Baker, 1959); John Calvin, *Institutes of the Christian Religion*, ed. J. T. McNeill and F. L. Battles (Philadelphia: Westminster, 1960), 1:6–10.

[18]Ibid., 1:5; A. Kuyper, *Lectures on Calvinism* (Grand Rapids: Eerdmans, 1931), pp. 110ff.; A. Lecerf, *Études Calvinistes* (Neuchâtel: Delachaux et Nièstlè, 1949), pp. 11ff.

[19]Ibid., pp. 115; H. H. Meeter, *Calvinism*, 2nd ed. (Grand Rapids: Zondervan, n.d.), pp. 27ff.

[20]T. H. L. Parker, *The Oracles of God: An Introduction to the Preaching of John Calvin*, (London Lutterworth, 1947), pp. 22ff.; J. Calvin, *Sermons*, ed. A-M. Schmidt and J. de Saussure, (Paris: Edits. "Je Sers," 1936). The latter contains a very enlightening preface on this subject. Cf. also W. Mulhaupt, *Die Predigt Calvins* (Berlin: De Gruyter, 1931), passim.

[21]Cf. W. S. Reid, "Calvin and the Founding of the Academy of Geneva," *Westminster Theological Journal* 18 (1955): 1ff; Parker, *Calvin*, pp. 126ff.

[22]Ibid., pp. 117ff.; Monter, *Calvin's Geneva*, pp. 93ff.; R. W. Collins, *Calvin and the Libertines of Geneva*, ed. F. D. Blackley (Toronto: Clark, Irwin, 1968), pp. 153ff.

[23]Monter, *Calvin's Geneva*, pp. 165ff.; C. H. Martin, *Les Protestants refugiés à Genève au temps de Calvin, 1555–1560* (Geneva: Jullien, 1915); H. de Vries de Heeklingen, *Genève, Pépinière de Calvinisme Hollandais* (Fribourg: Fragnière, 1918), 1:44ff.; J. Pannier, "Les rèsidences successives des étudiants écossais à Paris," *Association François-Écossaise*, Bulletin (1929) :33–34; A. A. van Schelven, *Het Calvinisme Gedurende zijn Bloeitijd*, 2 vols. (Amsterdam: ten Have, 1943).

[24]Parker, *Calvin,* pp. 101ff.; R. Stauffer, *L'humanité de Calvin* (Neuchâtel: Delachaux et Nièstlè, 1964), passim; Collins, *Calvin and the Libertines,* pp. 201ff.

[25]Bouvier, *Henri Bullinger,* pp. 110ff.; W. Nijenhuis, *Calvinus Oecumenicus* (The Hague: Nijhoff, 1959), pp. 92ff.

[26]Ibid., pp. 6ff.; J. D. Benoit, "Calvin the Letter-writer," in *John Calvin,* ed. G. E. Duffield (Nashville: Abingdon, 1966), pp. 67ff.

[27]B. B. Warfield, *Calvin and Calvinism* (New York: Oxford University Press, 1931), pp. 373ff.; Calvin, *Institutes,* ed. J. T. McNeill and F. L. Battles, Introduction.

[28]T. H. L. Parker, *Calvin's New Testament Commentaries* (Grand Rapids: Eerdmans, 1971), pp. 49ff.; T. H. L. Parker, "Calvin the Biblical Expositor," *Calvin,* ed. Duffield, pp. 176.

[29]*Tracts Relating to the Reformation by John Calvin,* ed. Henry Beveridge; D. A. Erichson, *Bibliographia Calviniana* (Nieuwkoop: de Graaf, 1960), pp. 6ff.

[30]F. M. Higman, *The Style of John Calvin in His French Polemical Treatises* (Oxford: Oxford University Press, 1967), passim; A. Veerman, *De Stijl van Calvijn in de Institutio Christianae Religionis* (Utrecht: Kemink & Zoon, 1943), passim; Warfield, *Calvin and Calvinism,* pp. 373ff.; P. E. Hughes, "The Pen of the Prophet," in Hoogstra, *John Calvin,* pp. 71ff.

[31]Chaunu, *Les Temps des Réformes,* pp. 523ff.; Collins, *Calvin and the Libertines,* pp. 32ff.; *Calvin's Commentary on Seneca's de Clementia,* ed. F. L. Battles and A. M. Hugo (Leiden: Brill, 1969), pp. 63ff.; J. Bohatec, *Budé und Calvin* (Graz: H. Böhlaus, 1950), pp. 119ff.

[32]W. S. Reid, "Calvin's Interpretation of the Reformation," *The Evangelical Quarterly,* 29 (1957): 4ff.; cf. also Atkinson, *Martin Luther,* pp. 275ff.; B. B. Warfield, *Calvin as a Theologian and Calvinism Today* (London: Sovereign Grace Union, 1951), pp. 5ff.; J. I. Packer, "Calvin the Theologian," in *Calvin,* ed. Duffield, pp. 149ff.

[33]Cf. W. S. Reid, "The Impact of Calvinism on Sixteenth Century Culture," *Bulletin of the International Association for Reformed Faith and Action* 10 (1967): 3ff.; J. T. McNeill, *The History and Character of Calvinism* (New York: Oxford University Press, 1954), pp. 226ff.

[34]J. T. McNeill, ed., *John Calvin on God and Political Duty,* (New York: Liberal Arts, 1950), pp. viiff. Cf. also L. Maimbourg, *Histoire du Calvinisme* 2nd ed. (Paris: Mabre-Camoisy, 1682), "Épître au Roy."

[35]M. Weber, *The Protestant Ethic and the Spirit of Capitalism,* ed. T. Parsons and R. H. Tawney (New York: Scribner, 1958), pp. 1ff., 98ff.

## Chapter 3

[1]*Corpus Reformatorum,* ed. G. Baum, E. Cunitz, E. Reuss (Beunsvigae: Schwetschke, 1870). *Calvini Opera Omnia (C.O.),* IX, col. 891–92: "Quand ie vins premierement en ceste eglise il n'y avoit quasi comme rien. On preschoit et puis c'est tout. On cerchoit bien les idoles et les brusloit-on, main il n'y avoit acune reformation. Tout estoit en tumulte."

[2]Amedée Roget, *Histoire du Peuple de Genève* (Nieuwkoop: B. DeGraaf,

repr. 1976), Vols. 2–7; E. William Monter, *Calvin's Geneva* (New York: Wiley, 1967), pp. 137–39; Robert Henderson, *The Teaching Office in the Reformed Tradition* (Philadelphia: Westminster, 1962), pp. 56–71.

³Philip Schaff, *History of the Christian Church,* vol. 8, (1960; reprint ed., Grand Rapids: Eerdmans, 1979), pp. 481–82; James Mackinnon, *Calvin and the Reformation* (London: Longmans, Green, 1936), pp. 77–81.

⁴Schaff, *History of the Christian Church,* p. 491.

⁵Thomas M. Lindsay, *History of the Reformation,* vol. 2, (Edinburgh: T. & T. Clark, repr. 1964), pp. 108–9. These laws existed throughout Europe until the end of the seventeenth century. Cf. Schaff, *History of the Christian Church,* pp. 493ff.; Gottfried W. Locher, *Die zwinglische Reformation im Rahmen der europäischen Kirchengeschichte* (Göttingen: Vandenhoeck & Ruprecht, 1979), p. 193.

⁶Philip E. Hughes, "The Geneva of John Calvin," *The Churchman* 78 (1964): 257. Cf. Mackinnon, *Calvin and the Reformation,* p. 81ff.

⁷Hughes, "Geneva," p. 261.

⁸Ibid., pp. 261–65.

⁹William Cunningham, *The Reformers and the Theology of the Reformation* (Edinburgh and Carlisle: Banner of Truth Trust, repr. 1967), pp. 224ff.; Lindsay, *History of the Reformation,* p. 111; George P. Fisher, *The Reformation* (New York: Scribner, 1888), p. 435; James I. Good, *History of the Swiss Reformed Church since the Reformation* (Philadelphia: Board of the Reformed Church in the U.S., 1913), pp. 16ff.; R. Staehelin, *Huldreich Zwingli, sein Leben und Wirken* II (Basel, 1897), p. 144.

¹⁰Robert C. Walton, "The Institutionalization of the Reformation at Zurich," *Zwingliana* vol. 13, no. 8 (1972), p. 505.

¹¹Bullinger even states his disagreement with Calvin. A.-I. Herminjard, *Correspondance des Reformateurs dans les pays de langue français,* vol. 9 (Geneva: George & Cie., 1897), pp. 116–21; Calvin says, "The church does not assume what is proper to the magistrate; nor can the magistrate execute what is carried out by the church." *Institutes* IV,11,3. Cf. R. Ley, *Kirchenzucht bei Zwingli* (Zurich: Zwingli Verlag, 1948), pp. 99–105.

¹²Calvin's ideas were implemented only in the French church and to a degree in the church of Knox. Cf. Schaff, *History of the Christian Church,* p. 473; Lindsay, *History of the Reformation,* p. 113.

¹³Hughes, "Geneva," p. 271. "Geneva, indeed, became the most famous haven for evangelical fugitives of the day."

¹⁴Ibid.

¹⁵*C.O.,* IX,31–32. "No one of us denies that the body and blood of Christ are communicated to us. But the question is . . ." Cf. Joseph N. Tylenda, "Calvin's Understanding of the Communication of Properties," *Westminster Theological Journal* 38: 63–66.

¹⁶Zwingli, *Expositio Christianae Fidei,* H. A. Niemeyer, *Collectio Confessionem in ecclesiis reformatis publicatarum* (Lipsiae: Klinkhardti, 1840), pp. 44–50. Cf. "On the Lord's Supper," *Library of Christian Clasics,* Zwingli and Bullinger, ed. G. W. Bromiley (Philadelphia: Westminster, 1953), pp. 189, 193, 199, 218, 225, 228; First Helvetic Confession, Article 23, Niemeyer, *Collectio* pp. 120ff.

[17]*C.O.*, XIII, 457; Calvinus Myconio 1549. Cf. W. Kolfhaus, "Der Verkehr Calvins mit Bullinger," *Calvinstudien*, ed. J. Bohatek (Leipzig: Rudolf Haupt, 1909), p. 47; E. Bizer, *Studien zur Geschichte des Abendmahlsstreits im 16. Jahrhundert*, repr. (Darmstadt, 1962), p. 285; Usteri, "Vertiefung der Zwinglischen Sakraments - und Tauflehre bei Bullinger," *Theologische Studien und Kritiken*, 1883 4:730ff.; O. E. Strasser, "Der Consensus Tigurinus," *Zwingliana* 9 (1949–53): 5.

[18]Kolfhaus, "Verkehr," p. 47.

[19]Cf. *The Decades of Henry Bullinger*, Parker Society 4:465 as cited in Pruett, "A Protestant Doctrine of the Eucharistic Presence," *Calvin Theological Journal* 10 (1975): 144. Bizer agrees, "Studien," p. 285.

[20]Pruett, "Eucharistic Presence," pp. 144–45.

[21]Kolfhaus, "Verkehr," pp. 47–48, 51; Schaff, *History of the Christian Church*, p. 471; Strasser, "Consensus Tigurinus," p. 4–5. In Bern, Calvin was called a Lutheran.

[22]*C.O.*, IX,514; Literalem sensum in his verbis; hoc est corpus meum, negamus fidei analogon esse: et simul asserimus a communi scripturae usu remotum, quotidies de sacramentis agitur."

[23]Ibid., 70; *Christi carne et Sanguine vere nos in sacra coene pasci. . . .*

[24]*Institutes*, IV,17, 5; IV,17, 11.

[25]*Institutes*, IV,17, 26; *C.O.*, IX,72, 221.

[26]*C.O.*, IX,33.

[27]Commentary on 1 Cor. 11:34, *C.O.*, XLIX,488.

[28]*C.O.*, IX,27.

[29]Ibid., 157.

[30]Ibid., 90.

[31]The helpful book by Uwe Plath, *Calvin und Basel in den Jahren 1552–1556* (Basler Beiträge zur Geschichtswissenschaft, Band 133 [Basel-Stuttgart: Helbring und Lichtenhahn, 1974]), sheds much light on the relationship between Calvin and the city on the Rhine. Especially after the execution of Servetus, Basel became rather hostile to Calvin. Cf. the review in *Renaissance Quarterly* 29 (1976) by W. Stanford Reid.

[32]Rudolf Pfister, *Kirchengeschichte der Schweiz*, Bd.II (Zurich: Theologischer Verlag), p. 299. Schaff, *History of the Christian Church*, says that Bibliander was "a distinguished Orientalist, 'the father of exegetical theology in Switzerland,' and a forerunner of Arminianism," p. 477.

[33]Pfister, *Kirchengeschichte*, p. 301, n. 301; Helmut Kressner, *Schweizer Ursprünge des anglikanischen Staatskirchentums*, Schriften des Vereins für Reformationsgeschichte, Nr. 170 (Gutersloh: C. Bertelsmann, 1953), pp. 46ff. Kressner also noted that England received, at least in part, her ideas of church government from Switzerland, pp. 73ff. Cf. Kurt Guggisberg, *Bernische Kirchengeschichte* (Bern: Paul Haupt, 1958), p. 173.

[34]Commentary on John 9:22, *C.O.*, XLVII,227; *C.O.*, VII,33–34; Commentary on 1 Cor. 5:11, *C.O.*, XLIX,386. Cf. F. W. Kampschulte, *Johann Calvin, seine Kirche und sein Staat* (Leipzig: Dunker & Humblot, 1869), p. 475; William A. Mueller, *Church and State in Luther and Calvin* (Garden City: Anchor Books, 1965), pp. 106–26; Benjamin C. Milner, Jr., *Calvin's Doctrine of the Church* (Leiden: Brill, 1970), pp. 175–79.

[35]The text may be found in Niemeyer, *Collectio,* pp. 462ff.; Schaff's English translation is found in *The Creeds of Christendom* (Grand Rapids: Baker, 1966), 3:831ff.

[36]Cf. Ernst Koch, *Die Theologie der Confession Helvetica Posterior,* Beiträge zur Geschichte und Lehre der Reformierten Kirche, Bd.27 (Neukirchen: Neukirchen Verlag, 1968); Charles Hodge, *Systematic Theology* (London: James Clarke, 1960), 3:634ff.; Schaff, *Creeds of Christendom,* 1:390–420; Pfister, *Kirchengeschichte,* pp. 308–12; Philip Hugues, ed., *The Encyclopedia of Christianity,* (Marshallton: The National Foundation for Christian Education, 1972), 3:102ff.

[37]E. William Monter, *Calvin's Geneva* (New York: Wiley, 1967), p. 201.

[38]Ibid., p. 209.

[39]W. Stanford Reid, "Calvin and the Founding of the Academy of Geneva," *Westminster Theological Journal* 18 (1955): 1–33.

[40]Pfister, *Kirchengeschichte,* p. 227.

[41]Monter, *Calvin's Geneva,* p. 212.

[42]This theory is propounded by Pfister, *Kirkengeschichte,* p. 228; Brian G. Armstrong, *Calvinism and the Amyraut Heresy* (Madison: University of Wisconsin Press, 1969), pp. 37–42; Walter Kickel, *Vernumft und Offenbarung bei Theodor Beza,* Beiträge zur Geschichte und Lehre der Reformierten Kirche, Bd.25 (Neukirchen: Neukirchen Verlag, 1967), pp. 159–69; Basil Hall, "Calvin against the Calvinists," in G. E. Duffield, ed., *John Calvin,* The Courtenay Studies in Reformation Theology, 1:25–28; Jack B. Rogers and Donald McKim, *The Authority and Interpretation of the Bible: An Historical Approach* (San Francisco: Harper and Row, 1979), pp. 162–65.

[43]Armstrong, *Amyraut Heresy,* p. 39.

[44]Cunningham, *Reformers,* pp. 349–412.

[45]Pfister, *Kirchengeschichte,* p. 411. Cf. Heiner Faulenbach, *Die Struktur der Theologie des Amandus Polanus von Polansdorf,* Basler Studien zur Historischen und Systematischen Theologie (Zurich: EVZ Verlag, 1967).

[46]Geoffrey W. Bromiley, *Historical Theology, An Introduction* (Grand Rapids: Eerdmans, 1978), p. 306. Bromiley also mistakenly notes that Wollebius took the chair of New Testament at Basel; it was actually the chair of Old Testament.

[47]Pfister, *Kirchengeschichte,* pp. 413–14.

[48]Besides Breitinger of Zurich, the following took part: Beck and Meyer of Basel, Diodati and Tronchin of Geneva, Rutimeyer of Bern and Koch of Schaffhausen. Cf. Good, *History of the Swiss Reformed Church,* pp. 18–31.

[49]Text in Niemeyer, *Collectio,* pp. 218–310; English in Archibald Alexander Hodge, *Outlines of Theology* (Grand Rapids: Zondervan, repr. 1972), pp. 656ff.

[50]A. A. Hodge, *Outlines of Theology,* p. 128.

[51]Schaff, *Creeds of Christendom,* 1:478–79; John Bowman, "A Forgotten Controversy," *The Evangelical Quarterly* 20 (1948): 52–55.

[52]Schaff, *Creeds of Christendom,* 1:481; Armstrong, *Amyraut Heresy,* his theology in its historical setting, pp. 120–57, his predestination teaching, pp. 169–221, et al.; C. Hodge, *Systematic Theology,* 2:332.

[53]It reappeared in the theology of Jonathan Edwards.

[54]Cf. Guillaume Eugène Theodore de Budé, *Vie de François Turretini, theologien genevois 1623–1687* (Lausanne: Georges Bridal Editeur, 1871).

[55]Turretin's work was also republished in 1847, and as Beardslee rightfully notices, this was important in light of Turretin's influence on the theology of Charles Hodge, *Reformed Dogmatics* (Grand Rapids: Baker, repr. 1977), p. 14.

[56]Rogers and McKim, *Authority and Interpretation*, pp. 174–75.

[57]Cf. Calvin's *Institutes*, I,7,4; I,8,1,3,5,12,13. Cf. Also Turretin, *Institutio Theologiae Elencticae*, Geneva, 1688, II,4,1; II,4,7; II,4,8; II,6,5.

[58]D. Paul Wernle, *Der schweizerische Protestantismus im 18. Jahrhundert*, Bd.I (Tübingen: Mohr, 1923), p. 494.

## Chapter 4

[1]Cf. *Eirenicon seu Synopsis doctrinae de natura et gratia* (Blois, 1633); Pierre Du Moulin, *Lettres au Synode d'Alençon en 1637 touchant les livres d'Amyraut et Testard ou Examen de leur doctrine* (Amsterdam, 1638); Lucien Rimbault, *Pierre Du Moulin* (Paris: Librairie philosophique J. Vrin, 1966), pp. 124ff.; Charles Delo, *Actes ecclésiastiques et civils de tous les Synodes nationaux des Eglises réformées de France* (La Haye, 1710), 2:571–76.

[2]John T. McNeill, ed., *Calvin: Institutes of the Christian Religion*, 2 vols., trans. Ford Lewis Battles (vols. 20 and 21 of The Library of Christian Classics) (Philadelphia: Westminster, 1960), 3.7.1.

[3]Cf. Samuel Mours, *Le Protestantisme en France au seizième siècle* (Paris: Librairie Protestante, 1959), p. 183.

[4]Pierre Courthial, ed., *Instruction et Confession de Foi*, modern French edition, Collection "Les Bergers et les Mages" (Paris, 1955), 79 pages.

[5]Claude Le Peintre and Pierre Le Clerc both became martyrs in the year of their appointment; cf. *Histoire ecclésiastique des Eglises réformées au Royaume de France* (Anvers: Imprimerie de Iean Remy, 1580), 1:42, 67.

[6]*Lettres de Jean Calvin* (Paris: Librairie Ch. Meyreuis, 1854), 1:301.

[7]Ibid., p. 431.

[8]Ibid., p. 371.

[9]Ibid., p. 382.

[10]*Histoire ecclésiastique*, 1:198.

[11]*Lettres de Jean Calvin*, 2:139.

[12]Ibid., p. 274.

[13]Ibid., p. 297.

[14]Agrippa d'Aubigné, *Histoire universelle*, (Paris: Librairie Renouard, 1897), 9:285.

[15]Michel Réveillaud, *La Confession de Foi chrétienne*, modern French edition La Revue Réformée (St. Germain-en-Laye, 1955).

[16]Paul Vulliaud, *La Clé traditionnelle des Evangiles* (Paris: Librairie Emile Nourry, 1936), pp. 8–9.

[17]Particularly noteworthy among du Moulin's works are the following: *Le Bouclier de la Foi (The Shield of Faith)* (1618), a rigorous and lively defense of the Confession of the Reformed Churches of the Kingdom of France; *Du Combat chrétien et des Afflictions (On the Christian Battle and Suffering)* (1622); *Traité de la Connaissance de Dieu (Treatise on the Knowledge of God)* (1625);

*De Juge des Controverses (On Judging Controversies)* (1630); and *L'Anatomie de la Messe (The Anatomy of the Mass)* (1636).

[18]Cf. R. Hooykaas, "Humanisme, Science et Réforme," *Free University Quarterly* (Amsterdam, 1958), pp. 167–294.

[19]The passages concerning the work of Bernard Palissy are taken from different volumes of the remarkable *Encyclopaedia Universalis,* in loc. (Paris, 1968ff.).

[20]Palissy is the author of *Traité des sels divers et de l'agriculture (A Treatise on Diverse Salts and Agriculture)* (1553); *Recepte véritable par laquelle tous les hommes de la France pourront apprendre à multiplier et augmenter leurs thrésors (The true means by which all Frenchmen may learn to multiply and increase their treasures)* (1563); and *Discours admirables de la nature des eaux et fontaines (Discourses that marvel at the nature of the activity of water and springs)* (1580).

[21]*Méthode de traiter les plaies faites par arquebuses et authres bâtons à feu et de celles faites par flèches, dards, et semblables (Method of Treatment for Wounds from Arquebuses and Other Firearms, and Those from Arrows, Darts and Suchlike)* (1545); *Brève collection de l'administration anatomique avec la manière de conjoindre les os. Et d'extraire les enfants tant morts que vivants du ventre de la mère lorsque nature de soi ne peut venir à son effet (Shorter Collection of Remedies of Anatomical Treatment with Instructions on how to Join Broken Bones Together, and for Extracting Infants Dead or Alive From Their Mother's Womb When Nature Cannot Itself Effect a Birth)* (1549); *Méthode curative des plaies et fractures de la tête humaine (Curative Method for Wounds and Fractures of the Human Head)* (1562); *Dix livres de la chirurgie avec le magasin des instruments nécessaires à icelle (Ten Books of Surgery With an Inventory of the Instruments Necessary for the Same* [Some of these instruments, with only minor modifications, are still in use today.]) (1564); *Traité de la peste, de la petite vérole et rougeole (Treatise on the Plague, Small Pox and Measles* [This book gives a detailed study of the phenomenon of contagion.]) (1568); *Des animaux et de l'excellence de l'homme (On Animals and the Excellence of Man)* (1579); *Le livre de la licorne (The Book of the Unicorn* [Paré demonstrates that this so-called animal does not exist.]) (1580).

[22]Cf. Paul Romane-Musculus, *La prière des mains,* Je sers (Paris, 1938).

[23]Among his more influential books are the following: *Recueil de petites Habitations (Collected Studies of Small Dwellings)* (1540, 1545); *Livre des Arcs (Book of Arches)* (1549); *Livre des Temples (Book of Protestant Church Buildings)* (1550); *Vues d'optique (Optical Diagrams)* (1551); *Livre d'Architecture (Book of Architecture)* (1559); *Monuments antiques (Ancient Monuments)* (1560); *Second Livre d'Architecture (Second Book of Architecture* (1561); *Livres des Edifices antiques et romains (Book of Ancient and Roman Edifices)* (1564).

[24]In *Introduction à la poësie française,* Nouvelle Revue Française (Paris, 1936).

[25]Cf. Albert-Marie Schmidt, *Jean Calvin et al tradition calvinienne,* Editions du Seuil (Paris, 1957).

[26]Cf. Emile G. Léonard, *Histoire générale du protestantisme* (Paris: Presses Universitaires de France, 1961), vols. 1–2; Auguste Lecert, *Etudes calvinistes*

(Paris: Delachaux et Niéstlé, 1948); Raoul Stephan, *Histoire du protestantisme français* (Paris: Club des Libraires de France, 1961).

## Chapter 5

[1]Cited in Emile Leonard, *A History of Protestantism* (London: Nelson, 1967), 2:80.

[2]John Calvin, "Petit Traicté monstrant que c'est que doit faire un homme fidèle cognoissant la verité de l'évangelie, quant il est entre les papistes," *Corpus Reformatorum,* vol. 34 (Brunswick, 1867), col. 566.

[3]Ibid., col. 572.

[4]Ibid., col. 580.

[5]Ibid., col. 571.

[6]Ibid., col. 568.

[7]Phyllis Mack Crew, *Calvinist Preaching and Iconoclasm in the Netherlands, 1544–1569* (London: Cambridge University Press, 1978).

[8]*Akten der Synode der Niederlaendischen Kirchen zu Emden vom. 4.-13. Oktober 1571,* herausgegeben von J. F. G. Goeters (Neukirchen-Vluyn: Neukirchen Verlag, 1971), p. 18.

[9]Belgic Confession, Article 29.

[10]James Arminius, *The Writings of James Arminius* (Grand Rapids: Baker, 1977), 3:489.

[11]Ibid., pp. 481, 491, 509.

[12]For the text see Howard B. Spaan, *Christian Reformed Church Government* (Grand Rapids: Kregel, 1968), p. 208.

[13]F. Ernest Stoeffler, *The Rise of Evangelical Pietism* (Leiden: Brill, 1965), p. 116.

[14]Ibid., pp. 127–33.

[15]Ibid., p. 116.

[16]*Reformed Dogmatics,* introduced and edited by John W. Beardslee III (New York: Oxford University Press, 1965), p. 10.

[17]Theodor Mueller-Krueger, *Der Protestantismus in Indonesien* (Stuttgart: Evangelisches Verlagswerk, 1968), p. 41.

[18]Matthijs Pieter Thomassen a Thuessink van der Hoop van Slochteren, *Kerk en Staat Volgens Groen Van Prinsterer* (Groningen: Oppenheim, 1905), p. 255.

[19]G. Groen Van Prinsterer, *The Anti-Revolutionary Principle,* trans. J. Faber (Grand Rapids: Groen Van Prinsterer Society, 1956), p. 42.

[20]Abraham Kuyper, *Calvinism: Six Stone Foundation Lectures* (Grand Rapids: Eerdmans, 1943).

[21]Frank Vanden Berg, *Abraham Kuyper* (St. Catharines, Ontario, Canada: Paedeia, 1978), p. 255.

## Chapter 6

[1]For Calvin's humanism, see Quirinus Breen, *John Calvin* (Grand Rapids: Eerdmans, 1931) and François Wendel, *Calvin et l'humanisme* (Paris: Presses Universitaire de France 1976).

[2]Still the best scholarly treatment of the interaction of Calvinism and

Lutheranism is Matthias Schneckenburger, *Vergleichende Darstellung des lutherischen und reformierten Lehrbegriffs* (Stuttgart: Metzler, 1855).

[3] Arthur C. Cochrane, *Reformed Confessions in the Sixteenth Century* (Philadelphia: Westminster, 1966), pp. 75–76; cf. references to the Reformed nature of worship, pp. 61–66, 71–72, 78–81.

[4] Studies showing the dependence of Lutheran Pietism on Reformed Puritanism include: F. Ernest Stoeffler, *The Rise of Evangelical Pietism* (Leiden: Brill, 1965) and August Lang, *Puritanismus und Pietismus* (Neukirchen: Erziehungsverein, 1941).

[5] Harold O. J. Brown, "John Laski, A Theological Biography" (Harvard University dissertation, 1967) is the best modern treatment of Laski.

[6] For "prophesyings" see Patrick Collinson, *The Elizabethan Puritan Movement* (Berkeley: University of California Press, 1967), passim; for "the exercise" see George David Henderson, *The Burning Bush* (Edinburgh: St. Andrew, 1957), chap. 2.

[7] Nevertheless, Luther's *Small Catechism*'s explication of the Ten Commandments is virtually indistinguishable from that of any Reformed catechism!

[8] J. Thomson, ed., *First General Presbyterian Council* (Edinburgh: Constable, 1877), pp. 28–51.

[9] Helpful studies of the Reformed/Lutheran conflicts over the Lord's Supper and the ascension and return of Christ, respectively, are Ernst Bizer, *Studien zur Geschichte des Abendmahlsstreits im 16. Jahrhundert* (Darmstadt: Wissenschaftliche Buchgesellschaft, 1962) and James B. Wagner, *Ascendit ad coelos* (Winterthur: Keller, 1964).

[10] James I. Good, *The Origin of the Reformed Church in Germany* (Reading, Pa.: Daniel Miller, 1887), pp. 203–13.

[11] Otto Weber, *Die Treue Gottes in der Geschichte der Kirche* (Neukirchen: Erziehungsverein, 1968), pp. 131–46.

[12] For insight into the significance of Ramus, see Perry Miller, *The New England Mind: the Seventeenth Century* (Boston: Beacon, 1954), chap. 7.

[13] Good, *Reformed Church in Germany*, p. 374.

[14] Jürgen Moltmann, *Christoph Pezel und der Calvinismus in Bremen* (Bremen: Einkehr, 1958).

[15] For covenant theology, the following are the most useful: Gottlob Schrenk, *Gottesreich und Bund* (Gütersloh: Bertelsmann, 1923); Charles S. McCoy, "The Covenant Theology of Johannes Cocceius" (Yale University dissertation, 1956); Heiner Faulenback, *Weg und zeil der Erkenntnis Christi* (Neukirchen: Erziehungsverein, 1973); Geerhardus Vos, *Redemptive History and Biblical Interpretation*, ed. Richard B. Gaffin, J.R. (Phillipsburg, N.J.: Presbyterian and Reformed, 1980).

[16] The Calvinistic non-Sabbatarian position was first expressed creedally in 1566 in the Second Helvetic Confession, where it is confessed that "we do not believe that one day is any holier than any other, or think that rest in itself is acceptable to God." (Cochrane, *Reformed Confessions,* p. 291).

[17] Some of the traditional Reformed attitude of resistance to unjust rulers can be seen in the Barthians' resistance to Hitler; it is significant that this was initiated in traditionally Reformed territory in Germany. See A. G. Cochrane *The Church's Confession Under Hitler* (Philadelphia: Westminster, 1962).

## Chapter 7

[1] According to recent research, the occupation of the Carpathian Basin took place in two phases, one in 670, the other in 896.

[2] Mihály Zsilinszky, *History of the Protestant Church in Hungary* (Budapest: Athenaeum Rt., 1907), p. 33.

[3] Ibid., p. 34.

[4] Peter Payne of Oxford, a Wyclifite refugee, first in Prague, then in Moldavia, exerted influence on the Hungarian "Hussite Bible" translation and the calendar attached to it. Cf. Sándor Fest, "Data Concerning the First Hungarian Translation of the Bible," in *Studies in English Philology* (Budapest: Pázmány University, 1937), 2:41.

[5] Zsilinszky, *Protestant Church in Hungary*, p. 34.

[6] Aladár Szabó, Jr., *History of the Reformed Churches in Hungary* (Debrecen: Debrecen, 1942), p. 4.

[7] Zsilinszky, *Protestant Church in Hungary*, p. 43.

[8] Ibid., pp. 36–39; Imre Revesz and George A. F. Knight, *History of the Hungarian Reformed Church* (Washington, D.C.: Hungarian Reformed Federation of America, 1956), p. 7.

[9] Zsilinszky, *Protestant Church in Hungary*, p. 43.

[10] Ibid., p. 39.

[11] Révész and Knight, *Hungarian Reformed Church*, p. 29; Szabó, *Reformed Churches in Hungary*, p. 5; Sándor Bíró et al., *The History of the Hungarian Reformed Church* (Budapest: Kossuth, 1949), p. 29.

[12] Zsilinszky, *Protestant Church in Hungary*, p. 84.

[13] Elemér Bakó et al., *History of Hungary* (Munchen: Hunnia, 1951), p. 74.

[14] János Csohány, "The Reformed Church in the Sixteenth Century and the Turks," in *Studia et Acta Ecclesiastica* (Budapest: Magyarországi Református Egyház, 1973), 3:891–901; Antal Földváry, *The Hungarian Reformed Church and the Turkish Occupation* (Budapest: Rábaközi, 1940), pp. 9–210.

[15] János Csohány, "Pal Thuri Farkas's Circular Letter," in *Studia et Acta Ecclesiastica*, 3:919.

[16] M. Eugene Osterhaven, "Transylvania," *Reformed Review* (Holland, Mich., 1968), p. 22.

[17] Révész and Knight, *Hungarian Reformed Church*, p. 8; Szabó, *Reformed Churches in Hungary;* Bíró et al., *Hungarian Reformed Church*, p. 31.

[18] Michael Bucsay, *Gregory Szegedi, Reformer in Debrecen, a Pioneer of the Calvinian Trend in Hungary* (Budapest: Balazs, 1945), pp. 10ff.; Jenő Zoványi, *Lexicon of Church History* (Budapest: Reformed Church in Hungary, 1977), p. 289.

[19] Michael Bucsay, *Gregory Belényesi, Calvin's Hungarian Student* (Budapest: Balázs, 1944), pp. 85–86.

[20] Bucsay, *Gregory Szegedi*, p. 10.

[21] Ibid., p. 14.

[22] Ibid., p. 11.

[23] Ibid., p. 12.

[24] Ibid., p. 11.

[25] Zoványi, *Lexicon*, p. 289.

[26] Ibid., p. 290; Zsilinszky, *Protestant Church in Hungary*, p. 87.

[27]Zsilinszky, *Protestant Church in Hungary*, p. 87; Géza Kathona, "Helvetic Theological Elements in the Theological Views of Stephen Szegedi Kis," in *Studia et Acta Ecclesiastica*, 3:23.

[28]Zoványi, *Lexicon*, p. 693.

[29]Osterhaven, "Transylvania," pp. 22-24.

[30]Kathona, "Helvetic Theological Elements," p. 15.

[31]Zoványi, *Lexicon*, pp. 48, 252, 584.

[32]Ferenc Balogh, *Details of the Hungarian Protestant Church History* (Debrecen, 1872), p. 73; Michael Bucsay, "Stephen Szegedi Kis's 'Speculum,'" in *Studia et Acta Ecclesiastica*, 3:110; Kathona, "Helvetic Theological Elements," pp. 16, 106.

[33]Zoványi, *Lexicon*, p. 584.

[34]Kathona, "Helvetic Theological Elements," pp. 13-106.

[35]Ibid., pp. 20-21.

[36]Ibid., pp. 17-19; Bucsay, "Stephen Szegedi Kis's 'Speculum,'" pp. 99-106.

[37]Kathona, "Helvetic Theological Elements," pp. 24, 101.

[38]Ibid., pp. 105-6.

[39]Professor Bucsay theorizes the possible identity of Gregory Belényesi as "Calvin's Hungarian student" and Gregory Szegedi as the "reformer in Debrecen, a pioneer of the Calvinian trend in Hungary."

[40]Bucsay, *Gregory Szegedi*, p. 4.

[41]L. Balázs, "Laskai Csókás Péter 'De homine' című művébek elő-szavából," in *Studia et Acta Ecclesiastica*, 3:1017ff.

[42]Bucsay, *Gregory Szegedi*, p. 36.

[43]Ibid., pp. 53-54.

[44]Ibid., pp. 48-49.

[45]Ibid., pp. 49-50.

[46]Ibid., pp. 60-61.

[47]Ibid., pp. 67-73. The communication of the properties of either nature to the person. *Institutes*, II.14.1.

[48]Géza Kathona, "The Work of Peter Melius," in *Studia et Acta Ecclesiastica* (1967), 2:113.

[49]Paul Thuri Farkas's distich on Calvin's *Institutes:* "Ever since the time of Christ, apart from the apostolic writings / The ages did not bear another book like this."

[50]István Botta identifies Melius with Peter Somogyi, teacher in Vágsellye in northwestern Hungary, who twice suffered imprisonment and whose prison diary is extant. Peter Melius occasionally signed his name "Peter Somogyi" (that is, of Somogy, his county of birth). This theory fills the time gap of 1557 to 1558—the time between his departure from Wittenberg and his arrival in Debrecen. Cf. István Botta, *The Youth of Peter Melius* (Budapest: Akadémiai Kiadó, 1978).

[51]Barnabas Nagy, "The Works of Peter Melius," in *Studia et Acta Ecclesiastica*, 2:193-301.

[52]Kathona, "The Work of Peter Melius," 2:106-7.

[53]Nagy, "The Works of Peter Melius."

[54]Ibid., p. 213.

[55] Ibid., pp. 205-6; Kathona, "The Work of Peter Melius," 2:127-30.

[56] Nagy, "The Works of Peter Melius," pp. 232-35.

[57] Ibid., p. 185.

[58] Kathona, "The Work of Peter Melius," 2:130-33; Nagy, "The Works of Peter Melius," pp. 206-9.

[59] Zoványi, *Lexicon*, p. 621.

[60] "Praeter Apostolicas post Christi Tempora Chartas Huic peperere libro / saecula nulla parem."

[61] Kathona, "The Work of Peter Melius," 2:138; Nagy, "The Works of Peter Melius," pp. 210-11.

[62] Endre Tóth, "History of the Second Helvetic Confession in Hungary," in *Studia et Acta Ecclesiastica*, 2:13-99; Endre Zsindely, "Heinrich Bullinger's Hungarian Connections" in *Studia et Acta Ecclesiastica*, 2:57-58.

[63] Kathona, "The Work of Peter Melius," 2:155-57.

[64] Ibid., pp. 157-58; Nagy, "The Works of Peter Melius," pp. 232, 235.

[65] Barnabas Nagy, "The Appearance, History, and Editions of the Heidelberg Catechism in Hungary in the Sixteenth and Seventeenth Centuries," in *Studia et Acta Ecclesiastica* (1965), 1:17-91.

[66] Ibid., p. 19.

[67] Ibid., pp. 22-23.

[68] Kathona, "The Work of Peter Melius," 2:151-53; Géza Kathona, "The Deformation of the Heidelberg Catechism in the Struggle Against Antitrinitarianism," in *Studia et Acta Ecclesiastica*, 1:93-129.

[69] Nagy, "The Heidelberg Catechism in Hungary," p. 29

[70] Ibid., p. 28.

[71] Nagy, "The Works of Peter Melius," pp. 267-71; Kathona, "The Work of Peter Melius," pp. 172-73.

[72] Zoványi, *Lexicon*, pp. 167, 182, 559.

[73] Ibid., p. 86; Zsilinszky, *Protestant Church in Hungary*, p. 95.

[74] *Epistolae Ioannis Calvini*, no. 2057, to the king of Poland, *Corpus Reformatorum* (Brusvigae: Schwetschke, 1876), col. 329.

[75] *Confession of Tarcal-Torda*, 1562, 1563.

[76] János Makár, *János Kanizsai Pálfi and His Life Work* (New Brunswick, N.J.: privately published, 1961), p. 101.

[77] Kathona, "The Deformation of the Heidelberg Catechism," pp. 159-61; Nagy, "The Works of Peter Melius," pp. 237-39.

[78] Imre Czegle, "The Way of Hungarian Bible Translation Till Caspar Károli," in *Studia et Acta Ecclesiastica*, 3:501-12.

[79] S. Jószef Szabó, "Caspar Károli's Life and Work," in *Károli Memorial Book*, ed. Béla Vasady (Budapest: Coetus Theologorum, 1940), pp. 7-25; Czegle, "Hungarian Bible Translation," p. 512.

[80] Caspar Károli, *Foreword to the Bible* (Visol: Mantskovit, 1590). Reprinted in *Studia et Acta Ecclesiastica*, 3:519-36.

[81] Szabó, "Caspar Károli's Life and Work," pp. 21-22.

[82] Károli, *Foreword*, p. 535.

[83] Personal communication from Kálmán Cs. Tóth. Also articles by G. Borsa and K. Cs. Tóth in "Magyar Zene" (1976), pp. 119-33; (1981), pp. 176-208.

[84] Nagy, "The Works of Peter Melius," p. 260.

[85]Ibid., pp. 268–69.

[86]K. Tóth, *Református*, pp. 217–22.


## Chapter 8

[1]John Foxe, *Acts and Monuments*, ed. J. Pratt, 4th ed. (London, 1843), III.589.

[2]Ibid., III.590.

[3]A. G. Dickens, *Lollards and Protestants in the Diocese of York, 1509–1558* (Oxford: University Press, 1959), p. 7.

[4]Foxe, *Acts and Monuments*, V.4.115.

[5]"Calvin against the Calvinist," in *John Calvin*, ed. G. E. Duffield (Grand Rapids: Eerdmans, 1966), p. 33.

[6]Author's translation from J. Calvin, *In Novum Testamentum Commentarii*, A. Tholuck, ed. (Berlin, 1834), VI, 331ff.

[7]*Letters of John Calvin*, trans. and ed. J. Bonnet (Edinburgh: Constable, 1858), II. no. CCXXIX, CCXLV.

[8]Ibid., II. no. CCLVII; *Original Letters Relating to the English Reformation*, Ed. H. Robinson (Cambridge: Parker Society, 1847), II. no. CCCXXXV.

[9]Ibid., II.548, 730.

[10]J. Calvin, *Commentary on the Prophet Isaiah*, ed. W. Pringle (Edinburgh: Calvin Translation Society, 1850), I.xixff.

[11]Calvin, *Commentary on the Epistle to the Hebrews, the Catholic Epistles, and the First and Second Epistles of Peter*, trans. W. B. Johnston (Grand Rapids: Eerdmans, 1963), p. 219ff.

[12]*Cal. Letts.* II.311, 315ff.

[13]*Orig. Letts.*, I. no. XIV.

[14]Ibid., I. no. CCCXXXVII; *Cal. Letts.*, II. no. CCXCIV.

[15]Ibid., II. no. CCXCVII; *Orig. Letts.*, II. no. CCCXXXVIII.

[16]*Cal. Letts.*, II. no. CCXCVIII.

[17]Ibid., II. no. CCCXL.

[18]Ibid., III. no. CCCLXXI; *Orig. Letts.*, II. no. CCCXXXIX. Under Elizabeth, Tremellius and Chevalier were successively professors of Hebrew at Cambridge.

[19]Ibid., I. no. LXXII.

[20]*Commentary on Isaiah*, I. xviff.

[21]*Cal. Letts.*, IV. no. DXXII.

[22]*Zurich Letters*, (Cambridge: Parker Society, 1845), II. no. XV; *Cal. Letts.*, IV. no. DXXXVII.

[23]Ibid., IV. no. DLIX.

[24]*Zurich Letts.*, II. no. XXI.

[25]*Cal. Letts*, IV. no. DLXV.

[26]Ibid., IV. no. DLXVI.

[27]*Zurich Letts.*, II. no. XLII.


## Chapter 9

[1]*Ioanni Calvini Opera* (Brunswick, 1863–1900), Calvin to Cranmer, Letter no. 1619, XIV, 313.

[2]*Original Letters* (Cambridge: Cambridge University Press, 1846), 1:48.

[3]C. H. Garrett, *The Marian Exiles,* (Cambridge: Cambridge University Press, 1938), pp. 32ff.

[4]S. K. Knox, "A study of the English Genevan Exiles" (B. L. H. thesis, Trinity College, Dublin, 1953), p. 130.

[5]John Strype, *Ecclesiastical Memorials,* (London: Wyat, 1721), III, iii, 42.

[6]The "middle way" of Elizabeth is that which was seen as somewhere between Roman Catholicism and the thorough reform many Protestants wanted.

[7]William Haller, *The Rise of Puritanism* (New York: Columbia University Press, 1938), p. 8.

[8]See Patrick Collinson, *The Elizabethan Puritan Movement* (London: Cape, 1967), pp. 29ff. See also Thomas Fuller, *The Church History of Great Britain* (Oxford: Oxford University Press, 1845), 4:327.

[9]S. L. Greenslade, *Cambridge History of the Bible* (Cambridge: Cambridge University Press, 1950), 3:158.

[10]F. F. Bruce, *The English Bible* (London: Lutterworth, 1961), p. 90.

[11]H. W. Robinson, *The Bible in Its Ancient and English Versions* (Oxford: Clarendon, 1940), p. 186.

[12]See Collinson, *Elizabethan Puritan Movement,* p. 140.

[13]Ibid., p. 110.

[14]Samuel Clarke, *The Marrow of Ecclesiastical History* (London: Miller, 1675), p. 415.

[15]Thomas Fuller, *Abel Redivivus* (London: Stafford, 1651), p. 434.

[16]Fuller, *Church History,* 5:170.

[17]Hereinafter called *Whether a Man.*

[18]*The Workes of that Famovs and Worthy minister of Christ in the Vniversitie of Cambridge, Mr. William Perkins* (Columbia: Legat, 1608–9) 1:356, 107ff.

[19]Beza's chart was produced in both *A Briefe Declaration* (London: Moptid and Mather, 1575) and *The Treasvre of Trueth* (1576). These books are exceedingly rare.

[20]T. Beza, *Briefe and Pithie* (London: Moptid and Mather, 1572), pp. 36–37.

[21]J. Calvin, *Concerning the Eternal Predestination of God* (Naperville, Ill.: Allenson, 1965), p. 135.

[22]For an exposition and defense of what may seem to some to be a controversial statement see my book: *Calvin and English Calvinism to 1649* (Oxford: Oxford University Press, 1979).

[23]"Does not the potter have the right to make out of the same lump of clay some pottery for noble purposes and some for common use?" (Rom. 9:21, NIV).

[24]*A Book of Christian Questions and Answers* (London: Harrison, 1572), pp. 84–85.

[25]John Calvin, *Institutes.* III. xxiii. 3.

[26]Translated as *A Christian and Plain Treatise of Predestination* in 1606.

[27]W. Perkins in preface, ibid.

[28]Hereinafter called *The Summe* (London: Young, 1633), this reached no fewer than eight editions in England between 1587 and 1633.

[29]Ursinus, *The Summe,* p. 94. Ursinus and his colleagues, including

Girolamo Zanchius (d. 1590), were preceded in this kind of thinking by
Wolfgang Musculus (d. 1563) and Henry Bullinger.

[30]Dudley Fenner, *Sacra Theologia* (Geneva: Vignon, 1589). Fenner may
have been the first Englishman to speak of this motif.

[31]Ursinus, *The Summe*, p. 39.

[32]Ibid., p. 95

[33]Ibid., p. 39.

[34]Perkins, *Workes*, 1:541.

[35]Ibid., 2:322.

[36]Ibid., 1:115.

[37]Ibid.

[38]Calvin, *Commentary*, 1 Cor. 1:9.

[39]*Institutes*, III.ii.38.

[40]*Commentary*, Joshua 3:10.

[41]*Institutes*, III.xiv.19.

[42]*Commentary*, 1 John 3:19.

[43]Ibid.

[44]*Commentary*, Romans 10:10.

[45]*Institutes*, II.iii.6.

[46]*Institutes*, III.ii.16.

[47]*Commentary*, Deuteronomy 29:4.

[48]Perkins, *Workes*, 1:126.

[49]Ibid., 1:362.

[50]Ibid., 1:290.

[51]T. Fuller, *The Holy State* (London: 1848), p. 82.

[52]M. M. Knappen, ed., *Two Elizabethan Diaries* (London, 1933), p. 109.

[53]*The Works of Thomas Goodwin* (Edinburgh: Nichol, 1861), 2:lviii.

[54]*Briefe Directions vnto a godly life* (1618), p. 30.

[55]*The Complete Works of Richard Sibbes, D.D.*, (Edinburgh: Nichol, 1862),
1:45.

[56]Ibid., p. 46.

[57]Ibid., 7:446.

[58]Ibid., 2:47.

[59]Ibid., 3:467.

[60]Perkins, *Workes*, 1:628.

[61]Sibbes, *Complete Works*, 6:522.

[62]J. Cotton, *Christ the Fountaine of Life* (London: Ibbitson, 1656), p. 40.

[63]Ibid., p. 41.

[64]Ibid., p. 43.

[65]See my "John Cotton—First English Calvinist?" *Westminster Conference
Papers* (1976).

[66]John Preston, *New Covenant* (London: Dawson, 1630), pp. 317–18.

[67]Ibid., pp. 321–25.

[68]Ibid., p. 358.

[69]Ibid., p. 389.

[70]Ibid., p. 392.

[71]John Preston, *The Breast-Plate of Faith and Love* (London: Jones, 1630),
1:63.

[72] Ibid., p. 64.

[73] I am indebted to J. I. Packer for this phrase. He used it in a conversation to describe certain "puritans."

[74] Giles Firman, *The Real Christian* (1670), p. 19.

[75] *Vnbeleevers Preparing,* (1638), p. 1.

[76] *The Soules Implantation* (London: Young, 1637), p. 26.

[77] *Vnbeleevers Preparing,* p. 120.

[78] W. Ames, *The Marrow of Sacred Divinity* (London: Griffin, 1643), pp. 8–9, passim.

[79] W. Ames, *An Analyticall Exposition of Both the Epistles of the Apostle Peter* (London: Rothwell, 1641), p. 4.

[80] Ibid.

[81] E. Calamy, *Gods Free Mercy to England* (London: Meredity, 1642), p. 20.

[82] *Journals of the House of Lords* (n.d.), 6:93.

[83] *Minutes of the Sessions of the Westminster Assembly of Divines* (Edinburgh: Blackwood, 1874), p. 270.

## Chapter 10

[1] John Knox, *The History of the Reformation in Scotland,* ed. W. C. Dickinson (Edinburgh: Nelson, 1949), 1:25.

[2] Ibid., p. 15.

[3] Ibid.

[4] Ibid., p. 69.

[5] Q. Kennedy, "Ane Compendius Tractive" (1558), in *The Wodrow Miscellany* (Edinburgh: Wodrow Society, 1844), p. 151.

[6] Knox, *History,* 1:290.

[7] Edward Irving, *Collected Writings* (London: Strahan, 1865), 1:602.

[8] P. Hume Brown, *John Knox* (Edinburgh: A. & C. Black, 1895), 2:148. Cf. also J. K. Cameron's edition of *The First Book of Discipline* (Edinburgh: St. Andrew, 1972).

[9] Knox, *History,* 2:29.

[10] A. Lang, *The History of Scotland* (Edinburgh: Blackwood, 1907), 2:86.

[11] Knox, *History,* 2:16.

[12] "The Reformation of Church Government in Scotland cleared from some Mistakes" (London: Bostock, n.d.).

[13] Cf. J. Kirk, ed., *The Second Book of Discipline* (Edinburgh: St. Andrew, 1980), pp. 51ff. for a different interpretation. (The Editor)

[14] Alexander Smellie, *Men of the Covenant* (Edinburgh: Melrose, 1924), p. 241.

[15] James Renwick, *Prefaces, Lectures and Sermons* (Glasgow: Bryce, 1776), p. 27.

[16] J. A. Froude, "The Influence of the Reformation on the Scottish Character," in *Short Studies on Great Subjects* (London: Longmans, Green, 1895), 1:180.

[17] G. Burnet, *History of His Own Time* (London: Evans, 1809), 1:410.

[18] A. R. Cousin, *Immanuel's Land and Other Pieces* (London: Nisbet, 1896).

[19] Geddes MacGregor, *Corpus Christi* (London: Macmillan, 1959), p. 85.

[20]N. MacLean, *Set Free* (London: Hodder & Stoughton, 1949), p. 212.

[21]*The United Kingdom Protestant Mission Handbook* (London: Evangelical Missionary Alliance, 1978), 2:12.

[22]Thomas Chalmers, *Works* (London: Constable, 1838–42), 21:175.

[23]Ibid., 9:459.

[24]Cf. the official *History of the Free Presbyterian Church* (Inverness: Free Presbyterian Church of Scotland Publications, 1975), pp. 156–63.

[25]Samuel Johnson, *Journey to the Western Islands of Scotland* (London: University Tutorial Press, n.d.), p. 115.

[26]D. A. Wilson and D. W. MacArthur, *Carlyle in Old Age* (London: Kegan Paul, 1934), p. 362.

[27]H. C. Whitley, *Thorns and Thistles* (Edinburgh: Edina, 1976), pp. 60ff.

## Chapter 11

[1]Francis A. Schaeffer, *How Shall We Then Live?: The Rise and Decline of Western Thought and Culture* (Old Tappan, N.J.: Revell, 1976), pp. 245, 249.

[2]Sydney E. Ahlstrom, *A Religious History of the American People* (New Haven: Yale University Press, 1972), p. 1090.

[3]"A Modell of Christian Charity," in Edmund S. Morgan, ed., *The Founding of Massachusetts: Historians and the Sources* (Indianapolis: Bobbs-Merrill, 1964), p. 191.

[4]Sacvan Bercovitch, *The Puritan Origins of the American Self* (New Haven: Yale University Press, 1975), p. 36.

[5]"A Modell of Christian Charity," pp. 202–4.

[6]"A Coppie of the Liberties of the Massachusetts Colonie in New England," in Edmund S. Morgan, ed., *Puritan Political Ideas, 1558–1794* (Indianapolis: Bobbs-Merrill, 1965), pp. 197–98.

[7]Roger Williams, "The Bloudy Tennet of Persecution," in *Puritan Political Ideas,* p. 208.

[8]"A Modell of Christian Charity," p. 203.

[9]Rousas J. Rushdoony, *This Independent Republic* (Nutley, N.J.: Craig, 1964), p. 32. Francis Schaeffer also makes much of this principle of *"Lex Rex"* in American history, *How Shall We Then Live?,* pp. 109–10.

[10]Thomas Paine, "Common Sense," in Loren Baritz, ed., *Sources of the American Mind* (New York: Wiley, 1966), 1:145.

[11]James Madison, "Federalist No. 10," in Baritz, *Sources of the American Mind,* 1:186.

[12]John Cotton, "An Exposition upon the 13th Chapter of Revelation" (London, 1656) in *The Puritans: A Sourcebook of Their Writings,* I., Perry Miller and Thomas H. Johnson, eds., (New York: 1963 [1938]), p. 213.

[13]John Adams, "A Dissertation on the Canon and the Feudal Law," (1765), in Baritz, ed., *Sources of the American Mind,* 1:115.

[14]I am indebted to the analysis of Nathan O. Hatch at this point, *The Sacred Cause of Liberty: Republican Thought and the Millennium in Revolutionary New England* (New Haven: Yale University Press, 1977). Hatch in turn cites Ernest H. Kantorowicz, *The King's Two Bodies: A Study in Political Theology* (Princeton: Princeton University Press, 1957), pp. 207–32 as the source of the

observations on secularization, Hatch, "Revolution and Religion: The Impact of Republican Thought Upon New England Millennialism. 1770–1800," unpublished paper, notes, p. 3.

[15]Abraham Keteltas, "God Arising and Pleading His People's Cause . . ." (Newburyport, Mass.: 1777), p. 30, quoted in Hatch, *Sacred Cause,* p. 61.

[16]Lyman Beecher, as quoted from an address of 1827 in Winthrop Hudson, *Religion in America: An Historical Account of the Development of American Religious Life,* 2nd edition (New York: Scribner, 1973 [1965]), pp. 112–13.

[17]Sydney Ahlstrom, "Thomas Hooker—Puritanism and Democratic Citizenship: a Preliminary Inquiry into some Relationships of Religion and American Civic Responsibility," *Church History,* vol. 32, no. 4 (December 1963), p. 423.

[18]Hendrikus Berkhof, *Christ and the Meaning of History* (1962; reprint ed., Grand Rapids: Baker, 1979), pp. 88, 181.

[19]H. Richard Niebuhr, *Christ and Culture* (New York: Harper and Row, 1951), pp. 149–222. I am also grateful to Professor C. T. McIntire of the Institute for Christian Studies in Toronto for valued criticism on these issues. A number of faculty members at Calvin College have also given me useful advice. I am especially indebted also to Professor Harry Stout for many good suggestions.

## Chapter 12

[1]In 1689 the French Huguenots, now exiled from their homeland by the Revocation of the Edict of Nantes, arrived in Ireland to aid the Scotch-Irish in the development of the successful linen trade.

[2]For a somewhat different view see R. J. Dickson, *Ulster Migration to Colonial America, 1718–1775* (London: Routledge and Kegan Paul, 1961).

[3]Leyburn estimates that by 1775 about 200,000 had arrived in the colonies and that by 1790 the Scotch-Irish comprised nearly 15 percent of the population of the new nation. James Leyburn, *The Scotch-Irish: A Social History* (Chapel Hill, N.C.: University of North Carolina Press, 1962), pp. 180, 183.

[4]*Scotch Irish in America: Proceedings and Addresses of the Third Congress,* (Nashville, 1891), p. 102.

[5]The Land Grant system of the New England colonies proved to be a formidable obstacle to the settlements of large groups, and patroonship in the Hudson Valley in New York offered the same problem. In Pennsylvania the Quakers were concentrated in the three easternmost counties, but the central and western areas lay open to them. In the north only in New Jersey could they find homes in the more established sections of the colony. From Maryland to South Carolina (and later Georgia), the prevalent plantation system left only the Shenandoah Valley and the Piedmont area of North and South Carolina available to them; it was here that they were concentrated in the southern colonies.

[6]William Warren Sweet, *Religion on the American Frontier,* vol. 2, *The Presbyterians, 1783–1840* (New York: Harper and Brothers, 1936), p. 4.

[7]Ibid., p. 23.

[8]In making such a statement I am well aware of the fact that Presbyterianism has long since ceased to claim the largest number of members of the churches in

this country, even if such a claim could ever have been made. Its strength did not arise from the size of its membership but from its inherent doctrinal strength and the vigor and strength of its ecclesiastical polity.

[9]*Records of the Presbyterian Church in the United States of America* (Philadelphia, 1841), pp. 7–8.

[10]Ibid., p. 8.

[11]*Records of the Presbyterian Church,* p. 61.

[12]Ibid., pp. 43–44.

[13]Ibid., p. 92.

[14]Ibid.

[15]For a fuller treatment of the subsequent history of this controversy see L. J. Trinterud, *The Forging of an American Tradition* (Philadelphia, 1949), pp. 49–56.

[16]Ibid., p. 51.

[17]There is in Trinterud's evaluation of this development a strong intimation that the synod Subscriptionists were more concerned with the preservation of correct doctrine than with preserving the ethical purity of the church and that the emphasis on Christian ethics was almost a monopoly of the Anti-Subscription Party.

[18]See Edwin S. Gaustad, *The Great Awakening in New England* (New Haven, Yale University Press, 1938). For an excellent account of the movement in these colonies see Charles Hartshorn, *The Great Awakening in the Middle Colonies* (Chicago: University of Chicago Press, 1920). Wesley M. Gewehr, *The Great Awakening in Virginia, 1740–1790* (Durham: Duke University Press, 1930) is very valuable for its statement on Presbyterianism.

[19]*Records of the Presbyterian Church,* p. 49.

[20]Ibid., p. 92.

[21]Trinterud, *Forging of an American Tradition,* p. 54. This thesis is open to some question in view of the fact that William Tennent had been trained in an Anglican school in Ireland and then had left that communion when he came to America. It seems strange that he would, within a very few years, revert to English Puritanism.

[22]*Records of the Presbyterian Church,* p. 108.

[23]Ibid., pp. 108–9.

[24]Ibid., p. 138.

[25]Ibid., pp. 285–88.

[26]Trinterud, *Forging of an American Tradition,* p. 122.

[27]Ibid., p. 108.

[28]John Robinson was a New Side minister who had visited Virginia in 1742–43. But he was not alone. Other New Side preachers preached in Hanover and other more western sections of the colony.

[29]*Christian Observer* (June 11, 1841), p. 95. Quoted in Ernest Trice Thompson, *Presbyterians of the South* (Richmond, Va.: John Knox, 1963), 1:362.

[30]Samuel J. Baird, *A Story of the New School* (Philadelphia: Claxton, Remsen, and Hoffelfinger, 1868), pp. 217–19.

[31]For a detailed discussion of this division see Thompson, *Presbyterianism of the South,* vol. 2, chapter 25, and Baird, *Story of the New School.*

[32]For the strength of the Old School theology see Thompson, *Presbyterianism of the South,* chapter 26.

[33]In 1861 the southern synods of the Old School again separated and formed the Presbyterian Church in the Confederate States of America. At the end of the conflict it became known as The Presbyterian Church in the United States. The Old School theology was the dominant theology in it.

[34]Lefferts Loetcher, *The Broadening Church* (Philadelphia: University of Pennsylvania Press, 1950), p. 8.

[35]The first such encounter took place while Francis Makemie was conducting his missionary tour in Virginia. Sometime later, Governor Gooch of that colony declared that it was his intention to grant such toleration as was permitted in England under the Acts of Toleration.

[36]Thompson, *Presbyterianism of the South,* pp. 106-7.

[37]Even when and where such congregations were formed, they were frequently without any pastoral leadership for long periods of time.

[38]*The Records of the Presbyterian Church* bear frequent testimony to this continuing problem.

[39]Leyburn, *The Scotch-Irish,* p. 294.

[40]Yet in both North and South Carolina, as well as in New York and Virginia, the Scotch-Irish could be found serving the Loyalist cause also.

[41]*Records of the Presbyterian Church,* pp. 466-69. The synod also requested that the church observe a day of fasting and prayer in behalf of the Second Continental Congress.

[42]Even if these charges were true, it would bring no discredit to the Scotch-Irish or any other Calvinistic group in Great Britain or in this country.

## Chapter 13

[1]Elton E. Eeningenburg, *A Brief History of the Reformed Church in America* (Grand Rapids: Douma, n.d.), p. 19.

[2]It ought to be added that this privileged position contributed in no small measure to the decline of Calvinism in the Netherlands in the eighteenth century as the state-church eventually became the state-dominated church.

[3]In fact one of the grievances presented by some New Netherlanders to the Dutch Estates General was to this effect: "The Directors [of the West Indies Co.] have made no effort to convert to Christianity either the Indians, or the Blacks or Slaves, owned by the company there." Cited by Gerald F. De Jong, "The Dutch Reformed Church and Negro Slavery in Colonial America," in *Church History* 40 (1971): 429.

[4]Charles E. Corwin, *A Manual of the Reformed Church in America, 1628-1922* (New York, Board of Publications and Bible School Work of the Reformed Church in America, 1922), p. 3.

[5]Edward R. Ellis, *The Epic of New York City* (New York: Coward-McCana, 1966), p. 31.

[6]By contrast New England, with its rugged climate and stony soil, had attracted a population of some 30,000 by 1640, twelve years after its founding. Undoubtedly its religious freedom was the determining factor.

[7]Once again, by contrast, the Puritans had adequate spiritual leadership. By

1632 they had 13 ministers, all college graduates, and by 1647 they had 130, all but two of them college-trained.

[8]Gerald F. De Jong, *The Dutch in America* (Boston: Twayne, 1975), p. 98.

[9]Queen's College opened in New Brunswick in 1771 with one instructor. In 1774 Matthew Leydt was its first graduate and he delighted the constituency by giving addresses in Latin, English, and Dutch at that first commencement.

[10]Other immigrant groups held similar convictions. Preservation of the faith was tied up inextricably with preservation of language.

[11]It is possible that reunion of the *Old Light* and *New Light* Presbyterians in 1758 spurred on the Dutch to end their schism.

[12]E. T. Corwin, *A History of the Reformed Church, Dutch* in *American Church History Series* (New York: Christian Literature, 1895), 8:112.

[13]William D. Brown, *History of the Reformed Church in America* (New York: The Board of Publications and Bible School Work, RCA, 1928), p. 91.

[14]Quoted by Corwin, *History of the Reformed Church, Dutch,* p. 175.

[15]*Acta* 1775, p. 57; *Acta* 1778, p. 69.

[16]Cited by John P. Luidens, "The Americanization of the Dutch Reformed Church" (1969 thesis, University of Oklahoma. Photocopy, Ann Arbor, Mich., University Microfilms, 1975) p. 202.

[17]Cited by Gerrit J. Ten Zythoff, "The Americanization of Albertus C. Van Raalte: A Preliminary Inquiry," *Reformed Review* 30 (1977): 85.

[18]Cited by De Jong, *The Dutch in America,* p. 134.

[19]Gordon J. Spykman, *Pioneer Preacher* (Grand Rapids: Heritage Hall Publications, No. 2, 1976), pp. 44ff.

[20]The Christian Reformed Church, which severed its connection with the Reformed Church in America in 1857, established Calvin College in 1876.

[21]Henry S. Lucas, *Netherlanders in America* (Ann Arbor: University of Michigan Press, 1955), p. 552.

[22]Ibid., p. 560.

[23]Ibid., p. 572.

## Chapter 14

[1]For more details see my article: "Protestant Pioneers in New France," *The Presbyterian Record,* vol. 97, no. 9 (Toronto, 1974), pp. 16–18. See also O. Zoff, *The Huguenots* (London: Allen & Unwin, 1943), pp. 248ff.; G. E. Rieman, *The Trail of the Huguenots* (Toronto: Allen, 1963), pp. 136ff.; J. S. Moir, *Enduring Witness* (Toronto: Bryant, n.d.), pp. 20ff.

[2]Reid, "Protestant Pioneers," p. 24; M. Trudel, *The Beginnings of New France, 1524–1663,* trans. P. Claxton (Toronto: McClelland & Stewart, 1973), pp. 54, 59, 110, 137–38; *The Journal of Captain John Knox,* ed. A. G. Doughty (Toronto: Champlain Society, 1914), 2:228.

[3]J. S. Moir, *Enduring Witness,* pp. 36–37; cf. K. J. Duncan, "Patterns of Settlement in the East," in *The Scottish Tradition in Canada,* ed. W. S. Reid (Toronto: McClelland & Stewart, 1976), pp. 49ff.

[4]Moir, *Enduring Witness,* pp. 38ff,; cf. W. S. Reid, "The Scottish Protestant Tradition," *The Scottish Tradition,* pp. 121–22.

[5]Moir, *Enduring Witness,* pp. 41, 43, 60.

[6]W. Kirkconnell, *The Baptists of Canada* (Toronto: Baptist Federation, 1958), pp. 4ff.

[7]Moir, *Enduring Witness,* pp. 43ff.; Reid, "Protestant Pioneers," p. 129.

[8]Moir, *Enduring Witness,* pp. 47ff.; J. R. Harper, *78th Fighting Frasers* (Laval, Que.: DEV-SCO, 1966), pp. 73ff.; G. M. Wrong, *A Canadian Manor and Its Seigneurs* (Toronto: MacMillan, 1926), pp. 22ff.

[9]Moir, *Enduring Witness,* pp. 48ff.; A. M. Evans, "William Bell, Upper Canadian Pioneer," in *Called to Witness,* ed. W. S. Reid (Toronto: Presbyterian Publications, 1975), 1:128ff.

[10]Moir, *Enduring Witness,* pp. 52ff.; Duncan, "Patterns of Settlement," p. 68.

[11]Moir, *Enduring Witness,* pp. 53ff.

[12]D. Allan, *St. Andrews Presbyterian Church, Guelph, Ontario, 1832–1932* (Guelph, 1932), p. 6; C. A. Burrows, *The Annals of the Town of Guelph* (Guelph: Herald, 1877), p. 49.

[13]S. Ivison and F. Rosser, *The Baptists in Upper and Lower Canada* (Toronto: University of Toronto Press, 1956), pp. 10ff, 20–21, 81–82, 122–23; Kirkconnell, *Baptists of Canada,* p. 7.

[14]R. Campbell, *The History of St. Gabriel St. Presbyterian Church, Montreal* (Montreal: Lovell, 1887), pp. 187ff.; D. C. Masters, *Protestant Church Colleges in Canada* (Toronto: University of Toronto Press, 1966), pp. 8–9.

[15]Moir, *Enduring Witness,* pp. 72ff., 85–86, 101–2.

[16]Ibid., pp. 110ff.; W. S. Reid, *The Church of Scotland in Lower Canada* (Toronto: Presbyterian Publications, 1936), pp. 135ff.

[17]Moir, *Enduring Witness,* pp. 137ff.; E. Scott, *Church Union" and the Presbyterian Church in Canada* (Montreal: Lovell, 1928), pp. 39ff.; W. Gregg, *A Short History of the Presbyterian Church in Canada* (Toronto: Robinson, 1892), pp. 188–89; W. S. Reid, "John Cook and the Kirk in Canada," in *Enkindled by the Word,* ed. N. G. Smith (Toronto: Presbyterian Publications, 1966), pp. 28ff.

[18]Kirkconnell, *Baptists of Canada,* pp. 9–10.

[19]J. H. MacVicar, *The Life and Work of Donald Harvey MacVicar* (Toronto: Westminster, 1904), pp. 173ff.; D. C. Masters, "The Rise of Liberalism in the Canadian Protestant Churches," *Canadian Catholic Historical Association Annual Report,* 1969, pp. 29–30.

[20]Moir, *Enduring Witness,* pp. 197ff.; Scott, *"Church Union,"* pp.127ff.

[21]Cf. articles by N. K. Clifford on Robert Campbell, by J. J. H. Morris on George McQueen, and by DeC. H. Rayner on Ephraim Scott in *Called to Witness,* vol. 1.

[22]Kirkconnell, *Baptists of Canada,* p. 10.

[23]Masters, *Protestant Church Colleges,* pp. 9, 112–13, 122.

[24]1971 Census of Canada: *Population, Religious Denominations.*

[25]R. L. Stevenson, "The Foreigner at Home," in *Memories and Portraits* (London: Collins, n.d.), pp. 28ff.

[26]P. Berton, *The National Dream* (Toronto: McClelland & Stewart, 1971), pp. 319–20.

[27]W. S. Reid, "The Scot and Canadian Identity," *Scottish Tradition,* pp. 307ff.

## Chapter 15

[1]Marcus L. Loane, *Hewn From the Rock* (Sydney: Anglican Information Office, 1976), p. 2.

[2]Ibid., p. 10.

[3]G. R. Balleine, *History of the Evangelical Party in the Church of England* (London: Church Book Room, 1951), pp. 106-7.

[4]A. T. Yarwood, *Samuel Marsden* (Melbourne: Melbourne University Press, 1977), pp. 89ff.; Loane, *Hewn From the Rock,* p. 11.

[5]L. L. Robson, *The Convict Settlers of Australia* (Melbourne: Melbourne University Press, 1970), Appendix 5, p. 189. It is also interesting to note that the Scottish convicts, both male and female, were the worst.

[6]C. M. H. Clark, *A History of Australia* (Melbourne: Melbourne University Press, 1963), 1:93ff.

[7]Archibald Gilchrist, *John Dunmore Lang 1799-1878* (Melbourne, 1951), p. 557.

[8]F. M. Bradshaw, "Presbyterian Church," in *Australian Encyclopaedia* (1965), 7:262-72.

[9]Aeneas Macdonald, *One Hundred Years of Presbyterianism in Victoria* (Melbourne: Robertson and Mullens, 1937), p. 35. "A massive preacher of great eloquence, he was a strong Evangelical, reared and content in the ways of the old Calvinism."

[10]Ibid., pp. 89, 90. See also "Rentoul, John Laurence," in *Australian Encyclopaedia,* 7:405-6.

[11]C. A. White, *The Challenge of the Years* (Sydney: Angus and Robertson, 1951), pp. 3-4.

[12]Macdonald, *One Hundred Years,* p. 81.

[13]Ibid., p. 126.

[14]"Strong, Charles," in *Australian Encyclopaedia,* 8:328.

[15]Macdonald, *One Hundred Years,* p. 128.

[16]Alexander Stewart and J. Kennedy Cameron, *The Free Church of Scotland 1843-1910* (Edinburgh and Glasgow: William Hodge, 1910). This gives a critical evaluation of the Declaratory Act adopted by the Free Church of Scotland in 1892, pp. 68-85.

[17]S. Angus, *Truth and Tradition* (Sydney, 1934). In his argument Angus makes use of the Declaratory Act as a basis for his freedom to teach doctrine in conflict with the Westminster Confession.

[18]Constitution and Regulations, The Uniting Church of Australia, Melbourne (1976), article 10, p. 9.

[19]Loane, *Hewn From the Rock,* pp. 45-66.

[20]Marcus L. Loane, *A Centenary History of Moore Theological College* (Sydney: Angus and Robertson, 1955), pp. 139-53.

[21]T. C. Hammond took an active interest in the "Red Book Case" and published the details in a volume, *The Bathurst Ritual Case.*

[22]The stand taken by the Presbyterian Church of Eastern Australia for Scottish Presbyterianism is convincingly set forth by J. Campbell Robinson in the volume, *The Free Presbyterian Church of Australia* (Melbourne: Hamer, 1947). Since the publication of this historical work the name of the denomination has been changed to the Presbyterian Church of Eastern Australia.

²³Rowland S. Ward, *Presbyterianism in Tasmania* (1977), pp. 36–78.

²⁴W. P. Morrell and D. O. W. Hall, *A History of New Zealand Life,* (Whitcombe and Tombs, 1957), pp. 29ff.

²⁵Noel S. Pollard, "Selwyn, George Augustus," in *New International Dictionary of the Christian Church,* (Grand Rapids: Zondervan, 1974), p. 895.

²⁶John Dickson, *History of the New Zealand Presbyterian Church* (Dunedin: Wilkie, 1899), pp. 17ff.

²⁷C. Stuart Ross, *The Story of the Otago Church and Settlement* (Dunedin: Wise, Caffin, 1887), pp. 20ff.

²⁸J. W. Deenik, *Will Presbyterianism Survive in New Zealand?* (Auckland: Reformed Publications, 1961), pp. 10ff.

²⁹John Haverland, *The Geering Controversy,* Church history essay assignment, third year, Reformed Theological College, Geelong, Australia. Geering denied the Calvinistic teaching on miracles, the infallibility of the Bible, the deity and power of Christ, the resurrection of Christ, and the immortality of the soul. At the trial in 1967 no action was taken by the General Assembly of the Presbyterian Church, New Zealand. In a pastoral letter to the churches the Assembly declared its "confidence in Professor Geering as a minister, theological teacher and Principal of our Theological College." Cf. D. F. Sage, "1967 Assembly," *Evangelical Presbyterian,* vol. 18 no. 1 (January-February, 1968). The author states that "the Presbyterian Church of N.Z. has ceased to be a confessional church since the decision of Assembly was passed" (p. 7).

³⁰J. F. H. Vander Bom, "Building a New Nation," *Trowel and Sword,* vol. 1, no. 1 (October 1954), p. 4.

³¹K. S. Latourette, *A History of the Expansion of Christianity* (1948; reprint ed., Grand Rapids: Zondervan, 1970), 5:197.

³²Ibid., p. 165.

³³J. Herbert Kane, *A Global View of Christian Missions* (Grand Rapids: Baker, 1971), pp. 526ff.

³⁴R. S. Miller, *Misi Gete. John Geddie, Pioneer Missionary to the New Hebrides* (The Presbyterian Church of Tasmania, 1975), p. 333.

³⁵Latourette, *History of Expansion,* p. 229.

³⁶Jean Cadier, *The Man God Mastered* (London: Inter-Varsity, 1960), p. 174.

## Chapter 16

¹Cf. the article "Calvinism," especially section 3 on the practical effects of Calvinism, in John E. Meeter, ed., *Selected Shorter Writings of Benjamin B. Warfield-II* (Nutley, N.J.: Presbyterian and Reformed, 1973).

²Cf. T. Huddleston, *Naught for Your Comfort* (London: Collins, 1956).

³Cf. W. A. de Klerk, *The Puritans in Africa: A Story of Afrikanerdom* (New York: Penguin, Pelican, 1976), ch. 12.

⁴De Klerk finds a discontinuity between Calvin and Puritanism and a continuity between Puritanism and Dutch Calvinism (cf. R. T. Kendall's recent study: *Calvin and English Calvinism to 1649* [New York: Oxford University Press, 1979]). This work is very interesting and full of historical information on South Africa.

[5]Prof. F. J. van Jaarsveld also ascribes the racial feeling to "Protestant Calvinism," but does not lay much emphasis on the doctrine of election in his book *From Van Riebeeck to Vorster 1652–1974* (Johannesburg: Perskor, 1975), p. 37.

[6]The traditional apologetic is of course an eminently biblical one and should not be abandoned (cf. Matt. 5:16).

[7]Cf. his *Het Calvinisme* (Kampen: Kok, 1959), p. 10.

[8]In his book *The History and Character of Calvinism* (New York: Oxford University Press, 1962), p. 418. Cf. De Klerk, *Puritans in Africa*, p. 102.

[9]Cf. Deneys Reitz: *No Outspan* (London: Faber and Faber, 1944), p. 14.

[10]"The distinguishing mark of Calvinism as over all other systems lies in its doctrines of 'efficacious grace,'" Meeter, *Writings of Warfield*, p. 415.

[11]In other words all those who accept the direct kingship of Christ over His church whether they be Congregational, Classical, or Conciliar Calvinists.

[12]Abridged editions have been published in Afrikaans. Dr. Simpson is now working on a translation of the 1559 edition of the Institutes.

[13]The Reformation is annually commemorated on October 31, but there are various other reasons for this fact.

[14]Cf. D. Kempff, *Bibliografie Van Suid-Afrikaanse Calviniana* (Potchefstroom: PU vir CHO, 1973).

[15]J. du Plessis, *A History of Christian Missions in South Africa* (London: Longmans, 1911), p. 21.

[16]Ibid., p. 23.

[17]P. B. van der Watt, *Die Nederduitse Gereformeerde Kerk 1652–1824* (Pretoria: N G Kerk, 1976) 1:10.

[18]De Klerk recognizes this: *Puritans in Africa*, p. 7.

[19]Ibid., p. 9.

[20]Cf. van der Watt, *Nederduitse Geregormeerde Kerk*, 1:25; Eric A. Walker, *A History of Southern Africa* (London: Longmans, 1962), p. 95; du Plessis, *History of Christian Missions*, p. 46.

[21]Du Plessis, *History of Christian Missions*, p. 44.

[22]Van der Watt, *Nederduitse Gereformeerde Kerk*, 1:20.

[23]Van Jaarsveld, *Van Riebeeck to Vorster*, p. 38.

[24]B. Spoelstra, *Die Doppers in Suid-Afrika* (Bloemfontein: Nasionale Boekhandel, 1963), p. 24.

[25]Cf. T. N. Hanekom, *Die Liberale Rigting in Suid-Afrika* (Stellenbosch, CSV, 1951), p. 100.

[26]Ibid., p. 107.

[27]Du Plessis, *History of Christian Missions*, p. 93.

[28]Van der Watt, *Nederduitse Gereformeerde Kerk*, 1:26.

[29]P. B. van der Watt, *Beroerders en Beroeringe* (Cape Town: N. G. Kerk, 1975), p. 24. Shand also refused to baptize children of ignorant and worldly parents and rarely administered Holy Communion. This led to a local schism that lasted for fifty years, but both synod and state supported Shand.

[30]P. B. van der Watt, *Die Nederduitse Gereformeerde Kerk 1824–1905* (Pretoria: N. G. Kerk, 1980) 3:44.

[31]Van Jaarsveld, *Van Riebeeck to Vorster*, p. 91.

[32] J. Whiteside, *The History of the Wesleyan Methodist Church of Suid-Afrika* (London: Stock, 1906), p. 206.

[33] Philip's willingness to believe accusations against the whites was certainly his weakness, but his Calvinism has been ignored by South African historians. Cf. Briggs and Wing, *The Harvest and the Hope* (Johannesburg: United Congregational Church, 1970), ch. 2, also p. 29.

[34] Du Plessis, *History of Christian Missions,* p. 227.

[35] The "Blood River" Covenant, as it is known, was conditional, more in line with the Old Testament vow, but both types include a binding promise and a confession of faith in God.

[36] Cf. "Verdagmaking teen Geloftedag," *Die Kerkbode* (September 14, 1977).

[37] J. J. Kotze and T. F. Burgers. About twenty more were in sympathy with liberalism as well as a few elders.

[38] N. J. Hofmeyr and Andrew Murray, Jr., were the most prominent.

[39] Van der Watt, *Nederduitse Gereformeerde Kerk,* 3:19.

[40] Earl Kitchener made use of scorched-earth tactics, comparable to those used in the American Civil War. Although only about 4,000 men lost their lives on the Republican side, 36,000 women and children died in concentration camps. Cf. van Jaarsveld, *Van Riebeeck to Vorster,* p. 204.

[41] Christian National Schools. Cf. van der Watt, *Nederduitse Gereformeerde Kerk,* 3:206.

[42] The "Cottesloe debacle." Cf. De Klerk, *Puritans in Africa,* p. 252.

[43] Many of these proposals have since that time been accepted by government, at least in principle.

[44] In his (as yet) unpublished lecture at the Calvin Congress for Africa in Pretoria, 1980: "Research on and influence of Calvin in the English-speaking Ecclesiastical sphere in South Africa." He said that the Afrikaner "contracted spiritually out of World War I, and were able to avoid the long term effects." But cf. note 57 below.

[45] The Nederduits Hervormde Kerk van Afrika.

[46] Accepted by the Cape church in 1814. As the first Synod did not meet until 1824 the oversight can be understood but not condoned.

[47] The new hymns, the liberal group in the Cape church, and cultural differences between the Cape ministers and members from the more remote districts all played a role in this process. The fact that the NHK was at that time state church of the Transvaal confounded the issues.

[48] In 1850 Thompson succeeded John Philip in this church, which was started by James Read in 1800 as a "Calvinistic Society." Cf. Briggs and Wing, *Harvest and Hope,* pp. 29, 105.

[49] Cf. T. N. S. Gqubule, "An Examination of the Theological Education of Africans in South Africa from 1860 to 1960" (Ph.D. thesis, Grahamstown: Rhodes University, 1977), p. 74.

[50] About 1.5 million, of whom one-third are black.

[51] The question is of course, What is the best sense? Even Presbyterians supported the British during the Anglo-Boer War in the name of patriotism. Cf. *The Christian Express* (October 1, 1900). This gives a report from the Presbytery of East London.

[52]Cf. T. R. H. Davenport, *The Afrikaner Bond* (Cape Town: O U P, 1966); D. A. Scholtz, "Ds. S J du Toit as kerkman en kultuurleier" (Th.D. thesis, Stellenbosch, 1975).

[53]The Afrikaner Bond is not to be confused with the Afrikaner Broederbond of much later date.

[54]Cf. L. D. Ngcongco, "John Tengo Jabavu," in Christopher Saunders, *Black Leaders in South African History* (London: Heinemann, 1979). (Jabavu was a Methodist.)

[55]Many individuals joined the war, of course.

[56]That was years before Kruger became president; cf. Spoelstra, *Die Doppers,* p. 209.

[57]This "rebellion" was meant to be a "non-violent armed protest," and the reasons were mixed. The direct reason was the refusal to occupy the territory of another nation (Germany), which is of course modern Namibia! Even the non-partisan ex-president M. T. Steyn could say, "Rather rebellion than to act unjustly towards a nation that did us no harm." Oberholster en Van Schoor, *President Steyn aan die Woord* (Bloemfontein: SA Calvinistiese Uitgewers, 1954), p. 191. Cf. F. J. van Jaarsveld, *Van Riebeeck to Vorster,* p. 236. General Koos de la Rey also intended to take part in the "armed protest" but he was accidentally killed a day before. Both Steyn and de la Rey warned against the 1899–1902 war, but both fought to the bitter end. All in all this was as near a "Puritan revolution" as one could hope for in South Africa.

[58]Or, never dominant.

[59]Du Plessis, *History of Christian Missions,* p. 233.

[60]M. T. S. Zeeman says that "LMS missionaries applied the ideas of J. J. Rousseau" ("Beleid van Afsonderlike Ontwikkeling Onchristelik?" *Die Kerkbode,* [February 25, 1981]). The reference is obviously to van der Kemp, i.a.

[61]Jane Sales, *Mission Stations and the Coloured Communities of the Eastern Cape* (Cape Town: Balkema, 1975), p. 11.

[62]Cf. an incident related by I. H. Enklaar during the "Oranjefurie" of 1787 in *De Levensgesheidenis van J. T. van der Kemp* (Wageningen: Veenman, 1972), p. 50.

[63]Du Plessis, *History of Christian Missions,* p. 128. As friend, teacher, and descendant of missionaries, du Plessis was sympathetic toward van der Kemp but he accepts the suggestion that van der Kemp was motivated by more than eccentricity and non-conformity plus the gospel, viz., by Rousseau's ideas.

[64]Du Plessis emphasizes his piety and devotion to Christ.

[65]I. J. van der Walt is technically correct when he says that van der Kemp "was not Reformed," because he was strongly interdenominational in his approach and did not like the binding authority of confessions and synods (although he used a catechism at Bethelsdorp). Cf. Enklaar, *Levensgeschiedenis,* ch. 7, for his "high Calvinism." Van der Walt does not specifically deny this in his book *Eiesoortigheid en die Sending* (Porchefstroom: Pro Rege, 1963), p. 318.

[66]Translated from the Dutch. The title of van der Kemp's commentary was *De Theodicee van Paulus;* Enklaar, *Levensgeshiedenis,* p. 80.

[67]Van Jaarsveld, *Van Riebeeck to Vorster,* p. 50.

68Ibid., p. 81.

69Corner remarked in 1815 that the people in that area were less desirous for the Word of God than others farther north. Cf. Spoelstra, *Die Doppers,* p. 23.

70The date of his conversion is uncertain. He also had contact with Joseph Williams of the LMS. Cf. B. Holt, *Joseph Williams* (Lovedale, 1954).

71Cf. Janet Hodgson, *Ntsikana's Great Hymn* (Cape Town: University of Cape Town, 1980).

72J. E. J. Capitein was ordained in Leyden in 1743 and S. A. Crowther in 1845, but they were both slaves for a period (which was not their fault!). Tiyo did not have similar compulsory advantages. Cf. Donovan Williams, *Umfundisi: A Biography of Tiyo Soga* (Lovedale, 1979).

73Niel Gunson believes that some missionaries anticipated "social Darwinism." Cf. his *Messengers of Grace* (Melbourne, O U P, 1978), p. 200.

74Cf. R. H. W. Shepherd, *Lovedale 1841–1941* (Lovedale, 1942).

75Du Plessis, *History of Christian Missions,* chs. 17, 27.

76E. Casalis, *My Life in Basutoland* (Cape Town: Struik, 1971).

77G. L. van Heerde, *Die Dag van Kleine Dinge* (Cape Town: N G Kerk, 1955), p. 20. De Buys had lived with various black women. In 1800 he met van der Kemp, who "taught him to pray." By 1862 his descendants were totally pagan.

78Ibid., p. 200.

79Compare the situation in the United States after the Civil War. E. T. Thompson, *Presbyterians in the South* (Richmond: John Knox, 1973) 2:309.

80C. W. de Kiewiet, *The Anatomy of South African Misery* (London: OUP, 1956), p. 22.

81Cf. de Klerk, *Puritans in Africa.*

82This is not to deny that nominal Christians may have used the Old Testament to justify war on the Bushmen. The pious, however, without practicing full social interrelationships, behaved differently. Cf. the records quoted by Spoelstra, *Die Doppers,* pp. 29–32.

83Cf. de Klerk, *Puritans in Africa,* p. 143. After writing a vivid description of Bogerman casting the Arminians "into outer darkness," he says, "Such would also be the effect of Dort on the Reformed Confession of the Afrikaners."

84Cf.Question and Answer 54, Heidelberg Catechism and the Belgic Confession, section 16.

85Cf. Meeter, *Writings of Warfield,* p. 431.

86Casalis, *My Life,* p. 89.

87Ibid., p. 90.

88Cf. van der Walt, *Eiesoontigheid,* pp. 406–10 for discussion of the 1857 synod.

89Ibid., p. 438.

90Cf. Pienaar and Scholtz, eds., *Glo in u Volk* (Speeches of Dr. Malan) (Cape Town: Tafelberg, 1964), p. 14. Most speeches are relevant to his theology.

91Ibid., p. 42. Cf. H. B. Thom, *Dr. D. F. Malan* (Cape Town: Tafelberg, 1979).

92Walker, *History of Southern Africa,* p. 152.

93Williams, *Umfundisi,* p. 128.

94Although Soga's children were sent to Scotland for their education, he strongly advised them to return to their father's people, ibid. pp. 88, 118. It is also of interest that Soga wanted to marry a Negro Christian from America (p. 26). For his Calvinism, cf. p. 126 and J. A. Chalmers, *Tiyo Soga* (Edinburgh: A. Elliot, 1877).

[95]Cf. A. P. Treurnicht, *Op die Keper* (Cape Town, 1965).

[96]Cf. A. B. du Preez, *Eiesoortige ontwikkeling tot Volksdiens* (Pretoria, 1959).

[97]Cf. de Klerk, *Puritans in Africa,* p. 338. De Klerk's own commitment is not clear.

[98]B. B. Keet, *Suid Afrika Waarheen?* (Quo Vadis?) (Stellenbosch, 1955).

[99]D. S. Bax, *A Different Gospel* (Presbyterian Church of South Africa, Johannesburg.)

[100]Published in the *Journal of Theology for South Africa,* no. 24 (September 1978).

[101]Meeter, *Writings of Warfield,* p. 412.

[102]Part of his famous hymn ''Lizalis' idinga lakho.'' Cf. Gqubule, ''Examination of Theological Education,'' p. 33, for circumstances.

# Index of Persons

# Index of Subjects

Absolutism, 117

Academy of Geneva, 45, 46, 65

Academy of Saumur, 76

Academy of Utrecht, 112

*Afscheiding* movement, 296-302

America: Christian, 241-44

American Revolution: and Calvinist clergy, 253

Anabaptists: banned from Hungary, 167; in the Netherlands, 97; and soul sleep, 42

Anglican church, 331, 332

Anglo-Boer War, 350

Anti-Revolutionary Party: the Netherlands, 118

Antitrinitarians: in Hungary, 145, 153, 154-55, 159

Apartheid: criticized by Calvinists, 362; supported by Calvinists, 360-61. *See also* Race discrimination.

Apocrypha: excluded from Scripture, 64

Architects: France, 89

Arminianism: in America, 275, 276; in Canada, 315; vs. conditional universalism, 69; in France, 75, 76, 85; in the Netherlands, 99, 104-9

Artists and painters: in France, 90

Association for a Christian University, 334

Astrology, 49

Atonement: extent of, 108, 205, 206; governmental theory of, 276; an issue in Australia, 329, 331; limited, 68, 209; particular, 67; in the Scots Confession of 1560, 221; universal, 69, 235; unlimited, 205

Augsburg Confession, 102, 125, 126, 132

Augsburg Diet (1530), 143

Authority: divine, 25; human, 25

Authorized Version (1611), 220

Baptists: on the American frontier, 275; in Canada, 313; 316; in South Africa, 352

Belgic Confession, 100, 101, 109, 118, 129, 290

Bible: authority, 15, 43, 52, 70, 80, 130, 175, 244; Dutch, 109; historico-grammatical exegesis, 48; and human reason, 17; Hungarian, 142, 162-64; Hussite, 142; inspiration of, 43, 69; inspiration of, modern view in Scotland, 236; interpretation of, 45, 113, 130, 137; interpretation of by Puritans, 246, 247; and the laity in Scotland, 226; message of, 174; origin of, 70; and preaching, 39

Bishop's Bible (1568), 200

Black Death, 34

Black Legion, 142

Book of Common Prayer, 178

Book of Common Order, 225

Bremen Confession, 136

Brethren of the Common Life, 96

Calling: divine, 28; influence on Americans, 255; Reformation idea of, 22; universal, 25; vocational, 51

Calvin, John: arrival of, in Germany, 125; and art, 15; on the arts, 231; on assurance, 208; and astrology, 15; on the authority of the Scriptures, 43, 50; and Beza, 66, 205-6; and the Bible, 28; on blasphemy, 179; and Bullinger on the Lord's Supper, 60-61; on calling, 22, 23, 25; vs. Calvinism, 199; catechism of, 49; on the catechism, 178; on Christian life, 45; and Canon law, 28; on the church, 23; and church and state, 58, 63; on church discipline, 46, 57; and church leaders, 57; commentaries of, 48; contact of, with the